Capital
Expenditure
Analysis

For Managers and Engineers

Capital
Expenditure
Analysis

For Managers and Engineers

Raymond R. Mayer
Walter F. Mullady Professor of Business Administration
Loyola University of Chicago

Waveland Press, Inc.
Prospect Heights, Illinois

For information about this book, write:
Waveland Press, Inc.
P.O. Box 400
Prospect Heights, Illinois 60070

To the memory of
Adam and Mary Majer

Contents

Preface   xi

1   The Capital Allocation Problem   1

*Topics: Types of investment alternatives/Determining the
alternatives/Describing the alternatives/Evaluating the alter-
natives/Considering the irreducibles/Making the post-audit/
Profit comparisons/Cost comparisons/Questions/Problems*

2   Relevant Costs and Factors   15

*Topics: Recurring costs/Capital costs/Methods of financing/
Operating cost estimates/Revenue estimates/Income tax esti-
mates/Depreciation methods/Devaluation expense estimates/
Cost of money estimates/Questions/Problems*

3   Compound Interest Formulas   55

*Topics: Simple interest/Compound interest/Nominal inter-
est/Effective interest/Single-amount future worth factor/Sin-
gle-amount present worth factor/Uniform-series future worth
factor/Future-amount annuity factor/Uniform-series present
worth factor/Present-amount annuity factor/Gradient-series
future worth factor/Gradient-series present worth factor/
Gradient-series annuity factor/Questions/Problems*

4   Uniform Annual Cost Comparisons   107

*Topics: A comprehensive uniform annual cost analysis/The
equal time-period requirement/Assumption regarding future
replacements/Irreducible factors/A replacement problem/
Economic life determination/Multiple-alternative problems/
Perpetual-service alternatives/Questions/Problems*

5   The Present Worth and Future Worth Criteria   141

*Topics: A comprehensive present worth analysis/A compre-
hensive future worth analysis/Assumption regarding reinvestment rates/A replacement problem/Multiple alternatives/Al-
ternate assumption regarding future replacements/Perpe-
tual-service problems/Capitalized costs/Valuation problems/
Choosing the analytical technique/Questions/Problems*

6   Rate of Return Computations   179

*Topics: Determining returns on total investment/An alter-
nate approach to the determination of returns on total in-
vestment/Determining returns on extra investment/An alternate approach to the determination of returns on extra in-
vestment/The equal time-period requirement/Weighted average returns/Questions/Problems*

7   The Rate of Return or Discounted Cash Flow Method   207

*Topics: A comprehensive rate of return analysis/A replace-
ment problem/Multiple-alternative problems/Internal returns
versus external returns/The case of multiple returns/The case
of no ascertainable return/Disadvantages and advantages of
the method/Questions/Problems*

8   Tax Determination and After-Tax Evaluations   257

*Topics: General approach to tax determination/Effective tax
rates/A comprehensive after-tax analysis/Determining returns
on equity investment/The return-on-equity criterion/A problem involving only tax differences/Investment tax credits/*

Treatment of gains and losses on disposal/Multiple-alternative problems/Questions/Problems

9   The Revenue Requirement Approach   315

Topics: General description of the method/The tax factor/ The tax formula/A comprehensive revenue requirement analysis/Multiple-alternative problems/A replacement problem/ Treatment of tax credits and of gains taxes/Evaluation of the approach/Questions/Problems

10   Break-even, Sensitivity, and Risk Analyses   361

Topics: The problem of estimation/Break-even point determination/Sensitivity analysis/Some fundamentals of probability/Analyses under the condition of risk/Estimation and inflation/Ranking investment alternatives/A final observation/Questions/Problems

Appendixes

A   Decision Trees for Decision Making   409

Topics: A problem involving uncertain events/Constructing the decision tree/Decision-event chains/Analyzing the alternatives/The "rollback" concept/Accounting for time differences/Evaluation of the approach

B   Derivations   425

Topics: Single-amount compound interest factors/Uniform-series compound interest factors/Gradient-series compound interest factors/The revenue requirement tax formulas

C   Interest Tables   439

*Topics: Summary list of future worth factors/Summary list
of present worth factors/Summary list of annuity factors/
Values of 2% to 50% compound interest factors*

Bibliography   465

Index   467

Preface

The efficient allocation of available capital entails the selection of the most attractive of alternative capital expenditure proposals. In those cases in which the most attractive alternative is defined as being the most economical one, the selection process calls for identifying that proposal which will generate the largest excess of revenues over costs. The need for making such an identification may be experienced by a private individual or by a member of an organization. When an organization is involved, the decision maker is likely to be either a manager or an engineer who functions in the area of operations, finance, marketing, purchasing, or research. The organization itself may be providing some other enterprise or the public with a product, service, or some combination of the two.

The purpose of this book is to provide concerned individuals and organizations with a knowledge and understanding of the analytical approaches by means of which the most economical capital investment alternative can be ascertained. It is intended for use under any one of a number of conditions. First, the book may be adopted as the basic text in an appropriate undergraduate or graduate course being offered by a school of business, a school of engineering, a college of science, or a school of agriculture. An appropriate course might be one in capital budgeting, engineering economics, managerial finance, capital investment analysis, or managerial economics. Second, it can serve as a supplementary text in courses in which only a portion of the total time is devoted to a financial evaluation of alternative courses of action. These might be courses in operations management, research and development, business finance, marketing management, agricultural economics, hospital administration, and government finance. Third, the book can be used as the text in training programs conducted by an organization for its managerial, financial, and engineering personnel. The organization may be a manufacturing company, a public utility, a processing firm, a government agency, or a service establishment. Last, it can be utilized by anyone who wants to engage in independent study of the subject. Such an individual could be someone who finds it necessary to make either decisions in the area of personal finance or financial decisions in his or her role as a member of an organization.

The nature of the presentation has been determined by my experiences when applying this material in practice and when presenting it to students of management and engineering and to participants in programs sponsored by firms, agencies, associations, and professional societies. In general terms, this presentation begins with a description of the nature of the capital allocation problem and of the elements of any rational approach to its solution. Next, a detailed explanation is provided of what must be known about the respective alternatives before their evaluation can begin. Then, because this evaluation must take into account the time value of money, consideration is given to the compound interest factors which enable one to provide for this time value of money when carrying out the analysis.

Some indication of the importance placed upon the foregoing topics is that approximately one-fourth of the book is devoted to their discussion. And it is only after this discussion has been completed that the various analytical techniques as such are presented. In the initial treatment of these techniques, the tax implications of alternative investment proposals are accounted for in an indirect manner. This permits the emphasis to be placed on the basic concepts which underlie the proposed methods of analysis. At the point at which there is reason to believe that a complete understanding of these concepts has been acquired, a direct method of providing for the impact of income taxes on the final decision is introduced.

Finally, cognizance is taken of the fact that the most sophisticated analytical approach may prove to be of little value if it is used to process inaccurate data. Hence, the presentation is brought to a close with a description of the ways by means of which one can alleviate the difficulties posed by the need to estimate the values of factors relevant to the analysis.

Questions and problems related to the topics covered in each chapter are presented to provide the reader with an opportunity to ascertain the degree to which he or she has mastered the material involved. These appear at the end of each chapter. The questions can also be used as a basis for classroom discussions, and the problems can be utilized to demonstrate applications other than those considered for illustrative purposes in the text. A solutions manual is available for use in conjunction with the problems.

Insofar as the details of the presentation are concerned, it might be noted that

- explanations of an intuitive nature supplement those of a rigorous nature whenever possible

- extensive use is made of cash-flow diagrams

- the implied alternative of making no investment of a certain type is always considered

- a distinction is made between alternatives that are mutually exclusive and those that are not

- cases in which a complete description of the alternatives' cash flows is possible and cases in which it is not possible are examined

- two-alternative and multiple-alternative problems are treated

- each of the analytical techniques is explained with the use of the same examples to permit a comparison of the results

- consideration is given to the relevancy of rates of return on total investment, extra investment, equity investment, and debt investment

- a distinction is made between internal and external rates of return

- the occurrence of multiple rates of return or no possible value for the rate of return is discussed

- analyses are made under the condition of certainty and the condition of risk

- the use of decision trees in decision making is described

- consideration is given to valuation problems, break-even point determination, perpetual service alternatives, economic service life determination, and sensitivity analyses

- the effect of inflation on capital investment decisions is investigated

- the ranking of investment alternatives is discussed

- the advantages and disadvantages of the respective analytical approaches are presented

- no one method of analysis is promoted as being the best under all possible circumstances

- the importance of irreducible, or intangible, factors is never ignored
- the continued need for judgment is stressed

The topics considered and their method of presentation are such that they should prove to be understandable to anyone who is acquainted with the fundamentals of algebra. No other background on the part of the reader is assumed. Teachers of students with this background are likely to find that the minimum amount of time required for a thorough treatment of the material will be equal to that available in a one-semester course at the college level. Those instructors who do not have this amount of time available or find it to be insufficient will have to use judgment when determining what should be omitted. Some may decide to exclude items of a special nature which appear in various chapters, while others may choose to ignore one or more chapters in their entirety. No specific recommendations with reference to such decisions are being made, because this type of decision must, of necessity, be subjective. Nevertheless, a word of caution is in order. This is that care should be taken to avoid the error of deleting something which is essential to an understanding of a subsequent topic of discussion. The risk of this kind of error is always present when steps are taken to modify a presentation which is designed to be a unified and integrated explanation of the subject.

Raymond R. Mayer

1

The Capital Allocation Problem

One of the few certainties in the area of managerial finance is that there are almost unlimited opportunities to invest capital. Another of these certainties is that the amount of money available for investment is limited. This somewhat unfortunate combination of circumstances creates a capital allocation problem, that is, a need for determining how available funds are to be distributed among the available investment alternatives.

It is important to note at the outset that there are two basic categories of capital investment alternatives. The one contains those alternatives that are mutually exclusive, and the other contains those that are not. The distinction between the two can be explained best with the use of examples. Suppose we have a business organization which is experiencing demands for expenditures for such things as product development, manpower training, production facilities, market research, raw material inventories, office equipment, plant expansion, data processing equipment, and promotional efforts. These respective investment opportunities can be described as not being mutually exclusive. This is because their natures are such that a decision to invest in one of them does not exclude the possibility of a decision to invest in one or more of the others at the same time. Therefore, in the case under consideration, management may decide to spend funds on manpower training *and* on production facilities *and* on data processing equipment, but not on the other items in the listing.

As a rule, once a decision has been reached to make a certain kind of investment, such as in data processing equipment, a need then arises for evaluating alternative methods of implementing this decision. To illustrate, in the case of a data processing installation, the equipment

1

required may be available from three different manufacturers of such equipment. These three sources represent a set of mutually exclusive alternatives because their natures are such that the selection of one of them precludes the selection of one or more of the others at the same time. Consequently, in the case under consideration, management must decide whether to obtain the equipment from the first manufacturer *or* the second *or* the third.

All this suggests, and correctly so, that two questions must be answered in the process of analyzing capital investment opportunities. The first is: What kinds of investments should be made? In the course of answering this question, it becomes necessary to pass judgment on alternatives that are not mutually exclusive. The second question is: Given a decision to make a certain kind of investment, what is the best way to execute this decision? In the course of answering this question, it becomes necessary to pass judgment on mutually exclusive alternatives.

We shall concern ourselves in this book with a description, explanation, and evaluation of the analytical techniques that have been developed for use in an attempt to answer these two questions. There is reason to believe that the application of these methods of analysis will prove to be more effective than the adoption of approaches based on judgment and intuition. However, as we shall see, judgment and intuition will continue to play a role in the solution of the capital allocation problem, albeit a greatly reduced one.

THE DECISION-MAKING PROCEDURE

In the course of our presentation, it will become necessary for us to define what is meant by the most attractive investment alternative in a given situation. This definition will be based on the assumption that the primary goal of the organization is the maximization of profits in the long run by means of legal and ethical methods of operation. This assumption is consistent with the fact that a given firm may have secondary goals. Examples of such goals may be management's desire to provide the work force with steady employment, to engage in philanthropic activities, or to acquire a reputation as an innovator in its field. Further, the assumption suggests that short-term gains might be sacrificed on the basis of long-term considerations. To illustrate, a firm is likely to sacrifice the immediate profits to be realized from a reduction in the quality of its services or in the safety of its products because future profits will be adversely affected by these kinds of actions. And, finally, the assumption takes cognizance of the fact that legal and ethical constraints exist which serve to eliminate certain courses of action from further consideration. Examples of such actions would be monopolistic practices, misleading advertising, and the use of coercion.

Given the stated primary goal of the organization, it follows that the decision-making process is one in which management must evaluate alternative legal and ethical courses of action with a view to identifying the one which will prove to be the most profitable in the long run. This particular course of action will be referred to as the most economical alternative.

One might argue that this description of the decision-making process would not be correct in those exceptional cases in which the firm is inclined to be governed by secondary considerations. It should be noted, however, that, even in those cases, a rational decision can be reached only after management identifies the most profitable alternative. Having done this, it can then go on to determine the cost of substituting its secondary goals for the primary goal and ascertain whether it can afford to incur this cost.

To summarize, an essential element of the decision-making process is the determination of the most economical alternative. When this has been accomplished, the firm can then conclude whether or not its secondary goals should take precedence over its primary goal.

In this book, we shall limit ourselves to a study of the decision-making process as applied in those cases in which the alternative courses of action involve capital expenditures. Let us begin with a general description of the steps in this process.

Determining the Alternatives. The most economical capital expenditure alternative is selected from a collection of available alternatives. Consequently, the decision-making procedure must begin with a determination of the investment alternatives in a given situation. The number of alternatives and their characteristics will depend on the nature of the problem. General illustrations in various fields will amplify this point. In the area of operations management, a choice may have to be made between special-purpose and general-purpose equipment for the performance of a specific manufacturing operation. In the area of finance, a choice may have to be made between selling bonds or stock to finance a planned expansion of a company. In the area of marketing, a choice may have to be made between private and public warehouses for the storing of a firm's products. In the area of accounting, a choice may have to be made between manual methods and the use of computers for data processing purposes. In the area of education, a choice may have to be made between one design and another for a school building which is to be constructed.

Even on the basis of these general illustrations, one can conclude that a determination of the alternatives calls for a specialized knowledge of the area in which a particular decision must be made. For example, alternative production methods can be ascertained only by someone who understands the manufacturing process involved and who is acquainted with the various kinds of equipment which are available for use in this process. Therefore, we shall have to content ourselves with simply stating that the selection of the most economical alternative begins with the determination of the available alternatives and that this determination is the responsibility of specialists in the area under consideration.

Describing the Alternatives. After the alternatives have been determined, management must go on to describe each of them in terms which will permit the subsequent identification of the most economical one. The elements of this description consist of such things as the alternative's initial cost, its service life, its terminal salvage value, its operating costs, and the revenues it will generate. Because these are factors which are common to all alternatives regardless of the field in which a decision is being made, we are able to discuss their nature in some detail and shall do so at a later point. This is not to suggest, however, that we shall consider how the value of each of these factors can be ascertained in a specific case. The estimation of these values calls for specialized knowledge of the activity involved, and this precludes our considering this aspect of the procedure.

Evaluating the Alternatives. Utilizing the data contained in its descriptions, the organization can go on to the next step in the analysis. This calls for translating all the costs and revenues to be associated with the respective alternatives into a form such that a comparison of the results will enable management to select the most economical alternative. A number of methods for doing this are available. Five of these, however, are of particular significance. They are (1) the uniform annual cost method, (2) the present worth method, (3) the future worth method, (4) the rate of return, or discounted cash flow, method, and (5) the revenue requirement method.

A treatment of these analytical techniques will serve as the core of this book. As will become evident, these methods are equally effective in their ability to identify the most economical alternative. This is to say that, in a given problem, each will identify the same alternative as being the most attractive. But for certain reasons, management may prefer one method under one set of circumstances, and some other under a different set. Hence, a knowledge of all five will prove to be beneficial.

It might also be mentioned that, as a rule, the impact of investment decisions on the firm's income tax liability cannot be ignored. Therefore, we shall find it necessary to consider the tax implications of alternative courses of action. But because the fundamentals of the analytical techniques are sufficiently complex in themselves, we shall begin with before-tax analyses, that is, with analyses of investment alternatives in which the tax consequences of the possible decisions are not ascertained but accounted for indirectly. Then, the equally complex topic of income taxes and their determination will be introduced and discussed so as to permit us to go on to the matter of direct after-tax comparisons of investment alternatives.

Considering the Irreducibles. In its attempt to apply any one of the available methods for evaluating investment alternatives, management will usually find that not all the relevant factors can be expressed in quantitative terms. For example, a relocation of an organization's administrative offices to a new building may result in, among other things, improved employee morale because of a more pleasant work environment, but it may be impossible to place a dollar value on this benefit. All such factors are known as irreducibles or intangibles.

Because such factors cannot be expressed in quantitative terms, they cannot be incorporated in the computations which are an integral part of the five methods we shall consider. Consequently, the results of these computations must be examined in light of the existing irreducibles. If the results being examined indicate that one of the alternatives is greatly superior to the others, the irreducibles may play a relatively minor role in the selection of the most desirable course of action. But if the results indicate that no one alternative is decidedly superior to the others, the final decision is often based on irreducibles. Given that these factors can, on occasion, assume such a major role, we shall find it necessary to consider their nature and to describe the manner in which they enter the analysis.

Making the Post-Audit. The final step in the decision-making procedure, as applied to the capital allocation problem, calls for a post-audit. This is nothing more than a determination, at a subsequent point, of whether the correct decision had been made.

Although the post-audit is not an integral part of the decision-making process, it is to management's advantage to make one to ascertain whether the selected investment alternative has yielded the results which were expected of it. A complete study of this type is not always feasible because the firm often does not know what would have actually happened had some other alternative been selected. But, even in those cases, a determination can be made of whether the estimates of such things as the selected alternative's first cost, service life, salvage value, operating costs, and revenues were correct. In the event that they were not, it may be possible to take steps to eliminate conditions which, for example, are causing operating costs to be excessive. Or, if nothing else, a knowledge of past errors in estimating may enable the firm to improve upon its future estimates.

The specific procedures to be followed when making the post-audit will vary from case to case and from company to company. As a result, we can say nothing about the exact nature of these procedures. At best, we can only state that, wherever possible, a given firm should establish and maintain a system which will prove to be appropriate for the aforementioned purposes.

The post-audit brings us to the end of our discussion of the decision-making process. As was brought out in this discussion, the procedure is designed to enable management to identify the most economical investment alternative, that is, the one which will maximize profits. Therefore, regardless of which analytical technique is used to evaluate available capital investment opportunities, a comparison of the results obtained with the selected method of analysis must be equivalent to a comparison of the profits that the respective alternatives are expected to generate. This permits us to say that the most economical alternative can be identified on the basis of a *profit comparison.* And yet, it is not unusual to find that, in the area of capital expenditure analysis, the results of a *cost comparison* of the alternatives are often used as a means for identifying the most economical one. Before going on, let us consider the question of whether a cost comparison can provide a solution to the capital allocation problem.

PROFIT VERSUS COST COMPARISONS

It will be recalled that underlying the position that a need exists for profit comparisons was the assumption that the primary goal of the firm is profit maximization. From this, it follows that underlying the position that a need exists for cost comparisons would be the assumption that the primary goal of the firm is cost minimization. In a way, it is unfortunate that the latter is not the case, because it is easier to minimize costs than to maximize profits. If cost minimization were the goal, management could attain this goal by simply terminating the business activity and, thereby, reducing costs to zero. But this is infrequently done because the resultant zero costs would be accompanied by zero revenues and, therefore, zero profits. In brief, the governing criterion is the expected effect of a proposed course of action on profits, not on costs. Of course, organizations that adopt the cost-comparison approach realize this, and, given that they do, we must ask whether there are any conditions under which a cost analysis proves to be appropriate. The question can be answered most clearly with the use of an illustration.

Some Examples.   Suppose that an organization is considering two mutually exclusive methods for carrying out a revenue-producing activity. The first method is alternative X, and the second is alternative Y. The most economical course of action is to be determined by a comparison of the average annual profits that can be expected from the alternatives. By means that we shall consider at a later point, the individuals making the study obtain the following results:

	Alternative X	Alternative Y
Annual revenues	$40,000	$40,000
Annual expenses	28,000	33,000
Annual profit	$12,000	$ 7,000

A comparison of these results reveals that, in the absence of irreducible factors, X is the more economical alternative because it yields a greater profit than does Y. But, at this point, there is a natural tendency to observe that a cost comparison would have revealed the same thing. Specifically, the annual profit will be $5,000 more with X than with Y because the annual expenses will be $5,000 less. But it is important to note that this is true only because the revenues in this instance are the same for each alternative. To demonstrate what might occur if this were not the case, let us suppose that the individuals making the study had determined the revenues, expenses, and profits to be as follows:

	Alternative X	Alternative Y
Annual revenues	$40,000	$49,000
Annual expenses	28,000	33,000
Annual profit	$12,000	$16,000

A profit comparison now shows that Y is the more economical alternative. A cost comparison would erroneously suggest that X is the more attractive. The error is attributable to the fact that a comparison of the costs fails to divulge that, although the annual expenses for Y exceed those for X by $5,000, this disadvantage is more than offset by the additional annual revenues of $9,000 that would be experienced with Y.

At this point, it is clear that a cost-comparison approach may be incapable of identifying the most economical alternative when revenues are affected by the choice of alternative. But this does not mean that a cost comparison will always prove to be satisfactory when revenues are equal. Even if revenues are the same for each alternative, the cost-comparison approach may fail to identify the best possible course of action. To demonstrate this, let us return to our illustration and now suppose that an analysis of the alternatives had produced the following results:

	Alternative X	Alternative Y
Annual revenues	$25,000	$25,000
Annual expenses	28,000	33,000
Annual profit	(−)$ 3,000	(−)$ 8,000

An examination of these data discloses that the revenues are the same for both alternatives, and, therefore, the alternative which minimizes costs maximizes profits. But there is a significant difference between this example and the earlier one in which revenues for both alternatives also were equal. In this case, as opposed to the earlier one, the revenues have a second characteristic in common; namely, they do not suffice to cover the expenses. As a result, it becomes necessary to observe that, under such circumstances, the alternative which minimizes costs simply serves to minimize losses. But it does not follow that this alternative is, therefore, the most economical. That this is so becomes evident when we take cognizance of the fact that the organization has still another alternative. This is not to engage in the activity being considered—with the result that no revenues or costs will be experienced. Because this course of action, which we shall call alternative Z, will generate no revenues or costs, its inclusion in the preceding analysis enables us to make the following comparison:

	Alternative X	Alternative Y	Alternative Z
Annual revenues	$25,000	$25,000	$0
Annual expenses	28,000	33,000	0
Annual profit	(−)$ 3,000	(−)$ 8,000	$0

Clearly, alternative Z is more attractive than X or Y, but to ascertain this, it was necessary to make a profit comparison. A cost comparison of alternatives X and Y would not have sufficed to disclose that their revenues, though equal, would not suffice to cover their costs.

A Summation.   The foregoing examples permit us to make the following general observation: A cost comparison can be used as a basis for capital expenditure decisions only when (1) revenues are unaffected by the choice of alternative and (2) revenues are known to exceed the costs. But whether these two conditions are satisfied can be determined only after consideration has been given to the revenues and costs to be associated with the respective alternatives. And a consideration of both revenues and costs is, in effect, a consideration of a combination which represents profit. Hence, we arrive at the conclusion that a profit comparison of investment alternatives, rather than a cost comparison, is needed.

This demonstrated need for profit comparisons can also be related to the earlier observations regarding alternatives that are not mutually exclusive as opposed to those that are. It was stated that the capital expenditure problem is one in which two questions must be answered. First, should any investment at all be made in an activity which happens to be one of a number of activities that are not mutually exclusive? And second, given a decision to make an investment in such an activity, which of a number of mutually exclusive ways of carrying out the activity is the most economical?

If we consider the income-producing activity in the illustration with which we have been working to be one of a number of possible activities that are not mutually exclusive, we can say that only a profit determination is capable of revealing whether any investment at all should be made in the activity. Then, if indications are that the activity will be profitable, we reject the alternative of not making an investment in it and proceed to the next step in the analysis. If alternatives X and Y are the mutually exclusive methods for carrying out the activity, this next step calls for making a profit comparison of these two alternatives so that the one which will maximize profits can be identified.

Having shown that rational decisions in the area of capital investment analysis can be reached only on the basis of a profit comparison, we shall now consider some of the difficulties which may be experienced in an attempt to apply this approach rather than the one based on a cost comparison.

CHOICE OF APPROACH

The application of a profit-comparison approach very often proves to be difficult because of the need it creates for an estimate of the revenues the respective alternatives can be expected to generate. And it so happens that the nature of many investment opportunities is such that it is impossible to ascertain what the revenues will be. For example, a large travel agency may be evaluating a proposal that its personnel's manual typewriters be replaced by a new electric model. When comparing the alternative of retaining the old machines with that of replacing them, management may be able to obtain fairly good estimates of the cost of each alternative, but it is questionable that anyone could determine what portion of the agency's revenues is attributable to the typewriters used by its employees. Consequently, a profit computation is not feasible. But because typewriters are a necessity in this type of business, management would probably assume that an investment in such equipment is a profitable one; as a result, the third alternative of disposing of the manual machines and not replacing them would be rejected. Next, on the basis of judgment, management would probably conclude that the agency's revenues will be unaffected by the kind of typewriters used; therefore, the kind that would minimize costs would maximize profits. In brief, since a determination of the profit for each alternative is not possible under the circumstances, the decision would be based on a cost comparison. This is not to say that the theoretical need for a profit comparison was rejected. Instead, the impact of revenues on the decision was evaluated on the basis of judgment because it was not possible to express this factor in quantitative terms.

In another case, there may be an owner of a warehouse who finds it impossible to estimate what revenues are generated by alternative types of materials handling equipment which are capable of satisfying his needs and which he is investigating with a view toward procuring the most economical type. Nevertheless, in his judgment, it is profitable to handle materials, and, hence, he begins by rejecting the alternative of making no investment in equipment required for this purpose. Also, in his judgment, the firm's revenues will be the same, regardless of the type of equipment selected. The result is that a final decision is reached by comparing expected costs, and it is correct to do so because of the one assumption that revenues will exceed costs and the other that revenues will be the same with each alternative.

As a final example, we might consider a public utility which supplies its customers with gas. It may be that three different types of pipe are being considered as a replacement for a corroded section of an existing pipe line. Although there is no way of knowing what revenues that section of the line yields, it is certain that these revenues will be unaffected by the choice of replacement pipe. Furthermore, the alternative of not replacing the corroded pipe is not a real one because of safety considerations and because the regulatory agency involved is unlikely to allow the utility to decide that it will simply stop supplying the affected customers with gas. Obviously, only a cost comparison of the remaining alternatives is possible, and, given the conditions, such a comparison will serve to identify the most profitable of these alternatives.

To summarize, on many occasions, it is impossible to obtain numerical values for revenues when appraising capital expenditure proposals and, therefore, impossible to calculate numerical values for profits. But if revenues can be assumed to exceed costs and if revenues can be assumed to be the same for the alternatives involved, a cost comparison becomes the equivalent of a profit comparison and can be substituted for it. However, if one or both of the aforementioned assumptions cannot be made, a profit comparison becomes a necessity.

Revenues as Costs. The fact that a profit analysis is mandatory in some capital allocation problems but can be replaced by a cost analysis in others proves to be somewhat troublesome. This is because it would be more convenient to be able to adhere to some single approach which would be suitable in all cases. We know that this single approach cannot be the profit-comparison approach, because there are instances when a calculation of profits is not possible. But this single approach can be the cost-comparison approach. Let us consider why this is so.

It was shown that a cost comparison suffices when revenues are equal and exceed costs. But this type of analysis can be adapted to those situations in which this is not the case. To explain how this can be done, we shall return to an earlier example in which the higher costs of one alternative were more than offset by its higher revenues. In that example, the following comparison was made:

	Alternative X	Alternative Y
Annual revenues	$40,000	$49,000
Annual expenses	28,000	33,000
Annual profit	$12,000	$16,000

At the time, it was explained why a profit analysis would and a cost analysis would not enable management to identify the most economical alternative. The task now is to develop a method for analyzing such situations by means of a cost comparison. Actually, this can be accomplished with little difficulty if we treat revenues as negative costs. Doing so will have the following consequences: All expenditures will be treated as positive costs, as they have been thus far. But because revenues are of opposite sign, they will be said to be negative costs. Therefore, the total annual cost of an alternative will be the sum of its positive costs and its negative costs, that is, the sum of its expenses and revenues. Applying this method to the preceding example, we obtain the following:

	Alternative X	*Alternative Y*
Revenues as a cost	(−)$40,000	(−)$49,000
Expenses as a cost	(+) 28,000	(+) 33,000
Total cost	(−)$12,000	(−)$16,000

These total annual costs must now be examined to determine which is the lower, because the more economical of the two alternatives will be the one that minimizes the total cost. This proves to be alternative Y, whose total annual cost of minus $16,000 is lower than the cost of minus $12,000 calculated for alternative X. Furthermore, Y is more economical than the alternative of making no investment in the activity because its total annual cost of minus $16,000 is lower than the cost of $0 that would be experienced if no investment were made; in other words, the fact that the total cost of alternative Y is negative reveals that its revenues will exceed its expenses. All this, of course, coincides with what we had concluded from the earlier profit comparison of these alternatives.

In brief, the most economical alternative can always be identified by a cost comparison if revenues are treated as negative costs. Therefore, a decision to treat them in this manner permits one to analyze every type of capital allocation problem by means of a cost comparison. Because this proves to be more convenient than analyzing some problems in this manner and others by means of a profit analysis, we shall, from this point on, consider revenues to be negative costs and expenditures to be positive costs and concern ourselves with a discussion of what can be referred to as *cost comparison techniques.*

Admittedly, the signs assigned to the relevant factors could have been reversed, that is, a positive sign could have been assigned to revenues and a negative one to expenses. But, as will be seen, numbers representing expenditures will appear much more frequently in our studies than will those representing revenues, and since most individuals find positive values easier to process than negative ones, it was decided to treat expenditures as positive values.

Having concluded that an evaluation of a given capital investment alternative entails the determination of its total cost in a way which will serve to reveal its profitability, we must now consider the various methods available for computing either this cost or its equivalent. But an application of these methods must be preceded by a suitable description of the respective alternatives. The form this description must assume can be appreciated only after one becomes acquainted with the elements of the calculated total cost. So let us go on to consider what these elements are.

QUESTIONS

1-1   Why is it said that a capital allocation problem exists?

1-2   What is the difference between capital investment alternatives that are mutually exclusive and those that are not? Give some examples of each.

1-3   How is the most economical investment alternative defined? Why is it defined in this manner?

1-4   Given that a firm may have goals other than profit maximization, why is it still recommended that management ascertain expected profits for alternative courses of action?

1-5   State and describe the steps in the decision-making procedure as it is applied to the capital allocation problem.

1-6   What are irreducible, or intangible, factors? Give some examples. When are they likely to assume an important role in capital investment analyses?

1-7   What is a post-audit? Why should one be made?

1-8   As a general approach, why is a profit analysis, rather than a cost analysis, selected as a means for evaluating investment alternatives?

1-9   Under what conditions will a cost comparison prove to be as suitable as a profit comparison when analyzing capital investment opportunities?

1-10 Is it always possible to calculate the profit that can be expected with some specific investment alternative? Explain.

1-11 In those cases in which no calculation of profits is made in the course of identifying the most economical alternative, does it follow that the profitability of the alternative was ignored?

1-12 Why shall we treat revenues as negative costs?

1-13 In a comparison in which expenditures are handled as positive costs and revenues as negative ones, what does the sign of the calculated total cost reveal about the profitability of a given alternative?

PROBLEMS

1-1   The owner of an automobile repair shop finds that the demand for service fluctuates significantly from day to day. If he conducts the business in a manner which will enable him to satisfy every request for service, his average annual revenues will be approximately $370,000, and his average annual costs will be about $325,000. An alternative is to establish a capacity for service which will reduce average annual costs to $280,000. However, he will then be unable to satisfy all the requests for service during periods of peak demand, with the result that his average annual revenues will probably decrease to $310,000. Determine the more economical alternative on the basis of (a) a profit comparison and (b) a cost comparison in which revenues are treated as negative costs.

1-2 A potential investor in rental property is giving consideration to the purchase of one of two available buildings. Each building will yield average revenues of $18,000 per year. Annual costs will be $13,000 with the first building and $11,000 with the second. Which building represents the more attractive alternative? Since revenues are expected to be the same with each building, could these revenues have been ignored in the analysis?

1-3 Three locations are available for the establishment of a restaurant. It is estimated that annual revenues will prove to be $160,000 at each location, but average annual costs will be affected by the choice of location. Specifically, these costs are expected to be as follows:

Location	Annual costs
A	$184,000
B	162,000
C	177,000

What course of action would you recommend? Base this recommendation, first, on a profit comparison of the alternatives and, then, on a cost comparison in which revenues are handled as negative costs.

1-4 Two different designs for a new product have been developed. The more complex design will generate annual revenues of $2,400,000 and annual costs of $1,900,000. The simpler design will serve to reduce revenues by 30 percent as compared with those to be associated with the complex design. This will be offset to some degree by the lower costs that will be experienced with the simpler design. What would these annual costs have to be to make the two designs equally attractive from the economic standpoint? (Ans. $1,180,000)

1-5 A firm has warehouses in three cities. One of its products is now stored in city X at an average cost of $89,000 a year. Storage costs in city Y would be 10 percent more than this amount, and, in city Z, they would be 17 percent less than this amount.

The cost of transporting the product from city X to the company's outlets is $62,000 a year. Transportation costs from city Y would be 8 percent less than this amount, and, from city Z, they would be 20 percent more than this amount.

The product will definitely be stored in one of these three cities. Furthermore, revenues generated by the product will be unaffected by the choice of location. Which warehouse would you select? (Ans. $151,000; $154,940; $148,270)

2

Relevant Costs and Factors

The total cost of an investment alternative consists of two elements. The first is *recurring costs*, and the second is *capital costs*. Each of these will now be examined in detail because an understanding of their nature will enable us to determine the manner in which a given alternative must be described before it can be analyzed by any one of the methods to be considered.

RECURRING COSTS

Recurring costs are represented by expenditures for items that will provide an organization or an individual with a service for a period of one year or less. The cost of direct labor is one example of an expense of this type. If employees are paid, say, every two weeks, the payment involved is for a service provided during a period of less than one-year duration. A second example is the cost of materials. Ordinarily, these are purchased in quantities which will be utilized within a one-year time period. Additional examples are expenditures for supervision, utilities, property taxes, maintenance, supplies, insurance, repairs, and administration. In brief, these are costs of a recurring nature which are experienced by the firm during the course of its operations, and, hence, we shall call them "operating costs."

Another item of a recurring nature is the income taxes the organization will have to pay periodically. These are also attributable to the firm's operations, but they are not being placed in the operating cost category for a special reason. It will be recalled that, for purposes of simplicity, we shall begin with a before-tax analysis of investment alternatives.

In such studies, the calculated total cost does not include the income tax expense, and, therefore, when we speak of operating costs in these studies, it will be helpful if we can simply assume that these operating costs will not contain income taxes. At a subsequent point when after-tax analyses are being made, the income tax expense can then be added as a distinct cost.

A final item of a recurring nature is the revenues the firm will realize from the sale of its products or services. Revenues are recurring in the sense that the organization will be realizing them at many points during a one-year time period. Because of our decision to treat them as negative costs, we shall place these revenues in the category of recurring costs.

To summarize, the total cost of an alternative will include recurring costs. In the most comprehensive case, that is, when the equivalent of an after-tax profit that can be expected from an alternative is being calculated, these recurring costs will consist of operating costs and income taxes, each of which will be handled as a positive expense, and of revenues, which will be handled as a negative expense.

CAPITAL COSTS

As opposed to recurring costs, capital costs are defined as expenditures for items that will provide an organization or an individual with a service for a period of more than one year. Examples of costs of this type are expenditures for buildings, automobiles, machine tools, office equipment, materials handling facilities, and computers—all of which have a service life of more than one year. Incidentally, such assets are called "fixed assets," whereas cash and other assets that will be converted into cash within one year are called "current assets."

Obviously, the capital costs that will be incurred must be taken into consideration in the course of calculating the total cost that will be experienced with a given investment alternative. However, as compared with recurring costs, capital costs prove to be somewhat more difficult to process when the techniques for analyzing capital expenditure opportunities are being applied. In anticipation of these difficulties, we shall now consider the nature of capital costs in greater detail.

Devaluation Expense. A capital expenditure causes the organization or individual making the expenditure to experience two types of expense. One of these is a *devaluation expense,* and the other is the *cost of money.* For the moment, let us consider only the first of these.

The devaluation expense is the amount by which an asset decreases in market value during some stipulated period. This period may be a day, a week, a month, a year, a decade, or any other span of time. For example, a firm may purchase an automobile for use by one of its salesmen for $5,000. If the market value of the automobile is $3,500 a year later, one of the costs of owning it during that year was the amount by which it decreased in value, that is, the devaluation expense of $5,000 minus $3,500, or $1,500, that was experienced. If the market value decreases to $2,600 by the end of the second year, a devaluation expense of $900 was incurred during the second year. Finally, if the market value decreases to $2,000 by the end of the third year, a devaluation expense of $600 was incurred during the third year. In total, the devaluation expense for the three-year period is the difference between the automobile's first cost of $5,000 and its $2,000 market value at the end of that period, or $3,000. If necessary, this total can be expressed as an average annual expense by dividing the $3,000 by the 3 years to obtain $1,000 per year.

The important thing, however, is that the capital cost of the investment in this automobile for the three-year period is not equal to the required initial capital expenditure of $5,000, because some of this expenditure can be recovered. The amount that can be recovered is equal to the $2,000 market value of the automobile at the end of 3 years. Therefore, ignoring the cost of money, we say that the capital cost will be equal to the difference between the original $5,000 expenditure and the $2,000 realizable market value. This difference of $3,000 represents the devaluation expense.

Thus, we are able to make the general observation that one of the elements of the capital cost of an investment alternative is the difference between the initial capital investment it requires and the terminal salvage value of the assets involved. Incidentally, although we are calling this difference the devaluation expense, it is sometimes referred to as the *depreciation expense.* We shall not call it this because the depreciation expense is usually interpreted as being the decrease in value reported for accounting purposes; this reported decrease may or may not coincide with the actual decrease in market value. Therefore, we shall consider the decrease as ascertained for accounting purposes to be the "depreciation expense" but the decrease as ascertained for cost-comparison purposes to be the "devaluation expense."

In any case, the devaluation expense is said to be a capital cost because it results from a capital expenditure. If assets did not decrease in value, a capital investment would not give rise to this cost, and there would be no need to consider it. But ordinarily, assets do decrease in value, which is to say that their terminal salvage value is less than their initial value, and, therefore, a devaluation expense is incurred. In those exceptional cases in which an asset maintains its value or even increases in value, we should simply say that the devaluation expense is zero in the one instance and negative in the other.

Cost of Money. The second expense experienced as a result of a capital expenditure was said to be the cost of money. This is the cost of financing the investment in an alternative, and it can assume the form of either an *interest expense* or an *opportunity cost*. Let us consider the first of these forms.

Suppose that a retail store is to be air conditioned and that a decision must be made regarding which of a number of different possible installations will be the most economical. One of these requires an initial investment of $20,000 in equipment of a certain type. Now, it may be that the management of the national chain, of which this store is a part, finds it necessary to finance such expenditures by means of debt capital. This is to say that the funds will be raised by borrowing, which will call for issuing notes, bonds, or debentures.

As we know, it is a fact of the business world that, if money is borrowed, some amount must be paid for the use of this money. This amount is the interest the lenders will demand. Therefore, if the retail chain obtains money by debt financing, the cost of this money may prove to be, say, 8 percent per year. Consequently, a decision to buy air-conditioning equipment which costs $20,000 is a decision which will necessitate borrowing $20,000. And borrowing $20,000 means paying an annual interest charge of $20,000 times 8 percent, or $1,600, for as long as the $20,000 is owed. In brief, a decision to buy the equipment is a decision which entails incurring an interest expense. If the investment were not made, the money would not be borrowed, and there would be no interest expense. It follows that, in a case such as this in which required funds are raised by borrowing, the resultant interest expense is one of the costs to be associated with the investment alternative involved.

When debt financing takes place, the cost of money is an out-of-pocket interest expense, and there can be no question but that the cost exists. But suppose that there is no need for a company to borrow money to finance capital expenditures because the firm engages in equity financing. In this type of financing, the money used belongs to the owners of the business. The owners may be an individual, as in the case of a sole proprietorship, or a number of individuals, as in the case of partners in a partnership and stockholders in a corporation. What is important, however, is that, if a capital expenditure is made, it will be made with the personal resources of the owners; these resources may be in the form of cash or in the form of assets which can be converted into cash for the purpose of financing the expenditure.

To relate this method of financing to our example, if the retail-store chain is able to procure the air-conditioning equipment with equity funds, no interest expense will be experienced. Nevertheless, we say that a cost of financing would continue to exist. But under these circumstances, the expense would assume the form of an opportunity cost instead of an out-of-pocket cost. It would be an opportunity cost in the following sense: If the investment were not made in this alternative, the company would have $20,000 more cash than it would have if the investment were made. This additional $20,000 could be invested elsewhere at a certain rate of return. Elsewhere could be in stocks, bonds, a new product or service, inventories, accounts receivable, and the like. Each of these investments would yield a return in one form or another. Stocks would provide dividends; bonds, an interest payment; a new product, increased profits; inventories, certain benefits to be associated with larger inventories; and accounts receivable, an ability to finance more customers and thereby increase sales and profits. This is not to say that each of these opportunities will be available to the store chain, but at least one of them will be. But if the firm chooses to invest the $20,000 in the air-conditioning equipment, it will forgo the opportunity to invest this money in sources from which a return could be realized. And, in principle, there is no difference between a decision which results in an out-of-pocket expense of some amount per year and a decision which results in the firm's not receiving some amount per year from another source. Therefore, if the company is using equity funds which could be invested elsewhere at a rate of return of, say, 8 percent per year, this opportunity cost is as much a cost as is an 8 percent annual interest charge the firm would incur if it found it necessary to borrow the money.

An analogous situation is one in which an individual buys a business. He can arrange to have the business managed under one of two possible arrangements. With the one, a manager could be hired and paid a salary of, say, $35,000 a year. A second possibility would be for the owner to manage the business himself. The first alternative generates an out-of-pocket expense, and, indubitably, the $35,000 annual cost would be considered to be one of the costs of owning the business. The second alternative generates an opportunity cost because it requires that the owner forgo the opportunity of selling his services to some other organization. If these services would command $35,000 a year, this is one of the costs of owning the business, and unless the business activity can yield sufficient revenues to cover, among other things, this expense, an investment in the activity could not be justified on the basis of financial considerations.

Thus, we conclude that a financing cost is always experienced when a capital investment is made. With debt financing, the cost is an interest expense; with equity financing, it is an opportunity cost. But we shall refer to this expense, regardless of the form it assumes, as the cost of money.

It was stated earlier that the cost of money is the second expense stemming from a capital expenditure. This is so because, as a rule, a significant amount of time elapses before the activity in which the investment is made is able to produce revenues sufficient to permit recovery of the capital invested. Meanwhile, there is a cost of financing the capital investment which remains at any one point. For example, money may be invested in facilities required to produce and distribute a new product. The venture will yield revenues which will compensate the firm for its operating costs and taxes soon after these expenses are incurred. Any remaining revenues will serve to compensate the firm for the initial investment in the facilities involved. But it might require a few years of operation to generate sufficient remaining revenues to recover the assets' initial cost. During this extended period, varying amounts of unrecovered capital remain committed to the activity. If it is debt capital, the result is an interest expense; if it is equity capital, the result is an opportunity cost.

To put this differently, if, say, $400,000 could be invested in an alternative which would instantaneously yield a revenue of $400,000, this capital expenditure would not create a cost of money. This is because, if the money was borrowed, it could be repaid at the moment of borrowing, and, therefore, there would be no interest expense. Or if equity funds were used, the money would be made available immediately for use elsewhere, and, hence, there would be no opportunity cost. But the usual situation is one in which investments are not recovered in a moment, with the result that funds are tied up for some time and a cost of money is experienced.

This is also an appropriate point at which to note that, very often, the presence of recurring costs necessitates a capital investment in addition to the one required for the procurement or construction of fixed assets. To illustrate, the costs of labor and materials expended in the processing of a product might be recovered very rapidly if the product is sold soon after it is produced. But even this relatively brief lag will usually create a need for working capital. Consequently, many capital expenditure proposals will require an investment in working capital; although the investment in working capital may not decrease in value, which is to say it will not give rise to a devaluation expense, it will bring about a cost of money which cannot be ignored.

To summarize all of the foregoing, the capital cost of a given investment alternative is represented by the two expenses which are incurred as a result of an investment in fixed assets and working capital. One of these expenses is the devaluation expense, and the other is the cost of money. If assets did not decrease in value and if there were no costs of financing or financing were unnecessary because of instantaneous capital recovery, there would be no capital cost. But things do decrease in value, there are financing costs, and capital recovery requires time. The result is a capital cost.

We now know that the total cost of an investment alternative will comprise the following: (1) operating costs, (2) income taxes, (3) revenues, (4) devaluation expense, and (5) cost of money. This knowledge permits us to go on to the consideration of the question of what must be known about a given alternative before its total cost can be ascertained. In this consideration, we shall deal with the most comprehensive case, that is, one in which all the costs and revenues to be associated with an alternative are to be expressed in quantitative terms.

OPERATING COST AND REVENUE ESTIMATES

Because of the need to include operating costs and revenues in the total cost computation, it becomes necessary to estimate the values of these factors for each of the investment alternatives being evaluated. As is to be expected, in many situations, these estimates prove to be difficult to make, but the need to do so cannot be avoided. Furthermore, the fact that estimating errors are likely to occur is accepted and treated as an irreducible when the final decision is made regarding the attractiveness of a proposed capital investment.

In an attempt to reduce the estimation problem to some degree, the practice has evolved of forecasting operating expenses and revenues on an annual basis rather than on a daily, weekly, or monthly basis, in spite of the fact that it is known that, during any one year, significant fluctuations in operating expenses and revenues might occur.

Insofar as operating cost estimates are concerned, a word of caution is in order. When estimating their values, the analyst should consider only those specific recurring expenses that are attributable to the alternative involved. For example, a telephone company might be in the process of analyzing a method for providing its customers with a new service. When estimating the operating costs that will be experienced with this method, the firm may find that there are certain kinds and amounts of direct labor and material that will have to be expended in the course of providing the customers with the service. In other words, if the service is not provided, no expenditures will have to be made for this labor and material. Clearly, these costs will, therefore, have to be included in the estimate of total operating costs. But to continue, it may also be found that the activity will require some floor space, supervision, indirect labor, and administration. However, suppose that no additional supervisors, indirect labor, or administrators will have to be hired because the personnel of this type that are currently on the firm's roll will be able to handle the additional work; similarly, suppose that no additional floor space will have to be obtained because unused space is available in the firm's buildings. Given that a decision to engage in the new activity will not serve to increase these specific costs, they should be ignored when total operating costs are being estimated.

The reason for making this distinction between those operating costs that will be affected by a decision to engage in an activity and those that will not is as follows: For cost accounting purposes, a company might classify a certain cost as being either a direct labor expense, a direct material expense, a factory overhead expense, a selling expense, or an administrative expense. Direct labor and direct material expenses are production costs that can be identified with a particular operation and, therefore, are charged to that operation. The remaining cost classifications contain such items as the cost of utilities, foremen's salaries, maintenance and repairs, materials handling, rent, salesmen's salaries, office supplies, advertising, officers' salaries, and depreciation as computed for accounting purposes; all these items are characterized by the fact that they represent expenditures which, for all practical purposes, cannot be identified with a particular operation, product, or activity. Consequently, for cost accounting purposes, the firm finds it practicable to allocate these indirect costs among its various products and services with the use of so-called overhead, or burden, rates. These rates assume various forms, but they might be expressed in terms of some dollar amount per hour of direct labor, per hour of machine time, per square foot of floor space, or per unit of output. However, it should be recognized that, although direct labor and material costs will be affected by a specific decision which will serve either to expand or contract the scope of the organization's operations, such a decision will not necessarily affect the level of all the indirect costs reflected in the overhead, or burden, rate. Therefore, in the course of estimating the total operating cost to be associated with a given capital investment alternative, it would be a mistake to use these overhead or burden rates as a means for estimating certain elements of the total operating cost.

All this permits us to return to our earlier observation that, when estimating the total operating cost, the analyst should consider only the elements of this cost that will be affected by a decision to make the investment, as opposed to a decision not to make it. These elements are said to be the relevant ones and are often referred to as the *marginal* or *incremental* costs.

Finally, it might be noted that the depreciation expense, as computed for accounting purposes, is not to be included as a part of the operating expense. This depreciation expense, which is intended to represent the decrease in the value of fixed assets, will be accounted for by the devaluation expense which we shall include, together with the cost of money, as a part of the capital cost at a subsequent point in the analysis. This is another reason for not using established burden rates when estimating operating costs, because these rates usually provide for the allocation of, among other things, depreciation expenses.

INCOME TAX ESTIMATES

If an after-tax analysis is being made of a capital expenditure proposal, the income taxes it can be expected to generate must be taken into account. Although the details of the tax calculation will be discussed later, a general description of the approach is necessary at this point so that we can determine what must be known about an alternative before this recurring expense can be ascertained.

The first step in the tax determination procedure calls for computing the taxable income; for reasons suggested when we discussed revenues and operating costs, this is done on an annual basis in capital investment analyses. Once the taxable income for a given year has been obtained, the tax rate is simply applied to this figure to arrive at the income tax for that year. Therefore, it becomes apparent that the federal and state income tax rates must be known. If current rates are expected to continue, no forecasting by the analyst is required; otherwise, estimates will have to be made of the rates that are likely to prevail during the alternative's life.

But to return to the taxable income, this is found by taking the difference between the revenues which the alternative will yield and the expenses which will be deductible for tax purposes. Its revenues will have already been estimated for inclusion in its total cost; so this required datum will be on hand for use in the tax calculation.

Insofar as the deductible expenses are concerned, the tax laws allow an organization to report its operating costs, the cost of borrowed money, and the depreciation expense as calculated for tax purposes. As in the case of revenues, operating costs will have been estimated earlier for inclusion in the alternative's total cost; so this item of information will also be available for use in the tax calculation. But the same is not true of the two remaining factors—interest expense and depreciation expense.

To arrive at the interest expense for an investment alternative, the analyst will have to be told by management what the cost of borrowed money is in terms of a rate per year. To convert this rate to a dollar cost, he must also know how much money will be borrowed to finance the expenditure and what the repayment plan will be. For example, management may have reason to believe that the cost of borrowed money will be 9 percent per year. Further, a certain kind of investment may call for borrowing $300,000 under an arrangement in which $100,000 will be repaid at the end of each year for 3 years. With this information at his disposal, the analyst will be able to determine that the interest expense will be 9 percent of $300,000 for the first year, 9 percent of $200,000 for the second, and 9 percent of $100,000 for the third. He need not concern himself with the cost of money to be associated with any equity funds that might be invested in the same alternative, because an opportunity cost is not a deductible expense.

This brings us to the remaining deductible expense, namely, the depreciation expense. What must be known to determine this expense can best be explained after we become acquainted with the three major methods used for arriving at this expense for tax purposes. These are the straight-line method, sum-of-the-years-digits method, and double-rate declining-balance method. We shall consider them in this order.

Straight-Line Depreciation. At one time, the most commonly used method for computing tax depreciation expenses was the straight-line method. To illustrate how it is applied, let us suppose that an asset has been purchased at a cost of $50,000 and is expected to have a service life of 5 years with a terminal salvage value of $5,000.

For tax purposes, the firm would not be allowed to claim the entire $50,000 as an expense because $5,000 of this amount is expected to be recovered at the end of the asset's life. Instead, the total amount that can be reported as a depreciation expense is the difference between the first cost and the salvage value, which represents the total expected decrease in the asset's value. Therefore, in our example, we obtain

Total depreciation expense = (first cost) − (salvage value)

$$= \$50,000 - \$5,000 = \$45,000$$

Next, the firm would not be permitted to claim the total depreciation as an expense during the first year of the asset's life, in spite of the fact that the capital expenditure was made at the beginning of that year. Instead, this total must be distributed over a time period equal to the asset's life. How this is done depends on the method of depreciation adopted. With the straight-line method, it is assumed that the asset decreases in value at a constant annual rate throughout its life, and, therefore, the total depreciation expense is divided by the asset's life to obtain the annual depreciation expense that can be claimed as a deductible expense. Applying this approach in our example, we obtain

Annual depreciation expense = (total depreciation expense) ÷ (life)

$$= \$45,000 \div 5 \text{ yrs} = \$9,000/\text{yr}$$

It might also be mentioned that, when an asset is purchased, it is entered into the company's "books" as having a *book value* equal to its first cost. This book value is reduced at the end of each year by an amount equal to the calculated depreciation expense for the year under consideration. If this is done in our example, the results are as follows:

Year	Depreciation expense	End-of-year book value
0	$ 0	$50,000
1	9,000	41,000
2	9,000	32,000
3	9,000	23,000
4	9,000	14,000
5	9,000	5,000
Total	$45,000	

As can be seen, the book value at the end of the assumed service life coincides with the expected salvage value. If all the estimates prove to be correct, the asset in our example will be sold at the end of the fifth year for $5,000 and removed from the company's books. However, the estimates may prove to be incorrect, and the asset might be sold at the end of the fifth year for $7,000; the $2,000 difference between this realized value and the book value would be treated as a *gain* for tax purposes and subject to a gains tax. Or the asset might be sold at the end of the fourth year of its life for $11,000; the $3,000 difference between this realized value of $11,000 and the book value of $14,000 would be treated as a *loss* and reported as such for tax purposes, with the result that a tax saving might be experienced. Another possibility is that the asset might be retained beyond the five-year period. If so, a depreciation expense may or may not be reported after the fifth year; whether it will be depends on what the terminal salvage value of the asset is expected to be.

All the foregoing observations have been made on the assumption that the firm will maintain *item*, or *single-asset*, accounts for depreciation purposes. With this arrangement, a separate account is established for each asset, and depreciation charges and book values are determined in the manner which has just been described. As opposed to this, a company may establish *multiple-asset* accounts for depreciation purposes. When this is done, a number of assets are placed into a single account. Then, on the basis of the estimated *average* life of those assets, a total annual depreciation expense is ascertained for the entire account. Consequently, while there is a book value at any one point for the account, there is none for any of the individual items in the account. Therefore, no gain or loss determination is ordinarily made when one of these assets is retired. But because of the complexity of multiple-asset accounting, we shall assume, in our analyses, that the firm maintains item accounts for tax depreciation purposes.

Another thing to keep in mind with respect to calculated depreciation expenses is that they do not represent expenditures at the points at which they are reported. In our example, if the estimates are accurate, there will be a cash outflow of $50,000 at the beginning of the five-year period and a cash inflow of $5,000 at its end. This actual pattern of cash flows can be depicted graphically as follows:

```
50,000                                             (5,000)
├──────────┼──────────┼──────────┼──────────┼──────────┤
0          1          2          3          4          5
```

Because we shall make extensive use of such diagrams, which can be called either "time lines" or "cash-flow lines," let us comment on them. The line shows the number of periods being considered in a given case and the amounts of money spent and received at various points during the time interval. Also, in keeping with the notation decided upon earlier, an expenditure is designated as a positive cost on the line, and a revenue as a negative cost. But because the use of negative signs on the line would prove to be cumbersome, we shall designate negative costs, that is, receipts, by means of parentheses. However, parentheses will be employed for this purpose on the time line only; elsewhere, a negative sign will be used.

In any event, the preceding cash-flow line reflects the fact that the firm in our example will spend $50,000 at the beginning of the first year and receive $5,000 at the end of the fifth. But for tax purposes, with straight-line depreciation, the company will have to describe the net cash outflow of $45,000 in the following manner:

```
        9,000     9,000     9,000     9,000     9,000
├──────────┼──────────┼──────────┼──────────┼──────────┤
0          1          2          3          4          5
```

This, of course, is not what actually occurs, but tax laws necessitate reporting the net cost as if this is what occurs. However, as will become apparent later, a distinction must be made, in the analyses of capital expenditure proposals, between cash-flow patterns actually experienced and the expense patterns reported for tax purposes.

Finally, it must be recognized that a reported depreciation expense will not necessarily coincide with the actual decrease in an asset's market value. In our example, the actual decrease in value during the first year might be $13,000 and not the calculated amount of $9,000. If it is the former, then the real expense to the firm will be $13,000, which means that, when computing its taxes for the year, the firm will be understating this expense by $4,000. But in a cost comparison of investment alternatives, the relevant figure would be the $13,000 because it represents what took place. It was to distinguish between an *actual* decrease in an asset's value and a *reported* decrease that it was decided earlier to refer to the actual decrease as the devaluation expense and the reported decrease as the depreciation expense.

Sum-of-the-Years-Digits Depreciation. We ended our discussion of the straight-line method of depreciation with the observation that a reported depreciation expense may often not be equal to the actual devaluation expense. As a matter of fact, this will usually be the case when the straight-line method is used because it yields a uniform series of depreciation expenses, whereas most assets decrease in value by a larger amount in the earlier years of their lives than in the later. In an attempt to obtain a more realistic pattern of calculated depreciation expenses, most organizations adopt some method of depreciation for tax purposes other than the straight-line method. One of these is the sum-of-the-years-digits method, which we shall describe by continuing to work with the asset which had a first cost of $50,000, an expected life of 5 years, and a salvage value of $5,000.

The first step in this approach is to compute the value of the total depreciation expense. As before, this is the difference between the first cost and the estimated salvage value of the asset. In our example, this was found to be $45,000. Next, the so-called sum-of-the-years-digits, *SYD*, is computed. How this is done can be described with the following expression, in which n represents the asset's life in years:

$$SYD = (n) + (n-1) + (n-2) + \cdots + 3 + 2 + 1$$

It can be shown, although we shall not do so, that this is always equal to

$$SYD = \frac{n(n+1)}{2}$$

Applying either of these expressions in our example, we obtain

$SYD = 5 + 4 + 3 + 2 + 1 = 15$

or

$$SYD = \frac{5(5 + 1)}{2} = 15$$

Continuing with the example, we should find the respective annual depreciation expenses in the manner shown in the following table and obtain the indicated book values:

Year	Depreciation expense	End-of-year book value
0		$50,000
1	(5/15)($45,000) = $15,000	35,000
2	(4/15)(45,000) = 12,000	23,000
3	(3/15)(45,000) = 9,000	14,000
4	(2/15)(45,000) = 6,000	8,000
5	(1/15)(45,000) = 3,000	5,000
Total	$45,000	

If an asset has, say, a 10-year life, the SYD will be found to be 55. The depreciation for the first year would be $10/55$ of the difference between the first cost and the salvage value; for the second, $9/55$ of the difference; for the third, $8/55$ of the difference; and so on until for the last year it would be $1/55$ of the difference.

But to return to our example, the preceding table reveals that the total reported depreciation would coincide with the $45,000 that would be reported with the straight-line method, and, hence, the end-of-life book value continues to be equal to the expected salvage value. However, the asset is said to be depreciated at a faster rate in the sense that larger values for the depreciation expense are obtained in the early years of the asset's life. As a result, the calculated taxable income would be lower during each of those years than it would be with the straight-line method, and, therefore, the annual taxes would be lower. Of course, smaller values for the depreciation expense are obtained in the later years than would be obtained with the straight-line method, and, consequently, the calculated taxable income for each of those years and the resultant annual taxes would be higher. Nevertheless, there is an advantage to be associated with an arrangement in which a portion of the tax expense is deferred.

In spite of the fact that the sum-of-the-years-digits method yields a pattern of depreciation expenses which is more likely to reflect the changes taking place in the asset's market value, it is still possible that a reported depreciation expense will not be equal to the actual devaluation expense experienced. This is to say that, at any point during the asset's life, there might be a discrepancy between its book value and its market value. The consequences of this are the same as those mentioned in the discussion of the straight-line method. It is also worth repeating that, regardless of the way in which they are calculated, depreciation expenses reported for tax purposes do not represent cash outflows.

Declining-Balance Depreciation. The sum-of-the-years-digits method is considered to be an accelerated method of depreciation, as compared with the straight-line method, because it results in the asset's being depreciated at a faster rate. Another such method is the double-rate declining-balance method.

To explain this method, let us begin with the term "double-rate." When the straight-line method is employed, the annual depreciation expense is obtained by dividing the total depreciation expense by the number of years which represent the asset's life. Specifically, in our example, we divided $45,000 by 5 years. This is to say that 1/5 of the total depreciation expense was reported every year. This fraction, which can also be expressed as 20 percent, is called the "appropriate straight-line rate." In general, this rate is equal to the reciprocal of the asset's life.

If an organization uses the double-rate declining-balance method for tax purposes, it is allowed to use a rate which is equal to twice, that is, double, the appropriate straight-line rate. Therefore, in our example, the double rate would be 2 times 20 percent, or 40 percent. In the declining-balance method, this double rate is applied as follows: The depreciation expense for any given year is found by multiplying the asset's book value at the beginning of that year by the double rate, which is obtained by dividing the asset's life, n, into 2. With the data in our example, this procedure will yield the following results:

Year	Beginning-of-year book value	Depreciation expense	End-of-year book value
1	$50,000	$50,000(0.40) = $20,000	$50,000 − $20,000 = $30,000
2	30,000	30,000(0.40) = 12,000	30,000 − 12,000 = 18,000
3	18,000	18,000(0.40) = 7,200	18,000 − 7,200 = 10,800
4	10,800	10,800(0.40) = 4,320	10,800 − 4,320 = 6,480
5	6,480	6,480(0.40) = 2,592	6,480 − 2,592 = 3,888

It is imperative to note that, at no point in this procedure, was consideration given to the $5,000 estimated salvage value of the asset. Or more specifically, with this method, the calculation begins with the application of the depreciation rate to the asset's first cost, rather than to the difference between this cost and the salvage value as it was in the preceding two methods. In any event, the result is that the end-of-life book value is not likely to coincide with the estimated salvage value; this proved to be the case in our example. As a matter of fact, unless a declining-balance rate of 100 percent is used, which would not be allowed for tax purposes, an infinite number of years would be required to arrive at an estimated salvage value of zero. Because of this, the firm will have to choose between two possible courses of action. One is to change to the straight-line method at some appropriate point, so as to arrive at a book value which is equal to the salvage value. To illustrate, in our example, the book value is $10,800 at the end of the third year. A book value of $5,000 could be obtained two years later by reporting a total of $5,800 in depreciation during the last two years. If the straight-line method were adopted for these years, the reported depreciation expense would be this $5,800 divided by 2, or $2,900, per year, instead of the amounts that would have been reported with the declining-balance method.

The alternative is to continue with the declining-balance method and then to report any difference between the final book value and the amount realized upon the disposal of the asset as a gain or loss. This, of course, assumes that single-asset rather than multiple-asset accounting is involved; it will be recalled that it was stated earlier that this is the assumption that would be made, for the sake of simplicity, in this presentation.

The double-rate declining-balance method of depreciation is the last one we shall consider. The pattern of depreciation charges it generates is similar to the one obtained with the sum-of-the-years-digits method, but, again, the respective values may or may not coincide with the devaluation expenses actually incurred.

A Summation.   The purpose of this entire section was to ascertain what would have to be known about a proposed investment alternative before an estimate could be made of the income tax consequences of the proposal. Keeping in mind that the annual tax will be a function of the tax rate and the taxable income, we can summarize our findings as follows: First, the federal and state income tax rates must be known. These are usually combined, in a manner to be described later, to arrive at an *effective* rate which reflects, for example, the fact that the state income tax may be treated as a deductible expense when computing the federal income tax.

Next, the annual revenues and operating costs that the alternative is expected to yield must be known because these will have an effect on the taxable income for a given year. This income will also be affected by the interest expense experienced with debt financing; so a need exists for knowing how much money must be borrowed to finance the investment, the repayment plan involved, and the annual interest rate. Finally, the taxable income for a given year will be affected by the depreciation expense reported for tax purposes, and, as we have just seen, this amount can be computed only if the method of depreciation is known; but the application of a specific method requires a description of the asset involved in terms of its first cost, estimated service life, and expected salvage value. With regard to the depreciation expense, it should be noted that, in our discussion of its determination, we assumed that the alternative being evaluated would require the procurement of an asset. But it may be that one of the alternatives calls for retaining an asset already owned by the firm; in that event, future annual depreciation expenses will depend on the depreciation method adopted at the time the asset was purchased and on how much of the total depreciation expense that was ascertained at that time remains to be reported.

THE DEVALUATION EXPENSE ESTIMATE

The annual income tax was the last item in the list of recurring costs that would be included in an investment alternative's total cost. So we can now turn to the second element of this total, namely, the capital cost, and consider the question of what must be known about an alternative before its devaluation expense and cost of money expense can be calculated. We shall begin with the devaluation expense.

The devaluation expense was defined as being the amount by which an asset decreases in value during some period of time. This time period, of course, will be the asset's service life, and, therefore, the value of this life must be estimated. Although this will be illustrated with a problem in a subsequent chapter, it is worth mentioning now that an attempt should be made to estimate the value of the asset's *economic* life. In general, this is the life that will place the alternative involved in the best possible light. This can be explained as follows:

When the life of an asset is increased, a decrease occurs in the average annual value of some of its costs. Let us take the average annual devaluation expense as an example. A unit of construction equipment may have a first cost of $70,000 and a salvage value of $30,000 at the end of 2 years of service; as a consequence, a two-year service life estimate would yield a total decrease in value of $40,000 and an average annual devaluation expense of $20,000. However, it may be that the estimated salvage value at the end of 4 years of service would prove to be $10,000; a four-year life estimate would, therefore, yield a total decrease in value of $60,000, which results in an average annual devaluation expense of only $15,000.

On the other hand, an increase in the service life estimate causes an increase in the average annual value of some of the alternative's other costs. To illustrate, with the aforementioned construction equipment, the average cost of maintenance and repairs may be $1,200 per year during the first 2 years of its life, but this average may increase to $1,900 per year if the asset is kept 4 years.

In brief, if we think of the total cost in terms of an average annual cost, some of the elements of this total will increase in value and others will decrease in value as the life estimate is increased. However, the sum of these increasing and decreasing cost elements will be a minimum for some service life, and it is this life that is called the "economic life." The analyst should attempt to estimate the value of the economic life because it may be that the proposed capital expenditure can be justified with this life estimate but not with some other.

In addition to a life estimate, a determination of the alternative's devaluation expense requires a knowledge of the value of the involved assets at the beginning of this life and a knowledge of their value at the end of this life. If the proposal being evaluated calls for the procurement of facilities which the firm does not currently own, the initial value is simply the first cost of the assets, which would include such things as the quoted price, delivery charges, and installation costs. The value of these assets at the end of the selected service period would, of course, be their salvage value, that is, the net proceeds the firm expects to realize from their disposal. Of these required items of information, each asset's price and cost of delivery will often be known, but the installation expense and terminal salvage value will always have to be estimated.

Currently-Owned Assets. The preceding discussion of what must be known about each asset to ascertain the future devaluation expense centered about an investment alternative which would require that a firm procure one or more assets it does not currently own. As an example, this alternative may stem from a proposal that a new unit of production equipment be purchased as a replacement for an old unit now located in the company's plant. But as this suggests, a second alternative that must be evaluated in the study is the one calling for the retention of the old equipment. This alternative is characterized by the fact that it involves an asset currently owned by the firm. Because such an asset does not require an actual capital expenditure at the present time, a question arises regarding what capital investment, if any, is required in an alternative of this type.

Before we answer this question, let us state something explicitly which, thus far, has only been implied. As individuals go through life, they invest different kinds of things in various kinds of activities. In some of these activities, there is an investment of time; in others, an investment of effort; in still others, an investment in the form of sacrificed opportunities, peace of mind, a way of life, and so on; in some, an investment of money; and in others, an investment of some combination of all these things. But in the area of finance, the investment in anything is considered to be simply the amount of money invested, or its equivalent. Therefore, the investment in, say, a proposed new machine tool would be the amount of money that would have to be spent to procure and install the asset. From this, it follows that the investment in a currently-owned asset is the amount of *money* currently invested in the facility. And for reasons we shall now consider, this amount of money is said to be the asset's present *market value*.

If a currently-owned asset has a market value of, say, $3,000, a decision to replace it will result in the asset's being sold for $3,000, which is to say that the firm will receive $3,000 in cash, or its equivalent. Conversely, a decision not to replace it will result in the retention of the asset, which is to say that the firm will not receive $3,000 in cash, or its equivalent. Hence, one of the questions in a replacement analysis is whether or not a currently-owned asset should be converted into an amount of money equal to its market value. It is clear that, if the decision is to retain the asset, an amount of money equal to its market value will not be received, and, therefore, a decision has been made to invest this amount in the alternative represented by the asset under consideration.

As this suggests, there is no difference in principle between a case in which a firm decides to procure a new unit of equipment at a cost of, say, $3,000 and a case in which a firm decides to retain an old unit of equipment which can be sold for $3,000. In either case, the firm will have $3,000 less than it otherwise would. Thus, it follows that the required investment in either case would be $3,000. But in the one case, the $3,000 happens to be the equipment's first cost, while in the other, it happens to be the equipment's market value. And incidentally, it is also correct to say that, even when the procurement of a new asset is being considered, the required investment is its market value, because the market value at that moment would be equal to its first cost.

At this point, however, it is necessary to consider a situation which sometimes arises. Very often, when currently-owned special-purpose equipment is involved, a company will find that the market value is quite low, because of the limited demand for used facilities of special design. However, the cost to replace the same equipment, given its unique characteristics, might be very high. As an example, some processing equipment in an oil refinery might have a market value, that is, a net disposal value of $14,000, but its replacement cost might be $200,000. Such situations, of course, raise the question of which of these two values represents the present value of the equipment. This question can be answered as follows:

If a decision to procure a new asset results in the disposal of the currently-owned asset, the present investment in the latter is its market value and not its replacement cost. We can see why with the aid of the oil refinery example. If the refining equipment will be sold in the event that a decision is made to replace it, the amount received will be the $14,000 market value and not the $200,000 replacement cost. Therefore, a proposal to retain the equipment is a proposal not to convert it into $14,000 or, in other words, a proposal to allow $14,000 to remain invested in the asset. Hence, this market value proves to be the present value of the equipment.

But, on occasion, a somewhat unusual set of circumstances exists. Specifically, a decision to buy new equipment may not result in the disposal of the old equipment because the company requires a replica of the old equipment for use elsewhere in its operations. If this is a requirement in the strict sense of the term, failure to retire the old equipment from its present application will necessitate the firm's buying an asset just like it to satisfy the other need. For example, let us suppose that, if the oil refinery does not retire the old equipment from its current function, it will have to purchase an asset just like it because this same kind of equipment is needed by some other operating unit in the organization. Naturally, the cost of the replica will be the replacement cost of $200,000 and not the market value of $14,000. In such situations, the present value of the old equipment is said to be its replacement cost rather than its market value, because a decision to retain it in its present capacity creates a need for spending an amount of money, equal to the replacement cost of the equipment, for an asset just like it for some other use.

Yet, even in these special cases, it can be argued, and correctly so, that the replacement cost is also a market value. To illustrate, in the case of the refining equipment, the market value was given as $14,000. This represented the amount the company would receive if it sold the asset to someone outside the organization. But then a condition was introduced which altered the nature of the market for the equipment.

This condition was that another customer appeared who was willing, because of necessity, to buy this kind of equipment for $200,000. This served to increase the market value from $14,000 to $200,000. The fact that this other customer was a member of the same organization is of no consequence, although it might be noted that that customer supposedly had been able to justify an investment of $200,000 in the activity in which he was engaged.

Just as a question arose regarding the relevancy of the replacement cost of a currently-owned asset, one might arise regarding the relevancy of its book value. We know that, when the book value of an asset does not equal the amount received upon the disposal of the asset, a gain or loss must be reported for tax purposes if the firm adheres to single-asset accounting. Therefore, the book value of a currently-owned asset is a relevant item of information in an after-tax analysis because it may enter into the determination of the tax consequences of the alternative which calls for retaining the asset. But it is of no relevancy for the purpose of determining the present value of such an asset.

As was pointed out earlier, any difference between book and market values simply represents the amount by which the depreciation expense has been overstated or understated. This is to say that, if at some point in the asset's life the book value is less than the market value, the amount by which the asset was shown to have depreciated in the company's books was too great and, therefore, this expense was overstated. As a result, the company's profit had been understated. Conversely, if at some point in the asset's life the book value is greater than the market value, the amount by which the asset was shown to have depreciated in the company's books was too small and, therefore, this expense was understated. As a result, the company's profit had been overstated.

There is usually no difficulty experienced in gaining acceptance of this line of reasoning when market values exceed book values. For example, if a building which an organization owns has a market value of $1,300,000 and a book value of only $750,000, it would be the rare individual in that organization who would maintain that the true value of the building is its book value, that is, that the present investment in the building is only $750,000. But if the building were to have a market value of $600,000 as compared with a book value of $750,000, there sometimes is an inclination to look upon the book value as the present investment in the asset and to maintain that selling the building at this time would generate a loss of $150,000. This inclination, however, must be overcome. The fact that the book value, in this case, exceeds the market value means that the actual decrease in market value which occurred exceeds the reported decrease by $150,000, with the result that past calculated profits were overstated by this amount. Anything that is done with the asset at this time will not change this fact. The $150,000 has already been "lost," and selling the asset now will simply compel management to reveal this by making the necessary adjusting entry in its accounts. Admittedly, for tax purposes, the loss would be treated as if it occurred when the asset was sold, but when determining the impact of an investment alternative on costs other than taxes, we must be governed by what actually has occurred or will occur rather than by what has been or will be reported as having occurred.

We know, from our discussion of tax depreciation methods, that discrepancies between book and market values are to be expected. Book values are affected by estimated service lives and terminal salvage values and by the choice of depreciation method, and it might be that the estimates are in error and that the selected depreciation method fails to generate an accurate pattern of depreciation charges. If so, the result is a series of reported depreciation expenses that does not coincide with the series of actual devaluation expenses and, therefore, book values that do not coincide with market values.

Incidentally, it is interesting to note that, in a given company, a single asset may have more than one book value. Because of the tax advantages to be associated with accelerated depreciation, the firm may use, say, the double-rate declining-balance method to obtain depreciation expenses and book values for tax purposes. But for reports to the stockholders and the public, the straight-line method might be used because the lower resultant depreciation charges and the corresponding higher book values during the early years result in higher calculated earnings which serve to place the firm in a more favorable light. And if the firm happens to be in a government-regulated industry, it may use a third method which serves to yield book values that will prove to be advantageous when the firm is dealing with regulatory commissions. In brief, it is not unusual for an asset to have more than one book value. Fortunately, the question of which of these represents the asset's present value does not have to be raised in capital investment analyses, since this present value is said to be the market value. This is true even in the special cases in which the replacement cost proves to be relevant, because we have seen that this replacement cost represents an amount someone in the firm is willing to pay for the asset, and, hence, it becomes a market value.

Let us now summarize what must be known about an investment alternative before its devaluation expense can be calculated. If the alternative requires the procurement of an asset the company does not currently own, the analyst must have data concerning the asset's first cost, service life, and terminal salvage value. If the alternative involves the retention of an asset the company currently owns, the analyst must have data concerning the asset's present market value, remaining service life, and future salvage value.

THE COST OF MONEY ESTIMATE

The expense that remains to be included in an alternative's total cost is the second expense that will be experienced as a result of a capital expenditure. This is the cost of money. The dollar value of this cost will be a function of two things. One is the amount of capital investment the alternative requires, and the other is the rate, or percent, in terms of which the interest expense or opportunity cost or both can be expressed.

It has just been ascertained that the required investment in an alternative will include either the first cost or the market value of the fixed assets involved. Earlier, it was noted that an additional investment may be required in working capital. Hence, the total investment in the alternative will be the sum of the respective investments in fixed assets and working capital. Because there was no need to estimate the necessary working capital for the purpose of determining revenues, operating costs, income taxes, and devaluation expenses, this estimate will have to be made at this point.

Insofar as the cost of money as a percent is concerned, it is simple enough to say that management must provide the analyst with this figure—usually in the form of a percent per year. However, one cannot escape the fact that the determination of this annual rate poses serious difficulties. At best, we can only identify the factors that must be taken into consideration in this determination. The nature of these factors stems from the reasons why investors demand a return from their investments, that is, why they charge someone for the use of their money. So let us become acquainted with these reasons.

Reasons for a Return Requirement. One reason an investor will charge for the use of his money is that the investment may involve an administrative cost. For example, a bank that lends an organization money can be thought of as making an investment in that organization's activities. But in order to be able to engage in such transactions, the bank will find it necessary to acquire a building, hire personnel, procure office equipment, obtain legal advice, and so on. Naturally, the cost of all this must be recovered, and this is done by requiring the borrower of the institution's funds to return more than he receives, that is, to pay interest. Therefore, the interest rate charged will have, as one of its elements, a certain percentage intended to compensate the bank for the administrative costs it experiences when making a loan. Or, in general, we can say that the higher the administrative costs to be associated with an investment, the higher will be the investor's rate-of-return requirement.

A second reason a return requirement exists is that every investment involves some risk. As an example, an individual might invest in a company's common stock. When doing so, he realizes that there is a chance that, at some future point, he may be unable to recover his entire investment because the business might not prove to be sufficiently profitable. The investor expects to be compensated for this risk by a return which can assume the form of dividends, an increase in the market value of his investment, or some combination of the two. And the greater the risk of loss, the greater will be the investor's rate-of-return requirement.

A third reason why a rate of return is demanded is that the purchasing power of the money invested may be decreasing. For example, a purchaser of government bonds may have every assurance that his original investment will be returned to him in five years. But if this happens to be a period of inflation, the dollars he receives are worth less than the dollars he invested. Naturally, he insists that he be compensated for this with interest payments that will offset the decrease in the real value of his investment. And the greater the inflation rate, the greater will be the investor's stipulated rate-of-return requirement.

The fourth and final reason why a return on investment is demanded is that the investor is postponing the satisfaction to be realized from the immediate use of available funds. For example, an individual who invests in an account in a savings institution could have spent the money instead on an automobile, entertainment, a vacation, clothing, a home, and so on. While it is true that he will still be able to make these expenditures when he withdraws his money from the account at some future time, he will have delayed experiencing the pleasures to be associated with such expenditures and, hence, will expect to be indemnified by means of a return on his investment. And of course, the higher the value individuals place on immediate utility, the higher will be their rate-of-return requirement.

All this explains why investors charge someone for the use of their money, but it does not reveal why an individual or an organization is willing to pay for the use of someone else's money. The reasons for this willingness are easily identified. Let us first consider an individual who seeks funds so as to be able to pay for consumer goods and services, such as an automobile, medical care, furniture, a painting, and so on. His willingness to pay for the use of these funds arises from the aforementioned value that people place on immediate utility, which explains the popularity of, say, installment plans in spite of the carrying charges involved. But individuals and organizations also seek funds for investment in "profit-making" ventures. When the anticipated return from such ventures exceeds the cost of obtaining the required capital, potential investors are willing to incur this cost.

So, on the one hand, we have people demanding a return on their investments, and, on the other, we have people willing to satisfy this demand. The result is that money evolves as a commodity whose acquisition entails some cost.

Return Requirement Determination. In the preceding discussion of why money must be paid for the use of money, extensive use was made of the term *rate of return*. This is because whatever rate, or amount, the supplier of capital receives for the use of his money can be said to represent the return he realizes on his investment. In brief, given the two parties involved in a financial transaction, whatever proves to be a cost to the one party proves to be a return to the other.

Keeping this in mind, let us return to the need for determining what rate, expressed as a percent per year, a firm should use in its determination of the cost of money to be associated with a proposed capital investment alternative. When considering this rate, however, we shall now think of it not only as a rate which represents a cost, but also as a rate which represents a return requirement. That it is correct to do so can be shown as follows: An investment in an activity is justified when the revenues from the activity suffice to cover its expenses, one of which is the cost of money. Another way of stating this is that an attractive investment alternative is one which is capable of generating revenues which enable the firm to recover, among other things, the cost of the money invested. Furthermore, an alternative which succeeds in doing this can be said to be yielding a satisfactory return. To illustrate, if the cost of money is 18 percent per year and if the activity involved yields revenues which just cover all the expenses, including this 18 percent cost of money, the activity is yielding a rate of return of 18 percent on the investment involved. Since this return is equal to the cost of money, it is defined as being satisfactory. From this, it follows that the cost of money represents the firm's minimum rate-of-return requirement, in the sense that, unless an investment is able to yield a return which suffices to cover the cost of money, it should not be made. This is so because, if the cost of money is the interest expense to be associated with borrowed capital, the alternative must be required to yield a return which will be at least equal to the interest rate being paid; and if the cost of money is an opportunity cost to be associated with equity capital, the alternative must be required to yield a return which will be at least equal to the rate that could be obtained from other available investment opportunities.

In theory, the rate-of-return requirement should be the rate which permits the firm to allocate its available capital in the most efficient manner. Selection of this rate requires that management determine its supply and demand schedules for capital. At various rates, different amounts of capital will be both made available to and required by the company for investment. In general, as management is willing to pay higher rates for the use of money, it will have more opportunities to obtain money, and its supply of capital will increase. However, as management demands higher rates of return from its investments, it will have fewer opportunities to invest money, and its demand for capital will decrease. At some rate, the capital supply and demand will be equal. If all available investment opportunities are of comparable risk and tax status, it is this rate which should be used as the rate-of-return requirement.

The reason it is necessary to speak in terms of comparable risk and tax status is easily demonstrated. With regard to the risk factor, a firm may estimate the potential annual return from a high-risk venture, such as introducing a new product, to be about 30 percent. At the same time, it may have an opportunity to invest the money in inventories, which involves less risk but will yield a return of only 14 percent. Because of the difference in the degree of risk, the 14 percent may actually be more attractive than the 30 percent. The same holds true when we consider the factor of tax status. Two bonds may be available which involve the same degree of risk. One pays an interest rate of 10 percent per year, but the interest payment is considered to be taxable income. The other pays an interest rate of only 7 percent, but the interest payment is tax exempt. Given this difference in tax status, the 7 percent bond may be more attractive to a given investor than the 10 percent bond.

Unfortunately, the determination of the minimum attractive rate of return is much more difficult in practice than it is in theory. To begin with, it is almost impossible for a given firm to ascertain what amounts of money are available at various rates. Therefore, the supply schedule of capital exists but cannot be accurately described. The same is true of the demand schedule. Its determination necessitates investigating all internal and external opportunities for investing funds and making the accurate estimates required to compute probable rates of return. For all practical purposes, this is impossible to do. But even if these obstacles to the determination of capital supply and demand schedules were overcome, the resultant rate would have a number of deficiencies. First, it would represent a state of equilibrium only at a given moment in time; this means that it would reflect neither future changes in investment opportunities nor future changes in capital availability. Next, the resultant rate would have to be modified to provide for the different levels of risk inherent in various investment opportunities and for the possible differences in the tax status of these investment opportunities; no completely satisfactory methods for doing so exist.

For these reasons, judgment plays an important role in the selection of the minimum rate-of-return requirement which, to repeat, is equal to the firm's cost of money. Let us now consider how this judgment is exercised. But before we do, it should be recognized that, in a before-tax analysis, the return requirement is a requirement *before* income taxes, whereas in an after-tax analysis, the return requirement is a requirement *after* income taxes. And as is to be expected, the after-tax requirement is the lower of the two. In any event, we shall begin with the before-tax case.

Average Cost of Money. Suppose an individual has an opportunity to invest $1,000 in a source which will yield a revenue of $1,260 one year later. If he decides to make the investment, he will have to borrow $200 because he has only $800 of his own money. Therefore, there would be 20 percent debt financing and 80 percent equity financing. The investor can borrow money at 10 percent per year and has an opportunity to invest his equity funds elsewhere, in situations of comparable risk and tax status, at a before-tax rate of 30 percent per year. Before he can evaluate the alternative under consideration, he finds it necessary to determine what cost of money will be experienced with this alternative.

This cost will be the average of the two different costs of money that will be incurred. One of these is the 10 percent interest expense that will be experienced with the debt portion of the total investment, and the other is the 30 percent opportunity cost that will be experienced with the equity portion of the total investment. However, these two values must be weighted in the process of being averaged to reflect the fact that debt capital will account for 20 percent of the total investment and that equity capital will account for 80 percent. Applying these weights, we obtain

Before-tax cost of money $= 0.20(10\%) + 0.80(30\%) = 26\%$

and, therefore, the minimum rate-of-return requirement should be 26 percent per year.

To continue the analysis, we were told that the $1,000 investment will yield $1,260 in one year. Of this amount, $1,000 will be the recovery of the original investment. The remaining $260 will be the dollar return on the $1,000 investment. In terms of a rate, this is 26 percent. Because this is equal to the investor's cost of money, the alternative is satisfying the established minimum rate-of-return requirement.

Before going on to an after-tax example, let us make a more detailed study of the cash flows that occur in this case. On a cash-flow line, we can break down the $1,000 total investment into two parts—the $200 debt investment and the $800 equity investment. Similarly, the $1,260 revenue can be broken down into two parts—the amount that will be claimed by the lender of the $200 and the amount that will remain for the investor of equity funds. The lender will receive his $200 plus 10 percent interest, or $220. The investor will receive the difference between the $1,260 and this $220, or $1,040. On a time line, all this would appear as follows:

```
  200              (220)
  800             (1,040)
 ─────            ───────
1,000            (1,260)
 ├────────────────────┤
 0                    1
```

When the cash flows are depicted in this manner, it becomes clear that the return on the $200 investment is $20, or 10 percent, and that the return on the $800 equity investment is $240, or 30 percent. This serves to demonstrate that the return of 26 percent on total investment enables the investor to meet the 10 percent interest expense generated by the debt portion of the investment and the 30 percent opportunity cost generated by the equity portion of the investment.

We shall now modify the problem by assuming that the investor wants to make an after-tax analysis in which he will take cognizance of the fact that his taxable income is subject to an effective tax rate of, say, 40 percent. This type of analysis requires that the cost of money after taxes be determined. In this determination, the cost of borrowed money remains unchanged, but the opportunity cost is altered.

Insofar as the cost of borrowed money is concerned, the interest rate which represents this cost remains unchanged in an after-tax analysis for the simple reason that the rate actually paid to the lender of funds is unaffected by the tax consequences of an investment alternative. Admittedly, the interest on debt will prove to be a tax-deductible expense. But this fact will be taken into account when the alternative's tax consequences are being ascertained, and it would be incorrect to take the tax effect of the interest expense into account a second time by adjusting the interest rate to reflect the fact that the interest expense is a tax-deductible expense. Therefore, in our example, the cost of debt would be said to remain at 10 percent in an after-tax analysis because, even though the investor's return is subject to a tax, he must continue to pay 10 percent for the use of the lender's $200.

However, the after-tax opportunity cost will differ from the before-tax opportunity cost. This is so because, if equity funds are invested in alternatives other than the one being evaluated, the return from these other investments will be subject to an income tax. Hence, the after-tax return generated by these other opportunities will be lower than the before-tax return, which is to say that the after-tax opportunity cost will be lower than the before-tax opportunity cost. To relate this to our example, if the $800 equity funds are invested elsewhere at 30 percent before taxes, the return after one year will be $240. But given a 40 percent tax rate, the tax on this return will be $96. As a result, the after-tax return will be the before-tax return of $240 minus the tax of $96, or $144, which is equal to 18 percent of the $800 invested. Therefore, the after-tax opportunity cost becomes 18 percent.

From all this, it follows that the average after-tax cost of money to the investor in our example will be the weighted average of the interest expense, which remains at 10 percent, and the after-tax opportunity cost, which is 18 percent. This weighted average is equal to

After-tax cost of money = 0.20(10%) + 0.80(18%) = 16.4%

and, therefore, the minimum after-tax rate-of-return requirement should be 16.4 percent per year.

As we did in the before-tax example, let us analyze the cash flows that will occur to determine whether the alternative satisfies this requirement. Of the $1,260 received at the end of one year, the lender's share will continue to be $220. But now, some of the remaining $1,040 will go to the government in the form of a tax payment. To compute the amount of this payment, we begin by noting that the investor of equity funds will have to report the entire $260 return on the $1,000 investment as income. But he can also report the $20 interest payment as a deductible expense, which serves to reduce his taxable income to $240. When the 40 percent tax rate is applied to this, a tax expense of $96 is obtained. In summary, the after-tax cash flows can now be described on a time line as follows:

```
  200              (220)
  800            (1,040)
                     96
 ─────           ───────
 1,000           (1,164)
 ├───────────────────┤
  0                  1
```

A study of these cash flows reveals that the $1,000 investment yields a total revenue after taxes of $1,260 minus $96, or $1,164. Of this total,

$164 is the after-tax return on the total investment of $1,000. This is a rate of 16.4 percent, which coincides with the 16.4 percent established as the minimum rate-of-return requirement after taxes. Hence, the requirement is being met.

Let us now demonstrate that this return on total investment will enable the investor to cover the 10 percent interest expense and the 18 percent opportunity cost. Returning to the preceding time line, we note that $220 will be available at the end of the year for payment of the $200 debt and the $20, or 10 percent, interest expense. Of the $1,040 balance, $96 will be used to pay the income tax, leaving $944 for the investor. Of this, $800 is a recovery of the $800 equity investment, and $144 is the return on this investment. This $144 is 18 percent of $800, and so the after-tax opportunity cost of 18 percent is being covered.

The results of the foregoing analyses permit us to say that the cost of money, which represents the minimum rate-of-return requirement, can be obtained, in terms of a percent per year, with the use of the following expression:

$$r_t = p_d(r_d) + p_e(r_e) \tag{2-1}$$

where

r_t = annual cost of money as a rate
    = minimum annual rate-of-return requirement on total investment
p_d = proportion of debt financing
r_d = annual interest as a rate applicable to debt investment
p_e = proportion of equity financing
r_e = annual opportunity cost as a rate applicable to equity investment

If a before-tax analysis is being made, the opportunity cost will be expressed as a before-tax rate, so that a before-tax cost of money can be obtained. If an after-tax analysis is being made, the opportunity cost will be expressed as an after-tax rate, so that an after-tax cost of money can be obtained. But the value of the interest rate applicable to debt is unaffected by whether a before-tax or an after-tax analysis is being made.

From Eq. (2-1), we are able to determine what must be known about an investment alternative before the analyst can ascertain the cost of money, as a percent per year, which will then be applied to the amount of money invested to obtain the cost of money in terms of dollars per year. These items of information are: (1) proportion of debt finanacing, (2) proportion of equity financing, (3) cost of borrowed money in terms of a percent per year, and (4) before-tax or after-tax opportunity cost in terms of a percent per year.

Insofar as the proportions are concerned, in the event that an amount of money is borrowed to finance a specific investment alternative, this known amount will permit the analyst to compute the values of the respective proportions. But, very often, debt is incurred to finance capital expenditures as a whole, and how much of this debt goes into a single investment is not known. When this is the case, whatever percent of total available capital is represented by debt is usually applied in every study for so long as this debt proportion remains at a certain level. If this level changes at some point, a revised proportion is used in subsequent studies.

A similar observation can be made with regard to the cost of borrowed money. If some amount is borrowed to finance a specific expenditure, the interest rate will be known, but this rate might be adjusted upward to account for any administrative and legal fees incurred in connection with the loan. However, if borrowing has occurred on a number of occasions to create a fund of debt capital for the financing of capital expenditures as a whole, a rate representing the average cost of this borrowed money will probably be used, and this average rate would also be increased by some amount if administrative and legal costs were incurred when the money was borrowed.

With respect to the opportunity cost, it can only be said that the firm will have to consider what return it believes could be realized from investments similar to the one being proposed. This means that the proposed investment must be examined, from the standpoint of the risk it entails and the tax treatment to which it will be subjected, and an estimate made of what returns can be expected from other investments of this type. The estimation problem is compounded by the fact that these other investment opportunities will be occurring throughout the life of the alternative being evaluated. Undoubtedly, there will be some fluctuation in available rates of return during that period, and, hence, the estimated opportunity cost must be an average of these rates.

Having shown what factors must be considered in the selection of a minimum rate-of-return requirement, we have reached the end of our discussion of what must be known about an investment alternative, in addition to the capital investment it requires, before the cost-of-money element in its total cost can be computed.

SUMMARY

The purpose of this chapter was to ascertain the manner in which a proposed capital investment alternative must be described to permit the determination of its total cost. We began by noting that this total cost will be made up of the following elements:

Capital costs:
  Devaluation expense
  Cost of money
Recurring costs:
  Revenues
  Operating costs
  Income taxes

A knowledge of these elements enabled us to go on to determine what must be known about an investment alternative before it can be analyzed by means of the techniques we shall consider. For the most comprehensive case, the required description was found to be as follows:

First cost or market value of fixed assets
Amount of required working capital
Service life of fixed assets
Terminal salvage value of fixed assets
Amount or proportion of equity financing
Amount or proportion of debt financing
Debt repayment plan
Cost of debt as a rate
Opportunity cost as a rate
Operating costs
Revenues
Method of tax depreciation
Income tax rates

This, of course, is a formidable list. Hopefully, it will serve to accomplish something in addition to describing what information must be obtained and suggesting the kinds of estimates that must be made. This is to bring out the fact that the application of any analytical technique must be preceded by what may prove to be an extremely difficult and time-consuming task of obtaining the data essential to the analysis.

QUESTIONS

2-1 How are recurring costs defined? Give some examples.

2-2 What is the difference between a before-tax and an after-tax analysis?

2-3 How are capital costs defined? Give some examples of capital expenditures.

2-4 What is a devaluation expense? Why is it said to stem from a capital expenditure?

2-5 What is meant by the cost of money? Why is this expense said to stem from a capital expenditure?

2-6 In what respect does an interest expense differ from an opportunity cost?

2-7 What is meant by debt financing? Equity financing?

2-8 Does the presence of operating costs create a need for a capital investment? Explain.

2-9 When estimating operating costs, why should the firm concern itself only with those that are marginal, or incremental?

2-10 What must be known about an investment alternative before a determination can be made of the effect it will have on an organization's income taxes?

2-11 In the process of ascertaining taxable income, what costs can be reported as deductible expenses?

2-12 How are depreciation expenses computed by the straight-line method? Sum-of-the-years-digits method? Double-rate declining-balance method?

2-13 What is meant by an asset's book value? Is it of any relevancy in the evaluation of a capital expenditure proposal? Explain.

2-14 How does single-asset, or item, accounting differ from multiple-asset accounting?

2-15 Is there any difference between a tax depreciation expense and a devaluation expense? Explain.

2-16 What must be known about an asset before its devaluation expense can be calculated?

2-17 How is the economic service life defined?

2-18 What is the present, or required, investment in a currently-owned asset?

2-19 Is an asset's replacement cost ever relevant? Explain.

2-20 What must be known about an investment alternative before the cost-of-money element of its total cost can be computed?

2-21 Why do investors demand a return on their investments?

2-22 How is the rate-of-return requirement affected by the administrative cost of making the investment? By the risk involved? By the income tax consequences? By expected changes in the purchasing power of money? By the value individuals place on immediate utility?

2-23 Why are people willing to pay for the use of other people's money?

2-24 What is the relationship between an investor's cost of money and his minimum rate-of-return requirement?

2-25 Describe the theoretical approach to the determination of a firm's rate-of-return requirement. What difficulties does this approach present in practice?

2-26 An organization's cost of money is said to be equal to the weighted average of the interest expense and the opportunity cost. Why is this so? How is this average computed?

2-27 What factors are considered in the selection of a minimum rate-of-return requirement before income taxes? After income taxes?

2-28 Summarize how a proposed investment alternative must be described before a determination can be made of the alternative's total cost, or of the equivalent of this cost.

PROBLEMS

2-1 A savings and loan association purchased some office equipment three years ago at a cost of $19,000. The market value of these assets at certain points in time proved to be as follows:

End-of-year	Market value
1	$11,000
2	7,000
3	5,000

What are the respective values of the annual devaluation expense? At what average annual dollar rate did the equipment decrease in value?

2-2 A vending machine firm purchased a coin sorter and counter for $2,000. During the four years that followed, the equipment decreased in market value by the following amounts:

Year	Devaluation expense
1	$550
2	420
3	270
4	190

Determine the asset's end-of-year market value for each of the four years.

2-3 An automobile leasing corporation operates with $400,000 of working capital. This entire amount has been obtained by borrowing at a cost of 11 percent per year. The terms of the loan call for paying the interest charge at the end of each year and for repaying the $400,000 principal at the end of 5 years. What will be the annual interest expense?

2-4 Suppose that the corporation in the preceding problem pays not only the interest charge at the end of each year but also repays $80,000 of the principal at the end of each year for 5 years. Compute the values of the annual interest expense which will be incurred with this revised repayment plan.

2-5 A retailer of women's clothing finances a $28,000 investment in new store fixtures with equity funds. The total investment in these facilities during any one year will be assumed to be equal to their market value at the beginning of the year under consideration. These values for the next six years are estimated to be as follows:

Beginning-of-year	Market value
1	$28,000
2	16,000
3	10,000
4	6,000
5	3,000
6	2,000

Given that the funds could have been invested elsewhere in sources of comparable risk and tax status at a return of 14 percent per year, compute the values of the retailer's annual opportunity cost in terms of dollars.

2-6 Suppose that the retailer in the preceding problem will finance only half of the $28,000 investment in fixtures by means of equity funds. The other half will be financed with debt capital at a cost of 10 percent per year. Furthermore, the debt repayment plan will be such that the amount of money owed during any one year will be equal to one-half of the assets' market value at the beginning of that year. What annual cost of money, in dollars, will the investment now generate?

2-7 Comment on the following:

a A painting contractor has already spent $200 in an attempt to obtain an order for a job. He is now told that the contract will be awarded to him if he is willing to do the work for a total of $6,900. However, he is inclined to reject the offer, because the job will result in his incurring a total cost of $7,000. This total consists of the $200 he has already spent and $6,800 of additional expenses which he will experience if he accepts the job.

b A processor of dairy products is thinking of replacing some packaging equipment. The direct labor cost with the new equipment would be about $47,000 a year. To estimate the annual cost of indirect labor and supervision which would be experienced with this equipment, an analyst multiplies this $47,000 by 32 percent. This is done because, at the present time, total plant indirect labor and supervisory costs are 32 percent of the firm's direct labor cost.

2-8 An architectural firm experienced revenues of $763,800 in a given year. Operating costs during that period were $412,600. Also, an interest expense of $9,100 was incurred. Finally, a depreciation expense of $24,400 was reported for tax purposes. If the firm's effective tax rate was 46 percent, what was the income tax for the year under consideration? (Ans. $146,142)

2-9 A telephone company has purchased an engraving machine, which it expects to use for 4 years, for $4,200. The equipment is expected to have a $200 salvage value at the end of its service life. Determine the asset's annual depreciation expenses and its end-of-year book values with the use of each of the following methods of depreciation:

  a Straight-line. (Ans. $1,000; $3,200, $2,200, $1,200, $200)
  b Sum-of-the-years digits. (Ans. $1,600, $1,200, $800, $400; $2,600, $1,400, $600, $200)
  c Double-rate declining-balance. (Ans. $2,100, $1,050, $525, $262; $2,100, $1,050, $525, $263)

2-10 Suppose that the company in the preceding problem begins with the double-rate declining-balance method of depreciation but changes to the straight-line method two years after the engraving equipment has been purchased. This is done to obtain an end-of-life book value which will be equal to the asset's estimated salvage value. What will be the reported depreciation expense for the third and fourth years? (Ans. $425)

2-11 A firm that engages in pressure filling of heavy viscosity materials has procured a unit of equipment at a cost of $18,000. Because the equipment will be used for only 8 years, this is the life that will be used for depreciation purposes. It is estimated that the terminal salvage value will be negligible. Calculate the respective annual depreciation expenses and the machine's end-of-year book values with each of the following methods:

  a Sum-of-the-years-digits.
  b Double-rate declining-balance.
  c Straight-line.

2-12 Given the data in the preceding problem, ascertain the resultant gain or loss for tax purposes under each of the following circumstances:

  a The tax depreciation expenses were reported on the basis of the sum-of-the-years-digits method, and the equipment was sold at the end of 4 years for $6,400. (Ans. $1,400 gain)
  b The tax depreciation expenses were reported on the basis of the double-rate declining-balance method, and the equipment was disposed of at the end of 8 years for a negligible amount. (Ans. $1,802 loss)
  c The tax depreciation expenses were reported on the basis of the straight-line method, and the equipment was disposed of at the end of 10 years for nothing.

2-13 It has been proposed that a currently-owned production facility be replaced. Five possible values for the asset's remaining service life have been selected. Average annual revenues, capital costs, and operating costs during these respective service periods are expected to be as follows:

Service life in years	Average annual amounts		
	Revenues	Capital costs	Recurring costs
1	$112,000	$58,000	$63,000
2	110,000	42,000	67,000
3	108,000	33,000	71,000
4	106,000	26,000	75,000
5	104,000	24,000	79,000

Which of these lives should be selected for the purpose of comparing the alternative of retaining this equipment with the alternative of replacing it? Why?

2-14 An electric utility is confronted by a power supply problem in a given area. One of the alternatives for increasing the supply to a satisfactory level calls for building two substations. The first of these is expected to cost $258,000, and the second to cost $217,000. Acquisition of the two substation sites will involve an additional expenditure of $10,000. Required source lines will cost about $790,000. Finally, distribution conversion costs of $960,000 will be experienced. If the firm selects this alternative, how large will its total investment be?

2-15 Comment on the following cases:

a   An individual owns common stock for which he paid $18,000. Its current market value is $14,000. Annual dividend payments are $1,260. He does not expect either the market value of the stock or the size of the dividends to change significantly in the foreseeable future. To arrive at the return he is realizing on his total investment, he divides the dividends of $1,260 by the original cost of $18,000 and obtains 7 percent. Because this is less than an 8 percent return he can realize by investing money in another source of comparable risk, he decides to sell the stock and invest the proceeds in the other source. His circumstances are such that there is no tax advantage to be associated with selling the stock at this time.

b   A delivery service pays the fines which result from traffic violations by the drivers of its trucks. One such driver was found guilty of an illegal turn, and the resultant fine was $15. Later, he was told the following by his supervisor: "That incident cost the company $30. Of that total, $15 is the fine, and the balance is the $15 we would have saved if you had not made that turn."

c   A fuel dealer has a supply of a certain type of coal which he purchased for $50 a ton. Because of price increases which have occurred, the cost of replacing this supply is $70 a ton. However, the dealer continues to sell the coal he has on hand for $65 a ton because his standard markup is 30 percent of cost.

d An overhead traveling crane has been in use in a foundry for a number of years. Its book value is $1,100. The company has decided to discontinue the foundry operation and, therefore, is attempting to sell all the equipment it will no longer need. This includes the crane. Representatives of about a dozen different organizations have expressed an interest in the crane. But without exception, every one offers only to dismantle and remove the installation at no cost to the owners of the foundry. The owners are reluctant to accept such an offer, because they believe that a decision to do so will result in their losing $1,100.

e An owner of an apartment building has decided to sell it because it is in an area in which property values are decreasing and will continue to do so. After months of advertising, the best offer the owner has been able to obtain is one for $130,000. But she considers this to be an unreasonable amount. Her reaction is based on the fact that the building is currently mortgaged for $175,000.

f The management of an oil refinery is considering a proposal that a new unit of processing equipment be purchased. If it is, a currently-owned unit, which is of special design, can and will be moved to another of the company's plants where it is badly needed. Otherwise, a replica of the currently-owned unit will have to be purchased for use at the other location. However, there is some disagreement regarding the value of the present investment in the old asset. Some individuals in the organization maintain that the investment is zero because this is the equipment's book value. Others insist that it is $500 because a dealer in used equipment is willing to buy and remove the unit for this amount. Still others point out that, since it would cost $2,700 to replace the equipment, this amount represents the present value of the asset and, hence, the amount invested in it at this time.

2-16 Calculate the average cost of money under each of the following circumstances:

a The proportion of debt financing is 0.30; the cost of borrowed money is 12 percent; and the opportunity cost to be associated with equity funds is 16 percent. (Ans. 14.8%)

b No debt financing is involved, but, if it were, the interest rate would be 9 percent. Equity funds can be invested elsewhere in situations of comparable risk and tax status at 15 percent.

c Only money borrowed at 8 percent will be used. If equity funds were available and used, an opportunity cost of 20 percent would be experienced.

2-17 Determine the following:

a The cost of debt financing if the average cost of money before taxes is 18 percent, the proportion of equity financing is 0.64, and the opportunity cost before taxes is 25 percent. (Ans.   5.6%)

b   The opportunity cost after taxes if the average cost of money after taxes is 9 percent, the proportion of debt financing is 0.10, and the cost of borrowed money is 6 percent.

2-18   A business executive has an opportunity to purchase a one-year note receivable at a cost of $10,000. To do so, he will have to borrow $5,000 at 7 percent per year and use $5,000 of his own money at a before-tax opportunity cost of 15 percent. Therefore, he concludes that the note will have to yield a minimum of $11,100 at the end of the year to enable him to cover his before-tax cost of money. Show how the executive arrived at this amount and that this amount will enable him to recover his before-tax cost of money and to realize a before-tax return of exactly 15 percent on his equity investment.

2-19   Suppose that the executive in the preceding problem estimates that his effective tax rate will be 33-1/3 percent and, hence, that his after-tax opportunity cost is 66-2/3 percent of 15 percent, or 10 percent. From this, he concludes that his minimum after-tax rate-of-return requirement should be 8.5 percent. Show how he arrived at this rate.

After having done so, demonstrate that, if the note yields the end-of-year receipt of $11,100 referred to in the preceding problem, the executive's after-tax return on total investment will be 8.5 percent and that his after-tax return on equity investment will be equal to his after-tax opportunity cost of 10 percent.

3

Compound Interest
Formulas

We know that what is a cost of money to one party in a financial transaction is a return to the other. Depending on the nature of the investment involved, this return may assume the form of interest, dividends, a reduction in operating costs, an increase in the market value of assets, and so on. Furthermore, this return can be expressed as a dollar amount, but it is usually more convenient to express it as a rate per year.

Regardless of the nature of the investment, it is always correct to speak in terms of the rate of return being realized. But if the investment happens to be a loan, a special term is often used when referring to the return. This term is the "interest rate." Therefore, the owner of bonds or notes receivable may state that he is realizing a *rate of return* of some amount, or he may state that he is receiving an *interest rate* of some amount. But while an owner of stock would state that he is realizing a rate of return of some amount, he would not state that he is receiving an interest rate of some amount. In brief, in the business world, the term "interest rate" is ordinarily employed with reference to money that has been lent or borrowed.

Unfortunately, this term is defined much more broadly in the area of capital investment analysis. Specifically, it is very often used as a substitute for the term "rate of return." And since a rate of return to one party in a transaction is a cost of money to another, the term "interest rate" is in effect also being used as a substitute for the term "cost of money." All this is said to be unfortunate because it can prove to be misleading when borrowing or lending is not involved. However, the subject matter of this chapter is drawn from an area of capital investment analysis in which it is customary to refer to the interest rate in the broad sense of the term. Hence, if we want to make use of the standardized terminology and notation that have evolved in this area, we are compelled to accept this broad definition of the term. But when we leave the topic of this chapter, we shall revert to our narrow definition of interest, which is that it is a rate being paid or received in connection with borrowed funds.

NEED FOR INTEREST CALCULATIONS

All the analytical techniques we shall consider will require computations in which it is necessary to work with an interest rate, as it is now being defined. These computations are sufficiently complex in themselves to warrant treating them independently of the analytical techniques. Our goal, at this point, is to acquire a knowledge of how these computations are carried out. Once this has been accomplished, we can go on to apply this knowledge in the analyses of capital investment alternatives.

We already know that the interest rate is used in the determination of an investment's capital cost. But a need also exists for taking the interest rate into consideration when processing data related to recurring costs, which include revenues. To illustrate, let us suppose that an individual is examining two pieces of rental property with a view toward purchasing one of them. The tenants of both properties have long-term leases, and, in each instance, the lease calls for the payment of an annual rent of $24,000. But the one agreement stipulates that this amount is to be paid in a single sum at the beginning of each year, while the other stipulates that it is to be paid by a series of $2,000 payments at the beginning of each month. Although $24,000 a year is involved in each case, the two payment plans are not equivalent to each other. Specifically, the more attractive one, from the standpoint of the investor, is the one in which he would receive the $24,000 at the beginning of each year. On the other hand, the more attractive one, from the standpoint of the tenants, is the one in which they pay $2,000 at the beginning of each month. This is so because money has a time value in the sense that a dollar received today is worth more than a dollar received at some future point. The reason for this is that the dollar received today can be invested at some interest rate to yield more than one dollar in the future. Similarly, a dollar received at some future point is worth less than a dollar received today because, at some interest rate, less than a dollar need be invested today to obtain a dollar at some future point. Hence, the investor in our example, when comparing the two rental properties, must somehow process the data related to the recurring revenues in a way which adjusts for the fact that, although the amounts received are the same for each alternative, the pattern of receipts differs. He does this by taking into consideration the time value of money, as represented by an interest rate.

To summarize, interest rates are used in the calculation of an investment's capital cost and also in the processing of data related to its recurring costs. And as has already been stated, this creates a need for becoming acquainted with the way in which the time value of money is handled under various circumstances.

SIMPLE INTEREST

We shall begin with the observation that there are two types of interest—simple and compound. Simple interest arrangements occur very infrequently. Nevertheless, let us consider them because an understanding of simple interest contributes to an understanding of compound interest.

A simple interest arrangement is said to exist when a borrower does not have to pay interest on the interest he owes. Insofar as the lender is concerned, it exists when he does not receive interest on the interest owed to him. For example, suppose someone borrows $1,000 at a simple interest rate of 10 percent per year and that the principal of the loan and the accrued interest are to be repaid in a single sum at the end of 2 years. The question is: How much is owed at that time? On a time line, the problem can be described as follows:

$$P = 1{,}000 \qquad F = ?$$

$$\vdash\!\!\!-\!\!\!-\!\!\!-\!\!\!+\!\!\!-\!\!\!-\!\!\!-\!\!\!\dashv$$

$$0 \qquad 1 \qquad n = 2$$

where

P = present sum of money
F = future sum of money
n = number of interest periods
i = interest rate per interest period

The interest charge for the first year would be calculated by taking the $1,000 owed at the beginning of that year and multiplying it by the 10 percent interest rate. This yields $100. Therefore, at the beginning of the second year, the borrower owes the $1,000 principal of the loan plus the accrued interest of $100, or $1,100. But the interest charge for the second year is not obtained by multiplying this $1,100 by 10 percent, but by again multiplying the $1,000 principal by 10 percent to obtain another $100. Consequently, the amount owed at the end of the second year is the $100 interest for that year plus the $1,100 owed at the beginning of that year, or $1,200. This means that no interest was paid on the interest owed during the second year.

A formula can be developed for determining the total amount owed at some future point, when simple interest is involved, by noting that this amount is the sum of the principal and the accrued interest. The principal is the present sum P. The interest charge per period is Pi, and the interest charge for the number of periods involved would be nPi. Therefore, we obtain

$$F = P + nPi \qquad\qquad (3\text{-}1)$$

If Eq. (3-1) were applied in our example, the result would be as follows:

$$F = \$1,000 + 2(\$1,000)(0.10) = \$1,200$$

which coincides with the result obtained earlier.

COMPOUND INTEREST

It so happens, however, that it is compound interest that prevails in the business world, and, hence, we shall be working with this kind of interest in all our analyses. Under a compound interest arrangement, no interest is allowed to accrue on which the borrower does not have to pay interest. This means that either (1) the interest owed is paid at the end of every interest period or (2) if not, interest is paid for the use of this interest during subsequent periods.

To return to our example, suppose that we are asked to determine how much is owed at the end of the second year, if the annual interest rate is 10 percent compounded *annually*. Annual compounding means that the interest charge is determined at the end of each year, which is to say that the length of one interest period is one year. But to continue, the interest charge for the first year would be, as before, 10 percent of the $1,000 owed at the beginning of that year, or $100; the amount owed at the end of that year would be, as before, the $1,000 plus the $100, or $1,100. But the interest charge for the second year would be 10 percent of the *total* amount owed at the beginning of that year, or 10 percent of $1,100, which yields $110. As a result, the amount owed at the end of the second year would be this $110 interest charge plus the $1,100 owed at the beginning of that year, or $1,210. This is greater than the $1,200 owed with a simple interest rate of 10 percent because interest is now being paid on the interest owed during the second year.

To summarize, the simple interest arrangement yielded the following cash flows for the lender, that is, the investor:

```
1,000            (1,200)
├────────┼────────┤
0        1        2
```

As compared with this, the compound interest arrangement yielded the following cash flows:

```
1,000            (1,210)
├────────┼────────┤
0        1        2
```

Equivalent Repayment Plans. None of this is intended to suggest that, in the presence of a compound interest rate, the borrower must allow interest to accumulate. As mentioned earlier, he can choose the alternative of paying the interest charge at the end of every interest period. In our example, this would call for the borrower's paying the $100 interest expense at the end of the first year. If he does, the interest for the second year would again be $100 because all he owes during that year is the principal of $1,000. The borrower can then pay this second $100 interest expense and return the $1,000 principal at the end of the second year. Hence, the lender will have experienced the following cash flows during the two-year period:

```
1,000    (100)    (1,100)
├────────┼────────┤
0        1        2
```

This is still a compound interest arrangement because at no time does the borrower retain owed interest at no cost. Yet, someone might note that the lender is receiving a total of $1,200, which is equal to the amount received under the simple interest arrangement. But it should be recognized that, in this case, $100 of that total is received one year sooner than it was in the simple interest case; therefore, given the time value of money, $1,200 received at the end of two years is not equivalent to $100 received at the end of one year and another $1,100 a year later.

While recognizing this, someone might then note that the fact remains that the investor receives only $1,200 as compared with the $1,210 he would receive were interest allowed to accrue. But, again, the difference in timing proves to be important. When the lender receives the $100 interest payment at the end of the first year, he is able to invest the money elsewhere at what we assume to be the prevailing interest rate of 10 percent. One year later, this other investment will yield an interest payment of 10 percent of $100, or $10, plus the repayment of the $100 invested, or a total of $110. When this is combined with the $1,100 that will be received from the initial investment, a total of $1,210 is obtained. These cash flows, from what is now a combination of two investments, can be described on a time line in the following manner:

```
1,000    (100)    (1,100)
          100      (110)
  |--------+---------|
  0        1         2
```

When the values that appear at the same points on the line are added, the result is

```
1,000              (1,210)
  |--------+---------|
  0        1         2
```

This enables us to conclude that the receipt of $100 in one year plus another $1,100 in two years is equivalent to the receipt of $1,210 in two years, when the interest rate is 10 percent compounded annually.

Let us consider just one more of many possible repayment plans involving compound interest. Suppose that the borrower in our example pays not only the $100 interest charge at the end of the first year, but also $400 of the $1,000 principal, that is, a total of $500. Because he now owes only $600 of the original loan during the second year, the interest charge for that year will be 10 percent of $600, or $60. If the borrower pays this $60 and the remaining principal of $600, or a total of $660, at the end of the second year, the investor's cash flows can be described as follows:

```
1,000    (500)    (660)
  |--------+---------|
  0        1         2
```

In this case, the lender will be able to reinvest the $500 he receives at the end of the first year. At 10 percent, this second investment will yield $550 one year later. Therefore, the combination of the initial investment of $1,000 and the second investment of $500 will generate the following pattern of cash flows:

```
1,000    (500)    (660)
          500      (550)
  |--------+---------|
  0        1         2
```

These can be summarized as follows:

```
1,000              (1,210)
├────────┼────────┤
0        1        2
```

So now we can say that the receipt of $500 in one year plus an additional $660 in two years is also equivalent to a single receipt of $1,210 in two years, when the time value of money is 10 percent compounded annually.

The three repayment plans we considered in our illustration suffice to demonstrate that cash flows experienced with a compound interest arrangement can assume one of a number of patterns. And, yet, each of these patterns reflects some single underlying compound interest rate. In our examples, this rate was 10 percent, and we saw that, with this rate, each of the various combinations of cash flows proved to be the equivalent of the investor's receiving $1,210 at the end of a two-year period. However, a very important assumption was made in the process of showing this to be true; namely, it was assumed that the cash flows generated by an investment could be reinvested at the interest rate involved in the original investment. As a rule, this is a realistic assumption because the interest rate involved is usually the one that prevails for an investment of that type. But if the assumption is not correct, one pattern of cash flows, which otherwise would be equivalent to some other pattern, may no longer be. But we shall concern ourselves with such instances in a subsequent chapter.

Frequency of Compounding. Although interest in the preceding illustration was compounded annually, more frequent compounding is not uncommon. For example, the interest rate in our problem could have been given as 10 percent compounded *semiannually.* Semiannual compounding means that each year is to contain two interest periods, in the sense that the interest owed will be computed at the end of every six-month period. Furthermore, the interest rate per interest period will be the annual rate divided by the number of periods per year. Therefore, if $1,000 is borrowed for 2 years at 10 percent compounded semiannually, we should say that $1,000 is borrowed for 4 interest periods at 5 percent per period. To determine how much is owed at the end of two years, we should begin by describing the problem as follows:

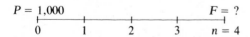

```
P = 1,000                      F = ?
├────────┼────────┼────────┼────────┤
0        1        2        3      n = 4
```

Then, the steps described in the following table would be carried out to arrive at the solution:

Interest period (a)	Amount owed at beginning of period (b)	Interest for period (c = b × 0.05)	Amount owed at end of period (d = b + c)
1	$1,000.00	$50.00	$1,050.00
2	1,050.00	52.50	1,102.50
3	1,102.50	55.12	1,157.62
4	1,157.62	57.88	1,215.50

It should be noted that the amount owed is now $1,215.50, as compared with the $1,210 obtained with annual compounding. This means that the true annual interest rate exceeds 10 percent in this case. To determine what it really is, we return to the preceding table and find that the amount owed at the end of the first year is $1,102.50. Therefore, the interest charge for the first year was $102.50, which is 10.25 percent of the $1,000 owed at the beginning of the year. This 10.25 percent is said to be the *effective* interest rate, whereas the stated rate of 10 percent is said to be the *nominal* interest rate. As this suggests, if interest is compounded annually, the effective rate is equal to the nominal rate, but if interest is compounded more frequently, the effective rate is greater than the nominal rate.

Suppose now that the interest rate had been given as 10 percent compounded *quarterly*. With quarterly compounding, each year would contain four interest periods, and the interest rate per period would be 10 percent divided by 4, or 2.5 percent. The amount owed at the end of the second year, that is, at the end of the eighth interest period, would be calculated as follows:

Interest period (a)	Amount owed at beginning of period (b)	Interest for period (c = b × 0.025)	Amount owed at end of period (d = b + c)
1	$1,000.00	$25.00	$1,025.00
2	1,025.00	25.62	1,050.62
3	1,050.62	26.26	1,076.88
4	1,076.88	26.92	1,103.80
5	1,103.80	27.60	1,131.40
6	1,131.40	28.29	1,159.69
7	1,159.69	28.99	1,188.68
8	1,188.68	29.72	1,218.40

Because an even larger amount is now owed than was owed with semiannual compounding, it is correct to assume that an increase has occurred in the effective interest rate. This can be easily verified. The data in the preceding table reveal that $1,103.80 is owed at the end of the first year, of which $103.80 is interest. This $103.80 is 10.38 percent of the $1,000 owed at the beginning of the year, and, therefore, the effective annual rate is 10.38 percent, as compared with the effective rate of 10.25 percent obtained with semiannual compounding. But the nominal rate would be, as before, 10 percent.

Suffice it to say that interest can also be compounded monthly, weekly, daily, hourly, and so on. The procedure followed in each of these cases to calculate the amount owed at some future point would be the one suggested by the procedure followed in our examples. The extreme case of frequency of compounding occurs when one year is divided into an infinite number of interest periods. When this is done, the compounding is said to be *continuous*. In any event, as the frequency of compounding increases, the effective interest rate per year increases, but the nominal rate remains the same. For example, if the annual interest rate is given as 10 percent compounded annually, the nominal rate is 10 percent, and the effective rate is also 10 percent. If the annual rate is given as 10 percent compounded semiannually, the nominal rate is still 10 percent, but, as was shown, the effective rate increases to 10.25 percent. If the annual rate is given as 10 percent compounded quarterly, the nominal rate continues to be 10 percent, but, as we saw, the effective rate increases still further to 10.38 percent. To summarize, the nominal rate is the stated rate *per year*, and the effective rate is the actual rate *per year*.

It was mentioned earlier that it is compound and not simple interest that prevails in the business world, and, hence, we shall adopt compound interest for use in our analytical techniques. Having acquired an understanding of what is meant by compound interest, we can proceed to a study of the methods for processing numerical data which call for taking the time value of money into consideration. As will be seen, in the course of processing these data, it will be necessary to perform one or more of nine basic operations. So let us begin with the first of these.

SINGLE-AMOUNT FUTURE WORTH FACTOR

Suppose that a company borrows $150,000 to increase its working capital. The money is obtained from a bank at a rate of 12 percent per year compounded annually. The terms of the loan require that the firm repay the principal and accrued interest in a single sum in 3 years. Management wants to know how much will be owed at that time.

In terms of the symbols introduced earlier, the problem to be solved can be described on a time line as follows:

$P = 150,000$ $F = ?$

```
├────────┼────────┼────────┤
0        1        2      n = 3
```

The steps in the solution of this kind of problem have already been described. If they are applied in this case, the results are as follows:

Year (a)	Amount owed at beginning of year (b)	Interest for year ($c = b \times 0.12$)	Amount owed at end of year ($d = b + c$)
1	$150,000	$18,000	$168,000
2	168,000	20,160	188,160
3	188,160	22,579	210,739

Obviously, this procedure can prove to be tedious and time-consuming when a large number of interest periods are involved. But, fortunately, an algebraic expression has been developed which enables one to obtain the value of the unknown in a much simpler manner. This expression is referred to as a *compound interest factor*. Before we discuss it, let us describe our problem in more general terms. This can be done on a time line as follows:

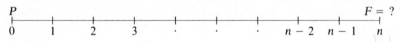

where, it will be recalled,

P = present sum of money
n = number of interest periods
i = interest rate per period
F = future sum of money n periods from now, which is equivalent to a present sum of money P at an interest rate i per period

It has been found that the following relationship exists among these four factors:

$$F = P(1 + i)^n \qquad\qquad (3\text{-}2)$$

Applying Eq. (3-2) in our problem, we should obtain

$$F = \$150,000(1 + 0.12)^3 = \$150,000(1.404928) = \$210,739$$

which is equal to the amount calculated earlier.

The term $(1 + i)^n$, which appears in Eq. (3-2), is the compound interest factor. We shall call it "the single-amount future worth factor" because it is used to find the future worth of a single amount of money. Since a knowledge of how this factor is derived is not essential to an understanding of its application, the derivation will not be shown in this chapter. The same will be true for the other eight compound interest factors with which we shall be working. However, the derivations for all nine factors are given in Appendix B.

In any case, it will prove convenient to designate this factor by means of a symbol when it appears in the solution of a problem. The symbolic notation we shall adopt is (F/P). As a result, Eq. (3-2) can also be expressed in the following form:

$$F = P(F/P) \tag{3-3}$$

which, of course, simply states that F is equal to F. But it also serves to explain why this notation was chosen; namely, the value of the multiplier must be the ratio of the future sum F to the present sum P.

However, when using Eq. (3-3) to solve our problem, we should state more specifically that

$$F = \$150,000\,(F/P)_{n=3}^{i=12}$$

because we want the value of the factor for an interest rate of 12 percent per period and for 3 interest periods.

Available Tables. One difficulty experienced when applying the single-amount future worth factor is that, if the exponent n is fairly large, logarithms must be used to obtain the numerical value of the factor. The same will be true for other compound interest factors. To eliminate the need for such computations, values of the factors, for various combinations of the interest rate and the number of interest periods, have been calculated and made available in table form. The tables presented in Appendix C are representative of those that have been developed. More complete sets are available in which values are given for many more interest rates and periods, but those presented will suffice for our purpose.

The tables in Appendix C are arranged in accordance with the interest rate involved, beginning with 2 percent and ending with 50 percent. To find the value of the single-amount future worth factor in our example, we should turn to the 12 percent table, Table C-6, find an n of 3 in the first column, move one column to the right which contains values of (F/P), and note that the value being sought is 1.4049.

Some of the values that do not appear in our tables can be found by interpolation. For example, suppose that we are seeking the value of the single-amount future worth factor for an i of 12 percent and an n of 36. In the given table, we find that

$(F/P)_{n=35}^{i=12} = 52.7996$

and that

$(F/P)_{n=40}^{i=12} = 93.0510$

Although the relationship between the value of any compound interest factor and the number of interest periods is not linear but curvilinear, no serious error occurs if we treat a small segment of the curve as if it were a straight line. Therefore, to obtain the value of the factor for an n of 36, we shall interpolate linearly between the values for an n of 35 and an n of 40. Doing so, we obtain

$$(F/P)_{n=36}^{i=12} = 52.7996 + \left(\frac{36-35}{40-35}\right)(93.0510 - 52.7996) = 60.8499$$

Similarly, there may be a need to find the value of a factor for an interest rate which does not appear in our tables. For example, a problem may call for the use of a single-amount future worth factor for an n of 3 and an i of 14 percent. With our tables, the closest we can get on either side of the desired value is

$(F/P)_{n=3}^{i=12} = 1.4049$

and

$(F/P)_{n=3}^{i=15} = 1.5209$

Again, we can engage in linear interpolation between two such values to obtain

$$(F/P)_{n=3}^{i=14} = 1.4049 + \left(\frac{14\% - 12\%}{15\% - 12\%}\right)(1.5209 - 1.4049) = 1.4822$$

This will be done in spite of the fact that the relationship between the value of any compound interest factor and the value of the interest rate is not linear but curvilinear. By doing so, we are treating, as we did earlier, a small segment of the curve as a straight line, but the resultant error is negligible.

Equivalence. Let us return to our problem in which $150,000 was borrowed for 3 years at a rate of 12 percent per year. But suppose we are now told that this rate is to be compounded semiannually. If so, the three-year period will contain 3 times 2, or 6, interest periods. Also, the interest rate per period will be 12 percent divided by 2, or 6 percent. Therefore, the amount owed at the end of the third year will be

$F = \$150,000(F/P)_{n=6}^{i=6} = \$150,000(1.4185) = \$212,775$

The reason for making this change in the problem was to stress the fact that, in all compound interest calculations, it is imperative that one work with the number of interest periods, which may or may not be equal to the number of years, and with the interest rate per interest period, which may or may not be equal to the interest rate per year. But we shall use the result of this latest computation as a basis for some other observations.

First, every result of a compound interest calculation should be examined to determine whether it appears to be correct. In our example, if $150,000 had been borrowed at an interest rate of 0 percent, the future amount owed would be $150,000; as this suggests, the value of the single-amount future worth factor for an i of 0 percent is 1.0000. But because the interest rate is greater than 0 percent, the amount owed can be expected to exceed $150,000, and the answer of $212,775 is consistent with this expectation. If a value of less than $150,000 had been obtained, an error was unquestionably made at some point in the computational process. Of course, an answer may appear to be correct and, yet, may not be, but the suggested check serves to reveal some of the times when a mistake was made.

A second observation that might be made is that the result obtained in this example permits us to say that $150,000 at the present time is equivalent to $212,775 in 3 years, if the time value of money is 12 percent compounded semiannually. This means that, given this time value of money, an expenditure of $150,000 now is the same as an expenditure of $212,775 in 3 years, or that a revenue of $150,000 now is the same as a revenue of $212,775 in 3 years. This can be explained as follows: A present debt of $150,000 can, of course, be repaid at this time by an expenditure of $150,000 or, if money has a value of 12 percent compounded semiannually, by an expenditure of $212,775 in 3 years. But instead of incurring the $150,000 expense at this time, the debtor can invest this amount at the 12 percent available rate and, by doing so, accumulate the $212,775 required to repay the debt in 3 years. Hence, given the stipulated time value of money, from the standpoint of the borrower, a debt repayment expense of $150,000 incurred now is the same as a debt repayment expense of $212,775 incurred 3 years from now. Similarly, from the standpoint of the lender, who is the investor, obtaining $150,000 from a borrower at this time is the same as obtaining $212,775 from him in 3 years. Given the stipulated time value of money, a revenue of $150,000 at this time would enable the lender to invest this amount elsewhere at 12 percent compounded semiannually, with the result that he would experience a revenue of $212,775 in 3 years. Consequently, he would consider a present receipt of $150,000 to be equivalent to a receipt of $212,775 in 3 years, if the interest rate is 12 percent compounded semiannually.

We might also note that, in our example, a present sum of money was considered to be an expense or a revenue that occurs right now. This will not always be the case. To illustrate, it might have been stated that the company will borrow $150,000 from the bank 1 year from now, will repay the loan 4 years from now, and wants to know how much it will owe at that time if the interest rate is 12 percent compounded semiannually. On a time line, this situation would be described as follows:

$$P = 150,000 \qquad\qquad F = ?$$

```
├──────┼───────┼───────┼──────┤
0      1       2       3      4
```

It should be apparent that interest will be accruing for 3 years in this case, just as it did in the preceding one, and, therefore, that the amount owed 4 years from now will be, as before, $212,775. This is to say that

$$F = \$150,000(F/P)_{n=6}^{i=6} = \$212,775$$

The reason the $150,000 is treated as a present sum of money is that point 1 on the time line is a present point *relative* to point 4 or, to put this differently, that point 4 is in the future *relative* to point 1. To generalize, an amount is either a present or a future amount as compared with an amount that appears at some other point in time.

Effective Interest Rate.   The difference between a nominal and an effective interest rate has already been discussed, and it was shown how the effective rate can be ascertained. But the availability of the single-amount future worth factor enables us to develop a method for determining the effective interest rate which is more efficient than the one presented earlier.

The development of this second method begins with the observation that the true, or effective, interest rate per year is the dollar interest charge for the year expressed as a percent of the amount owed at the beginning of the year. Further, the dollar interest charge for the year will be equal to the difference between the amount owed at the end of the year and the amount owed at the beginning of the year. To illustrate this, let us suppose that we are told that $2,000 is owed at the beginning of a given year and that $2,300 is owed at its end. On a time line, this would appear as follows:

$$P = 2,000 \qquad\qquad F = 2,300$$

```
├───────────────────────┤
0                       1
```

Therefore, the dollar interest charge for the year is $300, and the effective interest rate is $300 divided by $2,000, or 15 percent, per year.

But in terms of our symbolic notation, the respective amounts owed at the beginning and at the end of a year can be expressed in the following manner:

$$P \qquad F = P(1 + i)^n = P(F/P)_n^i$$

$$\vdash\!\dashv$$

$$0 \qquad\qquad\qquad\qquad 1$$

The dollar interest charge for the year, in terms of the same symbols, becomes

$$P(1 + i)^n - P = P[(1 + i)^n - 1] = P[(F/P)_n^i - 1]$$

and the effective interest rate r is found to be

$$r = \frac{P[(1 + i)^n - 1]}{P} = (1 + i)^n - 1 = (F/P)_n^i - 1 \qquad (3\text{-}4)$$

But since we are considering a one-year period, the i and n which appear in Eq. (3-4) are defined as follows:

i = interest rate per interest period
n = number of interest periods per *year*

Let us now apply this equation in a situation in which we are told that the annual interest rate is 40 percent compounded annually. To obtain the effective rate per year, we begin by noting that one year will contain 1 interest period and that the rate for this period is 40 percent. Substituting these values in Eq. (3-4), we obtain

$$r = (F/P)_{n=1}^{i=40} - 1$$

Table C-11 yields a value of 1.4000 for the single-amount future worth factor involved, and so the effective rate is

$$r = 1.4000 - 1 = 0.40 = 40\% \text{ per year}$$

If we were told that the annual interest rate is 40 percent compounded semiannually, one year would contain 2 interest periods, and the rate per period would be 20 percent. With these values, Eq. (3-4) yields

$$r = (F/P)_{n=2}^{i=20} - 1$$

From Table C-8, we obtain a value of 1.4400 for the single-amount future worth factor involved, and, therefore, the effective rate becomes

$$r = 1.4400 - 1 = 0.44 = 44\% \text{ per year}$$

As a final example, if the annual interest rate is given as 40 percent compounded quarterly, the use of Eq. (3-4) and Table C-5 would result in the following value for the effective rate:

$r = (F/P)_{n=4}^{i=10} - 1 = 1.4641 - 1 = 0.4641 = 46.41\%$ per year

We can use this last result to show that, when a problem calls for finding the future value of a present sum of money, an effective interest rate can be used in the computation in lieu of the nominal rate. For example, someone might want to determine how much is owed one year after $10,000 has been borrowed at 40 percent compounded quarterly. If Eq. (3-2), which contains the algebraic expression for the single-amount future worth factor, were used to arrive at this amount, the calculated value would be

$F = \$10,000(1 + 0.10)^4 = \$10,000(1.4641) = \$14,641$

However, we found that the effective rate in this case would be 46.41 percent, which means that 40 percent compounded quarterly is equivalent to 46.41 percent compounded annually. If we substitute this equivalent in Eq. (3-2), we obtain

$F = \$10,000(1 + 0.4641)^1 = \$10,000(1.4641) = \$14,641$

which coincides with the result obtained with the use of the nominal interest rate of 40 percent per year.

Having shown how the single-amount future worth factor can be applied in the determination of an effective interest rate and how an effective rate can be used in lieu of a nominal rate, we have completed our treatment of this factor.

SINGLE-AMOUNT PRESENT WORTH FACTOR

The next compound interest factor to be considered also serves to describe the relationship between a present sum of money and a future sum. However, in this case, the value of the future sum is known, and it is the value of the present sum that is unknown. As an example, a landscaper may have reason to believe that an appreciable amount of his equipment will require replacement in 7 years at a cost of $60,000. He is in a position to provide for this expenditure by investing a sum of money at the present time in a source which will yield a return of 8 percent compounded annually. Interest will be allowed to accrue during the seven-year period. He would like to know what present investment will satisfy his future need for $60,000.

This type of problem can be described, in general terms, as follows:

If an appropriate compound interest factor were not available, it would be necessary to use a trial-and-error approach to the solution of such a problem. Different values for P would have to be assumed until one was finally found which would prove to be equivalent to the desired future amount. However, this is not necessary because we already know that

$$F = P(1 + i)^n$$

which, when solved for P, yields

$$P = F \left[\frac{1}{(1 + i)^n} \right] \qquad (3\text{-}5)$$

The bracketed term in Eq. (3-5) is a compound interest factor which we shall call the "single-amount present worth factor" because it is used to find the present worth equivalent of a single sum of money which appears at some future point. As can be seen, it is the reciprocal of the single-amount future worth factor. This will be reflected in the symbolic notation for the factor, which will be (P/F) as compared with (F/P) which was used for the single-amount future worth factor. Therefore, in terms of this notation, we can say

$$P = F(P/F) \qquad (3\text{-}6)$$

To apply this factor in our problem, we begin by recalling that the time value of money was given as 8 percent compounded annually and that the other relevant information was as follows:

$$
\begin{array}{cccccccc}
P = \;? & & & & & & & F = 60{,}000 \\
\vdash & \dashv & \dashv & \dashv & \dashv & \dashv & \dashv & \dashv \\
0 & 1 & 2 & 3 & 4 & 5 & 6 & 7
\end{array}
$$

When appropriate substitutions are made in Eq. (3-6), the following is obtained:

$$P = \$60{,}000\,(P/F)^{i=8}_{n=7}$$

Values of this factor also are given in the tables in Appendix C. The value for the specific factor which appears in the preceding expression will be found to be 0.5835. Therefore, the amount the landscaper would have to invest at this time is

$$P = \$60{,}000\,(0.5835) = \$35{,}010$$

We can examine this result to determine whether it appears to be correct. If the landscaper were to earn no interest on his investment, it is apparent that he would have to invest \$60,000 to have \$60,000 in 7 years. This is to say that the value of the single-amount present worth factor is 1.0000 when the interest rate is 0 percent. But because he will be earning 8 percent, the landscaper can invest a smaller amount which, in this case, happens to be $35,010. Hence, we can say that $35,010 at this time is equivalent to $60,000 in 7 years when the time value of money is 8 percent compounded annually. The term "equivalent" has the same meaning in this instance as it had in the discussion of the result obtained with the use of the single-amount future worth factor.

It might also be noted that, in the application of the single-amount present worth factor, care must be taken not to lose sight of the fact that n is the number of interest *periods*, that i is the rate per *period*, and that an amount is a present sum *relative* to some other amount. And finally, to obtain certain values of this factor, it may be necessary to interpolate linearly when using the tables in Appendix C.

UNIFORM-SERIES FUTURE WORTH FACTOR

The third type of problem to be considered is one in which, as in our first problem, the unknown will be a future sum of money. In the earlier problem of this kind, the future value to be ascertained was the future worth of a single amount of money. But now, there will be a need to find the future worth of a *series* of amounts. However, a special kind of series will be involved, and its characteristics can be explained best with the use of an example.

Suppose that the administrators of an engineering college realize that some additional laboratory equipment will be required in 3 years. They want to build up a reserve to provide for a portion of the total procurement cost that will be incurred at that time. The administration will do so by taking $100,000 out of available funds at the end of each year for the next 3 years and investing these amounts at a rate of 10 percent compounded annually. The question is: How much will be in the reserve at the end of the three-year period, given that no withdrawals will be made during the period?

If we use F to represent the unknown future sum and A to represent the end-of-period investments, the situation can be described as follows:

$$F = \,?$$

$$A_1 = 100,000 \quad\quad A_2 = 100,000 \quad\quad A_3 = 100,000$$

0	1	2	3

This kind of problem can be solved with the use of single-amount future worth factors. The method calls for treating each of the $100,000 investments as a single amount, calculating the future worth of these respective single amounts, and adding these individual future worths to obtain the total future worth. In our example, these steps would yield

$$F = A_1(F/P)_{n=2}^{i=10} + A_2(F/P)_{n=1}^{i=10} + A_3(F/P)_{n=0}^{i=10}$$

$$= \$100,000(1.2100) + \$100,000(1.1000) + \$100,000(1.0000)$$

$$= \$331,000$$

This method can always be used to obtain the answer in such problems, but it proves to be tedious when the series involved is a long one. For this reason, a compound interest factor has been derived which enables one to obtain the answer in a more efficient manner. But this factor can be utilized only when a certain kind of series exists. Specifically, the series must have two characteristics. First, it must be a *uniform* series, and, second, it must be an *end-of-interest-period* series. Furthermore, application of the factor will yield the future worth of the series at the point at which the last amount in the series appears. In general terms, the factor has been derived for use under the following set of circumstances:

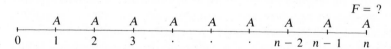

where

A = uniform end-of-period payment or receipt continuing for *n* periods at an interest rate *i* per period, which is equivalent to F

F = future sum of money *n* periods from now, which is equivalent to a series of uniform end-of-period amounts A continuing for *n* periods at an interest rate *i* per period

It might be noted that, although F is defined somewhat differently in this case than it was in the preceding two, it continues to represent a single amount which appears at point *n*, and that is why we continue to use the symbol F to represent this amount. Incidentally, A was chosen to represent the amounts in the series because it is the first letter in the word *annuity*, and the series can be thought of as being a special type of annuity. In any case, the relationship among the four factors in this type of problem can be described as follows:

$$F = A \left[\frac{(1 + i)^n - 1}{i} \right] \tag{3-7}$$

The bracketed term in the equation is the compound interest factor which is called the "uniform-series future worth factor" because it is used to find the future worth of a uniform series of amounts. The symbolic notation adopted for this factor is (F/A); so Eq. (3-7) can also be expressed in the following form:

$$F = A(F/A) \tag{3-8}$$

The fact that this results in the statement that F is equal to F explains why the given notation for the factor was adopted. But to continue, the application of Eq. (3-8) in our example yields

$$F = \$100,000(F/A)_{n=3}^{i=10}$$

As was to be expected, values of the uniform-series future worth factor are provided in the tables in Appendix C and can be found either directly in those tables or, if necessary, by linear interpolation between values in those tables. Substituting the available value for the factor in the preceding expression, we obtain

$$F = \$100,000(3.310) = \$331,000$$

which coincides with the result obtained when the problem was solved with the use of single-amount future worth factors. Furthermore, the answer appears to be correct. If no interest were being earned, three investments of \$100,000 each would provide \$100,000 times 3, or \$300,000, in the fund; as this suggests, the value of the uniform-series future worth factor is n when the interest rate is 0 percent. But because the college in our example will be earning 10 percent per year on its investments, the reserve will contain more than \$300,000 at the end of the third year.

The result obtained also enables us to say that \$100,000 at the end of each year for 3 years is equivalent to \$331,000 at the end of 3 years when the time value of money is 10 percent per year compounded annually. If the amounts represent expenditures, they are said to be equivalent because, instead of spending \$331,000 in 3 years, an individual could spend \$100,000 on an investment at the end of each year for 3 years and, at 10 percent, this series of expenditures would provide him with the \$331,000 he would need to satisfy an obligation of this size at that time. Or if the amounts are receipts, they are said to be equivalent because, instead of receiving \$331,000 in 3 years, an individual could receive \$100,000 at the end of each year for 3 years which could be invested at 10 percent to yield \$331,000 at the end of the third year.

Word of Caution.   Care must be taken not to apply the uniform-series future worth factor incorrectly. The risk of error can be minimized by understanding thoroughly the nature of the assumed conditions and what is occurring under these conditions. Let us begin by focusing our attention on what happens when the college in our example makes the series of $100,000 investments at an effective annual interest rate of 10 percent.

Because the first $100,000 investment is made at the *end* of the first interest period, it earns no interest during that period. Therefore, the fund will contain $100,000 at the end of the first year. During the second period, this amount will earn 10 percent interest, or $10,000. Therefore, the fund will contain $110,000 at the end of the second year. But at that point, another $100,000 is invested, and this serves to increase the amount in the fund at the end of the second year to $210,000. During the third year, this amount will earn 10 percent, or $21,000. Therefore, the fund will contain $231,000 at the end of the third year. But at that point, a final $100,000 is invested, and this serves to increase the amount in the fund at the end of the third year to $331,000.

Since this $331,000 is equal to the amount obtained with the use of the compound interest factor, it follows that the factor reflects the fact that (1) the individual investments were a *uniform* $100,000, (2) the individual investments were made at the *end* of each interest period for 3 years, and (3) the single-amount equivalent occurs at the end of the third year. Therefore, the factor could not be used to obtain the answer directly if the situation were as follows:

```
                              F = ?
          100,000     90,000      110,000
   |----------|----------|----------|
   0          1          2          3
```

or as follows:

```
                          F = ?
100,000      100,000     100,000
   |----------|----------|----------|
   0          1          2          3
```

or as follows:

```
                              F = ?
         100,000     100,000    100,000
   |----------|----------|----------|----------|
   0          1          2          3          4
```

However, the factor could be used under the following set of conditions:

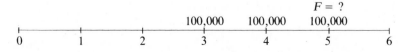

In this case, we should say that we have a uniform end-of-period series which begins at point 2 and ends at point 5. This series contains three periods, at the end of each of which a $100,000 amount appears, and, therefore, F, is equal to

$$F = \$100,000(F/A)_{n=3}^{i=10} = \$331,000$$

The n of 3 in this expression simply reveals that 3 end-of-period amounts are involved, and the factor, as derived, recognizes that the first of these amounts earns interest for only 2 periods, the second for only 1 period, and the third for 0 periods. In general, the n which appears in a series compound interest factor represents the number of end-of-period amounts in the series and not the number of periods during which any one amount is earning interest. As opposed to this, the n which appears in a single-amount compound interest factor represents the number of periods during which a single amount is earning interest. That this is true can be seen in the derivations presented in Appendix B.

It should also be noted that, throughout the entire discussion of the uniform-series future worth factor, reference has been made to end-of-*period* amounts and to interest rates per interest *period*. The reason for emphasizing the word "period" is that the assumption underlying the derivation of the factor is that a payment or a receipt occurs at the end of every interest period. More specifically, if annual compounding is involved, an end-of-year series is assumed; if quarterly compounding is involved, an end-of-quarter series is assumed; if weekly compounding is involved, an end-of-week series is assumed; and so forth. To illustrate this, let us suppose that the college in our example will make three end-of-year investments of $100,000 each, but that the interest rate is given as 10 percent compounded quarterly. The rate per period is now 2.5 percent, and the total number of interest periods is 12. But it would be incorrect to state that

$$F = \$100,000(F/P)_{n=12}^{i=2.5} = \$100,000(13.796) = \$1,379,600$$

A comparison of this answer with the earlier one of $331,000 suggests that something is wrong because increasing the frequency of compounding from once to four times a year certainly should not affect the result to this degree. What is wrong is that the preceding expression is applicable to a case in which $100,000 is invested at the end of each period for 12 periods and in which the interest rate is 2.5 percent per period. The college, however, is making only three $100,000 investments. Of course, something could be done in this case which would enable us to use the uniform-series future worth factor. This is to convert the nominal rate of 10 percent to an effective rate. If this were done, 10.38

percent would be obtained, and we could say

$$F = \$100,000(F/P)^{i=10.38}_{n=3}$$

But such necessary adjustments in the interest rate are sometimes difficult to make. This would be true, for example, if the interest rate in our problem were 10 percent compounded annually and the college were making, say, semiannual deposits. Unfortunately, we cannot simply say that the interest rate per semiannual period is 5 percent because, given annual compounding, it is not. Under the circumstances, a nominal rate compounded semiannually would have to be found which is equivalent to 10 percent compounded annually. This new rate, which would be less than 10 percent, could then be divided by 2 to obtain the rate per semiannual period.

In brief, then, the uniform-series future worth factor is used to calculate the future value of a series in which a uniform amount appears neither more nor less frequently than at the end of every interest period. Further, the future value found is the value at the point at which the last amount in the series appears. Finally, the amounts in the series can be either expenditures or revenues because what is an expenditure to one party is a revenue to some other.

FUTURE-AMOUNT ANNUITY FACTOR

The preceding problem was one in which the future worth of an annuity was unknown. The problem to be considered now is similar in the sense that it will also deal with the relationship between a future sum and an annuity, but, now, the annuity will be unknown.

As an example, suppose an airline company has issued bonds which are to be redeemed in 10 years at a cost of $5,000,000 to the firm. Management decides to provide for the redemption of the bonds by establishing a sinking fund for this purpose. Specifically, a uniform series of semiannual deposits will be made into the fund during the entire ten-year period. The first of these deposits will be made six months from now, and the last at the end of the tenth year. No withdrawals will be made during the period. All money in the fund will earn 8 percent compounded semiannually. The firm wants to know what the size of each deposit must be so that the required $5,000,000 will be on hand after the last deposit has been made.

This type of problem can be described, in general terms, as follows:

To obtain an expression which will enable us to solve for the value of A, we return to Eq. (3-7) which described the relationship between A and F to be as follows:

$$F = A\left[\frac{(1 + i)^n - 1}{i}\right]$$

Solving this equation for A, we obtain

$$A = F\left[\frac{i}{(1 + i)^n - 1}\right] \tag{3-9}$$

The bracketed term is our fourth compound interest factor, and it is called the "future-amount annuity factor" because it is used to find the annuity which is equivalent to a future amount of money. This factor is the reciprocal of the uniform-series future worth factor. Therefore, since we designated the latter with the symbol (F/A), we shall use (A/F) to represent the future-amount annuity factor. As a result, Eq. (3-9) becomes

$$A = F(A/F) \tag{3-10}$$

Of course, A continues to represent a uniform end-of-period payment or receipt, and F is a single amount at the end of the last period which is equivalent to the uniform series. The i in the algebraic expression for the compound interest factor involved continues to represent the interest rate per period, and n the number of interest periods at the end of each of which a payment or receipt occurs.

To apply Eq. (3-10) in our example, we begin with the following description of the problem:

It will be noted that the time line reflects the fact that, at an interest rate of 8 percent compounded semiannually, 10 years will contain 20 interest periods and also that a deposit will be made at the end of each of these periods. With a rate of 4 percent per period, the required size of the deposits will be found to be

$$A = \$5,000,000(A/F)_{n=20}^{i=4} = \$5,000,000(0.0336) = \$168,000$$

The value for the factor in this expression was found in the tables in Appendix C, and no interpolation was required because a 4 percent table was available. In any event, an examination of the result suggests that it is correct. If no interest were being earned on the deposits, the required size of each would be $5,000,000 divided by 20 deposits, or $250,000; this is to say that, at an interest rate of 0 percent, the future-amount annuity factor is equal to $1/n$. Because the company in our example will be realizing a return on its investment in the fund, it need deposit some series of amounts less than $250,000 each.

The result obtained also permits us to say that $168,000 at the end of each half-year for 10 years is equivalent to $5,000,000 at the end of the tenth year when the interest rate is 8 percent compounded semiannually. Equivalent has the same meaning here as it did in the discussion of the uniform-series future worth factor.

And, finally, as was true in the application of the uniform-series future worth factor, the correct application of the future-amount annuity factor requires that the number of interest periods per year be equal to the number of end-of-period payments or receipts per year.

UNIFORM-SERIES PRESENT WORTH FACTOR

We already know how to solve a problem in which it is necessary to find the present worth of a single amount that appears at some future point. Let us now turn to a problem in which it is necessary to find the present worth of a future series of amounts. The future series will have the characteristics of those series with which we dealt in the two preceding types of problems.

Suppose that an individual has won an amount of money in a lottery. He wants to invest some portion of that amount at this time in a source which will yield a return of 6 percent compounded annually. More specifically, the amount to be invested should just suffice to enable him to withdraw $1,000 at the end of each year for the next 4 years. This annual amount is what he believes will be required to cover the cost of a family vacation during each of the 4 years. We have been asked to calculate the value of the required investment.

This problem can also be described in the following manner:

$P = ?$

$A = 1,000 \quad A = 1,000 \quad A = 1,000 \quad A = 1,000$

0	1	2	3	4

It will be noted that A is being used to represent each of the amounts in the future series of receipts; this is because the series is a uniform end-of-period series of the type considered earlier, in which each amount was identified by the symbol A. Also, P is being used to represent the unknown value; this is because this value is a single amount which appears at a point in time which is a present point relative to the points at which the other amounts appear, and we have been identifying such present values by the symbol P.

If necessary, problems of this kind can be solved by calculating the respective present worths of the individual future amounts and then computing the sum of these present worths. This would call for the use of single-amount present worth factors which, in this case, would be applied as follows:

$$P = \$1,000(P/F)_{n=1}^{i=6} + \$1,000(P/F)_{n=2}^{i=6} + \$1,000(P/F)_{n=3}^{i=6}$$

$$+ \$1,000(P/F)_{n=4}^{i=6}$$

$$= \$1,000(0.9434) + \$1,000(0.8900) + \$1,000(0.8396) + \$1,000(0.7921)$$

$$= \$3,465$$

Because this approach is somewhat troublesome when a long series of amounts is being processed, a compound interest factor, whose derivation is given in Appendix B, has been developed for use under these circumstances. The exact circumstances can be described, in general terms, as follows:

$P = ?$

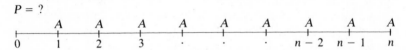

where

$\quad P \ = \ $ present sum of money at the beginning of the first of n periods, which is equivalent to a series of uniform end-of-period amounts A continuing for n periods at an interest rate i per period

$\quad A \ = \ $ uniform end-of-period payment or receipt continuing for n periods at an interest rate i per period, which is equivalent to P

With the derived factor, the relationship among the four factors in this type of problem can be described in the following manner:

$$P = A \left[\frac{(1 + i)^n - 1}{i(1 + i)^n} \right] \qquad\qquad (3\text{-}11)$$

The bracketed term is the compound interest factor. It will be called the "uniform-series present worth factor" because its function is to yield the present worth of a uniform series of end-of-period amounts. Our notation for this factor will be (P/A), and this enables us to express Eq. (3-11) in the following form:

$$P = A(P/A) \qquad\qquad\qquad (3\text{-}12)$$

An examination of this expression suggests why the notation involved was adopted; as the expression reveals, it is necessary that the factor represent the ratio of P to A.

The problem being considered can be solved with the use of Eq. (3-12) and the tables in Appendix C in the following manner:

$$P = \$1,000(P/A)_{n=4}^{i=6} = \$1,000(3.465) = \$3,465$$

This result coincides with that obtained earlier when single-amount present worth factors were applied. Furthermore, it appears to be correct. If the investment were to earn no interest, \$4,000 would be required at the present time to permit four future withdrawals of \$1,000 each; from this, we can conclude that, at an interest rate of 0 percent, the value of the uniform-series present worth factor is equal to n. But because a return of 6 percent will be realized on the investment, only \$3,465 is required.

We can also make the statement that \$3,465 at the present time is equivalent to \$1,000 at the end of each year for the next 4 years when the time value of money is 6 percent per year compounded annually. If these amounts are revenues, they are equivalent in the sense that, instead of receiving \$1,000 at the end of each year for 4 years, someone could receive \$3,465 at the beginning of the first year and invest this amount at 6 percent to obtain \$1,000 at the end of each year for 4 years. If these amounts are expenditures, they are equivalent in the sense that, instead of spending \$1,000 at the end of each year for 4 years, someone could spend \$3,465 in the form of an investment at the beginning of the first year at 6 percent and be able to withdraw \$1,000 at the end of each year for 4 years to cover the recurring expenses.

As with the other series factors, care must be exercised when applying the uniform-series present worth factor. This means that the factor should be used only when (1) the present worth of a series is being found at the beginning of its first interest period and (2) when the number of end-of-period amounts in the series is equal to the number of interest periods. As the second of these two conditions suggests, the value of n in the factor represents the number of end-of-period payments or receipts and not the number of periods during which any one amount is earning interest. That this is true becomes evident when we see what happens to the \$3,465 investment in our example in the ensuing 4 years during which the \$1,000 withdrawals are made. This is shown in Table 3-1 in which all values are rounded to the closest whole dollar.

But none of this means that the factor cannot be used in a situation in which some number of interest periods precede or follow the series.

Table 3-1   Determination of what happens when $3,465 is invested at 6 percent per year and 4 end-of-year withdrawals of $1,000 each are made

Amount invested at beginning of year 1	$3,465
Interest at 6 percent for year 1	+ 208
Amount invested at end of year 1	3,673
Withdrawal at end of year 1	−1,000
Amount invested at beginning of year 2	2,673
Interest at 6 percent for year 2	+ 160
Amount invested at end of year 2	2,833
Withdrawal at end of year 2	−1,000
Amount invested at beginning of year 3	1,833
Interest at 6 percent for year 3	+ 110
Amount invested at end of year 3	1,943
Withdrawal at end of year 3	−1,000
Amount invested at beginning of year 4	943
Interest at 6 percent for year 4	+ 57
Amount invested at end of year 4	1,000
Withdrawal at end of year 4	−1,000
Amount invested at beginning of year 5	$ 0

To illustrate, a problem might involve 8 interest periods, and, during these 8 periods, $1,000 amounts may occur at the points shown in the following time line:

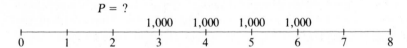

$$P = ?$$

If there is a need to find the single amount at point 2 that is equivalent to this series of $1,000 amounts, this can be done in the following manner if the interest rate is 6 percent per period:

$$P_2 = \$1,000(P/A)_{n=4}^{i=6} = \$1,000(3.465) = \$3,465$$

The factor has been used correctly because the series begins at point 2, ends at point 6, has a uniform amount at the end of every period contained in this time span, and the present worth is being found at the beginning of the first period of the series.

PRESENT-AMOUNT ANNUITY FACTOR

The sixth basic type of interest problem is a variation of the preceding one. In the preceding one, there was a need to find the present worth of a future uniform series of amounts, whereas in this one, there will be a need to find the future uniform series that is equivalent to a present sum of money. We shall consider an extremely simple example of this kind of problem because of the nature of the analysis to which the result will be subjected.

Let us assume that the employees of a firm form an association whose purpose is to organize recreational activities in which interested employees can participate. Management wants to contribute to the support of this organization. Its plan for doing so calls for its depositing, at this time, $4,000 in a savings institution which pays an annual interest rate of 8 percent compounded annually. At the end of each year for the next 2 years, the firm will withdraw a uniform amount from the account and give it to the employees' association; the size of these amounts will be such that, when the last withdrawal is made, the fund will be exhausted. When the two-year period ends, management will make a decision as to what the nature of its future support will be. A determination is to be made of the size of the two annual withdrawals.

The type of problem being considered can be described, in terms of the symbols with which we have been working, as follows:

$$P$$

$$A = ? \quad A = ? \quad A = ? \quad A = ? \quad A = ? \quad A = ? \quad A = ? \quad A = ? \quad A = ?$$

$$0 \quad 1 \quad 2 \quad 3 \quad \cdot \quad \cdot \quad \cdot \quad n-2 \quad n-1 \quad n$$

To obtain an expression which enables us to solve for the value of A directly, we return to Eq. (3-11) in which the relationship among P, A, i, and n was described as follows:

$$P = A \left[\frac{(1 + i)^n - 1}{i(1 + i)^n} \right]$$

Solving this equation for A, we obtain

$$A = P \left[\frac{i(1 + i)^n}{(1 + i)^n - 1} \right] \tag{3-13}$$

The bracketed term in this expression is our sixth compound interest factor, which we shall call the "present-amount annuity factor." This factor is the reciprocal of the uniform-series present worth factor, and it is used to determine the annuity which is the equivalent of a present amount of money. As before, the annuity A is a uniform end-of-period series of payments or receipts, and the present amount P, to which it is equivalent, appears at the beginning of the series' first period. Further, i continues to represent the interest rate per period, and n the number of periods in the series at the end of each of which a payment or receipt occurs.

Given that the symbol (P/A) was used for the uniform-series present worth factor, the symbol (A/P) will be used for its reciprocal, the present-amount annuity factor. Therefore, Eq. (3-13) becomes

$$A = P(A/P) \qquad\qquad\qquad (3\text{-}14)$$

To apply Eq. (3-14) in our example, we return to the question posed in the problem. This was as follows:

$P = 4,000$

$$
\begin{array}{ccc}
 & A = ? & A = ? \\
\vdash\!\!\!-\!\!\!-\!\!\!-\!\!\!-\!\!\!-\!\!\!+\!\!\!-\!\!\!-\!\!\!-\!\!\!-\!\!\!-\!\!\!\dashv \\
0 & 1 & 2
\end{array}
$$

With a time value of money of 8 percent per period, the maximum possible end-of-year withdrawal would be found to be

$$A = \$4,000(A/P)_{n=2}^{i=8} = \$4,000(0.5608) = \$2,243$$

The result suggests that the value of the compound interest factor, as obtained from the tables in Appendix C, is correct. If no return were being realized on the investment, a \$4,000 deposit would make possible two withdrawals of \$2,000 each because the value of the present-amount annuity factor is $1/n$ when the interest rate is 0 percent. But since a return of 8 percent is being experienced, a larger annual withdrawal can be made. And to return to the concept of equivalence, it can be said that \$4,000 at the present time is equivalent to \$2,243 at the end of each year for the next 2 years when the time value of money is 8 percent per year. In this case, as in all others, the present time is a point in time which precedes some other point.

An Elaboration. The present-amount annuity factor will prove to be a very important one in the analytical techniques to be considered because it will be used to convert the required investment in an alternative into its uniform annual equivalent, expressed as an end-of-year series of costs. To explain why it can be used for this purpose, let us return to our example and describe what is occurring in somewhat different terms.

The company in this example is making an investment in a fixed asset, namely, a savings account. The investment required by this alternative is the \$4,000 that must be spent to open the account. The life of this investment alternative is 2 years. And, finally, the salvage value of the asset involved, which is the account, is zero because the account will contain nothing after the last transaction is completed. But the consequences of this investment of \$4,000 in an asset that has a two-year life and no salvage value are that the firm will realize revenues of \$2,243 at the end of each year for 2 years. As we know, these consequences represent a return of 8 percent per year on the required investment.

From the standpoint of the savings institution, however, the situation can be described as follows: The institution is borrowing $4,000 at a cost of 8 percent per year compounded annually. The repayment plan calls for paying the lender, who is the investor, $2,243 at the end of each year for 2 years. When the last payment is made, the debt will have been repaid.

But let us now make a slight change in the circumstances, although we shall retain the numerical values of the factors involved. Suppose that, instead of considering a $4,000 investment in a savings account, the company is evaluating a proposal that a piece of production equipment be purchased. The equipment has a first cost of $4,000, an estimated service life of 2 years, and an expected terminal salvage value of zero. If the time value of money is 8 percent per year compounded annually, the required expenditure of $4,000 can be said to be equivalent to the following uniform end-of-year cost during the two-year life of the asset:

$$A = \$4,000(A/P)_{n=2}^{i=8} = \$4,000(0.5608) = \$2,243$$

This is so because, if the $4,000 first cost is to be financed with equity funds, these funds will not be available for investment elsewhere at 8 percent. Elsewhere could be the savings account mentioned earlier which, as we saw, would provide the firm with $2,243 at the end of each year during a time period equal to the equipment's life. Therefore, a decision to invest $4,000 in the equipment is a decision to give up the $2,243 a year for 2 years that could be realized from the savings account. Hence, the $4,000 capital expenditure on equipment generates an average annual cost of $2,243 during the asset's two-year life.

On the other hand, it might be that the proposed $4,000 expenditure for the equipment will be financed with debt capital. In this case, as we saw earlier, if the cost of borrowed money is 8 percent per year, the $4,000 loan would have to be repaid by a payment of $2,243 at the end of each year during a time period equal to the equipment's life. Therefore, a decision to invest $4,000 in the equipment is a decision to incur an obligation to pay someone $2,243 a year for 2 years. Hence, the $4,000 capital expenditure on equipment generates an average annual cost of $2,243 during the asset's two-year life.

The same line of reasoning would apply if the expenditure were to be financed by some combination of equity and debt funds. In that case, the 8 percent time value of money would represent the weighted average of the rate which represents the opportunity cost and of the rate which represents the interest expense.

It will be recalled, however, that, as stated in the preceding chapter, a capital expenditure generates a capital cost and that this capital cost consists of two elements. One of these elements is the devaluation expense, and the other is the cost of money. In these terms, then, we should say that, if the company in our example purchases the equipment for $4,000, it will experience a uniform annual capital cost of $2,243. Further, a portion of this cost will be the devaluation expense, that is, the average amount per year by which the asset decreases in value. Given that the value of the asset is $4,000 at the beginning of its two-year life and zero at the end, we are able to ascertain that the devaluation expense for the two-year period will be a total of $4,000, or $2,000 per year. It follows that, if $2,000 of the $2,243 capital cost is the average devaluation expense, the balance of $243 must be the average cost of money at 8 percent. That all this is true can be easily demonstrated. To do so, let us return to the alternative of investing $4,000 in a savings account at 8 percent and withdrawing $2,243 at the end of each year for 2 years. We shall now determine what is happening during the two-year period.

In the first year, the account will earn 8 percent of the $4,000 deposited, or $320. Consequently, the total investment at the end of the year will be $4,000 plus $320, or $4,320. At that point, $2,243 will be withdrawn, and the balance will be $2,077. Therefore, the asset will have decreased in value during the year by $4,000 minus $2,077, or $1,923. In brief, of the $2,243 withdrawn, $320 is interest and $1,923 represents devaluation.

In the second year, the account will earn 8 percent of the $2,077 it contains, or, to the closest whole dollar, $166. Consequently, the total investment at the end of the year will be $2,077 plus $166, or $2,243. At that point, $2,243 will be withdrawn, and the balance will be $0. Therefore, the asset will have decreased in value during the year by $2,077 minus $0, or $2,077. In brief, of the $2,243 withdrawn, $166 is interest and $2,077 represents devaluation. All this can be summarized as follows:

	Year 1	Year 2
Interest portion	$ 320	$ 166
Devaluation portion	1,923	2,077
Total withdrawal	$2,243	$2,243

The average of the two interest amounts in the foregoing table is $243, and the average of the two devaluation amounts is $2,000. Hence, we have shown that the earlier statement, regarding the respective values of these two cost elements, was correct; that is, if the company buys equipment for $4,000, it will experience an average annual cost of money of $243 and an average annual devaluation expense of $2,000, or a total average annual capital cost of $2,243. Of course, if a part of the original capital investment were to be recovered in the form of a salvage value, this annual capital cost would be reduced by an amount equal to the annual equivalent of the salvage value.

To summarize, the uniform annual capital cost of a fixed asset which has no salvage value is obtained by multiplying the initial investment in the asset by an appropriate present-amount annuity factor. This calculated capital cost consists of two elements—an average annual devaluation expense and an average annual cost of money. The devaluation expense is an average because the asset will not decrease in value by the same amount every year. The cost of money is also an average because, as the asset decreases in value, less money is invested in it as time goes by and a corresponding decrease takes place in the annual cost of money.

GRADIENT-SERIES FUTURE WORTH FACTOR

Three compound interest factors remain to be discussed. Each of these is used to find the equivalent of a series of payments or receipts. This series, like the one with which we have been working, will be an end-of-period series; that is, an amount will appear at the end of every interest period contained in the time interval under consideration. But unlike the series with which we have been working, this series will not be uniform; instead, the successive amounts in the series will be either increasing or decreasing in value by some constant. More specifically, the series will assume the form of an arithmetic progression.

As an example, let us take the case of an individual who has an opportunity to invest money at the unusually high rate of 24 percent per year compounded monthly. He decides to take advantage of this opportunity by investing some amount at the end of each month for a period of 12 months. His exact plan is to invest $50 the first month and then to increase the amount at a rate of $20 a month, with the result that his last investment will be $270. Further, no withdrawals will be made during the twelve-month period. We are asked to determine how much money will be in the fund right after the last payment has been made.

Continuing to use the symbol F to represent a single amount of money that appears at some future point, we should describe the problem on a time line in the following manner:

$$F = ?$$

50	70	90	110	130	150	170	190	210	230	250	270
0	1	2	3	4	5	6	7	8	9	10	11	12

The interest rate in this problem was given as 24 percent compounded monthly, and, therefore, the length of each interest period is 1 month and the interest rate per period is 2 percent. Because end-of-month deposits are to be made in the investment fund, we have an end-of-period series. However, it is not uniform, and, hence, its future worth cannot be found with the use of the uniform-series future worth factor. But it can be found by treating the monthly deposits as single amounts and applying appropriate single-amount future worth factors. This would be done as follows:

$$F = \$50(F/P)^{i=2}_{n=11} + \$70(F/P)^{i=2}_{n=10} + \cdots + \$250(F/P)^{i=2}_{n=1} + \$270$$

Obviously, this can prove to be a time-consuming method. Fortunately, a compound interest factor has been developed for use under these conditions. Its derivation is shown in Appendix B, and so we shall concentrate only on its application. To apply the factor, it is necessary to break down the given series into two equivalent series. One of these is a uniform series whose value is equal to the first amount that appears in the given series. The second series is a series of values equal to the difference between the given series and the uniform series. In our example, the two series that are equivalent to the given one would be as follows:

50	50	50	50	50	50	50	50	50	50	50	50
0	20	40	60	80	100	120	140	160	180	200	220
0	1	2	3	4	5	6	7	8	9	10	11	12

As a consequence, we are now saying that the deposit will be $50 plus $0 in the first year, $50 plus $20 in the second, and so on. In any event, if we find the future worth at point 12 of these two series, we shall have the future worth of the original series to which they are equivalent.

Since the $50 series is a uniform end-of-period series, its future worth F can be obtained by multiplying the $50 amount A by the uniform-series future worth factor. The remaining task is to obtain the future worth of the second series. Let us begin by noting that the amounts in this second series are increasing in value at a constant rate of $20 per period. This rate of change is referred to as the *gradient*, for which we shall use the symbol G. If we substitute this symbol for the $20 amounts in the second series, this series, which is called a "gradient series," assumes the following form: $0G$, $1G$, $2G$, . . . , $10G$, $11G$. It will be noted that the last term in this series is $(12 - 1)G$, which is equal to $(n - 1)G$. All this permits us to describe the original problem in the following general form:

$$F = \,?$$

	A	A	A	$\cdots$	A	A	A
	$0G$	$1G$	$2G$	$\cdots$	$(n-3)G$	$(n-2)G$	$(n-1)G$
0	1	2	3	$\cdots$	$n-2$	$n-1$	n

where

A = uniform end-of-period payment or receipt continuing for n periods at an interest rate i per period

G = constant arithmetic rate at which the successive amounts in an end-of-period series change in value

F = future sum of money n periods from now that is equivalent to a series of end-of-period amounts, which continues for n periods at an interest rate i per period and which can be described in the following terms: $[A + 0G]$, $[A + 1G]$, $[A + 2G]$, . . . , $[A + (n - 1)G]$

It might be mentioned that, in spite of the way in which F is now defined, it remains a single amount of money which appears at a future point. But to continue, its value in this type of problem will be the sum of the future worths of the *uniform* series and the *gradient* series. Since we know how to calculate the future worth of a uniform series, we need concern ourselves now with only the method for calculating the future worth F of the gradient series. This method calls for making the appropriate substitutions in the following expression:

$$F = G \left[\frac{(1 + i)^n - 1}{i^2} - \frac{n}{i} \right] \tag{3-15}$$

The bracketed term is our seventh compound interest factor, which is called the "gradient-series future worth factor" because it is used to compute the future worth of a gradient series that has the following form: $0G$, $1G$, $2G$, . . . , $(n - 1)G$. The symbolic notation for the factor is (F/G), with the result that Eq. (3-15) becomes

$$F = G(F/G) \tag{3-16}$$

Applying Eq. (3-16) to our example, in which the gradient is $20, the number of interest periods is 12, and the interest rate per period is 2 percent, we find the future worth F_G of the gradient series to be

$F_G = \$20(F/G)_{n=12}^{i=2} = \$20(70.60) = \$1,412$

The future worth F_A of the uniform series would be obtained in the following manner:

$F_A = \$50(F/A)_{n=12}^{i=2} = \$50(13.412) = \$671$

Therefore, the future worth of the series of total end-of-month deposits will be

$F = F_G + F_A = \$1,412 + \$671 = \$2,083$

We can check this result to ascertain whether it appears to be correct by calculating the amount the investment fund would contain if no interest were being earned on the monthly deposits. This amount would be

Sum of deposits $= \$50 + \$70 + \$90 + \ldots + \$250 + \$270 = \$1,920$

Because a return of 2 percent per month is being earned, we should expect the fund to contain a larger amount than this, and the calculated value of \$2,083 is consistent with this expectation. This result permits us to say that the given amounts at the end of each month for 12 months are equivalent to \$2,083 at the end of the twelfth month when the time value of money is 24 percent per year compounded monthly. In this statement, the term "equivalent" is defined as it was when it appeared in earlier statements of this type.

Before going on to the next factor, we might take cognizance of the fact that a series can contain a negative gradient. To illustrate, the investor in our example could have decided to invest \$270 the first month and then to *reduce* the monthly investment at a rate of \$20. The series of deposits would then be as follows:

```
   270   250   230   210   190   170   150   130   110    90    70    50
├─────┼─────┼─────┼─────┼─────┼─────┼─────┼─────┼─────┼─────┼─────┼─────┤
0     1     2     3     4     5     6     7     8     9    10    11    12
```

To calculate the future worth of this series at point 12, we should take the first amount of \$270 and construct a uniform series of this size. The gradient series would then assume the form shown on the following time line:

```
                                                                    F = ?
   270   270   270   270   270   270   270   270   270   270   270   270
   (0)   (20)  (40)  (60)  (80) (100) (120) (140) (160) (180) (200) (220)
├─────┼─────┼─────┼─────┼─────┼─────┼─────┼─────┼─────┼─────┼─────┼─────┤
0     1     2     3     4     5     6     7     8     9    10    11    12
```

It will be recalled that parentheses are being used on a time line to designate negative values. In any case, the value of the gradient is now minus $20; so the total future worth of the series of deposits is equal to

$$F = \$270(F/A)_{n=12}^{i=2} - \$20(F/G)_{n=12}^{i=2} = \$270(13.412) - \$20(70.60)$$

$$= \$2,209$$

This amount exceeds the $2,083 accumulated in the fund with the original series of deposits because, although the same total amount of money is being deposited, the larger deposits are now being made early in the year and, hence, the dollar amount of interest being earned is greater.

The only other thing that might be mentioned with respect to the gradient-series future worth factor is that, when determining the total number of interest periods for which the value of the factor is to be found in Appendix C, care should be taken to include, in this total, the period which precedes the first amount in the gradient series being processed. This first amount is always $0, but this is taken into account in the derivation of the factor. The same word of caution is in order for the two remaining factors to be considered, which will also be used to find the equivalent of a gradient series.

GRADIENT-SERIES PRESENT WORTH FACTOR

The next compound interest factor will be explained with the use of the following example: A public utility is considering a proposal that a two-cycle reciprocating engine, which is in current use at one of its compressor stations, be replaced. If the engine is not replaced now, it is expected that it will be kept for another 5 years. In the process of describing the alternative of retaining the old engine, the analyst estimates that operating, maintenance, and fuel costs with this engine will be $260,000 during the coming year but will increase at a rate of $19,500 a year thereafter. He chooses to treat these recurring expenses as if they will be incurred at the end of each year. The utility's cost of money is 15 percent per year compounded annually. The analyst wants to determine what expenditure at this time is equivalent to this future five-year series of recurring costs. On a time line, his question can be expressed as follows:

$P = ?$

```
        260,000    279,500    299,000    318,500    338,000
 |---------+----------+----------+----------+----------|
 0         1          2          3          4          5
```

The question could be answered with the use of single-amount present worth factors, which would be applied in the following manner:

$$P = \$260,000(P/F)_{n=1}^{i=15} + \$279,500(P/F)_{n=2}^{i=15}$$

$$+ \ldots + \$338,000(P/F)_{n=5}^{i=15}$$

But a compound interest factor is available which enables one to process such a series more efficiently. By such a series, we mean one which contains a gradient. The gradient in this case is $19,500, and so we are able to describe the given series as follows:

```
        260,000      260,000      260,000      260,000      260,000
              0       19,500       39,000       58,500       78,000
     ┝────────────┼────────────┼────────────┼────────────┤
     0            1            2            3            4            5
```

This description was obtained by taking the first amount in the original series and constructing a uniform series of this size. The remaining recurring costs yield a gradient series of the type considered earlier. The result is that we are able to describe the problem being considered in the following general form:

$P = ?$

```
        A            A            A    · · ·        A          A          A
       0G           1G           2G    · · ·    (n − 3)G   (n − 2)G   (n − 1)G
    ┝────────────┼────────────┼────────────┼────────────┼──────────┤
    0            1            2            3    · · ·    n − 2      n − 1        n
```

where

P = present sum of money at the beginning of the first of n periods that is equivalent to a series of end-of-period amounts, which continues for n periods at an interest rate i per period and which can be described in the following terms: $[A + 0G]$, $[A + 1G]$, $[A + 2G], \ldots , [A + (n − 1)G]$

The present worth of this series will be equal to the present worth P_A of its uniform portion plus the present worth P_G of its gradient portion. The uniform-series present worth factor will enable us to calculate the present value of the uniform series of A amounts, but we require a compound interest factor which will enable us to calculate the present worth of the gradient series. Such a factor can be developed by returning to Eq. (3-15) which stated that

$$F = G \left[\frac{(1 + i)^n − 1}{i^2} − \frac{n}{i} \right] \qquad (3\text{-}17)$$

But we know from Eq. (3-2) that

$F = P(1 + i)^n$

When we substitute $P(1 + i)^n$ for F in Eq. (3-17), we obtain

$$P(1 + i)^n = G\left[\frac{(1 + i)^n - 1}{i^2} - \frac{n}{i}\right]$$

which yields

$$P = G\left[\frac{(1 + i)^n - 1}{i^2(1 + i)^n} - \frac{n}{i(1 + i)^n}\right] \tag{3-18}$$

The bracketed term in this equation is our eighth compound interest factor, which is called the "gradient-series present worth factor" because it is used to find the present worth of a gradient series. Values of this factor are given in Appendix C for selected values of i and n, and, as with the other factors, linear interpolation can be employed when necessary. To reflect the fact that the value of the factor must be equal to the ratio of P to G, the symbolic notation for the factor will be (P/G). Therefore, we are able to express Eq. (3-18) in the following form:

$$P = G(P/G) \tag{3-19}$$

Applying all this to our example, we find the present worth of the estimated series of recurring costs to be

$$P = P_A + P_G = \$260,000(P/A)_{n=5}^{i=15} + \$19,500(P/G)_{n=5}^{i=15}$$
$$= \$260,000(3.352) + \$19,500(5.775) = \$984,132$$

This means that, with a time value of money of 15 percent per year, \$984,132 at the beginning of a five-year period is equivalent to \$260,000 at the end of the first year, \$279,500 at the end of the second, \$299,000 at the end of the third, \$318,500 at the end of the fourth, and \$338,000 at the end of the fifth. To relate this to our example, if the company were to invest \$984,132 at 15 percent at the beginning of the first year, the aforementioned amounts could be withdrawn from the established fund at the end of each year to cover the recurring expenses and, when the last withdrawal was made, the fund would be exhausted. If no return were being realized on such a fund, the required present investment would be simply the sum of the future recurring expenses, which is equal to

$$\text{Sum of expenses} = \$260,000 + \$279,500 + \cdots + \$338,000$$
$$= \$1,495,000$$

But at an annual return of 15 percent, the required amount should be less, and we found it to be $984,132.

GRADIENT-SERIES ANNUITY FACTOR

In the case we have just considered, the analyst was interested in determining the present worth of a future series of recurring costs which contained a gradient. But let us suppose that, instead of a present worth, he wants to calculate the uniform end-of-period equivalent of the series. More specifically, the new problem can be described as follows:

$$
\begin{array}{ccccc}
A = ? & A = ? & A = ? & A = ? & A = ? \\
260,000 & 279,500 & 299,000 & 318,500 & 338,000
\end{array}
$$

```
|-------+-------+-------+-------+-------|
0       1       2       3       4       5
```

If the present worth of such a series has already been found, its uniform end-of-period equivalent can be calculated with little difficulty. To illustrate, in the preceding example, we learned that the present worth of this series is $984,132. The actual series can be replaced by this single amount because the two are equivalent. When this is done, the problem then assumes the following form:

$P = 984,132$

$$
\begin{array}{ccccc}
A = ? & A = ? & A = ? & A = ? & A = ?
\end{array}
$$

```
|-------+-------+-------+-------+-------|
0       1       2       3       4       5
```

To compute the unknown value A, we apply the present-amount annuity factor to P and obtain

$$A = \$984,132(A/P)_{n=5}^{i=15} = \$984,132(0.2983) = \$293,567$$

This uniform series is said to be equivalent to the nonuniform series at an interest rate of 15 percent per year, and both are equivalent to a single amount of $984,132 at the beginning of the first period of either series. If this single amount were invested at 15 percent, the fifth withdrawal of $293,567 in a uniform series of withdrawals would exhaust the fund, as would the fifth withdrawal of $338,000 in the original nonuniform series.

Although this type of problem can always be solved by applying the present-amount annuity factor to the present worth of the series, a compound interest factor is available which eliminates the need for first finding the series' present worth. Like the two preceding factors, this factor is applicable only to a gradient series with the characteristics described earlier. The first step in its use calls for breaking down the given series into two parts—the uniform portion and the gradient portion. Since this was already done at an earlier point, we know that the result in our example would be as follows:

260,000	260,000	260,000	260,000	260,000
0	19,500	39,000	58,500	78,000

```
├────────┼────────┼────────┼────────┤
0        1        2        3        4        5
```

Our task now is to ascertain the single uniform end-of-period series that is equivalent to these two series. It is apparent that nothing need be done with the first series because it is already in the desired form. The question that remains to be answered can be presented in the following form:

$A = ?$	$A = ?$	$A = ?$	$A = ?$	$A = ?$
0	19,500	39,000	58,500	78,000

```
├────────┼────────┼────────┼────────┤
0        1        2        3        4        5
```

When the uniform series that is equivalent to this gradient series has been found, it can be added to the $260,000 uniform series to obtain the overall uniform annual equivalent of the given series of recurring costs. Therefore, the problem at hand can be described, in general terms, in the following manner:

$A = ?$	$A = ?$	$A = ?$	$\cdots$	$A = ?$	$A = ?$	$A = ?$
0G	1G	2G	$\cdots$	$(n-3)G$	$(n-2)G$	$(n-1)G$

```
├────────┼────────┼────────  · · · ────────┼────────┤
0        1        2        3    · · ·   n-2     n-1      n
```

where

A = uniform end-of-period payment or receipt continuing for n periods at an interest rate i per period, which is equivalent to a series of end-of-period amounts that can be described in the following terms: $0G, 1G, 2G, \ldots, (n-1)G$

We know from Eq. (3-18) that the present worth of the gradient series is equal to

$$P = G \left[\frac{(1+i)^n - 1}{i^2(1+i)^n} - \frac{n}{i(1+i)^n} \right]$$

and we also know from Eq. (3-11) that the present worth of a uniform end-of-period series is equal to

$$P = A \left[\frac{(1+i)^n - 1}{i(1+i)^n} \right]$$

Combining these two equations, we obtain

$$A\left[\frac{(1 + i)^n - 1}{i(1 + i)^n}\right] = G\left[\frac{(1 + i)^n - 1}{i^2(1 + i)^n} - \frac{n}{i(1 + i)^n}\right] \qquad (3\text{-}20)$$

When Eq. (3-20) is solved for A, the result is

$$A = G\left[\frac{1}{i} - \frac{n}{(1 + i)^n - 1}\right] \qquad (3\text{-}21)$$

The bracketed term in this equation is our ninth, and last, compound interest factor. It is used to find the uniform end-of-period annuity that is equivalent to a gradient series and, hence, is called the "gradient-series annuity factor." The symbolic notation for this factor is (A/G), with the result that Eq. (3-21) becomes

$$A = G(A/G) \qquad (3\text{-}22)$$

Eq. (3-22) and the values given for this factor in Appendix C can be used to find the uniform series that is equivalent to the gradient series in our example. The result would be as follows:

$$A = \$19{,}500(A/G)_{n=5}^{i=15} = \$19{,}500(1.723) = \$33{,}598$$

When this is added to the uniform \$260,000 portion of the original series of recurring costs, the total uniform end-of-year equivalent is found to be

$$A = \$260{,}000 + \$33{,}598 = \$293{,}598$$

It will be noted that this amount is slightly larger than the \$293,567 result obtained when a different approach to the solution of the problem was employed. Such insignificant differences will arise when two different methods for solving a problem do not involve the same compound interest factors; this is because of the way in which the factor values in Appendix C are rounded. In any event, we can now make our customary check to see whether the result appears to be correct. At an interest rate of 0 percent, the uniform end-of-year equivalent of the recurring costs in our example would simply be their arithmetic mean, which is equal to

$$\text{Average} = (1/5)(\$260{,}000 + \$279{,}500 + \cdots + \$338{,}000) = \$299{,}000$$

With a time value of money of 15 percent, we should expect some other, but similar, value for the average annual amount, and we found this other value to be \$293,598.

A final observation is in order regarding all three of the gradient-series factors we have considered. This is that they can also be applied to find the equivalent of a gradient series under a condition such as the following:

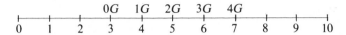

In this case, the series begins at point 2, ends at point 7, and contains 5 periods. Using an n of 5, we can find (1) the present worth of the series at point 2 with the gradient-series present worth factor, (2) the future worth of the series at point 7 with the gradient-series future worth factor, and (3) the uniform end-of-period equivalent of the series at points 3, 4, 5, 6, and 7 with the gradient-series annuity factor. And of course, in all cases, n represents the number of interest periods, and i the interest rate per interest period.

A SUMMATION

This might be an appropriate point at which to comment on why an end-of-period series was assumed in the derivation of all seven of the series compound interest factors. Admittedly, an end-of-period series is a natural one in some cases but not in all. For example, if a fund *has been* established, it is likely that a series of, say, annual withdrawals will be an end-of-year series so that the first withdrawal would occur one year after the investment had been made. But if a fund is *to be* established by means of a series of, say, annual deposits, it is likely that deposits will be made at the beginning of each year so that the last deposit would be made one year before the specified future amount is required. However, if some of the factors had been derived to treat an end-of-period series and others to treat a beginning-of-period series, it would be even more difficult than it already is to remember which factor is used under what circumstances. For this reason, an end-of-period series was assumed in all cases. Of course, a beginning-of-period series could have been assumed, but this was not done because, as we shall see, an end-of-period series is the more common of the two. However, should a beginning-of-period series occur, it can be converted to an equivalent end-of-period one by multiplying each amount in the series by the single-amount future worth factor for one interest period.

To minimize the difficulties experienced in an attempt to recall the names of the factors and the circumstances under which each is employed, it is useful to recognize that three classifications can be established for the nine available factors. The first classification contains the three factors used to find the *future worth* of something; this something might be (1) a single amount, (2) a uniform series, or (3) a gradient series.

Hence, we have the following future worth factors:

Single-amount future worth factor
Uniform-series future worth factor
Gradient-series future worth factor

The second classification contains the three factors used to find the *present worth* of something; this something might be (1) a single amount, (2) a uniform series, or (3) a gradient series. Hence, we have the following present worth factors:

Single-amount present worth factor
Uniform-series present worth factor
Gradient-series present worth factor

The third classification contains the three factors used to find the end-of-period *annuity* that is equivalent to something; this something might be (1) a present amount, (2) a future amount, or (3) a gradient series. Hence, we have the following annuity factors:

Present-amount annuity factor
Future-amount annuity factor
Gradient-series annuity factor

The algebraic expressions and the symbols for these factors are summarized on the first page of Appendix C, and, therefore, no summary listing is being presented here. And to repeat, complete derivations of the factors are given in Appendix B, and their values appear in Appendix C.

The discussion of these factors was a lengthy and detailed one, because an understanding of their application is essential to an understanding of the methods for analyzing capital investment alternatives. On the assumption that this understanding has been acquired, we shall go on to consider the first of these methods. But before doing so, let us recall that it was stated, at the beginning of this chapter, that, when we leave the topic of this chapter, we shall no longer use the term "interest rate" synonymously with the term "rate of return" or the term "cost of money." Therefore, from this point on, when we speak of a firm's rate-of-return requirement, the portion of this rate intended to cover the cost of debt capital will be referred to as the interest rate. But the portion intended to cover the cost of equity capital will be referred to as the opportunity cost. The symbol i, however, will continue to be used to represent the investor's rate-of-return requirement. This requirement is the cost and, therefore, the time value of money to the investor.

QUESTIONS

3-1 What is meant by the time value of money?

3-2 Why is it necessary to take the time value of money into consideration in the analysis of capital investment alternatives?

3-3 How do simple interest and compound interest differ?

3-4 With a compound interest arrangement, what does an interest period represent? An interest rate per interest period?

3-5 When interest is compounded more frequently than annually, how is the number of interest periods per year determined? The interest rate per period?

3-6 Define the nominal interest rate per year. The effective interest rate per year.

3-7 When is continuous compounding said to occur?

3-8 What is a compound interest factor?

3-9 Under what conditions is each of the following compound interest factors used:

a Single-amount future worth factor?
b Single-amount present worth factor?
c Uniform-series future worth factor?
d Future-amount annuity factor?
e Uniform-series present worth factor?
f Present-amount annuity factor?
g Gradient-series future worth factor?
h Gradient-series present worth factor?
i Gradient-series annuity factor?

3-10 What is the relationship among the following compound interest factors:

a Single-amount future worth factor and single-amount present worth factor?
b Uniform-series future worth factor and future-amount annuity factor?
c Uniform-series present worth factor and present-amount annuity factor?
d Gradient-series future worth factor, single-amount present worth factor, and gradient-series present worth factor?
e Gradient-series present worth factor, present-amount annuity factor, and gradient-series annuity factor?
f Gradient-series future worth factor, future-amount annuity factor, and gradient-series annuity factor?

3-11 At an interest rate of 0 percent, what are the values of the single-amount future worth factor and the single-amount present worth factor?

3-12 At an interest rate of 0 percent per period, what is the relationship between the number of interest periods and the values of the following compound interest factors:

    a   Uniform-series future worth factor?
    b   Future-amount annuity factor?
    c   Uniform-series present worth factor?
    d   Present-amount annuity factor?

3-13 How does a gradient series differ from a uniform series of payments or receipts?

3-14 Explain the concept of equivalence as it relates to cash flows.

PROBLEMS

3-1 The management of a metalworking firm has made a tentative decision to replace a turret lathe. The price of a suitable replacement is $57,500. To increase the probability of his getting the order, a supplier of the equipment makes the following offer: Instead of paying $57,500 at the present time, the firm can make an equivalent single payment 3 years from now. The annual interest rate during this period will be only 5 percent. Furthermore, the supplier volunteers to accept a simple interest arrangement. How much would have to be paid in 3 years? (Ans. $66,125)

3-2 Suppose that, in the preceding problem, the supplier of the lathe had stipulated that the interest rate would be 5 percent compounded annually. How much would the buyer of the equipment then owe at the end of 3 years? (Ans. $66,563)

3-3 A salesman needs a new automobile for business use. He is trying to borrow $6,200 with which to purchase the automobile. A friend of his will lend him this amount if the salesman agrees to repay $7,750 in 2 years. What annual simple interest rate would the salesman be paying?

3-4 To finance an advertising program, a manufacturer of digital watches will borrow $90,000 now and $90,000 at the beginning of each month for the next 5 months. One year from now, the $540,000 which had been borrowed and the accrued interest will have to be repaid. If the simple interest rate is 1 percent per month, what will the accrued simple interest prove to be? (Ans. $51,300)

3-5 A management consulting firm purchases a small office building for $120,000. This expenditure will be financed by borrowing the entire $120,000 at an annual interest rate of 10 percent compounded annually. The entire debt will be repaid by a series of four end-of-year payments.

    a   Determine the sizes of these respective payments if the interest owed is paid at the end of each year for 4 years and the principal of $120,000 is repaid at the end of the fourth year. (Ans. $12,000, $12,000, $12,000, $132,000)

    b   Determine the sizes of these respective payments if the interest owed and $30,000 of the principal is paid at the end of each year for 4 years. (Ans. $42,000, $39,000, $36,000, $33,000) c Determine the sizes of these respective payments if interest is allowed to accrue for 4 years at the end of which time this interest and the principal of $120,000 will be paid. (Ans. $0, $0, $0, $175,692)

    d Demonstrate that a uniform payment of $37,856 at the end of each year for 4 years will also serve to repay the debt. Do this by calculating the value of the remaining debt after each such payment is made.

3-6 If the consulting firm mentioned in the preceding problem is willing to make a down payment on the building equal to 40 percent of its first cost, the balance can be financed at a rate of 7 percent per year compounded annually. With this alternative, the debt would also be repaid by a series of four end-of-year payments.

    a Determine the sizes of these respective payments if the interest owed is paid at the end of each year for 4 years and the entire principal of the loan is repaid at the end of the fourth year.

    b Determine the sizes of these respective payments if the interest for the first 2 years is paid at the end of the second year and the interest for the second 2 years is paid at the end of the fourth year and the entire principal of the loan is repaid at the end of the fourth year.

    c Determine the sizes of these respective payments if the interest owed and one-fourth of the amount of the loan is paid at the end of each year for 4 years.

    d Determine the sizes of these respective payments if the interest owed is paid at the end of each year for 4 years and if one-half of the amount of the loan is repaid at the end of the second year and the other one-half at the end of the fourth year.

    e Determine the sizes of these respective payments if interest is allowed to accrue for 4 years at the end of which time this interest and the entire principal will be paid.

    f Demonstrate that a uniform payment of $21,256 at the end of each year for 4 years will also serve to repay the debt. Do this by calculating the value of the remaining debt after each such payment is made.

3-7 Ascertain the number of interest periods and the interest rate per interest period in each of the following cases:

    a Equity funds which could be invested elsewhere at 18 percent per year compounded monthly will be used to finance an investment in a freight car which has a life of 30 years. (Ans. 360, 1.5%)

    b Telephone poles whose life is 45 years will be purchased with debt capital obtained at a cost of 11 percent per year compounded annually.

    c A combination of equity and debt capital whose average annual cost is 13 percent compounded weekly will be invested in a market research study for a period of 1 year.

d Money obtained at an annual cost of 15 percent compounded quarterly will be spent for a sprinkler alarm system which will be used for 9 years.

e Funds will be deposited in a savings account for 6 years at an annual rate of 7.75 percent compounded daily.

f Municipal bonds can be purchased which yield a return of 6 percent per year compounded semiannually and which will be redeemed in 20 years.

3-8 What is the nominal interest rate and the effective interest rate under each of the following circumstances? If necessary, interpolate in the available interest tables.

a The interest charge is computed at the end of each month at a rate of 2 percent per month. (Ans.   24%, 26.82%)

b The rate is given as 16 percent per year compounded semiannually.

c The interest charge is computed at the end of each quarter at a rate of 4 percent per quarter.

d The rate is given as 30 percent per year compounded monthly. (Ans.   30%, 35.14%)

3-9 An individual invests $7,500 in government bonds at the age of 40. At the age of 65, she redeems them and recovers her original investment plus the accrued interest. What will this total be, given that the effective interest rate was 6 percent? (Ans. $32,189)

3-10 Suppose that the person in the preceding problem wanted to accumulate $50,000 by the time she reached the age of 65. How much would she have had to invest in the government bonds at the age of 40 to attain this goal?

3-11 The manager of an office building has developed a plan for making certain improvements in the building. The program entails an expenditure of $48,000 one year from now, $96,000 three years from now, $144,000 five years from now, and $192,000 seven years from now. If the time value of money is 20 percent per year compounded semiannually, what single expenditure at this time would be equivalent to the proposed future expenditures? (Ans. $199,925)

3-12 A gas utility has borrowed $230,000 to purchase a fleet of small trucks. This amount and all accrued interest is to be repaid at the end of a three-year period. If the annual interest rate is 13 percent compounded annually, how much is owed at the time payment is due?

3-13 A commerical laboratory has decided to establish a fund, into which three deposits will be made, to provide for the purchase of new testing equipment in 5 years. Specifically, $33,000 will be deposited immediately, $47,000 will be deposited one year later, and $71,000 will be deposited 2 years from now. The fund will yield an annual return of 8 percent compounded quarterly, and no withdrawals will occur until 5 years after the first deposit has been made. How much money will the fund contain at that time?

3-14 A development company is considering an investment of equity funds in a tract of land for which it will have a need in 30 years. It is estimated that the property will have a market value of $25,000,000 at that time. The available funds can be invested elsewhere in an alternative of comparable risk and tax status at a return of 23 percent per year compounded annually. What maximum amount should the company be willing to pay for the land at this time? (Ans. $60,000)

3-15 On his fortieth birthday, an individual decides to create a pension fund for himself. He will do this by making a uniform series of deposits in a savings account on which he will earn interest at an annual rate of 4 percent compounded annually.

   a If he deposits $1,200 on his forty-first birthday and every birthday thereafter up to and including his sixtieth, how much money will the fund contain after he has made his last deposit?

   b If he deposits $1,200 on his forty-first birthday and every birthday thereafter up to and including his sixtieth, how much money will the fund contain when he reaches the age of 65? (Ans. $43,477)

   c If he deposits $1,200 on his fortieth birthday and every birthday thereafter up to and including his fifty-ninth, how much money will the fund contain when he reaches the age of 60?

   d If he deposits $1,200 on his fortieth birthday and every birthday thereafter up to and including his fifty-ninth, how much money will the fund contain when he reaches the age of 65? (Ans. $45,214)

3-16 A steel company estimates that it will have to spend $4,250,000 five years from now for pollution control equipment. Management wants to provide for this expenditure by investing a uniform amount at the end of each year for the next 5 years in a source which will yield an annual return of 6 percent compounded annually. What must be the size of the annual investment?

3-17 Suppose that the steel company in the preceding problem had decided to make a series of uniform investments at the *beginning* of each year to accumulate the required $4,250,000 in 5 years. How much would it then have to invest each year? (Ans. $711,276)

3-18 A railroad wants to accumulate $20,000,000 in 10 years to provide for the retirement of a bond issue. It will do so by investing a uniform amount at the end of each quarter during the ten-year period. Given that a return of 8 percent per year compounded quarterly will be realized, how much will have to be invested each quarter?

3-19 The owner of a skiing resort would like to expand her operation. To enable her to do so, her bank agrees to lend her $50,000 at the end of each year for the next 5 years at an annual interest rate of 11 percent compounded annually. The entire debt is to be repaid by means of a single payment 6 years from now. What will be the size of the debt at the beginning of the fourth year of this six-year period? (Ans. $167,100)

3-20 Some time ago, a paper manufacturer financed the purchase of a forest by means of long-term debt. Specifically, the terms of the loan were such that the firm will have to repay $130,000,000 in a single sum 42 years from now. However, the manufacturer approaches the lending institution at this time with an offer to prepay the loan with a uniform series of 42 end-of-year payments at an annual interest rate of 10 percent compounded annually. If the lending institution agrees to the proposed revised repayment plan, how much will it receive at the end of each year for the next 42 years? (Ans. $252,200)

3-21 A city is going to deposit money in an account at this time for use in financing a program for the rehabilitation of the buses in its public transportation system. The rehabilitation program calls for spending $12,000 three months from now and another $12,000 every 3 months thereafter until a total of $96,000 has been spent. If the account will yield 8 percent per year compounded quarterly, what present deposit will suffice to cover the planned future expenditures?

3-22 In the preceding problem, it will have been found that the city intends to spend $12,000 at the *end* of each quarter for 8 quarters. But suppose that the plan had been to spend $12,000 at the *beginning* of each of those quarters. What effect would this change have on the total amount that would have to be deposited in the account at the beginning of the first quarter? (Ans. $89,664)

3-23 A company has purchased a grinder for $16,800. The estimated life of the asset is 14 years. The cost of money to the firm and, therefore, its minimum rate-of-return requirement is 20 percent per year compounded annually. Determine the uniform end-of-year equivalent of this capital expenditure.

3-24 It has been proposed that an electric utility spend $320,000 to improve some of its operating methods. The benefits of the improvement are expected to last for 38 years. What equivalent uniform end-of-year reduction in costs would the improvement have to generate to justify the proposed expenditure? The utility's annual rate-of-return requirement is 15 percent compounded annually. (Ans. $48,256)

3-25 A newspaper publisher has a fire insurance policy. Four annual premiums of $9,000 each remain to be paid. The first of these is due in 1 year. The insurance company is willing to grant a discount if the publisher chooses to prepay the remaining premiums by means of a single payment at the present time. Given that money is worth 8 percent a year compounded annually to the publisher, what maximum amount should she be willing to pay now in lieu of the four remaining annual payments?

3-26 An owner of two apartment buildings has sold one of them. He is now going to invest a portion of the proceeds in a source which will yield 12 percent per year compounded annually. The size of the investment is to be such that it will enable him to withdraw $7,500 each year for 10 years for the purpose of paying the annual real estate tax on the remaining building. However, the first withdrawal will not be made until 2 years after the fund has been established. How much of an investment is required? (Ans. $37,837)

3-27 A secretary has won $50,000 in a contest sponsored by a distributor of magazines. Although the winner has a right to demand immediate payment of the $50,000, she is offered an alternative which will enable her to receive a total of more than $50,000. The alternative calls for a series of six uniform semiannual payments. The first of these payments would be made right now. In the absence of tax considerations, what series of payments would be equivalent to the immediate single payment of $50,000 if the time value of money to the secretary is 12 percent per year compounded semiannually? (Ans. $9,594)

3-28 An automobile dealer is considering renting storage space for a period of 12 years. The terms of the available lease call for a payment of $24,000 at the *beginning* of each year for the first 5 years and $36,000 at the *beginning* of each year for the last 7 years. The dealer places a value on money of 25 percent per year compounded annually.

   a What expenditure at the beginning of the first year would be equivalent to the annual rental charges?

   b What uniform end-of-year series of payments would be equivalent to the stipulated annual rental charges?

   c What uniform beginning-of-year series of payments would be equivalent to the stipulated annual rental charges? (Ans. $27,344)

3-29 At the time his daughter is born, a father decides to establish a fund for her college education by opening a savings account in her name. Beginning with her first birthday, he will make a deposit in the account on every birthday up to and including her eighteenth. The initial deposit will be $100, and the succeeding ones will be increased at a constant rate of $50. The bank pays an effective interest rate of 6 percent.

   a How much money will the account contain after the last deposit is made? Make use of the gradient-series future worth factor in this determination.

   b What uniform series of end-of-year deposits would be equivalent to the planned series of deposits? Make use of the gradient-series annuity factor in this determination.

   c What uniform series of beginning-of-year deposits would be equivalent to the planned series of deposits? (Ans. $423)

   d What single deposit at the time of the girl's birth would be equivalent to the planned series of deposits? Make use of the gradient-series present worth factor in this determination.

3-30 When estimating the revenues it will realize from the sales of a new display rack it plans to produce, a company chooses to treat the revenues in any one year as if they would be realized at the end of the year. In any event, there is reason to believe that there will be a demand for the rack for a period of about 12 years. Annual sales âre expected to be $84,000 the first year but are expected to decrease thereafter at a constant rate of $2,000. The annual time value of money to the firm is 10 percent compounded annually.

a   What uniform series of end-of-year revenues would be equivalent to the estimated series? Make use of the gradient-series annuity factor in this determination. (Ans. $75,223)

b   What single receipt at the beginning of the first year would be equivalent to the estimated series of revenues? Make use of the gradient-series present worth factor in this determination.

c   What single receipt at the end of the twelfth year would be equivalent to the estimated series of revenues? Make use of the gradient-series future worth factor in this determination.

3-31   A finance corporation, which makes personal loans, charges interest at an annual rate of 36 percent compounded monthly. One of its clients is supposed to repay his loan today but is unable to do so. The company offers to accept the following series of payments instead: The individual is to make a payment at the end of each month for the next 2 years; the first payment is to be $20, and the succeeding payments will increase at a constant rate of $5. In the development of this plan, the firm used its customary interest rate. What is the amount of the present debt? (Ans. $1,210)

3-32   An automobile company is going to finance a program for the development of a new type of engine with a combination of equity and debt funds whose average cost is 15 percent a year compounded annually. The project is expected to last about 9 years, and the following are among the costs that will be experienced at certain points during this period:

End-of-year	Amount
3	$13,600
4	15,400
5	17,200
6	19,000

With the use of appropriate gradient-series compound interest factors, determine the following:

a   The single expenditure at the beginning of the nine-year period which would be equivalent to the foregoing costs. (Ans. $34,511)

b   The single expenditure at the end of the nine-year period which would be equivalent to these costs. (Ans. $121,400)

c   The uniform end-of-year series of costs, beginning with the third year and ending with the sixth, which would be equivalent to the given nonuniform series. (Ans. $15,987)

4

Uniform Annual Cost Comparisons

The first analytical technique we shall consider is the *uniform annual cost method*. The application of this approach begins with a description of a proposed investment alternative in the terms discussed in Chapter 2, so that all the expenses and revenues to be associated with the alternative during its life can be ascertained. Furthermore, the points in time at which these respective cash outflows and inflows are expected to occur must be noted. Then, with the time value of money being taken into consideration, the uniform annual equivalent of these cash flows is calculated. This annual equivalent is expressed as a uniform end-of-year series and can be thought of as representing the alternative's average annual cost.

In most cases, a number of mutually exclusive alternatives will be available for carrying out the activity with which the decision maker is concerned. As a consequence, it will be necessary to go through the steps in the foregoing procedure for each of these alternatives to obtain their respective total uniform annual costs. These totals can then be compared with a view to identifying the most economical of the mutually exclusive alternatives. In the absence of irreducible factors, this would be the alternative with the minimum average annual cost.

After the most economical of the mutually exclusive alternatives has been identified, the decision maker goes on to answer the question of whether the nature of this alternative is such that the investment it necessitates in the activity involved can be justified. This question is answered by examining the calculated value of the alternative's uniform annual cost. Given that expenses will be treated as positive costs and revenues as negative costs, an average annual cost that is either zero or negative would serve to reveal that the revenues will suffice to cover the expenses and, hence, that the investment in the activity can be justified. But a positive uniform annual cost would mean that expenses will exceed revenues and, hence, that the investment in the activity cannot be justified; in other words, it would be more economical to select the alternative of making no investment of this kind because this course of action would generate an average annual cost of zero dollars which is lower than the positive annual cost of making the investment. All this, of course, assumes that there are no offsetting irreducible factors.

In general, the uniform annual cost method for evaluating investment alternatives is designed to provide answers to the two questions that were developed in the introductory chapter of this presentation. One of these is: Which of a number of mutually exclusive alternatives for carrying out a given activity is the most economical? The second is: Given the nature of this alternative, can the required capital investment in the activity be justified?

We shall now go on to the specifics of this method of analysis. These will be explained with the use of an illustration in which an organization is confronted by a problem of a fairly comprehensive type. However, it will be assumed that an evaluation of the capital expenditure proposals involved is to be made on a before-tax basis. The explicit income tax consequences of investment decisions will then be studied in a subsequent chapter. As mentioned earlier, this method of presentation is being adopted to eliminate the need for dealing with two relatively complex topics at the same time.

THE ASSUMED PROBLEM

Suppose that a company is giving consideration to the production and marketing of a new product. On the basis of a detailed study, it is found that the item can be produced with the use of either of two manufacturing methods. One calls for a greater investment in production equipment than does the other. The more expensive type of equipment has the advantage of a longer life and a larger salvage value. It will also generate lower total annual operating costs, which consist of such things as direct material, direct labor, supervision, utilities, supplies, maintenance, property taxes, insurance, and marketing and administrative expenses.

Having labeled the lower-priced equipment as alternative K and the higher-priced equipment as alternative L, management summarizes its quantitative description of the two as follows:

	Alternative K	Alternative L
First cost	$84,000	$125,000
Service life	4 years	6 years
Salvage value	$0	$20,000
Annual operating costs	$30,000	variable
Annual revenues	$67,000	$67,000

The operating costs are given as being variable for alternative L because, unlike those for alternative K, they are not expected to be uniform. Instead, it is estimated that they will be $24,000 during the first year and, thereafter, will increase at a constant rate of $1,000 per year.

Management also estimates that each of these alternatives will necessitate an investment of $5,000 in working capital. This amount is expected to remain fixed throughout the period in which the product would be produced and will be recovered in its entirety at the end of that period.

Finally, the activity will call for some combination of debt and equity financing. Specifically, the proportion of debt financing will be 0.25, and the cost of this borrowed money will be 8 percent per year compounded annually. This means that the proportion of equity financing will be 0.75. The before-tax opportunity cost to be associated with the equity funds is estimated to average 24 percent per year during the service period to be considered; the relatively high value for this cost is attributable to the large degree of risk inherent in the activity. In any event, for reasons discussed when we developed Eq. (2-1), these data are processed as follows to obtain the firm's cost of money:

$$i = 0.25(8\%) + 0.75(24\%) = 20\%$$

It will be noted that i has been and will continue to be used to represent the cost of money expressed as a rate. Furthermore, unless there is a statement to the contrary, any such given rate is to be assumed, from this point on, to be a rate per year compounded annually. But to continue, because the cost of money before taxes is 20 percent, the firm selects 20 percent as its minimum before-tax rate-of-return requirement.

An analyst is asked to determine which of these two mutually exclusive alternatives is the more economical. After this alternative has been ascertained, it will be examined to determine whether it is more attractive than the alternative of not producing the product, that is, the alternative which calls for making no investment in the activity.

THE FIRST ALTERNATIVE

Let us begin the uniform annual cost comparison by considering alternative K. With the exception of the return requirement, the data which serve to describe this alternative can be summarized on a time line in the following manner:

```
84,000
 5,000                                          (5,000)
            30,000      30,000      30,000      30,000
           (67,000)    (67,000)    (67,000)    (67,000)
 ├──────────┼───────────┼───────────┼───────────┤
 0          1           2           3           4
```

As was to be expected, the four-year life of the alternative is reflected in the length of the cash-flow, or time, line. Also, the required initial investment of $84,000 in equipment is shown at its point of occurrence, namely, at the beginning of the first year. The same is true for the required investment of $5,000 in working capital. But because this latter amount is not expected to decrease in value, it is shown as having a salvage value of $5,000 at the end of the four-year service period; to designate the fact that this amount represents a revenue and, hence, a negative cost, it is enclosed in parentheses. No revenue stemming from a salvage value is shown at point 4 for the equipment because its terminal salvage value was estimated to be zero.

It will also be noted that all annual operating costs and revenues are shown as occurring at the end of the respective years. The reason for this originates in the difficulty of the estimation process. Although it is realized that operating costs and revenues may be experienced every hour, day, week, or month during a single year, no firm is likely to attempt to describe these recurring costs and revenues in terms of the exact points in time at which they will occur. At best, an analyst can be expected to make a fairly good estimate of annual costs and revenues, and, therefore, this is all he is usually asked to do. Of course, a need now arises for selecting a point during the year at which these costs and revenues will be assumed to have occurred. Any point midway in the year is ordinarily rejected because, with annual compounding, the selection of such a point might necessitate working with a number of interest periods which is not a whole number, and this would prove to be troublesome. Therefore, only two possible points remain. One is the beginning of the year, and the other is the end of the year. Suffice it to say that the practice has evolved of showing annual operating costs and revenues as occurring at the end of the year, and we shall adhere to this custom. This is one of the reasons why an end-of-period series was assumed in the derivation of the series compound interest factors. Therefore, throughout this presentation, an annual cost or revenue will always be treated as an end-of-year amount, unless a specific statement is made to the effect that it will occur at the beginning of a year.

In spite of the aforementioned end-of-year convention, a few firms choose to treat annual operating costs and revenues as if they were distributed uniformly throughout the respective years. When this is done, it becomes necessary to use compound interest factors derived on the basis of continuous compounding, in which it is assumed that the number of interest periods per year approaches infinity. However, the difference between the respective results obtained with end-of-year and continuous-flow conventions is very rarely of any practical significance. When this is coupled with the fact that *estimated* cash flows are being processed and that compound interest factors based on continuous compounding are somewhat more difficult to apply, the reason for the end-of-year convention becomes apparent.

Having explained the reasoning which underlies the cash-flow pattern constructed for alternative K, we can go on to determine the uniform annual equivalent of these cash flows.

The Capital Cost. It will be recalled that, in the uniform annual cost method, the annual equivalent of an alternative's cash flows is expressed as an end-of-year series, and this is another reason why an end-of-period series of amounts was assumed in the derivation of the series compound interest factors. As a consequence, a need arises for converting the $84,000 first cost of the equipment in alternative K into an equivalent uniform end-of-year series. This is done by applying the present-amount annuity factor for a period of 4 years, which coincides with the asset's life, and for a rate of 20 percent, which coincides with the firm's minimum return requirement. Doing so, we obtain

Uniform annual capital cost $= \$84,000(A/P)_{n=4}^{i=20} = \$32,449$

It will be noted that the value of the compound interest factor, as obtained from Appendix C, has not been shown because there is no reason to do so. When a reason does arise, such values will be given in expressions of this type, but, otherwise, from this point on, they will not. Also, it should be noted that the calculated annual equivalent is called the "uniform annual capital cost." This is because the $84,000 expenditure will provide the company with a service for a period in excess of one year, and, by definition, it becomes a capital cost, and its uniform annual equivalent becomes a uniform annual capital cost. Furthermore, we should recall that this average annual capital cost consists of two elements—the devaluation expense and the cost of money. The devaluation expense portion can be easily calculated. Given that the asset has an initial value of $84,000 and a terminal salvage value of zero, the total devaluation expense is $84,000 during the four-year service period. This yields an average of $84,000 divided by 4, or $21,000, per year. If $21,000 is the average annual devaluation expense, the difference between this amount and the $32,449 annual capital cost, which is $11,449, must be the average annual cost of money at 20 percent; this average reflects the fact that the value of the asset and, therefore, the investment in the asset decreases as time goes by.

However, this $32,449 per year is not the entire capital cost because an additional $5,000 will be invested in working capital for a period of 4 years. The annual equivalent of this amount will be

$$\$5,000(A/P)_{n=4}^{i=20} = \$1,932$$

But we must now adjust for the fact that this investment will have a salvage value of $5,000 at the end of the four-year period. This is to say that the calculated cost of $1,932 must be reduced by the annual equivalent of this salvage value. Keeping in mind that this salvage value is a negative cost and that the annual equivalent of a future amount is obtained by applying the future-amount annuity factor, we compute the desired annual equivalent to be as follows:

$$(-)\$5,000(A/F)_{n=4}^{i=20} = (-)\$932$$

In summary, the uniform annual capital cost generated by the $5,000 investment in working capital is equal to

$$\text{Uniform annual capital cost} = \$5,000(A/P)_{n=4}^{i=20} - \$5,000(A/F)_{n=4}^{i=20}$$

$$= \$5,000(0.3863) - \$5,000(0.1863)$$

$$= \$5,000(0.20)$$

$$= \$1,000$$

The reason for showing the values of the compound interest factors contained in the preceding expression is to demonstrate that, in this case, the average annual capital cost proves to be equal to the $5,000 investment times the 20 percent annual cost of money. The explanation for this is as follows: Because the $5,000 investment in working capital does not decrease in value, the devaluation expense per year is zero, and, further, the amount invested every year remains at $5,000. Therefore, the annual capital cost is equal only to the cost of money, and this cost is obtained by multiplying the constant annual investment of $5,000 by the 20 percent annual cost of money, which yields $1,000. This fact also serves to reveal the relationship that exists between the present-amount annuity factor and the future-amount annuity factor; this is that, for the same time value of money and the same number of interest periods, the difference between these factors is equal to the time value of money expressed as a rate per period.

The Total Annual Cost. At this point, we know that the uniform annual equivalent of the $84,000 first cost of the equipment is $32,449. We also know that the uniform annual equivalent of the $5,000 investment in working capital is $1,932. Finally, we know that the uniform annual equivalent of the $5,000 salvage value of the working capital is (−)$932. Substitution of these three series for the corresponding three single amounts in the original cash-flow line yields the following:

```
    32,449      32,449      32,449      32,449
     1,932       1,932       1,932       1,932
      (932)       (932)       (932)       (932)
    30,000      30,000      30,000      30,000
   (67,000)    (67,000)    (67,000)    (67,000)
 ├──────────┼───────────┼───────────┼──────────┤
 0          1           2           3           4
```

An examination of this line reveals that, because the estimated annual operating costs and revenues assume the form of a uniform end-of-year series, no processing of these data is required. Therefore, all the cash flows to be associated with alternative K are now expressed in the required way, and its total uniform annual cost will simply be the sum of the five uniform series we now have. This sum is equal to

Item	Amount
Annual equivalent of equipment's first cost	$32,449
Annual equivalent of working capital investment	1,932
Annual equivalent of working capital's salvage value	(−) 932
Annual equivalent of operating costs	30,000
Annual equivalent of revenues	(−) 67,000
Total uniform annual cost	(−)$ 3,551

The Interpretation. Before we go on to the second alternative, let us pause to analyze the value of the total annual cost obtained for alternative K. To do so, it will be helpful to present the results contained in the preceding table in a slightly different manner.

It will be recalled that $21,000 of the equipment's $32,449 annual capital cost is a devaluation expense and that the balance of $11,449 is the cost of money. Also, the entire $1,000 annual capital cost of the working capital investment is a cost of money. When the $11,449 cost of money is added to the $1,000 cost of money, a total cost of money of $12,449 per year is obtained. Therefore, the total uniform annual cost of alternative K can be described as follows:

Item	Amount per year
Devaluation expense	$21,000
Cost of money	12,449
Operating costs	30,000
Total positive expense	$63,449
Revenues	(−) 67,000
Total cost	(−)$ 3,551

When the results are presented in this way, certain things become evident. Specifically, it is apparent that the expected revenues in our example suffice to reimburse the firm for the operating costs, the devaluation expense, and the cost of money. Since the cost of money is the cost at a rate of 20 percent per year, this means that the revenues suffice to satisfy the firm's minimum rate-of-return requirement of 20 percent. However, they do more than this. Because the annual revenues exceed the total positive expense by $3,551, we can say that this additional $3,551 serves to increase the firm's rate of return to some amount greater than 20 percent. In brief, a negative total annual cost means that the alternative under consideration will generate a return, on the total investment in the alternative, which is greater than the rate used in the determination of this total annual cost. We say "greater than the rate used in the determination of this total annual cost" because, if a higher rate had been used, the annual cost of money would exceed $12,449, and an increase would take place in the alternative's total positive expense. And it might be that the higher rate will serve to raise this total positive expense to a level such that the total annual cost is no longer negative, which means that the actual return would be less than the higher rate used in the computation of the total annual cost.

But suppose that the analyst in our example had been told that the annual revenues with alternative K were estimated to be exactly $63,449. The results of his computations could now be summarized as follows:

Item	Amount per year
Devaluation expense	$21,000
Cost of money	12,449
Operating costs	30,000
Total positive expense	$63,449
Revenues	(−) 63,449
Total cost	$ 0

In this case, the total annual cost proves to be zero because the revenues succeed in just enabling the firm to cover its operating costs, devaluation expense, and 20 percent cost of money. Because nothing remains after these expenses are recovered, the company has simply covered, among other things, its 20 percent cost of money, and, therefore, the alternative is exactly satisfying the established minimum rate-of-return requirement. From this, it follows that, if the total uniform annual cost of an alternative is zero, the rate of return on the total investment will be equal to the rate used in the determination of that annual cost.

Finally, let us suppose that the annual revenues in this illustration had been given as being $62,000. The results would then have been as follows:

Item	Amount per year
Devaluation expense	$21,000
Cost of money	12,449
Operating costs	30,000
Total positive expense	$63,449
Revenues	(−) 62,000
Total cost	(+)$ 1,449

Under these circumstances, the revenues enable the company to recover $21,000 a year for 4 years, or $84,000, to offset the first cost of the equipment. Also, they are sufficient to permit management to meet its annual operating costs of $30,000. But, now, only $11,000 remains per year to reimburse the company for the $12,449 cost of money generated by the 20 percent rate used in the computations. This $12,449 cost exceeds the $11,000 remaining revenues by $1,449, and, as a consequence, the total annual cost becomes (+)$1,449. Obviously, the revenues are not adequate from the standpoint of their ability to compensate the firm for its cost of money of 20 percent, and the alternative would be yielding a return of less than 20 percent per year on the total investment of $84,000 in equipment and $5,000 in working capital. Hence, we say that, if the total annual cost is positive, the return on the total investment in a given alternative is less than the rate used in the determination of that total cost.

The significance of all this is as follows: In the absence of irreducible factors, a proposal that an investment be made in a given alternative should be rejected unless the indicated return on the total investment in that alternative is equal to or exceeds the established minimum rate-of-return requirement. This is so because this requirement reflects the investor's cost of money, and this cost, like any other cost, must be recovered. Or to state this in other terms, an investment proposal should be given further consideration only if its calculated total annual cost is zero or negative, and should be rejected if this cost is positive. Another way of explaining this is to note that the annual cost of making no investment in the activity under consideration, which in our example is the production and marketing of a new product, is zero. Unless an alternative for carrying out the activity yields a cost equal to or less than this cost of zero, it is more economical not to make an investment of this type. In other words, a positive annual cost exceeds the cost of making no investment, and, consequently, an investment in an alternative which yields a positive cost cannot be justified.

But to return to alternative K, whose average annual cost was found to be $(-)\$3,551$, we conclude that, since this cost is negative, it is better to produce and market the item by means of this alternative than not to produce and market the item at all. The remaining question is: Will it be even more economical to produce and market the item by means of alternative L? To answer this question, we must calculate the uniform annual cost of this remaining alternative.

THE SECOND ALTERNATIVE

The data made available to the analyst with respect to alternative L enable him to describe the cash flows to be associated with this alternative in the following manner:

```
125,000                                                              (20,000)
  5,000                                                               (5,000)
         24,000      25,000     26,000      27,000     28,000     29,000
        (67,000)    (67,000)   (67,000)    (67,000)   (67,000)   (67,000)
   |_____|_____|_____|_____|_____|_____|
   0         1          2          3          4          5          6
```

The uniform annual capital cost of the equipment will be the uniform annual equivalent of its first cost less the uniform annual equivalent of its salvage value. Noting that the service period in this case is 6 years, we should find this cost to be

Uniform annual capital cost $= \$125,000(A/P)_{n=6}^{i=20} - \$20,000(A/F)_{n=6}^{i=20}$

$$= \$35,574$$

If we want to ascertain what portion of this amount is the devaluation expense, we can take the $\$105,000$ total decrease in the asset's value and divide this total by the asset's life of 6 years to obtain $\$17,500$ per year. The balance of $\$18,074$ is the average annual cost of money at 20 percent.

As with alternative K, the annual capital cost caused by the $5,000 investment in working capital will be the annual equivalent of this amount less the annual equivalent of its terminal salvage value of $5,000. This difference is equal to

$$\text{Uniform annual capital cost} = \$5,000(A/P)\,{}^{i=20}_{n=6} - \$5,000(A/F)\,{}^{i=20}_{n=6}$$

$$= \$1,000$$

Next, the uniform annual equivalent of the nonuniform series of operating costs must be computed. We begin by recognizing that this series contains a gradient of $1,000. Therefore, we take the first value of $24,000 which appears in the series and establish a uniform series of this size. The remaining operating costs yield a gradient series whose annual equivalent can be found with the use of the gradient-series annuity factor. When the annual equivalent of the gradient series is added to the $24,000 uniform series, we find that

$$\text{Uniform annual operating costs} = \$24,000 + \$1,000(A/G)\,{}^{i=20}_{n=6}$$

$$= \$25,979$$

The remaining values on the cash-flow line are the $67,000 annual revenues. These require no processing because they already are in the form of a uniform end-of-year series. Consequently, the actual pattern of cash flows for alternative L can now be described in terms of the following equivalent pattern:

35,574	35,574	35,574	35,574	35,574	35,574
1,000	1,000	1,000	1,000	1,000	1,000
25,979	25,979	25,979	25,979	25,979	25,979
(67,000)	(67,000)	(67,000)	(67,000)	(67,000)	(67,000)

```
+----+----+----+----+----+----+
0    1    2    3    4    5    6
```

The total uniform annual cost of alternative L can be obtained by finding the sum of these four uniform series. When this is done, the result is as follows:

Item	Amount
Annual cost of equipment	$35,574
Annual cost of working capital	1,000
Annual operating costs	25,979
Annual revenues	(−) 67,000
Total annual cost	(−)$ 4,447

Since this cost is negative, we conclude that the revenues with this alternative more than suffice to recover its positive costs, which include a 20 percent cost of money, and, hence, that the rate of return on the total investment of $130,000 required by the alternative more than satisfies the firm's minimum return requirement. This coincides with what we found to be true of alternative K. Thus, we have succeeded in learning that either alternative K or L is to be preferred to the alternative of making no investment in the activity. But we must now choose between K and L.

THE COMPARISON

If we identify the alternative of not producing the product as alternative J, the results we have obtained thus far can be summarized as follows:

	Alternative J	Alternative K	Alternative L
Total uniform annual cost	$0	(−)$3,551	(−)$4,447

Because these respective totals represent costs, we say that the most economical alternative, in the absence of irreducible factors, is the one that minimizes costs. From this, it follows that, as was seen earlier, alternative J should be rejected because a cost of zero is larger than the negative costs to be associated with the other two alternatives. At this point, there is a natural inclination to go on to note that a cost of (−)$4,447 is lower than a cost of (−)$3,551 and, therefore, to conclude that L is the more economical of the two remaining alternatives. Unfortunately, in theory, this kind of comparison cannot be made because each of these costs is not expressed in the same units. Specifically, the cost of alternative K is (−)$3,551 *per year for 4 years,* and the cost of alternative L is (−)$4,447 *per year for 6 years.* This permits one to say only that alternative K is more costly than alternative L for 4 years but does not permit one to reach any conclusion regarding what will take place after 4 years have elapsed.

All this suggests that equal time periods must be compared in any attempt to select the more economical investment alternative. The need to do so can be explained as follows: The fact that the company in our example estimated a six-year life for the equipment represented by alternative L means that the firm plans to produce and market the product involved for at least 6 years; the period may be even longer if the equipment is replaced at the end of 6 years by other facilities which will continue to provide the same service. But it is certain that at least 6 years of service will be required. Consequently, if the equipment represented by alternative K were selected, it would be necessary to replace this equipment at the end of its four-year life by new facilities. Furthermore, it is possible that the new facilities available at that time will be so economical that it will be to the firm's advantage to produce the product in a relatively expensive manner for the first 4 years in order to be in a position to procure the much more economical equipment that will be available at the end of that time.

To illustrate this, let us suppose that, 4 years from now, equipment to produce the product will be available which has a first cost of $47,000, a life of 2 years, a salvage value of zero, annual operating costs of $22,000, and expected annual revenues of $67,000; with this equipment, a $5,000 investment in working capital will continue to be required, which means that the initial working capital investment would now be recovered 2 years later than before, that is, at the end of 6 years. Therefore, if management were to select alternative K at the present time, it would replace K in 4 years by the equipment just described. As a result, all the costs and revenues that would be experienced during the next 6 years with this arrangement are as follows:

84,000				47,000		
5,000						(5,000)
	30,000	30,000	30,000	30,000	22,000	22,000
	(67,000)	(67,000)	(67,000)	(67,000)	(67,000)	(67,000)
0	1	2	3	4	5	6

This alternative has a life of 6 years, as does alternative L, and consists of equipment K, which has a life of 4 years, followed by its replacement, which has a life of 2 years. Our task is to convert the cash flows involved to their uniform annual equivalent, expressed as a cost per year for 6 years. This can be done in a number of different ways, but, in this case, it might be best to begin by finding the single amount at point 0 that is equivalent to all the costs and revenues which will be experienced during the six-year period. Then, the uniform annual equivalent of this present amount can be calculated. The value of the present amount can be obtained in the following way:

$$\text{Present worth} = \$84,000 + \$5,000 + \$47,000(P/F)_{n=4}^{i=20}$$

$$- \$5,000(P/F)_{n=6}^{i=20}$$

$$+ \$30,000(P/A)_{n=4}^{i=20} + \$22,000(P/F)_{n=5}^{i=20}$$

$$+ \$22,000(P/F)_{n=6}^{i=20} - \$67,000(P/A)_{n=6}^{i=20}$$

$$= (-)\$18,968$$

The equivalent of this present worth in terms of six uniform end-of-year amounts would be obtained as follows:

Annual equivalent $= (-)\$18{,}968(A/P)_{n=6}^{i=20} = (-)\$5{,}704$

It can now be said that the total uniform annual cost of this alternative, which consists of equipment K and its replacement, is $(-)\$5{,}704$ a year for 6 years. Because equal time periods have been considered, this cost can be compared directly with the calculated cost of $(-)\$4{,}447$ a year for 6 years for alternative L. It is interesting to note that, because of the nature of its replacement, alternative K now proves to be more economical, whereas alternative L appeared to be the more attractive when the difference in the time periods involved was ignored. This is true, of course, only because of the nature of K's replacement; with another type of replacement, a different conclusion might be reached. In any event, what happens beyond the six-year service period considered is of no relevance because, whether it selects equipment K and its replacement or alternative L, management will have the same choice of alternatives 6 years from now.

A Simplifying Assumption. The foregoing suggests that, if two or more mutually exclusive investment alternatives have different service lives, the investor must forecast the nature of the future replacements for each until equal time periods are obtained. As one might suspect, this creates certain problems. For example, in our illustration, it might have been that equipment K, whose service life is 4 years, was expected to be replaced by facilities with a service life of 5 years. This would yield a total time period of 9 years, which now exceeds the six-year life of alternative L. Therefore, the nature of L's replacement would have to be predicted; if it were estimated to have an eight-year life, we now would have a total period of 14 years as compared with 9 years for the other alternative. We could go on this way, but this suffices to bring out the magnitude of the estimation problem involved.

  Given the difficulty of describing existing alternatives in terms of the costs and revenues they will generate, it is almost impossible to exaggerate the difficulty of estimating the characteristics of what may prove to be a series of future replacements. Consequently, with few exceptions, assumptions are made about the nature of these replacements. Although these assumptions vary, all serve to generate the cash-flow patterns which will characterize future replacements and, thereby, eliminate the need for forecasting what these patterns will be.

  One of the most common assumptions, and it is the one we shall adopt when the nature of future replacements is not given, is that, regardless of which of the presently-available alternatives is selected, it will be replaced at the end of its service life by a series of alternatives just like it.

To relate this to our illustration, it would be assumed that alternative K will be replaced at the end of its four-year life by equipment which will also have a four-year life and will generate the same pattern of cash flows as did the original equipment. Furthermore, it would be assumed that this first replacement will be followed by a second replacement just like it, and so on.

Insofar as alternative L is concerned, it would be assumed that, at the end of their six-year life, the assets involved will be replaced by equipment which will also have a six-year life and generate the same pattern of cash flows as did the original equipment. Also, it would be assumed that the first replacement will be followed by a second replacement just like it, and so on.

Specifically, the number of replacements that would be assumed for each alternative would be that number which yields equal time periods. In our illustration, given a four-year life for alternative K and a six-year life for alternative L, two replacements would be assumed for K and one for L because the total service period would then be 12 years in each case. As a result, if we omit the thousands for convenience, the selection of alternative K at this time would be expected to bring about the following cash flows during the twelve-year period:

84			84			84					
5			5			5					
			(5)			(5)					(5)
30	30	30	30	30	30	30	30	30	30	30	30
(67)	(67)	(67)	(67)	(67)	(67)	(67)	(67)	(67)	(67)	(67)	(67)
0	1	2	3	4	5	6	7	8	9	10	11	12

Similarly, the selection of alternative L at this time would be expected to yield the following cash flows during the same twelve-year period:

125					125						
					(20)						(20)
5					5						
					(5)						(5)
24	25	26	27	28	29	24	25	26	27	28	29
(67)	(67)	(67)	(67)	(67)	(67)	(67)	(67)	(67)	(67)	(67)	(67)
0	1	2	3	4	5	6	7	8	9	10	11	12

Thus far, we have demonstrated that the assumption eliminates the need for forecasting the nature of future replacements. We shall now show that it also serves to simplify the computations.

When the nature of K's replacement was predicted at an earlier point, the resultant equal time periods proved to be 6 years in length, and it became necessary to ascertain each alternative's average cost per year for 6 years. With the assumption regarding the nature of future replacements, the resultant equal time periods prove to be 12 years in length, and it becomes necessary to ascertain each alternative's average cost per year for 12 years. How this can be done will be explained with the use of alternative K for purposes of illustration.

To obtain the average cost per year for 6 years for alternative K and its predicted replacement which had a two-year life, it was necessary to process every value that appeared in the cash-flow pattern that was forecast for the six-year period. This was done by calculating the total present worth of these values and, then, computing the annual equivalent of this total. It would be only natural to assume that a need now exists for processing every value that appears in the twelve-year cash-flow pattern for alternative K and its assumed replacements to obtain its average cost per year for 12 years. As we shall see, this happens not to be true, but, for the moment, let us suppose it is and proceed accordingly.

If we return to the twelve-year cash-flow line for alternative K, an examination of the values it contains reveals that, at points 4 and 8, a $5,000 expenditure is offset by a $5,000 revenue; so these four values can be ignored. A study of the following expression will reveal how the annual equivalents of the remaining values can be obtained.

$$\text{Annual cost} = \$89{,}000(A/P)_{n=12}^{i=20} + \$84{,}000(P/F)_{n=4}^{i=20}(A/P)_{n=12}^{i=20}$$

$$+\$84{,}000(P/F)_{n=8}^{i=20}(A/P)_{n=12}^{i=20} - \$5{,}000(A/F)_{n=12}^{i=20}$$

$$+ \$30{,}000 - \$67{,}000$$

$$= (-)\$3{,}551$$

As is shown, if the indicated steps are carried out, the result is a cost of (−)$3,551 per year for 12 years. But this coincides with what we had obtained much earlier when we processed the cash flows for only the first 4 years. A moment's thought will reveal why this is true. To repeat, we had found earlier that the cost of alternative K is (−) $3,551 per year for 4 years. But if the assumed first and second replacements have alternative K's characteristics, it should be apparent that they also will generate an average annual cost of (−)$3,551. Therefore, there is no need for making any additional computations. We can simply say that, if alternative K is selected, the result will be a cost of (−)$3,551 a year for 12 years.

Similarly, if alternative L yields a cost of (−)$4,447 a year for 6 years, a replacement with the same characteristics will, of course, generate an annual cost of (−)$4,447 for another 6 years. This permits us to say that, if alternative L is selected, the result will be a cost of (−)$4,447 a year for 12 years. Hence, as with alternative K, there is no need to process all the values that appear in the twelve-year cash-flow pattern for alternative L.

Finally, because equal time periods are now involved, we can compare these annual costs directly and conclude that, in the absence of any irreducible factors, L is the more economical alternative since a cost of (−)$4,447 is lower than a cost of (−)$3,551.

To summarize all this, when the alternatives have unequal service lives, two approaches are possible. One calls for predicting the nature of future replacements until equal time periods are obtained and computing the respective resultant uniform annual costs. The second calls for making the assumption we have made with regard to the nature of future replacements. With this second approach, the average annual cost of each alternative is calculated on the basis of the estimated service life of the assets it involves. Then, it is assumed that these respective annual costs will continue until equal time periods are attained. This eliminates the need for making additional computations and permits one to compare the calculated average annual costs directly. Unless stated otherwise, we shall employ this second approach in each of the analyses we shall be making.

But to return to our problem, it is sometimes helpful to describe the results, such as those we obtained, in somewhat different terms. Specifically, it can be said that the effect of an investment in alternative K will be that the firm will experience a net gain of $3,551 a year, whereas the comparable figure for alternative L is $4,447. Values of this kind, which represent the profit after the cost of money has been taken into account, are often called the "economic profit." Therefore, alternative L would be considered to be more attractive than K because it is expected to yield a higher economic profit. But as an earlier computation demonstrated, a different conclusion might have been reached had the characteristics of the *actual* future replacements been known.

IRREDUCIBLE FACTORS

When an assumption such as the one that has just been described is made, it is taken into account as one of a number of irreducible, or intangible, factors which are capable of causing management to make a decision other than the one suggested by a comparison of the calculated uniform annual costs. To illustrate, although a quantitative description of future replacements may prove to be impossible in the preceding example, there may be reason to believe that, in 4 years, equipment K can be replaced by equipment whose cost will be lower than $84,000 and whose annual operating costs will be less than $30,000. Since the calculated average annual cost of alternative K is only $896 higher than that of L, it might be decided, on the basis of judgment, to select alternative K at this time in anticipation of these lower future costs.

On the other hand, management may suspect that, because of rising prices, future replacement and operating costs will exceed those generated by the assumption. In our example, such an expectation might place alternative L in an even more favorable light because this alternative would postpone the need for incurring those higher future costs until 6 years from now, as compared with 4 years with alternative K.

Having noted that the implications of our assumption are treated as an irreducible in the analysis, we might go on to consider other examples of factors of this type. One of these is the risk of error to be associated with any prediction of cash flows. In our example, management might note that, although alternative K has the higher calculated average annual cost, this cost is based on an assumed zero salvage value, whereas a $20,000 salvage value was estimated for alternative L. The estimate of zero is certainly more conservative than the one of $20,000, and this realization might have an effect on the final decision. Alternative K also has an advantage stemming from the fact that it required forecasts of cash flows for the next 4 years, as compared with 6 years for alternative L, and a four-year forecast is more likely to be accurate than is a six-year forecast.

To continue with examples of a more general nature, if management suspects that the cost of borrowed money will decrease in the future, it will be disposed toward the currently-available alternative which will minimize the amount of debt capital that must be raised at this time. As another example, the shorter-lived of the presently-available alternatives would be preferred when indications are that particularly attractive investment opportunities will be available in the relatively near future. In another case, the firm would favor the alternative which reduces the required amount of materials and labor when indications are that the prices of these factors of production might increase in the future.

As final examples, management would lean toward that alternative which will (1) provide it with greater output capacity which might possibly be required in the future, (2) result in increased safety for its employees or the users of its products, (3) improve the quality of its output, (4) enable it to make faster deliveries to its customers, (5) improve employee morale, (6) render more reliable service, or (7) bring about better public relations.

Obviously, the development of an exhaustive list of such factors is not possible, but those presented suffice to suggest their nature. In general, they assume a major role in the decision-making process when a comparison reveals that the total costs generated by the alternatives are not significantly different. Under such circumstances, the final decision is very often based on such factors. Of course, if a dollar value can be assigned to any of these or similar factors, they cease to be irreducibles.

COST RELEVANCY

It was mentioned in the introductory chapter of this presentation that, for certain reasons, the analyst may not be able to obtain a complete description of the consequences of a proposed investment alternative. Let us consider this type of situation. We shall begin by returning to the results of the analysis we have just completed. These results can be summarized as follows:

	Alternative K	Alternative L
Annual capital cost	$33,449	$36,574
Annual operating costs	30,000	25,979
Total annual expense	$63,449	$62,553
Annual revenues	(−) 67,000	(−) 67,000
Total annual cost	(−)$ 3,551	(−)$ 4,447

A comparison of these results reveals that alternative L is more economical than K by $896 a year. But suppose that the facts of the case were as follows: Before beginning his computations, the analyst examines the descriptions of the respective alternatives that had been made available to him. He discovers that no estimate of annual revenues has been provided. In reply to his inquiry, he is told that management simply did not feel that a meaningful estimate was possible. However, the consensus was that the revenues would be the same with each alternative and that they would exceed the positive costs. Therefore, the analyst is instructed to proceed with the analysis on that basis.

In the absence of information regarding revenues, the only comparison possible is a comparison of the alternatives' respective capital and operating costs. This comparison would yield the following:

	Alternative K	Alternative L
Annual capital cost	$33,449	$36,574
Annual operating costs	30,000	25,979
Total annual expense	$63,449	$62,553

A comparison of these results reveals that, as before, alternative L is more economical than K by $896 a year. This was to be expected because each of the earlier totals was changed by the same amount, namely, (−)$67,000. But the fact that the new "totals" are positive is of no significance since they are not totals in the strict sense of the term and, therefore, are not capable of telling us anything about the rate of return. Yet, they do suffice to identify which of these two alternatives is the more economical. And this is all that is necessary, if the firm decides, on the basis of judgment, that the revenues will exceed the positive costs and, hence, that the rate of return on the total investment in each of the alternatives is satisfactory. Such a decision is one to exclude the alternative of making no investment in the activity under consideration. Given a decision of this type, anything is permissible that does not alter the *difference* between the calculated values of the "total cost" of the remaining alternatives. We demonstrated this by ignoring the revenues to be associated with alternatives K and L. As another example, if the cost of materials with each of these alternatives happened to be $10,000, this cost could also be ignored; each of the values for the calculated total annual cost would now be reduced by $10,000, but the difference between them would remain at $896 in favor of alternative L.

To summarize, as explained earlier, there are circumstances under which an investor cannot obtain a complete description of the cash flows to be associated with each of a set of mutually exclusive investment alternatives. Consequently, he must use judgment and intuition to decide whether the activity involved will yield a satisfactory return on total investment. If the decision is that it will, the analysis begins with a rejection of the alternative of making no investment. To continue the study, the remaining alternatives need be described only in terms of those factors whose values are affected by the choice of these alternatives. This means that those revenues and expenses which are the same for each of the remaining alternatives can be ignored. As a matter of fact, only the differences between the affected revenues and expenses need be estimated should it prove to be convenient to estimate differences rather than totals. But to repeat, the average annual costs calculated on the basis of such descriptions do not represent the true total average annual costs, and, hence, they reveal nothing about the rates of return on the respective total investments. This is to say that, with this approach, it is of no significance whether the calculated average annual cost of a given investment alternative is positive, negative, or zero. But let us now apply all this to a type of problem which differs from the one with which we have been working.

A REPLACEMENT PROBLEM

Suppose that a building contractor owns a unit of construction equipment which he purchased 3 years ago. It has been proposed that the equipment be replaced by a new unit of improved design. The old equipment can be sold at this time for $3,600. If it is retained, it will be kept for either 1 or 2 years, depending on which of these service periods proves to be the more economical. The salvage value is expected to be $1,000 in 1 year, and $800 in 2 years. Repair and maintenance costs are estimated to be $960 for the coming year, and $1,140 for the year after. Annual fuel costs are expected to be $190 higher each year than they would be with the new equipment.

The proposed replacement has a first cost of $11,900, an estimated life of 4 years, and an expected terminal salvage value of $3,900. Its annual repair and maintenance costs during the four-year service period are estimated to be $120, $200, $310, and $540, respectively.

The contractor believes that his total revenues will be the same whether he retains or replaces the old asset. However, he is unable to estimate what such equipment contributes to these revenues, but he intends to stay in business and, to do so, he must have this kind of equipment. Therefore, he rejects the alternative of selling the old asset and not replacing it by a new unit because he assumes that this would be uneconomical. Given this decision, he does not bother to estimate the working capital requirements and differences in operating costs other than repair, maintenance, and fuel since these items will probably be unaffected by the choice of equipment.

In brief, the question is: Should the old equipment be replaced at this time? This question is to be answered on the basis of a before-tax uniform annual cost comparison, in which the analyst is to use a rate of 15 percent as the contractor's annual cost of money.

Economic Life Determination. The analysis can begin with a determination of the old equipment's economic life, that is, the life which will minimize its average annual cost. This can be ascertained by simply computing and comparing this cost for each of the two proposed lives. Insofar as the one-year service life is concerned, the cash flows during this period would be as follows:

```
3,600    (1,000)
           960
           190
|——————————|
0          1
```

The uniform annual equivalent of these amounts will be an end-of-year series of only one-year duration. Therefore, the equivalent of each of these four amounts at the end of 1 year must be found. The salvage value and recurring expenses already appear in the form of an end-of-year series whose length is 1 year; so only the required investment of \$3,600 remains to be converted into this form. When this is done, the total uniform annual cost is found to be equal to

Annual cost $= \$3,600(A/P)_{n=1}^{i=15} - \$1,000 + \$960 + \$190$

$\qquad = \$4,290$

If the asset is kept for 2 years, the cash-flow pattern would be as follows:

```
3,600                   (800)
          960           1,140
          190           190
  |--------+------------|
  0        1            2
```

This pattern yields the following uniform annual cost:

Annual cost $= \$3,600(A/P)_{n=2}^{i=15} - \$800(A/F)_{n=2}^{i=15} + \$960$

$\qquad + \$180(A/G)_{n=2}^{i=15} + \$190$

$\qquad = \$3,076$

An examination of this expression will reveal that the two-year series of repair and maintenance costs has been broken down into a \$960 uniform series and a \$180 gradient series. But to continue, in the absence of information related to the nature of future replacements, we assume that, if the equipment is kept 1 year, its replacements will also yield a cost of \$4,290 per year and that, if the equipment is kept 2 years, its replacements will also yield a cost of \$3,076 per year. This enables us to compare these two costs directly and to conclude that the economic life of the asset is 2 years because this life yields the lower annual cost. It is this cost of \$3,076 per year that should be compared with the annual cost of the proposed new equipment.

The Proposed Equipment. To obtain the uniform annual cost of the proposed replacement, we begin by taking into account the cash flows of this alternative. These can be described in the following manner:

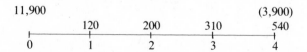

```
11,900                                        (3,900)
          120        200        310           540
  |--------+----------+----------+------------|
  0        1          2          3            4
```

The nature of the nonuniform series of recurring expenses is such that we must first find their total present worth before calculating their uniform annual equivalent. Keeping this in mind, we should compute the average annual cost of this alternative as follows:

$$\text{Annual cost} = \$11,900(A/P)_{n=4}^{i=15} - \$3,900(A/F)_{n=4}^{i=15} + [\$120(P/F)_{n=1}^{i=15}$$
$$+ \$200(P/F)_{n=2}^{i=15} + \$310(P/F)_{n=3}^{i=15}$$
$$+ \$540(P/F)_{n=4}^{i=15}] (A/P)_{n=4}^{i=15}$$
$$= \$3,657$$

It will be recalled that the average annual cost of retaining the old equipment for 2 years was found to be $3,076. Our assumption regarding the nature of future replacements enables us to make a direct comparison of this $3,076 with the cost of $3,657 obtained for the new equipment. This comparison reveals that, in the absence of irreducible factors, the contractor would be advised to retain the old asset because that alternative has the lower annual cost.

It is interesting to note that, if the economic life of the old equipment had not been determined, a different and incorrect decision might have been reached. This can be seen from a summary of the results of the complete analysis. This summary is as follows:

Alternative	Uniform annual cost
Retain old equipment 1 year	$4,290
Retain old equipment 2 years	3,076
Replace old equipment now	3,657

A comparison of these costs reveals that a one-year life estimate would have called for replacement at this time at a cost of $3,657 per year, whereas a two-year life estimate results in the selection of an alternative whose cost is only $3,076 per year.

We might also observe that, because revenues and certain recurring expenses were ignored, these average annual costs are not total annual costs. Therefore, they are incapable of telling us anything about the rate of return that would be realized on the total investment in each of the three alternatives. This is to say that the fact that these costs are positive is of no significance. However, this is not to suggest that an investor under such circumstances is unconcerned with whether his minimum rate-of-return requirement, as represented by the cost of money, is being satisfied. Instead, for reasons already given, the investor, under such circumstances, finds it necessary to reach a conclusion regarding his rate of return on the basis of judgment rather than on the basis of a quantitative analysis. If his assumption that revenues will exceed costs and, hence, that the return will be satisfactory happens to be incorrect, thé decision reached by means of a study of this type will at least succeed in minimizing his economic loss.

Also, it should be realized that, in a problem of this type, the specific values obtained for the alternatives' uniform annual costs will be affected by how the analyst treats some of the relevant cash flows. To illustrate, it was stated that the annual fuel costs would be $190 higher with the old equipment than with the new. Had this amount been handled as a saving to be associated with the new equipment rather than as an additional cost to be associated with the old equipment, each alternative's uniform annual cost would have been $190 less than what we calculated it to be. However, differences among the alternatives' uniform annual costs would have remained the same, and it is these differences which serve to identify the most economical alternative.

Finally, cognizance should be taken of the fact that a decision, other than the one indicated by the cost comparison, might be reached if irreducible factors remain to be evaluated. Similarly, the indicated decision might be altered if the contractor chooses to forecast the nature of future replacements rather than to accept the cash-flow patterns generated by the assumption we have made about the nature of these replacements.

Before going on to another type of problem, we might note that, in this illustration, three investment alternatives were being analyzed, as compared with two in the preceding "new product" problem. When more than two alternatives are to be compared, the problem is said to be a "multiple-alternative problem." Suffice it to say that, when the uniform annual cost method is being employed, a multiple-alternative problem simply requires that the annual cost of each of the available alternatives be ascertained. This must be done for the same time period in each case, and these equal time periods can be attained either by forecasting the nature of future replacements or by making our assumption regarding their nature. The resultant annual costs can then be compared to identify the most economical alternative.

PERPETUAL-SERVICE ALTERNATIVES

One more type of problem remains to be considered before we end our treatment of the uniform annual cost method. This is a problem in which one or more of the alternatives involves an asset which has an infinite service life.

To illustrate, suppose that a distributor of food products is expanding his operations. As a result, he will require a warehouse in an area which he does not currently service. One of the alternatives is to lease the required space. Another is to purchase an available tract of land for $750,000 and then to construct and maintain a suitable building on the site. It is estimated that the building will call for an initial investment of $1,500,000, that its economic life will be 30 years, and that its terminal salvage value will be $300,000. The annual cost of maintaining the building is expected to be $40,000 during the first 10 years of its life, and $60,000 during the last 20 years.

The distributor has definitely decided to acquire the additional space and wants to compare the two aforementioned methods for doing so by making a before-tax comparison of their respective uniform annual costs. He realizes that equal time periods must be considered for each alternative and decides this period should be of infinite duration. This decision is based on the assumption that his organization will operate forever and that the warehouse facility will be required for that length of time.

Insofar as the alternative of acquiring land and then building the warehouse is concerned, the distributor recognizes that, although the land will have an infinite life, the warehouse will not; therefore, he must take into account the nature of the infinite series of replacements which the building will require. To simplify the analysis, he is willing to assume that the cash-flow pattern generated by the initial building will be repeated every 30 years. The distributor also states that the average cost of money during the entire study period is estimated to be 8 percent per year.

We are asked to demonstrate to the distributor's financial analyst how to calculate the average annual cost of the alternative of acquiring land and constructing and maintaining an infinite series of warehouses. The analyst will then be able to make a similar determination for the alternative of leasing the required space.

The Cost Calculation.   What distinguishes this investment alternative from the others we have considered thus far is that one of the assets it involves has an infinite life. Specifically, the $750,000 investment in land will provide the distributor with perpetual service, and, consequently, the uniform annual equivalent of this amount must be found for an infinite number of years. This equivalent can be calculated by multiplying the $750,000 by the present-amount annuity factor for a rate of 8 percent and a number of years equal to infinity. The resultant expression would be as follows:

$$\text{Annual equivalent} = \$750,000(A/P)_{n=\infty}^{i=8}$$

But this raises the question of what value this compound interest factor assumes when the number of periods is infinite. The question could be answered by taking the algebraic expression for the factor and finding its limit as n approaches infinity. But there is a simpler way. Suppose that the distributor's 8 percent cost of money in our problem represents what he could realize by investing money in some other source of comparable risk and tax status. For example, let us assume that he could establish a fund of some type which would yield an annual return of 8 percent in the form of an interest payment. If he and his heirs wanted to make an infinite number of uniform end-of-year withdrawals from this fund, the maximum possible withdrawal would be equal to the interest earned each year which is

Annual interest = $750,000(0.08) = $60,000

An annual withdrawal of this size would leave the capital investment intact, so that $60,000 per year would continue to be earned and could be continued to be withdrawn indefinitely. If even $1 more than this amount were withdrawn per year, the fund would, in time, be exhausted; that is, it would not have an infinite life. This means that

$$\$750,000(A/P)_{n=\infty}^{i=8} = \$750,000(0.08)$$

which enables us to conlude that the value of the present-amount annuity factor (A/P) for an n equal to infinity is equal to i. Since the uniform-series present worth factor (P/A) is the reciprocal of the present-amount annuity factor, it follows that the value of this factor for an n equal to infinity is $1/i$. To illustrate, someone may want to know how much must be invested now to provide for an infinite series of $60,000 end-of-year withdrawals in which the first withdrawal is to be made 1 year from now. If the return on the investment will be 8 percent compounded annually, the required investment would be

$$\$60,000(P/A)_{n=\infty}^{i=8} = \$60,000(1/0.08) = \$750,000$$

But to return to our warehouse problem, we can, therefore, say that the annual cost generated by the investment in land will be equal to

Annual cost of land = $750,000(A/P)_{n=\infty}^{i=8} = $750,000(0.08)

= $60,000

The annual cost of constructing and maintaining the building can be ascertained by processing the cash flows to be associated with this portion of the investment. These, in thousands of dollars, are as follows:

```
1,500                                                    (300)
     40   40   · · ·   40   60   60  · · · · · · ·   60
   ├────┼────┼─ · · ─┼────┼────┼─ · · · · · · · ─┤
   0    1    2   · · ·  10   11   12  · · · · · · ·  30
```

The uniform annual equivalent of these amounts can be found in the following manner:

$$\text{Annual cost of building} = \$1,500,000(A/P)_{n=30}^{i=8} - \$300,000(A/F)_{n=30}^{i=8}$$

$$+ [\$40,000(P/A)_{n=10}^{i=8}$$

$$+ \$60,000(P/A)_{n=20}^{i=8}(P/F)_{n=10}^{i=8}] (A/P)_{n=30}^{i=8}$$

$$= \$178,624$$

Given the assumed nature of the building's replacements, we should say that this $178,624 will continue for an infinite number of years. When this cost is added to the $60,000 annual cost of owning the land for an infinite number of years, a total annual cost of $238,624 is obtained for the alternative being considered.

Another Approach. To emphasize the fact that a given combination of cash flows can be processed in more than one way, let us calculate the total uniform annual cost of this alternative by means of a slightly different approach. We could begin by noting that the total necessary investment at this time is the sum of the $750,000 required for land and the $1,500,000 required for the first building, or $2,250,000. This specific total expenditure will be made only once during the infinite time period, and, therefore, it can be depicted, in thousands of dollars, as follows:

```
2,250
 ├─────────────────────────────────────────┤
 0                                          ∞
```

The annual equivalent of this expenditure would be calculated as follows:

$$\text{Annual equivalent} = \$2,250,000(A/P)_{n=\infty}^{i=8} = \$180,000$$

At the end of every 30-year period, another $1,500,000 would have to be spent for the building's replacement; but because the building being replaced has a salvage value of $300,000, the net expenditure for the replacement would be the difference between these two amounts, or $1,200,000. With the given recurring expenses, the cash flow pattern, in thousands of dollars, that would now repeat itself every 30 years would be as follows:

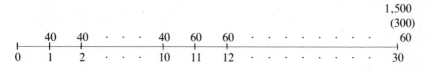

The annual equivalent of this pattern could be obtained in the following manner:

Annual equivalent $= \$1,200,000(A/F)_{n=30}^{i=8} + \$40,000$

$$+ \$20,000(P/A)_{n=20}^{i=8}(P/F)_{n=10}^{i=8}(A/P)_{n=30}^{i=8}$$

$$= \$58,624$$

The assumption regarding the nature of future replacements permits us to add this result to the \$180,000 annual equivalent of the initial expenditure of \$2,250,000. When we do, we find that

Annual cost $= \$180,000 + \$58,624 = \$238,624$

which coincides with the value obtained earlier.

In any event, the analyst would go on to ascertain the uniform annual cost of the other alternative in the same general manner. The distributor would then base his decision on a comparison of these respective totals, as modified to reflect the presence of existing irreducible, or intangible, factors.

A SUMMATION

This brings us to the close of our discussion of the uniform annual cost method for analyzing investment alternatives. Two basic types of problems were considered. In the one, the economic profit that would be generated by a certain kind of investment could be computed because a complete description of each alternative in a set of mutually exclusive investment alternatives was possible. In the other, the economic profit that would be generated by a certain kind of investment could not be computed because the mutually exclusive alternatives involved could not be described in terms of all the costs and revenues they would generate. But in both types of problems, consideration was given to the questions of whether any investment at all should be made in a certain activity and, if so, which of the available mutually exclusive alternatives was the most economical.

The specific examples used to analyze these two types of problems are representative of those that will be encountered in this area of decision making. Furthermore, the cash-flow patterns assumed for purposes of illustration were selected with a view to showing how various combinations of costs and revenues can be processed to obtain their uniform annual equivalents.

No attempt will be made, at this point, to pass judgment on this approach to capital investment analysis because its advantages and disadvantages can be better appreciated after we have become acquainted with the other analytical techniques.

QUESTIONS

4-1 Describe, in general terms, the uniform annual cost approach to the determination of the most economical investment alternative.

4-2 How is the uniform annual equivalent of each of the following found:
  a   The required investment in an alternative?
  b   The terminal salvage value of an asset?
  c   A series of uniform recurring expenses or revenues?
  d   A series of nonuniform recurring expenses or revenues?

4-3 When all the costs and revenues generated by an alternative have been taken into account, what can be said about the rate of return on the total investment in that alternative when its total uniform annual cost is found to be zero? To be negative? To be positive? Explain.

4-4 Why is it necessary to consider equal time periods when comparing mutually exclusive investment alternatives?

4-5 In some of the examples in this chapter, the respective total annual costs were computed for alternatives which had different lives, and, yet, a direct comparison was made of these costs to determine which was the lowest. On the basis of what assumption was this done?

4-6 It has been stated that, on occasion, revenues and costs that are unaffected by the choice of alternative might be ignored in a cost comparison. Under what circumstances would this be done? Do the resultant calculated total annual costs tell one anything about the returns on total investment being realized with the respective alternatives? Does this mean that the investor is not concerned with whether an established minimum rate-of-return requirement is being satisfied?

4-7 Define economic profit.

4-8 How is a multiple-alternative problem analyzed by means of the uniform annual cost method?

4-9 Can it be said that the uniform annual equivalent of the first cost of an asset with an infinite service life is equal to the investor's minimum rate-of-return requirement times the asset's first cost? Explain.

4-10 Define irreducible, or intangible, factors. How do they enter into the decision-making process? Under what conditions do they assume a major role when investment alternatives are being compared? Give some examples of such factors and explain how each would affect the firm's choice of alternative.

PROBLEMS

4-1 An organization which operates automobile parking facilities is evaluating a proposal that it erect and operate a structure for parking in a city's downtown area. Three designs for a facility to be built on an available site have been developed. In general, the resultant structures would differ from each other from the standpoint of first cost, operating expenses, and capacity. More specifically, the three alternatives can be described as follows:

	Design A	Design B	Design C
Cost of site	$240,000	$240,000	$240,000
Cost of building	$2,100,000	$1,800,000	$1,200,000
Annual revenues	$720,000	$650,000	$500,000
Annual recurring costs	$390,000	$360,000	$310,000
Service life	50 years	50 years	50 years

There is reason to believe that, at the end of the estimated service period, whichever facility had been constructed would be torn down and the land would be sold. It is estimated that the resale value of the land will be equal to the cost of clearing the site.

Any capital that is invested will consist of 30 percent debt funds raised at a cost of 8 percent and 70 percent equity funds for which the annual opportunity cost is 18 percent.

Which of the three designs yields the minimum uniform annual cost? Should this parking facility be built and operated? (Ans. $21,234, $16,204, $26,144)

4-2 A manufacturer of chemicals is going to install a system for transporting materials from one location to another. Two types of pipe are found to be suitable for this purpose. The cost of the first type is such that the entire installation will entail an initial expenditure of $14,800 and will have a life of 10 years. The second type of pipe is made of somewhat more durable material which will serve to increase the life of the installation to 15 years but will also increase the required initial expenditure to $19,700. Neither installation will have a salvage value, and annual operating expenses will be the same for each. If the firm's minimum rate-of-return requirement is 30 percent per year, which of these alternatives will appear to be the more economical on the basis of a uniform annual cost comparison?

4-3 Suppose that the manufacturer in the preceding problem is willing to assume that the life, salvage value, and operating expenses of any future replacement will be equal to those of the original installation. However, he is not willing to assume the same insofar as a replacement's first cost is concerned. Instead, he estimates that the cost to replace either type of pipe will increase at a rate of 6 percent per year compounded annually. What effect will this have on the respective uniform annual costs? (Ans. $5,094, $6,188)

4-4 A manufacturer of duplicating equipment currently purchases a part which is used in the assembly of one of his machines. The firm estimates that, if it continues to buy the part, the total purchase cost will be $50,500 next year and that this total will increase at a rate of $1,600 a year thereafter. Ordering and receiving costs will also be incurred, and these will amount to a fixed $700 a year.

The company could manufacture the part in its own plant. Doing so would call for an investment in production facilities which would have a first cost of $62,900, a service life of 7 years, and a salvage value equal to 20 percent of their first cost. Incremental disbursements for such things as labor, materials, supervision, utilities, and property taxes would probably be $43,000 a year during the first 3 years and $48,000 a year during the last 4 years of the facilities' life.

By means of a uniform annual cost comparison for a seven-year period, ascertain whether the part should be bought or manufactured in the future. Money costs the firm 12 percent a year.

4-5 A financial institution has decided to open a branch office. Two locations have been suggested. For cost comparison purposes, management will assume that, regardless of which of these is selected, the branch office at that location will be maintained forever.

At the first location, an initial capital investment of $4,675,000 will be required in land, a building, equipment, and furnishings. Every 8 years, beginning 8 years from now, $160,000 will be spent to either replace or rehabilitate obsolete and deteriorated equipment and furnishings. Every 30 years, beginning 30 years from now, $1,300,000 will be spent to rehabilitate the building. Annual recurring costs will average $720,000.

At the second location, the required initial capital investment will be $5,230,000. Every 10 years, beginning 10 years from now, $170,000 will be spent on equipment and furnishings. Every 40 years, beginning 40 years from now, $1,500,000 will be spent on the building. Annual recurring costs will average $660,000.

Keeping in mind that an infinite service period is involved, determine the total uniform annual costs that will be experienced at the respective locations if the cost of money to the institution is 6 percent per year. (Ans. $1,033,170, $996,453)

4-6 The uniform annual costs of two tractors are to be compared. The farmer, who has decided to buy one of them, has learned that the first cost of the smaller tractor is $17,000. He estimates its salvage value to be $2,600 at the end of its expected life of 5 years.

The larger tractor will require an investment of $24,000. It could be operated 2 years longer than the smaller tractor and would have a terminal salvage value of about $3,200.

Insofar as annual operating costs are concerned, those of the larger tractor will exceed those of the smaller one by $1,300. However, as compared with the smaller one, the larger tractor will enable the farmer to realize additional revenues of $900 a year.

Given a rate-of-return requirement of 9 percent, which is the more economical of these two units of equipment?

4-7 An investor is considering the purchase of one of four different bonds. Each will be redeemed in 8 years. All are alike in the sense that they will each yield $1,000 at the time of redemption. Meanwhile, each entitles the owner to a semiannual interest payment, beginning 6 months from now, during the entire eight-year period. These interest payments and the present market value of the bonds are as follows:

	Bond E	Bond F	Bond G	Bond H
Market value	$612	$575	$750	$438
Interest payment	$41	$32	$48	$27

Because of the very low rating these bonds have, the investor has established a rate-of-return requirement of 16 percent compounded semiannually. Which, if any, of these securities should she purchase? (Ans. Bond H)

4-8 A printing establishment has just completed a methods analysis of one of its activities at a cost of $2,800. The result is a proposal that a change be made in the way the operation is now being carried out.

The proposed method would serve to reduce the cost of direct materials by $4,100 in the first year, but this saving would decrease thereafter at an annual rate of $550. There would also be a reduction in the number of man-hours required to perform the tasks involved. Specifically, one of the employees currently assigned to this work could be transferred to another job where more manpower is needed; his annual wages and fringe benefits are expected to be $16,000 next year and will probably increase at an average rate of $960 in the years that follow.

Furthermore, there would be a 25 percent reduction in the amount of required supervisory time. The present cost of supervision is $22,000 a year, and it is expected to remain at this level even if the new method is adopted because, although less supervision will be needed, a decrease in the number of supervisors will not occur.

The cost of introducing the new method, which could be adhered to for 4 years, would be $53,000; this does not include the $2,800 which has already been spent on the methods analysis. The company's minimum rate-of-return requirement is 20 percent. Does a uniform annual cost analysis suggest that the new method should be adopted?

4-9 Six manually powered low-lift pallet trucks are being used in one area of a soap manufacturer's plant. The present and future market values of the trucks are negligible. With a reasonable amount of maintenance and repair, they can continue to be operated for another 3 years. During this period, annual operating costs, which include labor, will be about $45,000.

These trucks can be replaced by four electrically powered trucks of the same general type. The first cost of the new trucks, including batteries, will be approximately $22,000. Their salvage value and average annual operating costs will depend on the number of years they are kept in operation. More specifically, for the following possible service lives, these amounts are likely to be as follows:

Service life (years)	Terminal salvage value	Average annual operating costs
3	$4,100	$35,000
4	3,300	36,000
5	2,700	37,500
6	2,300	39,500

At a cost of money of 25 percent, do the new trucks represent an economical investment? Answer this question by, first, determining the economic life of these trucks and, then, comparing their uniform annual cost for this period with the uniform annual cost of retaining the old trucks. (Ans. $45,183, $44,744, $45,353, $46,750; $45,000)

4-10 The owner of a reproduction service has not been able to obtain certain kinds of orders because she does not have the equipment which would enable her to do the work involved. A supplier of this equipment has two types available. The following data serve to describe the cash-flow pattern that would be generated by each type:

	Type I	Type II
Required investment	$37,000	$28,000
Service life	9 years	5 years
Salvage value	$3,000	$5,600
First-year revenues	$22,000	$19,000
First-year operating costs	$6,400	$4,700
Cost of money	40%	40%

After the first year, revenues are expected to increase at an annual rate of $1,100 with the first type of equipment and at a rate of $900 with the second. Similarly, operating costs are expected to increase at an annual rate of $800 with the first type of equipment and at a rate of $700 with the second.

The owner of the business is confronted by two questions: Should she invest in this type of equipment? And if so, which of the two is the more attractive investment? You are asked to answer these questions on the basis of a uniform annual cost analysis.

4-11 In the preceding problem, suppose it was decided not to assume that the nature of future replacements is such that the respective calculated uniform annual costs will continue until the same point in time is reached with each alternative. Instead, it is estimated that if equipment of Type II is procured, it will be replaced in 5 years by equipment which will require an investment of $35,000, have a four-year service life and an $8,000 terminal salvage value, and result in average annual recurring costs of $5,900 and average annual revenues of $24,300. What effect will this have on the decision reached in the preceding problem? (Ans. −$719, −$1,220)

4-12 Water is to be supplied to a location which will be the site of a new community. A decision must be made with regard to which of two proposed routes the required installation should follow. Uniform annual costs to be associated with the two routes are to be compared on the assumption that the two installations will be maintained forever. The time value of money is considered to be 10 percent.

If route S is selected, a total present investment of $2,900,000 will be necessary. Of this amount, $1,100,000 will be for work which will never have to be repeated. The balance of $1,800,000 will be for facilities which will have a life of 60 years and a salvage value of $90,000; all their future replacements are expected to have these same characteristics. Finally, it is estimated that, during every such 60-year period, the relevant recurring expenses will be $12,600 the first year and that these will increase at a rate of $1,300 a year.

In the event that route L is selected, an initial cost of $3,100,000 will be incurred, of which $1,500,000 will be for work of a permanent nature. The remaining $1,600,000 will be for facilities whose terminal salvage value will be about $70,000 in 50 years; their future replacements are likely to have these same characteristics. During every 50-year period, relevant recurring expenses are expected to be $13,000 per year for the first 20 years and $15,000 per year for the last 30 years.

Can the extra investment called for by route L be justified? (Ans. $315,856, $324,660)

4-13 Additional problems to be solved on a before-tax basis by the uniform annual cost method appear at the end of chapters 5 and 7. Analyze those for which you choose to or are asked to provide solutions.

5

The Present Worth and Future Worth Criteria

The second analytical technique to be considered is the *present worth method*. This approach to the evaluation of capital investment alternatives is applied in the following general manner: If it is at all possible to do so, each of a set of mutually exclusive alternatives is described completely in terms of the costs and revenues it is expected to generate during a given service period. This service period must be of the same duration for each alternative. Then, with the time value of money being taken into consideration, a determination is made of the single sum of money at the present time which is equivalent to all the cash flows to be associated with a given alternative. This single sum of money is called the "present worth" of the alternative. After this determination has been made for all the mutually exclusive alternatives, the results are compared to ascertain which alternative is the most economical.

In the absence of irreducible factors, the most economical alternative is defined as being the one with the lowest present worth. This is because every item in a cash-flow pattern is treated as a cost. More specifically, a cash outflow, that is, an expense, is processed as a positive cost, and a cash inflow, that is, a receipt, is processed as a negative cost. Consequently, the total present worth of any given alternative represents its total cost expressed as a single sum of money, expended at the present time, which is equivalent to the actual cash-flow pattern that will be experienced with the alternative. Because the calculated present worths are total costs, the investor's goal becomes cost minimization, and, hence, we say that the most economical of a set of mutually exclusive alternatives is the one that minimizes the total cost, that is, the total present worth.

Either after or at the time this alternative has been identified, consideration is given to the question of whether this alternative is more attractive than the one calling for making no investment in the activity involved. This latter alternative will yield neither expenses nor receipts, and, therefore, its present worth will be zero. As this suggests, no investment of the type that has been proposed is warranted unless a present worth equal to or less than zero is obtained for the most economical of the mutually exclusive alternatives that call for a capital expenditure at this time.

In brief, the present worth method has been designed to provide answers to the two basic questions that arise in the area of capital investment analysis. One, should an investment of a certain type be made? And two, if so, which specific investment alternative of this type is the most economical? We shall now go on to a consideration of the details of the present worth approach. These will be presented with the use of the example with which we began the explanation of the uniform annual cost method, so that a comparison can be made of the results obtained with the respective methods. Furthermore, for the time being, we shall continue to limit ourselves to a before-tax analysis of this and the subsequent problems to be considered in this chapter.

THE NEW PRODUCT PROBLEM

Let us begin with a summary of the relevant data with which the analyst was provided in the problem to which we are returning. The company was giving consideration to the production and marketing of a new product. Two alternatives, K and L, were available for carrying out this activity. Alternative K was characterized by (1) equipment which had a first cost of $84,000, a life of 4 years, and a salvage value of zero, (2) a required investment in working capital of $5,000 which would not decrease in value, (3) annual operating costs of $30,000, and (4) annual revenues of $67,000. Alternative L was characterized by (1) equipment which had a first cost of $125,000, a life of 6 years, and a salvage value of $20,000, (2) a required investment in working capital of $5,000 which would not decrease in value, (3) annual operating costs of $24,000 the first year but which would increase at a rate of $1,000 per year thereafter, and (4) annual revenues of $67,000. Also, the firm's minimum rate-of-return requirement was 20 percent per year.

The Equal Time-Period Requirement. Before processing these data, we shall pause for a moment to explain why it is necessary to consider equal time periods in a present worth comparison of investment alternatives. This will be done with the use of a simple example.

Suppose that the operator of a theater has decided to purchase an insurance policy which will provide him with a certain kind and amount of coverage. The firm which is issuing the policy offers a variety of plans for payment of the premiums. Among these are the following two: The one calls for a single payment of $2,100 at the present time to obtain the protection involved for a period of 3 years. The other calls for a single payment of $3,000 at the present time to obtain the protection involved for a period of 5 years. In other words, the single payment equivalents at the present time of all the cash flows to be associated with the two alternatives are $2,100 and $3,000, respectively, which is to say that the respective present worths of the alternatives are $2,100 and $3,000.

A comparison of these two present worths would suggest that, since a total cost of $2,100 is less than a total cost of $3,000, the more economical policy is the one whose cost is $2,100. But, obviously, such a conclusion may not be correct because it fails to take into account that the policy with the higher cost is also the policy with the longer life. And it may be that this policy's additional cost of $900 will be more than offset by the additional 2 years of coverage which it will provide. That this is true can be easily demonstrated. Ignoring the time value of money and the nature of future replacements for purposes of simplicity, we can say that $2,100 for a three-year policy yields an average cost of $700 per year, whereas $3,000 for a five-year policy yields an average cost of only $600 per year. This rough calculation of the average annual cost suffices to show that, unless equal time periods are considered, a direct comparison of the respective present worths of a set of mutually exclusive investment alternatives may not reveal which of these alternatives is the most economical. Keeping all this in mind, let us return to the new product problem.

The Computation. Because alternative K has a four-year life and alternative L has a six-year life, the equal time-period requirement compels the analyst to take into consideration the alternatives' future replacements. As we know, the cash flows to be associated with such replacements can be generated either by estimates or by an assumption of the kind made when the application of the uniform annual cost method was discussed. We shall begin by accepting the assumption.

It will be recalled that the assumption yielded cash flows for a twelve-year period for each of the alternatives. With alternative K, the resultant pattern of expenses and receipts, in thousands of dollars, was as follows:

```
84                      84                      84
5                        5                       5
                        (5)                     (5)                              (5)
   30   30   30   30   30   30   30   30   30   30   30   30
  (67) (67) (67) (67) (67) (67) (67) (67) (67) (67) (67) (67)
 |----|----|----|----|----|----|----|----|----|----|----|----|
 0    1    2    3    4    5    6    7    8    9   10   11   12
```

The single present sum of money which is equivalent to all these amounts can be computed in the following manner:

$$\text{Present worth} = \$89,000 + \$84,000(P/F)_{n=4}^{i=20} + \$84,000(P/F)_{n=8}^{i=20}$$

$$- \$5,000(P/F)_{n=12}^{i=20} - \$37,000(P/A)_{n=12}^{i=20}$$

$$= (-)\$15,763$$

As can be seen from an examination of this expression, the calculations were simplified by combining the uniform series of operating costs with the uniform series of revenues and by noting that a \$5,000 expense at points 4 and 8 is canceled by a \$5,000 receipt at each of these points.

But to continue, insofar as alternative L is concerned, the given data and the assumption regarding future replacements yielded the following cash-flow pattern, in thousands of dollars, for the same twelve-year period:

```
125                           125
                             (20)                             (20)

5                              5
                              (5)                              (5)
   24   25   26   27   28      29   24   25   26   27   28   29
  (67) (67) (67) (67) (67)    (67) (67) (67) (67) (67) (67) (67)
 |----|----|----|----|----|----|----|----|----|----|----|----|
 0    1    2    3    4    5    6    7    8    9   10   11   12
```

Combining certain amounts that appear at the same points on the time line, we should find that the present worth of these costs and revenues is as follows:

$$\text{Present worth} = \$130,000 + \$105,000(P/F)_{n=6}^{i=20} - \$25,000(P/F)_{n=12}^{i=20}$$

$$+ \$24,000(P/A)_{n=12}^{i=20} + \$1,000(A/G)_{n=6}^{i=20} (P/A)_{n=12}^{i=20}$$

$$- \$67,000(P/A)_{n=12}^{i=20}$$

$$= (-)\$19,740$$

A word of explanation may be in order about how the present worth of the nonuniform operating costs was found. First, each of the two nonuniform series was translated into a \$24,000 uniform series and a

$1,000 gradient series. Because the $24,000 series lasts for 12 years, its present worth was computed accordingly. However, each of the gradient series lasts for only 6 years, and so the annual equivalent of the first of these series was found by applying the gradient-series annuity factor for an n of 6. But because the same gradient series occurs in the second six-year period, the annual equivalent of this second series is equal to that of the first. This means that the calculated annual equivalent continues for a total of 12 years, and its present worth is determined by applying the uniform-series present worth factor for an n of 12 to the uniform annual equivalent of the first gradient series.

Another possible expression for the present worth of the two gradient series would be

$$\$1{,}000(P/G)_{n=6}^{i=20} + \$1{,}000(P/G)_{n=6}^{i=20} (P/F)_{n=6}^{i=20}$$

which is to say that

$$\$1{,}000(A/G)_{n=6}^{i=20} (P/A)_{n=12}^{i=20} = \$1{,}000(P/G)_{n=6}^{i=20}$$
$$+ \$1{,}000(P/G)_{n=6}^{i=20} (P/F)_{n=6}^{i=20}$$

In all such cases, the choice of computational method depends on the analyst's personal preference. But to continue, the results of the present worth computations and of the earlier uniform annual cost computations can now be summarized as follows:

Alternative	Present worth	Uniform annual cost
J	$ 0	$ 0
K	(−) 15,763	(−) 3,551
L	(−) 19,740	(−) 4,447

Alternative J, which appears in the preceding table, represents, as it did in the analysis of this problem by the uniform annual cost method, the alternative of not producing and marketing the product, that is, of making no investment in the activity. Because this alternative generates no costs or revenues, the present worth of these zero values will also be zero, as was their uniform annual equivalent.

The Comparison. A comparison of the calculated present worths tells us that the minimum total cost, expressed in terms of a single amount at the present time, will be attained with alternative L. Not only is this alternative more economical than alternative K, but it is also more economical than the alternative of not making this kind of investment. Another way of recognizing this is by interpreting the calculated present worths as follows: If the product is not produced, the resultant cash flows are equivalent to the firm's experiencing an increase of $0 in its net worth at this time. But if the product is produced and marketed by means of alternative K, the resultant cash flows are equivalent to the firm's experiencing an increase of $15,763 in its net worth at this time. And, finally, if the product is produced and marketed by means of alternative L, the resultant cash flows are equivalent to the firm's experiencing an increase of $19,740 in its net worth at this time. It is apparent that, in the absence of irreducible factors, this last occurrence is the most desirable of the three.

A review of the results, as summarized in the preceding table, also serves to remind us that alternative L was found to be the most economical by means of the uniform annual cost method. This was to be expected because the present worth method will rank alternatives in the same order of attractiveness as will the uniform annual cost method. Why this is so can be easily explained. When the average annual cost of alternative K is found to be $(-)$3,551$, this uniform annual equivalent can be substituted for the actual cash-fow pattern that will occur during a twelve-year period with this alternative. Therefore, to calculate the present worth of the alternative, we could have determined the present worth of the uniform twelve-year series of $(-)$3,551$ amounts, instead of the present worth of the amounts that appeared in the actual cash-flow pattern. Doing so, we should have obtained

$$\text{Present worth} = (-)\$3,551(P/A)_{n=12}^{i=20} = (-)\$15,763$$

which coincides with the value found by means of the first computational method.

Similarly, the present worth of alternative L could be obtained by calculating the present worth of its $(-)$4,447$ annual cost for a period of 12 years. This would yield

$$\text{Present worth} = (-)\$4,447(P/A)_{n=12}^{i=20} = (-)\$19,740$$

which also coincides with the result obtained earlier.

In brief, the present worths of a set of mutually exclusive investment alternatives can be found by multiplying their respective uniform annual costs by the uniform-series present worth factor for a number of years equal to the length of the study period involved. Since this number of years must be the same for each alternative, the uniform annual costs are, in effect, being multiplied by a constant. Therefore, the alternative with the minimum annual cost will prove to be the alternative with the minimum present worth.

From this, it also follows that an alternative with a negative annual cost will have a negative present worth, that an alternative with a positive annual cost will have a positive present worth, and that an alternative with an annual cost of zero will have a present worth of zero. Now, in the preceding chapter, we learned that, if an alternative has been described completely in terms of all the costs and revenues it will generate, the value of its uniform annual cost enables us to ascertain whether the return on the total investment in the alternative will be greater than, less than, or equal to the established minimum rate-of-return requirement, which is the rate used in the computation of the uniform annual cost. Specifically, a negative annual cost indicates a return greater than that required; a positive annual cost, a return less than that required; and a zero annual cost, a return equal to that required. But since a negative annual cost produces a negative present worth, we can also say that a negative present worth for an investment alternative indicates that the alternative will yield a return on total investment greater than the investor's rate-of-return requirement. Similarly, a positive present worth indicates that the alternative will yield a return on total investment less than the investor's minimum rate-of-return requirement. And finally, a present worth of zero indicates that the alternative will yield a return on total investment equal to the investor's minimum rate-of-return requirement. Hence, we say that, unless at least one of a set of mutually exclusive investment alternatives yields a present worth which is negative or zero, an investment of the type being proposed cannot be justified.

To relate all this to our example, we conclude that the results of the present worth analysis are consistent with the results of the uniform annual cost analysis. In both instances, alternative L was found to be more economical than alternative K. Furthermore, because alternative L's present worth, like its annual cost, is negative, the firm's return on the total investment in this alternative will exceed the 20 percent rate used in the determination of its present worth. Since this 20 percent represents the firm's cost of money and, hence, its minimum rate-of-return requirement, alternative L can be said to yield a satisfactory return on total investment and, as a consequence, is preferable to the remaining alternative of not producing and marketing the product.

At this point, we might also note that, just as a calculated uniform annual cost can be used to ascertain the corresponding present worth of an alternative, a calculated present worth can be used to ascertain the corresponding uniform annual cost. To illustrate, suppose we had been told that the present worth of alternative K for a twelve-year period is $(-)$15,763$ at a rate of 20 percent. By applying the present-amount annuity factor to this value, we could find the equivalent uniform annual cost as follows:

$$\text{Annual cost} = (-)\$15,763(A/P)_{n=12}^{i=20} = (-)\$3,551$$

And if we had been told that the present worth of alternative L for a twelve-year period is $(-)\$19,740$ at a rate of 20 percent, we could have calculated its uniform annual cost in the following manner:

Annual cost $= (-)\$19,740(A/P)_{n=12}^{i=20} = (-)\$4,447$

Both of these annual costs, of course, coincide with those obtained when the earlier approach to their determination was employed.

The reason for showing that a present worth can be translated into a uniform annual cost is that, on occasion, a combination of cash flows will exist whose nature is such that, from a computational standpoint, it may be simpler to find their uniform annual equivalent, if this is what is desired, by first calculating their present worth. But, as we know, a uniform annual equivalent can also be converted to a present worth, and, with a given combination of cash flows, a desired present worth may be more easily obtained by first calculating the uniform annual equivalent; this is particularly true when two alternatives with unequal service lives are being compared. For example, one of these alternatives may have an estimated life of 7 years, and the other a life of 13 years. With our assumption regarding the nature of future replacements, cash flows for a total of 91 years would have to be compared to satisfy the equal time-period requirement. To obtain the present worth of either of these alternatives without first calculating its uniform annual cost, we should have to describe its cash flows for 91 years and then calculate the present worth of the resultant cash-flow pattern. Undoubtedly, it would be simpler to begin by computing the uniform annual cost of the one alternative for 7 years and of the other for 13 years and, then, to obtain the respective present worths by multiplying each of these annual costs by the uniform-series present worth factor for an n of 91.

A Forecasted Replacement.   The present worths of alternatives K and L were ascertained on the basis of an assumption regarding the nature of their future replacements. The fact that an assumption of a certain kind had been made would be among the irreducibles considered in the course of reaching a final decision in this case. However, it is worth repeating that, if an investor is adverse to making such an assumption, he is free to forecast the nature of future replacements. And it may be that the consequences of his forecast will encourage him to make a decision other than the one he would be inclined to make on the basis of the assumption. This was demonstrated in the presentation of the uniform annual cost method, and it will now be demonstrated with the use of the present worth method.

It will be recalled that, at one point in the analysis of the new-product problem by the uniform annual cost approach, we supposed that the analyst estimated that the equipment involved in alternative K would be replaced at the end of its four-year life by an asset which would continue to require $5,000 of working capital and would have a first cost of $47,000, a life of 2 years, a salvage value of zero, annual operating costs of $22,000, and expected annual revenues of $67,000. As a result, the cash-flow pattern, in thousands of dollars, generated by alternative K and this replacement became as follows:

```
84                    47
5                            (5)
    30    30    30    30    22    22
   (67)  (67)  (67)  (67)  (67)  (67)
 ├─────┼─────┼─────┼─────┼─────┼─────┤
 0     1     2     3     4     5     6
```

   Let us now suppose that this is the cash-flow pattern the analyst wants to adopt for the purpose of making a present worth comparison of alternatives K and L. No additional estimates are necessary because alternative K and its replacement now involve a six-year time period, and this coincides with alternative L's life. Therefore, the present worth of alternative K and its replacement could be found in the following manner:

$$\text{Present worth} = \$89,000 + \$47,000(P/F)_{n=4}^{i=20} - \$5,000(P/F)_{n=6}^{i=20}$$

$$+ \$30,000(P/A)_{n=4}^{i=20} + \$22,000(P/A)_{n=2}^{i=20} (P/F)_{n=4}^{i=20}$$

$$- \$67,000(P/A)_{n=6}^{i=20}$$

$$= (-)\$18,968$$

   For alternative L, the cash flows during the same six-year period were given as

```
125                        (20)
5                          (5)
    24    25    26    27    28    29
   (67)  (67)  (67)  (67)  (67)  (67)
 ├─────┼─────┼─────┼─────┼─────┼─────┤
 0     1     2     3     4     5     6
```

and their present worth can be obtained as follows:

$$\text{Present worth} = \$130,000 - \$25,000(P/F)_{n=6}^{i=20} + \$24,000(P/A)_{n=6}^{i=20}$$

$$+ \$1,000(P/G)_{n=6}^{i=20} - \$67,000(P/A)_{n=6}^{i=20}$$

$$= (-)\$14,791$$

   A comparison of this present worth with the one computed for alternative K and its forecasted replacement reveals that alternative L is no longer the more attractive of the two alternatives. This agrees with what was found when a uniform annual cost analysis had been made of the same cash-flow patterns. But it should be stressed that none of this is intended to suggest that a forecasted replacement will lead to one decision and that an assumed replacement will lead to another. This happened to occur in this instance because of the nature of the forecasted replacement. But this type of replacement was selected intentionally to show that this kind of occurrence is a possibility.

FUTURE WORTH METHOD

Before going on to other applications of the present worth method, we might note that its distinguishing characteristic is that it serves to describe the consequences of a specific proposed investment in terms of a single sum of money. The fact that this single amount appears at the beginning of the alternative's life is of secondary importance. In other words, there is no reason why the consequences of an investment cannot be described in terms of a single sum of money at some other point in the alternative's life. We shall explain this by returning to alternatives K and L and to their cash flows during the twelve-year service period generated by the assumption regarding future replacements. These cash flows for alternative K were as follows:

```
84                        84                        84
 5                         5                         5
                          (5)                       (5)                       (5)
      30    30    30       30    30    30    30       30    30    30    30    30
     (67)  (67)  (67)     (67)  (67)  (67)  (67)     (67)  (67)  (67)  (67)  (67)
  ├─────┼─────┼─────┼─────┼─────┼─────┼─────┼─────┼─────┼─────┼─────┼─────┤
  0     1     2     3     4     5     6     7     8     9    10    11    12
```

The present worth of these costs and revenues was found to be $(-)\$15,763$, and it was stated that this result could be interpreted as follows: The consequences of an investment in this alternative are equivalent to the investor's receiving $15,763 at the present time or, to put this differently, to the investor's experiencing an increase of $15,763 in his net worth at the present time. But it would be just as logical to ascertain the consequences of an investment in this alternative in terms of their effect on the investor's net worth at the end of the twelve-year study period. This would call for finding the *future worth* of the alternative at point 12. The following expression describes how this can be done:

Future worth $= \$89,000(F/P)_{n=12}^{i=20} + \$84,000(F/P)_{n=8}^{i=20}$

$$+ \$84,000(F/P)_{n=4}^{i=20} - \$5,000 - \$37,000(F/A)_{n=12}^{i=20}$$

$$= (-)\$140,552$$

The fact that the result is negative tells us that the future value of the receipts exceeds the future value of the expenses. More specifically, we can say that, given a time value of money of 20 percent per year, the cash flows with this alternative are such that the investor's net worth will be \$140,552 greater 12 years from now than it otherwise would be. But, and this is extremely important, the assumption is being made that any net receipts realized by the investor at any point during the twelve-year period can and will be reinvested at a rate equal to the investor's cost of money which, in this case, is 20 percent; if the return on reinvested funds were some percent other than 20, an amount other than \$140,552 would be accumulated. However, if the cost of money has been estimated correctly, this assumption is a realistic one. Let us consider why.

It will be recalled that the firm in our example arrived at the 20 percent rate by taking into consideration that one-fourth of the financing would be debt financing at a cost of 8 percent per year, and that three-fourths would be equity financing at a cost of 24 percent per year. As a result, a weighted-average cost of money of 20 percent per year was obtained. In terms of these data, the specific assumption is that, if the firm chooses to produce and market the product by means of alternative K, it will use a part of the periodic net receipts being realized to reduce its debt, and the balance of the net receipts will be reinvested in activities whose risk and tax status are comparable to those of producing and marketing the new product. The portion of the net receipts used to repay debt can be said to be earning 8 percent because debt repayment serves to eliminate an 8 percent interest expense; the remaining portion, which is reinvested in other activities, can be said to be earning 24 percent because this is the firm's opportunity cost. Given the implied assumption that the proportion of debt financing remains constant, the average return on reinvested funds becomes 20 percent. This return is sometimes referred to as the "external return" because it represents the average return realizable from external sources.

In any event, this is the assumption with regard to the return that can be realized from the reinvestment of periodic net receipts being generated by an alternative. To summarize, the assumption is that these net receipts can be invested elsewhere at a rate equal to the rate which is used to represent the cost of money when actual cash flows are processed to obtain their equivalents. This assumption is made when either the uniform annual cost, present worth, or future worth of an investment alternative is being ascertained.

But to continue with our future worth analysis of the new-product problem, we can calculate the future worth of alternative L at the end of its twelve-year service period by returning to its cash-flow pattern for that period. This was as follows:

```
125                          125
(20)                                                      (20)
5                            5
(5)                                                        (5)
24    25    26    27    28    29    24    25    26    27    28    29
(67)  (67)  (67)  (67)  (67)  (67)  (67)  (67)  (67)  (67)  (67)  (67)
|-----|-----|-----|-----|-----|-----|-----|-----|-----|-----|-----|
0     1     2     3     4     5     6     7     8     9    10    11    12
```

The future worth of these costs and revenues can be found in the following manner:

$$\text{Future worth} = \$130,000(F/P)_{n=12}^{i=20} + \$105,000(F/P)_{n=6}^{i=20} - \$25,000$$

$$+ \$24,000(F/A)_{n=12}^{i=20} + \$1,000(F/G)_{n=6}^{i=20}(F/P)_{n=6}^{i=20}$$

$$+ \$1,000(F/G)_{n=6}^{i=20} - \$67,000(F/A)_{n=12}^{i=20}$$

$$= (-)\$176,017$$

This means that the consequences of the firm's producing and marketing the product by means of alternative L are equivalent to an increase of $176,017 in its net worth at the end of the twelve-year service period. The comparable amount for alternative K was only $140,552, and, therefore, in the absence of irreducible factors, alternative L is the more economical of the two alternatives. Furthermore, since a decision not to produce the product would contribute $0 to the firm's future net worth, we go on to conclude that alternative L is also more attractive than the alternative of making no investment in the activity.

It should be noted that a direct comparison of the calculated future worths was made possible by the fact that they all appear at the same future point in time, namely, point 12. If we were told that one course of action would yield some amount of money, say, 4 years from now and that another course would yield some other amount of money, say, 6 years from now, a comparison of these amounts would not serve as a basis for decision making because they are separated by 2 years, and it might be that a smaller amount at one point is worth more than some larger amount 2 years later. As this suggests, the equal time-period requirement must be satisfied in a future worth analysis, just as it must be in uniform annual cost and present worth analyses.

Although the results of our future worth computations were interpreted to represent contributions to the firm's future net worth, they also represent total costs. This is to say that, in terms of a single amount at the end of the twelfth year, the total cost is (−)$140,552 for alternative K and (−)$176,017 for alternative L. Therefore, alternative L has the lower cost and is the more attractive of the two. Furthermore, because this cost is negative, the revenues more than offset the costs, which include the firm's 20 percent cost of money, and, consequently, the minimum rate-of-return requirement is being more than satisfied. In other words, the investment should be made. As this suggests, a calculated negative future worth means that the return on total investment exceeds the rate used in the computation of this future worth; a calculated positive future worth means that the return on total investment is less than the rate used in the computation of this future worth; and a calculated future worth of zero means that the return on total investment is equal to the rate used in the computation of this future worth. From this, it becomes apparent that, in the absence of irreducible factors, unless the future worth is negative or zero, no investment of the kind being considered should be made.

As was to be expected, the same alternative proves to be the most economical regardless of whether an annual cost, present worth, or future worth analysis is made. To emphasize this, the following summary of the results obtained with all three methods is being presented. In this summary, alternative J is the alternative of not producing and marketing the product.

Alternative	Uniform annual cost	Present worth	Future worth
J	$ 0	$ 0	$ 0
K	(−) 3,551	(−) 15,763	(−) 140,552
L	(−) 4,447	(−) 19,740	(−) 176,017

For a given alternative, any one of the costs that appear in this table can be converted to either of the other two forms by the application of an appropriate compound interest factor; as an example, the respective future worths can be obtained by multiplying each of the uniform annual costs by the uniform-series future worth factor for an i of 20 and an n of 12. Such conversions will not be demonstrated here because the procedure for making them was illustrated at an earlier point.

In any event, the future worth method has been presented to show that it is possible to evaluate a set of mutually exclusive investment alternatives by calculating their respective single payment equivalents at some point other than the present. But the fact is that, with very few exceptions, those firms that prefer to make a comparison of single amounts, rather than a comparison of a uniform series of amounts, do so by comparing present worths and not future worths. Why this is so is not known.

A REPLACEMENT PROBLEM

The present worth method and the future worth method were explained with the use of an example in which the alternatives involved were described in terms of *all* the costs and revenues they were expected to generate. But as was pointed out in the discussion of the uniform annual cost method, there are instances in which such complete descriptions are not feasible. When this is the case, the potential investor decides, on the basis of judgment, whether the rate of return on the required total investment in an activity of a certain type will be satisfactory. If he decides that it will be, the available mutually exclusive alternatives for carrying out the activity involved are described in terms of their relevant costs and revenues, that is, in terms of the costs and revenues which will be affected by the choice of alternative. These values are then processed to identify the most economical alternative. We shall now consider how this is done by means of the present worth method.

So that we can compare the results obtained with the respective approaches, let us return to the illustration employed when this type of problem was analyzed with the use of the uniform annual cost approach. This was an illustration in which a building contractor was giving consideration to the replacement of a unit of construction equipment which he currently owned. The relevant data were as follows:

Three alternatives were to be evaluated. One was to retain the old equipment for 1 year. The second was to retain the old equipment for 2 years. And the third was to replace the old equipment at this time by a new unit.

The old equipment had a present market value of $3,600. One year from now, this value would drop to $1,000, and two years from now to $800. Repair and maintenance costs were estimated to be $960 for the first year, and $1,140 for the second. Also, annual fuel costs would be $190 higher than with the new equipment.

The new equipment had an $11,900 first cost, a four-year service life, and a $3,900 terminal salvage value. Its repair and maintenance costs were expected to be $120 in the first year, $200 in the second, $310 in the third, and $540 in the fourth. Finally, the firm's annual cost of money was given as 15 percent.

The Analysis. A present worth analysis of this problem must begin with the contractor's recognizing that the present worths of the three alternatives by which he is confronted must be ascertained for equal time periods. Because the alternatives have different service lives, the equal time-period requirement calls for taking into consideration the nature of future replacements. We shall suppose, as we did earlier, that the contractor chooses to assume that whichever alternative he selects will be followed by a series of identical investments until the same point in time is reached with each currently-available course of action. Given that the alternatives' respective lives are 1 year, 2 years, and 4 years, this assumption will generate cash flows for a total period of 4 years. For the alternative of keeping the old equipment for 1 year, these cash flows will be as follows:

```
3,600   3,600   3,600   3,600
       (1,000) (1,000) (1,000) (1,000)
         960     960     960     960
         190     190     190     190
  ├───────┼───────┼───────┼───────┤
  0       1       2       3       4
```

One way of obtaining the present worth of these amounts is to begin by combining the values that appear at any one point on the time line. When this is done, the following is obtained:

```
3,600   3,750   3,750   3,750    150
  ├───────┼───────┼───────┼───────┤
  0       1       2       3       4
```

The present worth of this series of values is equal to

Present worth $= \$3,600 + \$3,750(P/A)_{n=3}^{i=15} + \$150(P/F)_{n=4}^{i=15}$

$$= \$12,248$$

which is to say that the cash flows to be associated with this alternative during the next 4 years are equivalent to the contractor's spending $12,248 at the present time. Or another way of expressing this is as follows: If the contractor were to deposit $12,248 at this time in a fund that would earn 15 percent per year compounded annually, he could immediately withdraw $3,600 to provide for the initial required investment in the asset. Then, continuing with the values that appear at subsequent points on the preceding time line, we should say that he could withdraw another $3,750 at the end of each year for 3 years to cover the net expenses that would be incurred at those points. Finally, he could withdraw $150 at the end of the fourth year to cover the net expense that occurs at that point. And it would be found that this last withdrawal would exhaust the fund.

Turning to the alternative of keeping the currently-owned equipment for 2 years, we should obtain the following cash-flow pattern for the four-year study period:

```
3,600        3,600
            (800)        (800)
     960    1,140   960  1,140
     190     190    190   190
  |-----+-----+-----+-----|
  0     1     2     3     4
```

which can be simplified to yield the following:

```
3,600  1,150  4,130  1,150   530
  |-----+-----+-----+-----|
  0     1     2     3     4
```

The present worth of these amounts would be as follows:

Present worth $= \$3,600 + \$1,150(P/F)_{n=1}^{i=15} + \$4,130(P/F)_{n=2}^{i=15}$

$$+ \$1,150(P/F)_{n=3}^{i=15} + \$530(P/F)_{n=4}^{i=15}$$

$$= \$8,782$$

This tells us that, with a 15 percent time value of money, an expenditure of $8,782 by the investor at this time is equivalent to all the costs he will experience with this alternative during the four-year period. And again, we can also think of this in terms of his investing $8,782 now at 15 percent, making the necessary withdrawals to meet the alternative's net expenses as they arise, and finding that the fund is exhausted when the last withdrawal of $530 is made at the end of the fourth year.

Finally, the present worth of the alternative of buying the new unit of construction equipment can be obtained by processing the expenses and receipts it will yield, and these are equal to

```
11,900                    (3,900)
      120    200    310    540
  |-----+-----+-----+-----|
  0     1     2     3     4
```

The resultant present worth will be as follows:

Present worth $= \$11,900 + \$120(P/F)_{n=1}^{i=15} + \$200(P/F)_{n=2}^{i=15}$

$$+ \$310(P/F)_{n=3}^{i=15} - \$3,360(P/F)_{n=4}^{i=15}$$

$$= \$10,440$$

The same interpretation is to be placed on this result as on the ones obtained for the other alternatives, which is to say that the selection of this alternative is equivalent to incurring a single expense of $10,440 at the present time.

The Comparison. In summary, a present worth analysis of the problem under consideration yields the results contained in the following table, in which the results of the earlier uniform annual cost analysis of the same problem are also shown:

Alternative	Present worth	Uniform annual cost
Retain old equipment 1 year	$12,248	$4,290
Retain old equipment 2 years	8,782	3,076
Replace old equipment now	10,440	3,657

An examination of these findings reveals that the outcome of a present worth analysis coincides with that of a uniform annual cost analysis. First, the economic life of the old equipment is found to be 2 years, as indicated by the fact that the total cost, in terms of a present worth, is only $8,782 when this life is assumed, but $12,248 when a one-year life is assumed. Next, it is not economical to replace the old asset at this time, because a cost of $8,782 is lower than the total cost of $10,440 obtained for the new unit. Finally, it should be noted that a different decision would have been reached had care not been taken to ascertain the old equipment's economic life; specifically, a single life estimate of 1 year for the currently-owned unit would have incorrectly suggested that its immediate replacement would be the most economical course of action.

Future Worths. If the investor prefers, a future worth analysis can be substituted for a present worth analysis in a problem of this type. In the example under consideration, the respective future worths would have to be found at the end of the fourth year for each alternative to satisfy the equal time-period requirement. These future worths would probably be calculated by finding the sum of the individual future worths of the specific costs and revenues that appear in the cash-flow lines for the respective alternatives. But they can also be computed by, first, finding a given alternative's present worth or uniform annual cost and, then, ascertaining the future worth of either of these values. We shall employ this latter approach in our example because we already have the present worths and the annual costs of the alternatives involved. Applying this approach, we obtain the results shown in the following table:

Alternative	Future worth		
Retain old equipment 1 year	$12,248(F/P)_{n=4}^{i=15} =	$4,290(F/A)_{n=4}^{i=15} =	$21,421
Retain old equipment 2 years	8,782(F/P)_{n=4}^{i=15} =	3,076(F/A)_{n=4}^{i=15} =	15,359
Replace old equipment now	10,440(F/P)_{n=4}^{i=15} =	3,657(F/A)_{n=4}^{i=15} =	18,260

Each of these future worths represents the single expenditure at the end of the fourth year which is equivalent to the cash flows generated by the corresponding alternative during the four-year study period. On the basis of a comparison of these future worths, we should rank the three alternatives in the same order of attractiveness as we did on the basis of their present worths and uniform annual costs. This, of course, was to be expected because, as the preceding table reveals, the respective future worths are equal to the respective present worths or uniform annual costs multiplied by an appropriate constant.

The fact that the present worths and future worths obtained in this example are positive is of no significance. This is true for the reason given when the uniform annual costs of these alternatives were interpreted in the preceding chapter; namely, the sign of an alternative's cost is capable of telling us whether the return on the total investment in that alternative is satisfactory only if the calculated cost is a *total* cost. But the type of problem being considered here is one in which the investor decided, on the basis of judgment, that his minimum rate-of-return requirement would be satisfied. Hence, he began by rejecting the alternative of making no investment in the activity involved and continued the analysis by processing only those expenses and receipts that would be affected by his choice of the remaining alternatives. As a result, the computed costs are not total costs.

Also, it is important to recognize that the contractor's final decision may be other than the one suggested by a comparison of the calculated present or future worths, if irreducible factors remain to be evaluated or if he chooses to forecast the nature of future replacements rather than to assume their nature.

Finally, this illustration serves to demonstrate that the application of the present worth or future worth method presents no special difficulties when a multiple-alternative problem is being solved. With either of these analytical techniques, as many single-payment equivalents are computed as there are alternatives, and the resultant values are then compared. Of course, the same study period must be selected for each alternative in such a set of mutually exclusive investment alternatives.

ALTERNATE ASSUMPTION REGARDING REPLACEMENTS

We have seen that the nature of the assumption regarding future replacements is such that, when an *annual cost* determination is being made, the cash flows generated by the assumption do not have to be taken into consideration explicitly in the computations. For example, in the preceding replacement problem, to obtain the uniform annual cost of keeping the old equipment one more year, it was necessary to process only the values of the expenses and receipts that would occur during that one-year period. The assumption, in effect, was that this same annual cost would be experienced during each succeeding one-year period, and so there was no need to describe and calculate the uniform annual equivalent of the assumed cash-flow pattern during each of those succeeding one-year periods.

We also saw that, after a uniform annual cost has been ascertained, it is possible to convert it to a present worth by multiplying it by an appropriate uniform-series present worth factor. In the replacement problem, this factor was the one for an n of 4. But, very often, the determination of the present worth is not preceded by the determination of the uniform annual cost. Instead, the cash flows for the entire study period are described, and their present worth is computed directly. This is to say that every expense and receipt generated by the assumption is taken into consideration explicitly in the computation. To return to the alternative of keeping the old equipment for 1 year in the replacement problem, it will be recalled that the values actually processed in the course of obtaining the present worth of this alternative were as follows:

3,600	3,600	3,600	3,600	
	(1,000)	(1,000)	(1,000)	(1,000)
	960	960	960	960
	190	190	190	190
0	1	2	3	4

When the assumed pattern of future cash flows is expressed in such a vivid manner, as it usually is in a present worth analysis, the investor often cannot help but recognize that the assumption being made in a given situation simply does not make sense. Specifically, in our replacement example, it is very unlikely that a decision to retain the old equipment for one more year will also be a decision to replace this asset in the future by a series of old units of the same type; instead, what is likely is that a currently-owned asset will be replaced eventually by a new one. In brief, to assume, as we have, that a new asset will be replaced eventually by a replica of itself is one thing, but to assume, as we also have, that an old asset will be replaced eventually by a replica of itself is another thing.

For this reason, an assumption other than the one we have adopted is sometimes made regarding future replacements in a problem in which one of the alternatives calls for retaining a currently-owned asset. The other assumption is that this asset will be replaced at the end of its estimated remaining life by a series of assets which are like the new asset that is available at this time. As applied to our example, this would mean that, if the old unit of construction equipment is kept for one more year, its replacements will be a series of new units, each of which will yield a cash-flow pattern identical to that of the currently-available new unit. Consequently, the following pattern of costs and revenues would now be obtained for the alternative of keeping the old unit one year and then replacing it:

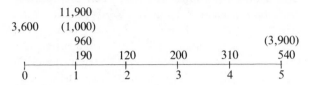

Similarly, the alternative of keeping the old unit two more years and then replacing it would now be characterized by the following cash flows:

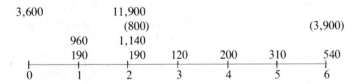

However, the new assumption, like the original one, is that, if a new asset is procured at this time, it will be replaced by a series of replicas of itself. Applying this assumption to the alternative of investing in a new unit of construction equipment at this time, we should obtain the following cash-flow pattern for the new unit and its first replacement:

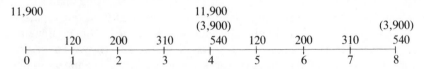

Although only one of the assumed replacements was shown for each of the three alternatives, it is evident that the equal time-period requirement necessitates assuming additional replacements of the same kind. But it is also evident that, because every additional replacement will serve to extend each of the time lines by another 4 years, equal time periods cannot be attained unless an infinite series of replacements is assumed. This means that, with the new assumption regarding future replacements, the analyst will have to work with a study period of infinite duration for each alternative. We shall now consider the effect of this requirement on the computational procedure.

Annual Cost Determination. Let us suppose that the analyst wants to make a uniform annual cost analysis of the three alternatives in the replacement problem for what will now be an infinite number of years. Obviously, we cannot depict the expenses and revenues that will occur during this entire period on a time line; so it will be necessary to work with their equivalents. How this is done will now be shown for the first alternative.

At an earlier point, it had been found that the annual cost of keeping the old equipment for one more year would be $4,290 and that the annual cost of the new equipment would be $3,657. Therefore, if the old equipment is retained at a cost of $4,290 for 1 year and then replaced by an infinite number of new units, each of which will yield an annual cost of $3,657, the resultant cost pattern will be as follows:

```
     4,290  3,657  3,657  3,657  3,657    ·        ·        ·        ·     3,657
  |-----+------+------+------+------------------------------------------------|
  0     1      2      3      4      5      ·        ·        ·        ·       ∞
```

Insofar as keeping the old unit for 2 years is concerned, the resultant annual cost was calculated to be $3,076. If this is followed by an infinite series of new units whose annual cost will be $3,657, the resultant cost pattern will be as follows:

```
     3,076  3,076  3,657  3,657  3,657    ·        ·        ·        ·     3,657
  |-----+------+------+------+------------------------------------------------|
  0     1      2      3      4      5      ·        ·        ·        ·       ∞
```

Finally, given that the annual cost of the new equipment will be $3,657, the following cost pattern will be experienced if this equipment is purchased now and replaced by a replica of itself an infinite number of times:

```
     3,657  3,657  3,657  3,657  3,657    ·        ·        ·        ·     3,657
  |-----+------+------+------+------------------------------------------------|
  0     1      2      3      4      5      ·        ·        ·        ·       ∞
```

Only the last of these three cost patterns is in the form of a uniform annual series. Therefore, it appears that there is a need to find the respective uniform annual equivalents of the first two cost patterns. However, if a uniform annual cost analysis is to be made, this apparent need is not a real one for the following reason: An examination of the first time line will reveal that the average of the amounts involved will, in effect, be the average of the two different values which these amounts assume, namely, $4,290 and $3,657; consequently, the average will be *greater than* $3,657. Similarly, the average of the amounts involved in the second time line will, in effect, be the average of the two different values which these amounts assume, namely, $3,076 and $3,657; consequently, the average will be *less than* $3,657. Therefore, the second alternative will have a lower average annual cost than will the first.

The analyst can now go on to the third alternative which has an average annual cost of $3,657. Comparing this to the average annual cost of the second alternative which is known to be *less than* $3,657, he would conclude that the second alternative is also more attractive than the third and, therefore, the most economical of the three.

What the foregoing demonstrates is that the series that begins with the lowest average annual cost will always prove to be the most economical one. This is because, as a result of the assumption, each of the respective beginning series is followed by another uniform series of infinite length, and this other series will be of the same size for each alternative. This being the case, the lowest overall average will be realized with the alternative which begins with the lowest average annual cost.

In brief, the application of the new assumption requires that the analyst ascertain only the beginning values in each of the series. These values can be determined by computing the respective uniform annual equivalents of the cash flows generated by the alternatives that head the respective series. This would be done just as it was with the original assumption. As we know, these uniform annual equivalents were as follows:

Alternative	Uniform annual equivalent
Retain old equipment 1 year	$4,290 for 1 year
Retain old equipment 2 years	3,076 for 2 years
Replace old equipment now	3,657 for 4 years

To repeat, because each of these cost patterns will be followed by a uniform annual cost of $3,657 which continues into infinity, the contractor should select that alternative which will minimize the average annual cost he will experience before he begins to incur the $3,657 annual cost. This is the alternative of retaining the old equipment for 2 years.

To summarize, with the alternate assumption as with the original one, there is no need for processing the cash flows generated by the assumption when a uniform annual cost analysis is being made. Furthermore, either assumption results in the same alternative's being identified as the most economical one. However, in a replacement problem, the new assumption proves to be a more realistic one, and, given that it does not create any computational difficulties, there is no reason why it should not be adopted in lieu of the original one. But as we shall see, this is true only when the alternatives in a replacement problem are being evaluated by the uniform annual cost method.

Present and Future Worth Determinations. Unfortunately, the alternate assumption regarding future replacements does present computational difficulties when a present worth or a future worth analysis is to be made. This is because, with either of these approaches, the single payment equivalent of an infinite series of costs and revenues must be calculated to satisfy the equal time-period requirement. Let us see what this involves by returning to our example.

To obtain the present worth of the alternative of keeping the old equipment for 1 year, the analyst can begin by enumerating the cash flows that will occur during this one-year period. But, obviously, he cannot go on to enumerate the specific costs and revenues that will be experienced with the infinite series of assumed replacements. Instead, he must first ascertain the uniform annual equivalent of these costs and revenues and then substitute this equivalent for the actual cash-flow pattern that would be generated by the replacements. This annual equivalent was already found to be $3,657, and so there is no need to determine it at this point. In any case, given the actual cash flows during the first year and the uniform annual equivalent of the cash flows in the succeeding years, the alternative under consideration would be described in the following manner:

```
3,600  (1,000)
         960
         190   3,657   3,657   3,657   3,657    ·      ·      ·      ·    3,657
   ├───────┼───────┼───────┼───────┼───────┼                              ┤
   0       1       2       3       4       5     ·      ·      ·      ·     ∞
```

Before beginning the present worth calculation, the analyst must recognize that the number of years from point 1 on is infinite and recall that the value of the uniform-series present worth factor for an infinite number of periods is $1/i$. If he does, he will find the present worth of this alternative to be

$$\text{Present worth} = \$3,600 + \$150(P/F)_{n=1}^{i=15} + \$3,657(P/A)_{n=\infty}^{i=15}(P/F)_{n=1}^{i=15}$$

$$= \$24,931$$

In the same manner, the alternative of keeping the old equipment for 2 years would be described as follows:

```
3,600            (800)
         960    1,140
         190     190   3,657   3,657   3,657    ·      ·      ·      ·    3,657
   ├───────┼───────┼───────┼───────┼───────┼                              ┤
   0       1       2       3       4       5     ·      ·      ·      ·     ∞
```

and the present worth of these amounts would prove to be

Present worth $= \$3,600 + \$1,150(P/F)_{n=1}^{i=15} + \$530(P/F)_{n=2}^{i=15}$

$\qquad\qquad\qquad + \$3,657(P/A)_{n=\infty}^{i=15} (P/F)_{n=2}^{i=15}$

$\qquad\qquad = \$23,435$

And, finally, the alternative of procuring the new equipment at this time would be described as follows:

$$
\begin{array}{ccccccccc}
3,657 & 3,657 & 3,657 & 3,657 & 3,657 & \cdot & \cdot & \cdot & 3,657 \\
\hline
0 & 1 & 2 & 3 & 4 & 5 & \cdot & \cdot & \cdot & \cdot & \infty
\end{array}
$$

and the present worth of this uniform series would be found to be

Present worth $= \$3,657(P/A)_{n=\infty}^{i=15} = \$3,657(1/0.15)$

$\qquad\qquad = \$24,380$

A comparison of these results reveals that the alternatives will be ranked in the same order of attractiveness as they were when the present worths were computed on the basis of the original assumption regarding future replacements. This can be seen in the following table:

	Present worth	
Alternative	*Original assumption*	*Alternate assumption*
Retain old equipment 1 year	$12,248	$24,931
Retain old equipment 2 years	8,782	23,435
Replace old equipment now	10,440	24,380

Incidentally, the present worths obtained with the new assumption can be converted to their uniform annual equivalents by multiplying each by the present-amount annuity factor for an n equal to infinity. Doing so, we obtain

$\$24,931(A/P)_{n=\infty}^{i=15} = \$24,931(0.15) = \$3,740$

for the first alternative, and

$\$23,435(A/P)_{n=\infty}^{i=15} = \$23,435(0.15) = \$3,515$

for the second alternative, and

$\$24,380(A/P)_{n=\infty}^{i=15} = \$24,380(0.15) = \$3,657$

for the third alternative.

It will be recalled that, because there was no real need to do so, the values of these annual costs were not ascertained in the preceding section when a uniform annual cost analysis was being made of the effect of the new assumption. But the statement was made that these annual costs would yield the same ranking of the alternatives as did the annual costs based on the original assumption. That this is true can be seen in the following table:

| | Uniform annual cost | |
Alternative	Original assumption	Alternate assumption
Retain old equipment 1 year	$4,290	$3,740
Retain old equipment 2 years	3,076	3,515
Replace old equipment now	3,657	3,657

Insofar as the future worths of the alternatives are concerned, suffice it to say that, in this case, the nature of the new assumption precludes our being able to evaluate the alternatives on this basis. Because the assumption generates an infinite series of costs for every alternative, the value of these amounts an infinite number of years from the points at which they occur would be equal to an infinite number of dollars for each alternative. It is clear that no meaningful comparison of such results can be made.

We might also note that, in this discussion of the implications of the alternate assumption regarding future replacements, no cognizance has been taken of an important possibility in a replacement problem. This is that more than one new asset may be available for replacement purposes at this time. For example, the contractor in our illustration may find that the old asset could be replaced now by either of two different models of the new equipment and that each of these models will yield a different combination of costs and revenues. As a result, the problem would contain four alternatives, of which two would involve a new asset. Therefore, a need exists for deciding which of these new assets will represent the assumed series of future replacements. The decision is reached, in such cases, by first computing the uniform annual cost of each new asset for a number of years equal to its service life. These respective annual costs are then compared to determine which of the new assets is the most economical. Next, it is assumed that all future replacements will consist of this most economical of the currently-available new assets. Following this, the analysis proceeds in the manner described in our example.

To summarize all this, in the analysis of a replacement problem, the same alternative will be identified as being the most economical whether the original or the alternate assumption regarding future replacements is made. However, because the alternate assumption can prove to be more difficult to apply in certain types of analyses, it has not been widely adopted, even though there is general agreement that it generates a more realistic pattern of future cash flows. Given the potential difficulties of applying the alternate assumption and the fact that both assumptions yield the same ranking of investment alternatives, we shall adhere to the original assumption from this point on. But this is not intended to discourage anyone else from adopting the alternate assumption in a replacement problem and applying it in the manner which has been explained.

PERPETUAL-SERVICE PROBLEMS

We have just considered a situation in which, given a certain kind of assumption regarding future replacements, it was necessary to process cash flows for a service period of infinite duration. But as we learned in the presentation of the uniform annual cost method, it may also be necessary to accept a study period of this length because an investor is evaluating an opportunity to invest in an asset which has an infinite service life and he has reason to believe that the activity involved will be engaged in for that length of time. Let us take an investment alternative of this type and analyze it by means of the present worth method. No consideration will be given to a future worth analysis since, as we saw earlier, the future worth of an infinite series is infinity, and values of this type cannot serve as a basis for passing judgment on a given alternative.

So suppose that an oil company has decided to construct a road in one of its refineries. Different types of road can be built, but one of those being proposed has the following characteristics: It will call for an initial expenditure of $43,000 per mile of road for preparation of a base and subsurface and for surfacing. However, it is estimated that the road's surface will have to be replaced every 9 years at a cost of $24,000 per mile. Also, during each nine-year period, maintenance costs are expected to be $300 per mile the first year but will increase at a constant rate of $200 per year. Finally, the company's before-tax cost of money is 6 percent per year. An analyst has been asked to calculate the cost of perpetual service with this alternative. This cost is to be expressed in terms of a present worth, which will then be compared with the present worths of the other alternatives for constructing the road under consideration.

The determination can begin with the observation that the present worth of the required initial expenditure is $43,000. To obtain the present worth of the remaining costs, the analyst must note that these costs will form the following pattern during every nine-year period:

$$
\begin{array}{ccccccccc}
 & & & & & & & & 24{,}000 \\
300 & 500 & 700 & 900 & 1{,}100 & 1{,}300 & 1{,}500 & 1{,}700 & 1{,}900 \\
\hline
0 & 1 & 2 & 3 & 4 & 5 & 6 & 7 & 8 \quad 9
\end{array}
$$

The uniform annual equivalent of these expenditures will be as follows:

Annual equivalent $= \$300 + \$200(A/G)_{n=9}^{i=6} + \$24{,}000(A/F)_{n=9}^{i=6}$

$$= \$3{,}111$$

Since the given nine-year cost pattern will repeat itself an infinite number of times, the calculated annual equivalent will continue for an infinite number of years, and its present worth will be equal to

Present worth $= \$3{,}111(P/A)_{n=\infty}^{i=6} = \$51{,}850$

When this is added to the \$43,000 present worth of the initial expenditure, the following total is obtained

Total present worth $= \$43{,}000 + \$51{,}850 = \$94{,}850$

Had a uniform annual cost determination been desired, the annual equivalent of this present worth could be found in the following manner:

Annual cost $= \$94{,}850(A/P)_{n=\infty}^{i=6} = \$5{,}691$

In any case, the present worths of the other alternatives would be calculated in the same general way as was the present worth of this alternative. A comparison of the results would then serve to identify the most economical course of action. Naturally, any irreducible factors that might prove to be relevant would also have to be taken into consideration before a final decision could be reached. It might also be noted that the fact that the computed present worth for the described alternative is positive is of no significance because the road's contribution to revenues has been ignored. Therefore, we must conclude that the company's management is assuming that this contribution will be the same for each type of road and that it will suffice to offset the positive costs that will be experienced. As a final observation, it might be mentioned that the present worth of an alternative for a perpetual service period is sometimes called the *capitalized cost*.

A SUMMATION

The foregoing problem is the last example we shall consider in this presentation of the present worth method and the future worth method. These examples served to demonstrate that, when either finite or infinite service periods are involved, the investor can substitute the present worth method for the uniform annual cost method in his attempt to identify the most economical of a set of mutually exclusive investment alternatives. Furthermore, when finite service periods are involved, the future worth method becomes another means for ascertaining the most economical alternative. But it should be stressed that the present worth and future worth approaches are similar in the sense that each converts the cash flows to be associated with a given alternative into an equivalent single sum of money at some point in time, and this single sum in no way represents the "worth" of the alternative. This is being mentioned because the names of these analytical techniques can erroneously suggest that they yield a value which represents the worth or value of the assets involved in the alternative under consideration. But as we have seen, what they do yield is a value which represents the single net receipt or expenditure in terms of which the consequences of a given investment can be described. However, it might be noted that the present worth approach can be adapted for use in the solution of what are referred to as "valuation problems." We shall now consider how this is done.

A Valuation Problem. Suppose that a corporation issued bonds of $1,000 denomination 6 years ago. The bonds were to be redeemed in 20 years; this means that a current owner of such a bond will receive $1,000 from the company in 14 years. To continue, the bonds called for an interest payment of 10 percent compounded semiannually; this means that a current owner of such a bond will receive an interest payment of 5 percent times $1,000, or $50, at the end of every six-month period for the next 14 years.

During the past 6 years, however, interest rates have risen. Also, the company has been experiencing financial difficulties with the result that its bonds have a relatively low rating at this time. As a consequence, a potential purchaser of one of these bonds concludes that the investment can be justified only if his rate of return will be at least 16 percent compounded semiannually. His question is: Given this minimum return requirement, what is the present value of one such bond?

The analysis begins by our noting that, if a bond is purchased now, the resultant cash flows will be as follows:

$P = ?$									(1,000)
	(50)	(50)	(50)	·	·	·	·	·	(50) (50) (50)
0	1	2	3	·	·	·	·	·	26 27 28

The time line is shown to contain 28 interest periods because of the semiannual compounding that will occur during the 14-year remaining life of the bond. Also, cognizance is taken of the fact that a $50 interest payment will be received at the end of each of these periods and that the $1,000 principal amount will be received at the end of the last interest period. However, the amount P to be invested in the bond at this time is designated as an unknown; the reason for this is that the investor wants to determine what present investment P will result in a realized return of 16 percent compounded semiannually, that is, of 8 percent per interest period.

The approach to the determination of this amount becomes clear when we recall that, if the present worth of an investment alternative is found to be zero, the return on the total investment in that alternative is equal to the rate used in the calculation. In other words, the need here is for the determination of the present expenditure P which will result in a present worth of zero for this alternative at the specified interest rate of 8 percent per period. This is to say that the stipulated requirement is as follows:

$$P - \$50(P/A)_{n=28}^{i=8} - \$1,000(P/F)_{n=28}^{i=8} = 0$$

Solving for P, we obtain

$$P = \$50(P/A)_{n=28}^{i=8} + \$1,000(P/F)_{n=28}^{i=8}$$
$$= \$669$$

Therefore, the present value of this bond is $669 to an investor whose minimum rate-of-return requirement is 16 percent compounded semiannually. If the bond can be purchased for this or a lower amount, the investment can be justified; otherwise, it cannot.

This, then, is how the present worth approach can be used to obtain the present value to an investor of an asset of some type. But such problems are valuation problems, and not problems in which the goal is the identification of the most economical of a set of mutually exclusive investment alternatives.

Choice of Method. We have seen that, if a finite service period is involved, the most economical investment alternative can be identified with the use of any one of the three analytical techniques considered thus far. Which of these approaches should be employed in such a situation is a matter of personal preference. Some individuals select the uniform annual cost method because they feel most comfortable with the concept of an average annual cost, while others select the present worth or future worth method because they feel most comfortable with the concept of a single payment equivalent at some point in time. Or some individuals select the uniform annual cost method because they find it easier to evaluate irreducible factors by examining the difference between calculated average annual costs, while others select the present worth or future worth method because they find it easier to evaluate irreducible factors by examining the difference between calculated single payment equivalents.

From the computational standpoint, no one of the methods has a decided advantage. This becomes apparent when it is recalled that a uniform annual cost can be easily converted to a present worth or a future worth by the application of an appropriate compound interest factor and that a present worth or a future worth can be easily converted to a uniform annual cost by the application of an appropriate compound interest factor.

Finally, of those individuals who prefer to compute and compare single payment equivalents, some find it easier to interpret the meaning of a present worth, while others find it easier to interpret the meaning of a future worth. Of course, as pointed out earlier, the future worth approach is not a feasible method of analysis when an infinite time period is being considered because it yields a future worth of infinity for each alternative.

So, to repeat, the choice of method is a matter of personal preference. And there is no reason why the same analytical technique must be used in every study in a given organization. Some of the firm's decision makers may be disposed toward a particular approach, and others toward another approach; if so, the result may be that all three methods of analysis will be applied in a single organization. As a matter of fact, the number may even exceed three because, as had been stated earlier, additional analytical techniques have been developed for the evaluation of investment alternatives. We shall now go on to consider one of these additional approaches.

QUESTIONS

5-1 Give a general description of the present worth and future worth approaches to the determination of the most economical investment alternative.

5-2 Why must equal time periods be compared when evaluating investment alternatives by the present worth method? By the future worth method?

5-3 If an alternative has been described completely in terms of the costs and revenues it will generate, what can be said about the rate of return on the total investment in that alternative when its total present worth or future worth is found to be positive? To be negative? To be zero? Explain.

5-4 Under what conditions can the expenses and revenues which are unaffected by the choice of alternative be ignored when comparing investment alternatives by the present worth or future worth method?

5-5   What specific compound interest factor can be used to convert a calculated uniform annual cost to a present worth? A calculated present worth to a uniform annual cost? A calculated uniform annual cost to a future worth? A calculated future worth to a uniform annual cost? A calculated present worth to a future worth? A calculated future worth to a present worth?

5-6   What assumption is made in the uniform annual cost, present worth, and future worth methods regarding the return that will be realized from the reinvestment of the periodic net receipts being generated by an investment alternative?

5-7   How is a multiple-alternative problem analyzed by means of either the present worth or future worth method?

5-8   In a replacement problem, the assumption is sometimes made that a currently-owned asset, if retained, will be replaced in the future by a series of assets which are like the most economical of the replacements being proposed at the present time. What is the effect of this assumption in a uniform annual cost analysis? In a present worth analysis? In a future worth analysis?

5-9   Does the future worth method lend itself for use as an analytical technique when a service period of infinite duration must be considered? Explain.

5-10 Can the present worth of an investment alternative with an infinite life be obtained by dividing the alternative's uniform annual cost by the investor's minimum rate-of-return requirement? Explain.

5-11 In some cases, the result of a present worth or future worth analysis is interpreted as representing an investment alternative's effect on an investor's net worth. In others, the result is interpreted as representing a single expenditure which is equivalent to the actual cash flows that will be experienced with an investment alternative. Under what conditions is the first of these interpretations appropriate? Under what conditions is the second of these interpretations appropriate?

5-12 Describe the approach to be employed in the determination of an asset's "present worth" in a valuation problem.

5-13 Up to this point, the uniform annual cost, present worth, and future worth methods of analysis have been considered. What determines which of these techniques will be adopted for use in the evaluation of a set of mutually exclusive investment alternatives?

PROBLEMS

5-1   On the basis of a seven-year sales forecast for a new product, a manufacturer of spraying equipment has developed a probable production schedule and three operating plans by means of which the schedule can be met.

The first plan calls for the procurement of an amount of equipment such that no overtime work would be required and for hiring and laying off employees as the demand for manpower varies. This plan would necessitate a $400,000 investment in facilities which would have a salvage value of $60,000 at the end of the seven-year period. Annual operating costs would be $128,000.

A second plan requires a much smaller investment in equipment. Specifically, only $300,000 would have to be invested in facilities which are expected to have a $45,000 salvage value at the end of 7 years. Furthermore, the plan calls for fewer employees than does the first one but for significantly more overtime work with the result that annual operating costs would be $150,000.

The third plan necessitates an investment in equipment which exceeds that involved in the second plan but which is less than that involved in the first. Some overtime work would be scheduled, and excess employees would be kept on the roll during slack periods. The result of all this is that $340,000 would be invested in equipment whose salvage value would be $52,500 in 7 years and that annual operating costs would be $139,000.

Regardless of which plan is selected, the necessary capital investment will be financed by 50 percent debt funds, which will cost 8 percent per year, and 50 percent equity funds, with which management associates an opportunity cost of 16 percent per year.

With the use of the given data, ascertain which of the three plans is the most economical. Do this by the following means:

a A present worth approach.
b A future worth approach in which you do not employ the calculated total present worths.
c A uniform annual cost approach in which you do not employ either the calculated total present worths or the calculated total future worths.

5-2 The management of a chain of drug stores wants to open another one. Four alternative locations have been proposed. The consequences of acquiring and operating a store at each of these locations are expected to be as follows:

	Site 1	Site 2	Site 3	Site 4
First cost	$950,000	$700,000	$840,000	$620,000
Service life	15 years	30 years	10 years	30 years
Salvage value	$510,000	$250,000	$600,000	$370,000
Annual operating costs	$880,000	$810,000	$1,000,000	$690,000
Annual revenues	$1,230,000	$990,000	$1,370,000	$860,000

In addition to the initial investment indicated in the preceding table, each location will require an investment of $150,000 in working capital which will not decrease in value. Given that management's minimum rate-of-return requirement is 25 percent, determine the most economical alternative in the following manner:

a   By means of a present worth analysis. (Ans.   −$283,562, $130,412, −$460,522, $90,218)

b   By means of a future worth analysis in which you do not make use of the calculated total present worths. (Ans.   −$229,059,680, $105,346,030, −$372,006,900, $72,877,523)

c   By means of a uniform annual cost analysis in which you do not make use of either the calculated total present worths or the calculated total future worths. (Ans.   −$70,996, $32,635, −$115,276, $22,575)

5-3   A lumber company is going to purchase a forklift truck. A choice must be made between one powered by gasoline and one powered by electricity. Each type will have a five-year service life and a terminal salvage value equal to 10 percent of the initial investment it requires. The purchase of either truck will be financed with the use of equity funds which cost the firm 20 percent per year.

The electric-powered truck, including a battery and a charger, costs $18,300. This exceeds the cost of a gasoline-powered truck of the same capacity by $4,000. However, annual operating costs will be lower with the electric-powered truck. More exactly, when those expenses which will be the same with each type are ignored, it is estimated that recurring costs with the electric truck will be $3,500 the first year and that these will increase at an annual rate of $200. With the gasoline truck, they will probably be $4,700 in the first year, $5,000 in the second, $5,400 in the third, $5,900 in the fourth, and $6,500 in the fifth.

Compare these alternatives by means of each of the following methods:

a   A present worth analysis.

b   A future worth analysis in which you do not make use of the calculated total present worths.

c   A uniform annual cost analysis.

5-4   It has been recommended that an existing packaging line be replaced. If it is, the old equipment will be sold for $24,000. However, its book value is $30,000, its replacement cost is $27,000, and $18,000 of the original cost remains to be paid.

The proposed new equipment has a list price of $110,000. There would also be a delivery charge of $2,200 and an installation cost of $3,600.

The economic service life of the old equipment is estimated to be 6 years and that of the new equipment to be 12 years. The terminal salvage value of the old equipment is expected to be zero and that of the new equipment to be $27,000. Relevant annual operating costs will average $95,000 with the existing line and $81,000 with the proposed line.

If the firm's minimum rate-of-return requirement is 10 percent, can the extra investment required by the new equipment be justified? Base your answer to this question on the following:

a A before-tax comparison of present worths. (Ans. $684,878, $659,132)

b A before-tax comparison of future worths which you do not obtain with the use of the calculated total present worths. (Ans. $2,149,320, $2,068,531)

c A before-tax comparison of uniform annual costs which you do not obtain with the use of either the calculated total present worths or the calculated total future worths. (Ans. $100,510, $96,735)

5-5 In the preceding problem, suppose that we are provided with the following additional data: If the old packaging line is retained, it will be replaced at the end of its remaining service life by new equipment which will require an initial investment of $56,000 and which will have a life of 6 years, a salvage value of $13,000, and annual operating costs of $75,000. What effect will these additional data have on the respective alternatives' present worths? Future worths? Uniform annual costs? Can the extra investment in the new equipment now be justified? (Ans. $649,620, $659,132; $2,038,767, $2,068,531; $95,364, $96,735)

5-6 Unless stated otherwise, our assumption always is that the cash-flow pattern of each currently-available investment alternative will continue to repeat itself in the future. But suppose that, in problem 5-4, the analyst chooses to assume that the future replacements for both the old packaging line and the proposed new line will generate cash-flow patterns which coincide with that of the currently-available new line. Consequently, he will have to take into consideration an infinite series of replacements when evaluating each of the two alternatives. What will he find the respective total present worths to be? The respective total uniform annual costs? Is the decision reached in problem 5-4 affected by this new assumption? (Ans. $983,790, $967,350; $98,379, $96,735)

5-7 A promissory note is for sale. Whoever purchases it will receive an end-of-month interest payment of $150 for the next 52 months and an additional single payment of $18,000 at the end of that time period. At what price would a buyer of the note realize a return of exactly 24 percent compounded monthly on his investment?

5-8 Two business properties are for sale. Each contains stores and offices. An individual wants to determine which, if either, of these properties she should purchase for investment purposes.

Building T is available for $175,000, and building V for $140,000. Either building would be kept for only 3 years. It is estimated that, during that period, the market value of such property will increase at an annual rate of 4 percent compounded annually based on the present asking price. Insofar as annual property taxes are concerned, they will probably average 2 percent of a building's current price.

For the three-year period, annual receipts from rents and annual operating expenses other than property taxes are expected to be as follows:

| | Building T | | Building V | |
Year	Receipts	Expenses	Receipts	Expenses
1	$127,000	$66,000	$99,000	$45,000
2	131,000	69,000	94,000	43,000
3	129,000	67,000	98,000	44,000

You are asked to make a recommendation regarding the most economical course of action for this investor whose rate-of-return requirement is 40 percent. Do so on the basis of each of the following:

a A future worth comparison.

b A present worth comparison.

c A uniform annual cost comparison.

5-9 In the preceding problem, it will have been found that, for building T, annual property taxes were estimated to be $3,500 and that the building's resale value was estimated to be $196,858. The comparable amounts for building V were $2,800 and $157,486, respectively.

Suppose that these values and the values of the estimated annual receipts and operating expenses prove to be correct. What maximum present amount should the investor offer to pay for building T so as to realize a return of 40 percent on her total investment? For building V? (Ans. $163,971, $137,209)

5-10 A gas company finds that there is room for the installation of only one main along a proposed route. One alternative is to install a 4-inch main at this time at a cost of $110,000. This would be adequate from the standpoint of capacity for only 10 years. It would then be necessary to remove the 4-inch main and replace it by a 12-inch main which, for all practical purposes, would have an infinite service life. The net cost of replacing the 4-inch main in 10 years is estimated to be $420,000; this takes into account the salvage value and removal cost of the old main and also the prices that are likely to prevail 10 years from now.

A second alternative is to install a 12-inch main at the present time to take advantage of current prices and installation costs. This can be done at a total cost of $280,000. The resultant capacity would be adequate throughout the main's assumed infinite life.

Average annual maintenance and repair costs with the first alternative would be about $1,100 during the life of the 4-inch main and $1,500 during the life of its 12-inch replacement. With the second alternative, these costs would be approximately $1,400 a year.

Given that the involved regulatory commission allows the company to realize a return on total investment equivalent to 20 percent a year before income taxes, what are the alternatives' present worths? Uniform annual costs? (Ans. $183,652, $287,000; $36,730, $57,400)

5-11 The owner of a unit of earth-moving equipment is leasing it to a construction firm. At this point in time, the contract calls for the owner's receiving six more semiannual payments of $11,000 each; the first of these is due within a few days. Three years from now, he will take possession of the equipment and probably can then dispose of it for about $9,000.

Because he has an immediate need for cash, the owner of the equipment is attempting to sell it. The buyer would, of course, acquire title to the asset and be entitled to the payments due under the aforementioned leasing arrangement. What is the present worth of the equipment to a potential buyer whose minimum rate-of-return requirement is 12 percent compounded semiannually? (Ans. $63,677)

5-12 One of two milling machines is going to be purchased by a firm that engages in metalworking operations. Machine P requires a total investment of $124,000, of which $31,000 will be recovered at the end of the asset's eight-year life. Recurring expenses will average $62,000 a year. Also, a $7,000 overhaul will be needed at the end of the fifth year.

Machine Q will require an initial investment of $186,000, of which $39,000 will be recovered at the end of its twelve-year life. Annual recurring expenses with this equipment will average $47,000. The asset will need a $12,000 overhaul at the beginning of the eighth year of its life. Finally, as compared with machine P, it will provide the firm with an average annual revenue advantage of $3,000.

Using 12 percent for the cost of money and a study period of 24 years, evaluate the two alternatives in each of the following ways:

a By comparing their total future worths.
b By comparing their total present worths.
c By comparing their total uniform annual costs.

5-13 In the preceding problem, our standard assumption regarding the nature of future replacements created a need for comparing the alternatives for a service period of at least 24 years. This is because, if it is assumed that machine P is replaced by a series of machines like P and that machine Q is replaced by a series of machines like Q, the equal time period requirement can be satisfied by comparing a series of three machines of type P with a series of two machines of type Q. Each of these series proves to be 24 years long.

However, the equal time period requirement can also be satisfied by assuming that machine P will be replaced by an infinite number of machines of type P and that machine Q will be replaced by an infinite number of machines of type Q. If this were done, what would be the alternatives' respective total annual costs? Total present worths? Is it surprising that machine Q continues to be the more economical of the two? Explain. (Ans. $85,241, $73,281; $710,342, $610,675)

5-14 When a number of currently-available assets are being compared, it is sometimes assumed that each will be replaced at the end of its life by an infinite series of the most economical of the currently-available assets. In problem 5-12, the more economical of the two assets would be found to be machine Q. Therefore, with the aforementioned assumption, one would suppose that machine P would be replaced at the end of its eight-year life by an infinite series of machines like machine Q and that machine Q would be replaced at the end of its twelve-year life by an infinite series of machines of the same kind. What effect would this have on the alternatives' respective total present worths? On their total uniform annual costs? Is it surprising that machine Q continues to be the more economical of the two? Explain. (Ans. $670,129, $610,675; $80,415, $73,281)

5-15 The owner of a patent is negotiating with a firm which wants to produce and distribute the item covered by the patent. The firm estimates that, during the patent's remaining 16-year life, the annual output of the item will be as follows:

Year	Output, units	Year	Output, units
1	4,000	9	7,800
2	4,600	10	7,400
3	5,200	11	7,000
4	5,800	12	6,600
5	6,400	13	6,200
6	7,000	14	5,800
7	7,600	15	5,400
8	8,200	16	5,000

These data have been made available to the patent holder, and after examining them, she asks that she be paid an annual end-of-year royalty equal to $0.50 times the number of units to be produced in any given year. Management accepts this as a reasonable demand but states that it would prefer to purchase the right to produce the item by making a single payment at the present time. If the patent owner places a time value on money of 15 percent, for what present sum of money should she sell this right?

5-16 A telephone company is going to compare the cost of retaining one of its service trucks with the cost of replacing it by a new one. When doing so, it wants to take care to select a remaining service life for the old truck which will place it in the most favorable light. Therefore, it considers the possibility of retaining the truck for one more year

or two more years or three more years. The cash flows that will
be affected by the choice of service life are those related to the market
value of the truck and to the recurring maintenance and repair
expenses. What these are expected to be can be described as follows:

Year	End-of-year market value	Recurring costs
0	$1,300	$ —
1	750	240
2	500	820
3	450	1,000

Which of the three possible service lives should be selected for use
when evaluating the proposal that the truck be replaced at this time?
Answer this question using a rate-of-return requirement of 10 percent
and employing each of the following:

a   A future worth analysis. (Ans. $7,099, $7,924, $8,094)
b   A present worth analysis.
c   A uniform annual cost analysis.

5-17   Additional problems, to be solved on a before-tax basis by the present
worth, future worth, and uniform annual cost methods, appear at
the end of chapter 7. Analyze those for which you choose to or are
asked to provide solutions.

6

Rate of Return Computations

The technique for analyzing investment alternatives that is to be considered next is the *rate of return method,* which is sometimes referred to as the *discounted cash flow method.* For now, suffice it to say that this analytical technique calls for calculating the rate of return on the total investment in a given alternative and for calculating the rate of return on the extra investment in one alternative as compared with another. Therefore, the presentation of the rate of return method must be preceded by an exposition of the mechanics of computing such rates of return. A mastery of the procedures involved will enable us to go on to a study of the method as such.

RETURN ON TOTAL INVESTMENT

It has been pointed out that one characteristic of a satisfactory investment alternative is that it will yield a return on the total investment it requires which is equal to or exceeds the investor's minimum rate-of-return requirement. In the uniform annual cost, present worth, and future worth methods, the presence or absence of this characteristic was revealed by the nature of the calculated total cost of an alternative. Specifically, if all the costs and revenues to be associated with an alternative had been considered, a total cost which was zero or negative indicated that the established rate-of-return requirement was being satisfied, whereas a total cost which was positive indicated that it was not. But in the rate of return method, it is necessary to determine what the *specific* value of the return on total investment will be for a given alternative.

179

Whether this return is satisfactory is ascertained by comparing it with the established requirement.

There are two basic approaches to the calculation of the specific value of the rate of return that will be realized on a total investment. These will now be presented with the use of appropriate examples.

The First Approach. Suppose that a hospital has received a contribution of $100,000 from a philanthropic organization. The hospital's administrators plan to invest the entire amount in a source which will enable them to make a series of end-of-year withdrawals such that the last withdrawal will exhaust the fund. This type of investment is being considered because the periodic receipts will serve to cover a portion of the institution's operating costs.

One investment opportunity of this kind can be described as follows: If an investment of $100,000 is made at this time, $36,040 can be withdrawn at the end of each year for 3 years. On a time line, the resultant cash flows would be described in the following manner:

```
100,000    (36,040)    (36,040)    (36,040)
├───────────┼───────────┼───────────┤
0           1           2           3
```

Let us now assume that the hospital's administrators want to know what return they would be realizing on the $100,000 investment should they decide to select this alternative. To determine this return, we begin by recalling that, if an alternative's *total* uniform annual cost, present worth, or future worth is zero, the return being realized on the total investment in the alternative is equal to the rate i used in the computation which yielded a total cost of zero. Therefore, the return on the $100,000 investment will be equal to the rate i which will yield a uniform annual cost or a present worth or a future worth of zero for the alternative under consideration. In other words, using the uniform annual cost approach for purposes of illustration, we can say that, at some unknown rate i, the uniform annual cost of this alternative will be equal to zero and that the return on total investment will be equal to this rate i. To determine what this rate is, we start by expressing the first part of the preceding statement in the following form:

Annual cost $= \$100,000(A/P)_{n=3}^{i=?} - \$36,040 = 0$

To obtain the value of i, we solve this expression for the unknown value of the compound interest factor it contains. Doing so, we obtain

$(A/P)_{n=3}^{i=?} = \$36,040/\$100,000 = 0.3604$

Next, we turn to the compound interest tables in Appendix C to find the rate which will yield a value of 0.3604 for this present-amount annuity factor for an n of 3. When we reach the table for an i of 4 percent, we discover that this is the rate we have been seeking. Therefore, the rate of return on the total investment will be 4 percent per year.

The unknown rate could also have been ascertained by beginning with the statement that the return will be equal to the unknown rate i which will yield a present worth of zero for the alternative. This statement would assume the following form:

Present worth $= \$100,000 - \$36,040(P/A)_{n=3}^{i=?} = 0$

Solving this expression for the unknown uniform-series present worth factor, we should find that

$(P/A)_{n=3}^{i=?} = \$100,000/\$36,040 = 2.775$

Again, an examination of the compound interest tables in Appendix C would reveal that, for an n of 3, the value of this factor is 2.775 for an i of 4 percent. Consequently, the return on the total investment will be 4 percent per year.

A third way of obtaining the unknown rate would be to start with the observation that the return will be equal to the rate i which will yield a future worth of zero for the alternative. In equation form, this is to say that

Future worth $= \$100,000(F/P)_{n=3}^{i=?} - \$36,040(F/A)_{n=3}^{i=?} = 0$

Unfortunately, this expression contains two unknown factors, and, hence, we cannot solve directly for their values. When an expression such as this is obtained, it becomes necessary to use a trial-and-error approach to determine the value of i. How this is done will be explained at a subsequent point. For now, suffice it to say that, if possible, such expressions should be avoided. We have seen that it is possible to do so in this case by working with either an annual cost or present worth expression; so we shall simply conclude that the future worth approach would be an inefficient one under the circumstances which prevail in this example.

Let us now suppose that the hospital's administrators have another opportunity for investing the $100,000 and that they would like to calculate the return on total investment which would be experienced with this alternative. The alternative will generate end-of-year receipts of only $27,300, but these withdrawals can be made for a period of 4 years. On a time line, the cash flows involved would appear as follows:

```
100,000   (27,300)   (27,300)   (27,300)   (27,300)
|----------|----------|----------|----------|
0          1          2          3          4
```

The return on the total investment of $100,000 in this alternative can be ascertained by beginning with any one of the three expressions with which we began the analysis in the preceding example. But we shall arbitrarily select the present worth expression for purposes of illustration. This expression will assume the following form:

Present worth $= \$100,000 - \$27,300(P/A)^{i=?}_{n=4} = 0$

from which we obtain

$(P/A)^{i=?}_{n=4} = 3.663$

Turning to Appendix C to find the unknown rate, we now discover that there is no interest rate which yields this exact value for the factor. Specifically, at 2 percent, the value of the factor is 3.808, which is greater than the desired value of 3.663, and, at 4 percent, the value of the factor is 3.630, which is lower than the desired value of 3.663. At best, this enables us to conclude that the rate is an amount between 2 and 4 percent, but this amount cannot be found directly because Appendix C does not contain compound interest tables for rates between 2 and 4 percent. When this situation arises, we shall engage in linear interpolation. How this is done can be best explained by beginning with a graphical description of the situation. This description, in which the values of the compound interest factor and the corresponding values of i are shown, is as follows:

```
  3.808                 3.663    3.630
  ├──────────────────────┼─────────┤
i = 2%                 i = ?    i = 4%
```

As an examination of this diagram reveals, the linear interpolation would be carried out in the following manner:

$$i = 2\% + \left(\frac{3.808 - 3.663}{3.808 - 3.630}\right)(4\% - 2\%) = 3.6\%$$

This result is likely to contain a slight error because the relationship between the rate i and the value of any compound interest factor is not linear but curvilinear. However, if we get as close as we can to the correct value of i in the available tables before interpolating, the resultant error will be negligible.

In any event, the return on the total investment in the alternative under consideration would be, as indicated, 3.6 percent per year.

The Second Approach. In each of the preceding two examples, the rate of return could be obtained by solving for the value of an unknown compound interest factor and then finding the corresponding rate i in the compound interest tables. The fact that interpolation in the tables was necessary in one of the cases did nothing to alter the basic nature of the approach.

But in one of the examples, it was found that the cost expression, with which the rate of return determination begins, may contain more than one unknown compound interest factor. When this occurs, the rate cannot be ascertained from the compound interest tables. Admittedly, it so happened that, in the example involved, the problem this posed could be eliminated by turning to another cost expression, but, very often, this is not possible. When it is not, the rate of return must be arrived at by a second approach, namely, trial and error. To explain this approach, we shall return to the example in which the hospital administrators had an opportunity to invest $100,000 in a source which would yield end-of-year revenues of $36,040 for a period of 3 years.

It will be recalled that, when an attempt was made to solve for the return on total investment with the use of a future worth expression, the following was obtained:

$$\text{Future worth} = \$100,000(F/P)_{n=3}^{i=?} - \$36,040(F/A)_{n=3}^{i=?} = 0$$

When this point was reached, the approach was abandoned because the expression contained two unknowns, as compared with the one unknown contained in the annual cost and present worth expressions. Therefore, each of the latter expressions was used to solve the problem, and the return was found to be 4 percent per year. But we shall now suppose that a decision was made to continue to work with the future worth expression.

To solve the problem with this expression, it is necessary to estimate the rate of return, find the values of the two compound interest factors at that rate, substitute these values in the future worth expression, and determine whether the resultant future worth is zero. If it is not, another rate must be selected, and the entire procedure repeated. This would continue until a rate is found which will yield a future worth of zero. To illustrate, suppose that an initial estimate of 2 percent had been made. At this rate, the future worth would be found to be

$$\text{Future worth} = \$100,000(F/P)_{n=3}^{i=2} - \$36,040(F/A)_{n=3}^{i=2} = (-)\$4,162$$

Because the result is negative, the actual return will exceed the 2 percent rate used in this first trial; so a higher rate would now be estimated. If the new estimate is 6 percent, the following would be obtained:

$$\text{Future worth} = \$100,000(F/P)_{n=3}^{i=6} - \$36,040(F/A)_{n=3}^{i=6} = (+)\$4,349$$

The positive result discloses that the actual return will be less than the 6 percent rate used in this second trial; so a lower rate would now be estimated. If the new estimate is 4 percent, the following would be obtained:

Future worth $= \$100,000(F/P)_{n=3}^{i=4} - \$36,040(F/A)_{n=3}^{i=4} = \$0$

Given that a rate of 4 percent yields a future worth of zero, we conclude that the return will be 4 percent per year, which coincides with what was found in a more direct manner by beginning with either a uniform annual cost or present worth expression.

It so happens that the cash flows in this case were such that the rate which generated a future worth of exactly zero by means of the trial-and-error approach was a rate which was represented in our tables of compound interest factors. But, more often than not, this will not be the case. For example, let us assume that the hospital in our illustration has still another alternative for investing the $100,000. This one will permit a series of end-of-year withdrawals for a period of 5 years. The first of these withdrawals will be $20,000, and the subsequent ones will increase at a rate of $2,000 per year. On a time line, this cash-flow pattern would appear as follows:

```
100,000   (20,000)   (22,000)   (24,000)   (26,000)   (28,000)
├──────────┼──────────┼──────────┼──────────┼──────────┤
0          1          2          3          4          5
```

If the determination of the return on total investment begins with a uniform annual cost expression, the following equation will be obtained:

Annual cost $= \$100,000(A/P)_{n=5}^{i=?} - \$20,000 - \$2,000(A/G)_{n=5}^{i=?} = 0$

This equation contains more than one unknown compound interest factor, and so would a present or future worth expression. Hence, we are confronted by a case in which we have no choice but to employ the trial-and-error approach. If, in the course of doing so, we estimated the returns to be 6 percent and 8 percent, respectively, substitution of these values in the preceding equation would yield the following annual costs:

Rate	Annual cost
6%	(−)$ 28
8	(+) 1,358

These calculated annual costs disclose that the return must be between 6 and 8 percent. But because the tables in Appendix C do not contain values of compound interest factors for rates between these two percentages, it becomes necessary to obtain the unknown rate by interpolation. This will be done linearly, and the method for doing so becomes apparent when the point we have reached in the analysis is described graphically. This description, which shows the relationship between the rate i and the calculated uniform annual cost, is as follows:

$$
\begin{array}{lll}
(-)28 & 0 & (+)1{,}358 \\
\hline
i = 6\% \quad i = ? & & i = 8\%
\end{array}
$$

As this diagram suggests, the interpolation would be carried out in the following manner:

$$
i = 6\% + \left(\frac{\$28}{\$28 + \$1{,}358} \right)(8\% - 6\%) = 6.04\%
$$

Therefore, the return on the total investment in this alternative would be said to be 6.04 percent per year. This is said with the realization that the use of linear interpolation introduces a slight error in the result because the relationship between the rate i and the calculated cost of an alternative is not linear but curvilinear. However, if the analyst succeeds in getting as close to the correct rate as the available compound interest tables enable him to, the error attributable to the linear interpolation that follows is negligible.

This, then, is the second approach to the determination of the rate of return on the total investment in an alternative. In brief, it is a trial-and-error approach that must be employed when the annual cost, present worth, or future worth expression, with which the determination begins, is found to contain more than one unknown compound interest factor. As opposed to this, the first approach considered is one in which the return can be found in the compound interest tables after the analyst has ascertained that the annual cost, present worth, or future worth expression, with which the determination begins, contains only one unknown compound interest factor. We have also seen that, in both approaches, a need for interpolation may arise.

It will be noted that, after the returns on total investment had been computed in our examples, no attempt was made to use the results to pass judgment on the alternatives involved. This is because our only goal for now is to become acquainted with the mechanics of computing such returns.

RETURN ON EXTRA INVESTMENT

Mention has been made of the fact that the application of the rate of return method also necessitates taking into consideration the return that will be realized on the extra investment called for by one alternative as compared with another. We shall now discuss the procedure for determining such returns. Again, as was the case with returns on total investment, there are two basic methods available for this purpose. Each will be presented with the use of an example.

The First Method. Suppose that an insurance company has had a study made of its office procedures. As a result, two different proposals have evolved for improving upon these procedures. The implementation of the first proposal, R, requires a present expenditure of $24,000, with the result that $13,090 per year will be saved in operating costs during the next 2 years. The second proposal, S, calls for an expenditure of $36,000 at this time, but, as a consequence, an annual saving of $20,190 will be experienced during the next 2 years. The firm wants to determine the following: (1) the return that would be realized on the total investment of $24,000 in proposal R, (2) the return that would be realized on the total investment of $36,000 in proposal S, and (3) the return that would be realized on the extra investment of $12,000 that proposal S requires as compared with proposal R.

If the savings in operating costs are treated as end-of-year amounts, proposal R can be described as follows:

```
24,000     (13,090)     (13,090)
├────────────┼────────────┤
0            1            2
```

To calculate the return on the total investment of $24,000, the firm can begin with the following uniform annual cost expression:

$$\text{Annual cost} = \$24,000(A/P)_{n=2}^{i=?} - \$13,090 = 0$$

When this equation is solved for the unknown present-amount annuity factor it contains, a value of 0.5454 is obtained, and the compound interest tables reveal that this corresponds to an i of 6 percent.

Similarly, the determination of the return on the total investment of $36,000 in proposal S would begin with a description of its cash flows, which are as follows:

```
36,000     (20,190)     (20,190)
├────────────┼────────────┤
0            1            2
```

Next, the following uniform annual cost expression can be constructed:

$$\text{Annual cost} = \$36,000(A/P)_{n=2}^{i=?} - \$20,190 = 0$$

The value of the unknown present-amount annuity factor in this case proves to be 0.5608, and this is found to correspond to an i of 8 percent in the compound interest tables.

Thus far, of course, the computational procedure is one with which we are already familiar. The only thing that might be noted is that present or future worth expressions could have been substituted for the uniform annual cost expressions with which the preceding determinations began. But let us now turn to the question of what return would be realized on the extra investment of $12,000 in proposal S.

The one method for ascertaining this begins with a statement of the amount of the required extra investment; in our example, this is $12,000. Then, the consequences of the extra investment in the one alternative, as compared with the other, are determined; this is done by making a period-by-period comparison of the alternatives' respective cash flows. In our example, a year-by-year comparison of the cash-flow lines for proposals R and S discloses that, by investing an additional $12,000, the company can increase the annual saving from $13,090 to $20,190, or by $7,100, for a period of 2 years. On a time line, this would appear as follows:

```
12,000      (7,100)      (7,100)
 |-----------|-----------|
 0           1           2
```

The question now becomes: If $12,000 is invested and an annual saving of $7,100 for a period of 2 years results, what return will be realized on the $12,000 investment? As this question suggests, the final step in the method calls for finding the rate i which will yield a value of zero dollars for the uniform annual equivalent, present worth equivalent, or future worth equivalent of this cash-flow pattern. Continuing to work with a uniform annual equivalent expression, the firm in our example would begin this final step with the following equation:

$$\text{Annual equivalent} = \$12,000(A/P)_{n=2}^{i=?} - \$7,100 = 0$$

The value of the present-amount annuity factor which this equation contains would be calculated to be 0.5917. From the compound interest tables, the rate i would be found to be 12 percent, which means that the prospective return on the extra investment of $12,000 is 12 percent per year. How this result is used to pass judgment on the alternative involved is something with which we shall not concern ourselves at this point because our sole interest for now is the method for calculating such returns.

Before going on, however, we might make certain observations with regard to this example. First, when the period-by-period consequences of the extra investment in proposal S were ascertained, the resultant combination of cash flows was such that the expression for the uniform annual equivalent of these cash flows contained only one unknown compound interest factor; furthermore, the calculated value of this factor was such that no interpolation was required in the compound interest tables to obtain the unknown rate i. But it should be realized that, in some other problem, a similar cash-flow pattern might exist, but it may be necessary to interpolate in the interest tables to obtain the rate i that corresponds to some calculated value of a compound interest factor. Also, in some other problem, a dissimilar cash-flow pattern might be obtained whose nature is such that a trial-and-error approach and interpolation would have to be employed to find the rate i which yields an equivalent of zero for the cash flows generated by the extra investment and its consequences. Suffice it to say that, in all such cases, the interpolation and trial-and-error procedures would be identical to those used in the process of ascertaining returns on total investment. This will be demonstrated when we get to the rate of return method as such.

Another relevant observation is that the analysis in our example was simplified by the fact that the two alternatives had equal lives. To explain this, we can begin by noting that, when a return on total investment is being determined, this return is something which is inherent in the alternative under consideration and is independent of anything that might occur with some other alternative. Consequently, in the process of ascertaining that the return on the total investment in proposal S would be 8 percent, the firm in our illustration found it necessary to take into consideration only the life of proposal S and the costs and revenues that would be experienced during this period. Nothing about some other alternative's life or cash flows could alter the fact that the consequences of a total investment of $36,000 in proposal S generate a return of 8 percent on that investment.

But the characteristics of some other alternative no longer prove to be irrelevant when a return on the extra investment in a given alternative is being computed. This is because the computational procedure involved calls for a period-by-period comparison of the two alternatives. If their respective service lives are not equal, a difficulty is experienced when an attempt is made to carry out such a comparison. To illustrate, suppose that the insurance company had a third alternative, T, for improving its office procedures. This one requires an initial expenditure of $45,000 and will bring about an annual saving of $16,000 for 4 years. On a time line, this would appear as follows:

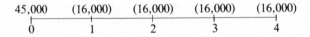

Let us now assume that the firm wants to calculate the return on the extra investment in this proposal, as compared with proposal S which had the following characteristics:

```
36,000      (20,190)    (20,190)
├───────────┼───────────┤
0           1           2
```

A year-by-year comparison of proposals T and S reveals that proposal T necessitates an extra investment of $9,000 and will reduce the annual saving in operating costs by $4,190 during each of the first 2 years of its life. But it is not possible to determine how it will differ from proposal S during the third and fourth years of its life, because we do not know what will occur during those years if the company chooses alternative S. Hence, the analysis cannot proceed unless a description is provided of proposal S's replacement. As we know from our discussion of the other analytical techniques, when an investor is confronted by this need, he can either forecast or assume the nature of future replacements until equal time periods are obtained. In this case, should the insurance company choose to make the assumption that proposal S will be replaced by an alternative which will yield an identical cash-flow pattern, proposal S and its assumed replacement would be expected to generate the following cash flows:

```
36,000                  36,000
        (20,190)    (20,190)    (20,190)    (20,190)
├───────────┼───────────┼───────────┼───────────┤
0           1           2           3           4
```

Because this service period is equal to that of proposal T, the year-by-year comparison can continue, and it would be found that proposal T differs from proposal S in the following way:

```
9,000                   (36,000)
        4,190       4,190       4,190       4,190
├───────────┼───────────┼───────────┼───────────┤
0           1           2           3           4
```

If it were decided to begin with, say, a present worth expression, the return on the $9,000 extra investment could now be found by solving the following equation for the unknown rate i:

$$\text{Present worth} = \$9,000 - \$36,000(P/F)_{n=2}^{i=?} + \$4,190(P/A)_{n=4}^{i=?} = 0$$

Since more than one unknown compound interest factor is involved, a trial-and-error approach would have to be employed.

But the important thing is that, as has just been shown, when the return on the extra investment in one alternative as compared with another is being calculated, it is mandatory that the same service period be considered for both alternatives. Given that the determination of the return on extra investment is an integral part of the rate of return method, it follows that the equal time-period requirement must be satisfied with this method just as it must be with the uniform annual cost, present worth, and future worth methods.

A Second Method. There is a second basic method for ascertaining the return that will be realized on an extra investment. This approach differs from the one just described in that it eliminates the need for a period-by-period comparison of the two alternatives being analyzed. Instead, it requires that the analyst find the rate *i* which equates the uniform annual costs of the two alternatives being compared. This is because the rate, which yields the same annual cost for one alternative as it does for another, represents the rate that the investor will be realizing on the extra investment called for by one of the alternatives. But this is more easily demonstrated than explained, and so let us return to the example which involved the insurance company.

With the first method, the determination of the return on the extra investment in proposal S as compared with proposal R began with an examination of proposal R's cash-flow pattern, which was as follows:

```
24,000      (13,090)    (13,090)
|-----------|-----------|
0           1           2
```

and with an examination of proposal S's cash-flow pattern, which was as follows:

```
36,000      (20,190)    (20,190)
|-----------|-----------|
0           1           2
```

A comparison of the two disclosed that the extra investment in proposal S and the consequences of this investment were as follows:

```
12,000      (7,100)     (7,100)
|-----------|-----------|
0           1           2
```

The return on this extra investment was ascertained by equating the uniform annual equivalent of these cash flows to zero and solving for the rate *i*. The specific equation developed was as follows:

$$\$12,000(A/P)_{n=2}^{i=?} - \$7,100 = 0 \tag{6-1}$$

With the second method for determining this rate, we should again begin by describing the cash flows for alternatives R and S. But instead of continuing by making a year-by-year comparison of these respective cash-flow patterns, we simply set up an expression in which the uniform annual cost of alternative S is shown to be equal to the uniform annual cost of alternative R at some unknown rate i. When this is done, the following is obtained:

$$\$36,000(A/P)_{n=2}^{i=?} - \$20,190 = \$24,000(A/P)_{n=2}^{i=?} - \$13,090$$

If the terms on the right side of this equation are moved to the left side, the result is as follows:

$$\$36,000(A/P)_{n=2}^{i=?} - \$24,000(A/P)_{n=2}^{i=?} - \$20,190 + \$13,090 = 0$$

which is to say that, if two annual costs are equal, the difference between them will be zero. Going on to combine terms in this expression, we obtain

$$\$12,000(A/P)_{n=2}^{i=?} - \$7,100 = 0 \qquad\qquad (6\text{-}2)$$

But a comparison of this equation with Eq. (6-1), which was the result of the first method for obtaining the unknown return on extra investment, reveals that the two are identical. Therefore, the two methods will yield the same result. This means that, as before, the return will be found to be 12 percent. Incidentally, this rate will yield an annual cost of $1,111 for each of the two alternatives, but this value is of no significance.

To summarize, the second method calls for setting up an expression in which the uniform annual cost of the one alternative is shown to be equal to the uniform annual cost of the other alternative at some unknown rate i. Then, the terms from one side of the equation are moved to the other, and any terms that can be are combined. The result will be an expression of the type shown as Eq. (6-2). If the resultant expression contains only one unknown compound interest factor, the value of this factor can be calculated and the corresponding rate i obtained from the compound interest tables. But if it contains two or more unknown compound interest factors, a trial-and-error approach must be employed to find the value of i.

Although it has been demonstrated with the use of an example that the two methods will yield the same result, it might be helpful to show why this is so in more general terms. Suppose one alternative, M, generates the following cash flows, designated by letters, during a two-year period:

```
a        b        c
├────────┼────────┤
0        1        2
```

and that a second, N, generates the following:

```
d        e        f
├────────┼────────┤
0        1        2
```

Ignoring the time value of money, we can say that, for alternative M, the average cost per year for 2 years will be

$$\frac{a + b + c}{2}$$

and that, for alternative N, it will be

$$\frac{d + e + f}{2}$$

Now, in the second method for finding the return on extra investment, two such average annual cost expressions would be equated to obtain

$$\frac{a + b + c}{2} = \frac{d + e + f}{2}$$

which yields

$$\frac{a + b + c}{2} - \frac{d + e + f}{2} = 0$$

which is also equal to

$$\frac{a + b + c - d - e - f}{2} = 0$$

which can also be expressed as

$$\frac{(a - d) + (b - e) + (c - f)}{2} = 0 \qquad (6\text{-}3)$$

As compared with this, in the first method for finding the return on extra investment, the average annual value of the year-by-year differences between the two alternatives would be equated to zero. These differences for alternatives M and N are as follows:

$$\begin{array}{c c c} a - d & b - e & c - f \\ \vdash\!\!\!\!\!{-}\!\!\!\!\!-\!\!\!\!\!-\!\!\!\!\!\!+\!\!\!\!\!-\!\!\!\!\!-\!\!\!\!\!\!\vdash \\ 0 & 1 & 2 \end{array}$$

Ignoring the time value of money as we did before and equating the two-year average of these differences to zero, we obtain the following:

$$\frac{(a - d) + (b - e) + (c - f)}{2} = 0 \qquad (6\text{-}4)$$

But this coincides with Eq. (6-3). Therefore, we conclude that, if the difference between the respective averages of two annual series of numbers is zero under a given set of circumstances, the average of the year-by-year differences between these two annual series of numbers will also be zero.

In any event, the advantage of the second method is that it eliminates the need for ascertaining the period-by-period differences between the two alternatives being compared. This proves to be important in those instances in which relatively long service periods are involved. To illustrate, it may be that one alternative has a seven-year life, and another has a nine-year life. If the customary assumption is made that the "seven-year" alternative will be replaced by a series of alternatives identical to itself and that the "nine-year" alternative will be replaced by a series of alternatives identical to itself, a 63-year service period would be obtained. It is clear that a year-by-year comparison under such circumstances would be a tedious process. A simpler approach would be to equate the uniform annual cost expressions for the two alternatives; in these expressions, the rate i would appear as an unknown. And, of course, in an extreme case, the service period may be infinite, as it was in some of the problems we have already considered, and, obviously, a year-by-year comparison would prove to be impossible.

It might also be mentioned that the rate i which yields equal uniform annual costs will yield equal present worths and equal future worths. But there would be no computational advantage to be associated with a method for determining the return on extra investment in which the rate i is found which equates the present or future worths of two alternatives rather than their annual costs. If the assets contained in the respective alternatives have equal service lives, the respective uniform annual cost expressions are as easily developed as are present worth or future worth expressions. And if the assets do not have equal service lives and the aforementioned assumption is made regarding their future replacements, uniform annual cost expressions are more easily developed than are present worth or future worth expressions. For example, in the case just referred to in which one alternative had a seven-year life and the other had a nine-year life, cash flows for 63 years would have to be processed to obtain the present worth or future worth expressions. As opposed to this, with the uniform annual cost approach, the annual equivalent of the seven-year cash flows for the one alternative could simply be equated to the annual equivalent of the nine-year cash flows for the other, because of the assumption that these respective annual equivalents will continue until the same future point in time is reached with each alternative.

Therefore, in our discussion of the rate of return method, when we ascertain returns on extra investments by the second method for doing so, we shall ordinarily find the rate i which yields the same value of the uniform annual cost for each of the two alternatives being compared. Otherwise, we shall adopt the first method, in which the year-by-year differences between the two alternatives are ascertained and the rate is found which yields a value of zero for the uniform annual equivalent, present worth, or future worth of these differences.

WEIGHTED AVERAGE RETURNS

One more observation remains to be made and explained before we go on to our presentation of the rate of return, or discounted cash flow, method. The observation is that one of three interrelated rates of return is the weighted average of the other two. The explanation will be based on a very simple example.

An individual is considering buying one of two promissory notes that are for sale. Insofar as he is concerned, the two alternatives are mutually exclusive, because he has sufficient funds to buy one of the notes but not both. The first note is for sale for $24,000 and will result in the investor's receiving a payment of $25,440 in one year. This can be described as follows:

24,000 (25,440)
├──────────┤
0   1

To calculate the return on the total investment in this note, the potential investor could set up the following future worth expression:

Future worth $= \$24,000(F/P)_{n=1}^{i=?} - \$25,440 = 0$

The value of the unknown single-amount future worth factor would be found to be 1.06, and this corresponds to a rate i of 6 percent in the compound interest tables. Therefore, the return on the total investment of $24,000 would be 6 percent.

The second note is for sale for $36,000, and it calls for paying the holder of the note $38,880 in one year. On a time line, these cash flows appear as follows:

36,000 (38,880)
├──────────┤
0   1

In this case, the determination of the return on total investment could begin with the following future worth expression:

Future worth $= \$36,000(F/P)_{n=1}^{i=?} - \$38,880 = 0$

The value of this single-amount future worth factor proves to be 1.08. From the compound interest tables, the corresponding rate i is found to be 8 percent; so the return on the $36,000 total investment would be 8 percent.

A comparison of these two alternatives discloses that the second note requires an extra investment of $12,000, as a result of which the investor will experience an additional receipt of $13,440 in one year. This can be shown on a time line in the following manner:

```
12,000   (13,440)
├──────────┤
0          1
```

The return on this extra investment can be computed with the use of the following future worth expression:

$$\text{Future worth} = \$12,000(F/P)_{n=1}^{i=?} - \$13,440 = 0$$

The value of the single-amount future worth factor which this equation contains would be found to be 1.12, which corresponds to a rate i of 12 percent in the compound interest tables. Therefore, the return on the extra investment of $12,000 would be 12 percent.

The results of this analysis can be summarized as follows:

	Alternative	
	First note	Second note
Total investment	$24,000	$36,000
Return on total investment	6%	8%
Extra investment	—	$12,000
Return on extra investment	—	12%

For reasons that will become apparent later, it is worth recognizing that the following interpretation can be placed upon these results: The investor has an opportunity to invest $24,000 at 6 percent *plus* an extra $12,000 at 12 percent. If he takes advantage of this opportunity, he will have invested a total of $36,000, which is to say that he will have purchased the second note. Consequently, the $36,000 investment in the second note can be thought of as consisting of two parts. The one part is $24,000 which will yield $25,440, or 6 percent, in one year; the second part is $12,000 which will yield $13,440, or 12 percent, in one year. In other words, the cash flows generated by the second note can be described in the following manner:

$$
\begin{array}{ll}
24{,}000 & (25{,}440) \\
\underline{12{,}000} & \underline{(13{,}440)} \\
36{,}000 & (38{,}880)
\end{array}
$$

```
|—————————|
0         1
```

From this, it follows that the return on the total investment of $36,000 must be the average of the 6 percent and 12 percent returns being realized on the component parts of this investment. But this average must be weighted to reflect the fact that the 6 percent will be earned on $24,000 and that the 12 percent will be earned on only $12,000. The value of this weighted average can be obtained as follows:

$$
\text{Weighted average return} = \frac{\$24{,}000(6\%) + \$12{,}000(12\%)}{\$36{,}000}
$$

$$
= (2/3)(6\%) + (1/3)(12\%)
$$

$$
= 8\%
$$

As was to be expected, this result coincides with the 8 percent that had been calculated earlier as representing the return on the total $36,000 investment in the second note.

Although this concept of a weighted average return is correct and will prove to be useful at a later point, it is imperative to note that, as a rule, it should not be used as a basis for calculating the value of one of three related returns when the other two are known. This is because the weighted average calculation, as carried out in this example, assumes that the respective weights are constant throughout the time period involved in the analysis. But, more often than not, this will not be true. Let us consider why this is so.

Returning to the preceding computation, we observe that 2/3, or 0.67, of the total investment of $36,000 is shown to be invested at 6 percent, and that 1/3, or 0.33, is shown to be invested at 12 percent. Because this alternative has a life of only 1 year, these respective proportions remain unchanged throughout this one-year service period. But with some other cash flow pattern, the proportions may change as time goes by. To illustrate, it may be that one promissory note, which will yield $42,980 in 10 years, is for sale for $24,000 and that a second note, which will yield $77,720 in 10 years, is for sale for $36,000. Therefore, the cash flows to be associated with the first note are as follows:

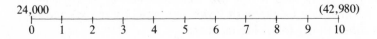

whereas those to be associated with the second are as follows:

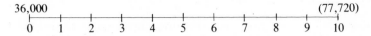

If we begin, as we did before, with a future worth expression for each of these alternatives and equate it to zero, the return on the $24,000 investment would again be found to be 6 percent, and the return on the $36,000 investment would again be found to be 8 percent.

To obtain the return on the $12,000 extra investment in the second note by means of the same approach, we should start by noting that the consequences of this extra investment will be an additional receipt of $34,740 in 10 years. On a time line, this would be described in the following manner:

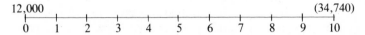

Equating the future worth of these amounts to zero and solving for the rate i which would satisfy this equation, we should obtain a return of 11.2 percent on the extra investment. But suppose that, at this point, someone decides to use the weighted-average approach to see whether it will yield the 8 percent we obtained for the return on the total investment of $36,000 in the second note. He observes that, according to our computations, $24,000 can be invested at 6 percent and that an extra $12,000 can be invested at 11.2 percent. Then, he calculates the weighted average of these respective returns with the use of the following expression:

$$\text{Weighted average return} = \frac{\$24,000(6\%) + \$12,000(11.2\%)}{\$36,000}$$

$$= 0.67(6\%) + 0.33(11.2\%)$$

$$= 7.7\%$$

Obviously, something is wrong, since the expected result of 8 percent has not been obtained. What is wrong is that the weighted-average approach has not been applied properly in this case, and, consequently, the calculated value of 7.7 percent is incorrect. It is incorrect because it stems from a calculation in which it was assumed that the proportion of the total amount invested at 6 percent is 0.67 throughout the entire ten-year period and that the proportion of the total amount invested at 11.2 percent is 0.33 throughout the entire ten-year period. And it so happens that the cash flows involved are such that the respective proportions are not constant; instead, they change with each passing year. To demonstrate this, we shall consider what has occurred after 1 year has elapsed.

At the beginning of the first year, the total investment of $36,000 in the second note can be shown on a time line as being the sum of the following two amounts:

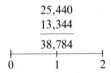

But we know that 6 percent will be earned on the $24,000 portion and that 11.2 percent will be earned on the $12,000 portion. Therefore, by the beginning of the second year, the $24,000 will grow to $24,000 times 1.06, or $25,440; similarly, the $12,000 will grow to $12,000 times 1.112, or $13,344. Because no money is recovered from the alternative at this point, the total investment in the second note during the second year will be as follows:

```
        25,440
        13,344
       ────────
        38,784
├───────────┼───────────┤
0           1           2
```

During the second year, the first portion of the total investment of what is now $38,784 will continue to earn 6 percent, and the second portion will continue to earn 11.2 percent. But this first portion of $25,440 is now equal to 0.65 of the total investment of $38,784, and the second portion of $13,344 is 0.35 of the total investment of $38,784. By comparison, during the first year, the proportion of the total investment that was earning 6 percent was $24,000 divided by $36,000, or 0.67, and the proportion that was earning 11.2 percent was $12,000 divided by $36,000, or 0.33. In brief, to obtain the correct return of 8 percent on the initial total investment in the second note by means of the weighted-average approach, the investor would have to take into account the fact that, in this case, the weights to be assigned to the respective components of this return are not constant throughout the entire service period. It was shown that they changed after one year, and it could be shown, in the manner indicated, that they will continue to change with each passing year.

Since the most common pattern of cash flows generated by an investment alternative is one which causes the values of the appropriate weights to vary from year to year, it will be found that any attempt to apply the weighted-average approach correctly to the determination of an unknown return would necessitate the calculation of the values of these inconstant weights. This will usually prove to be significantly more difficult than what is involved in the approach in which the return is calculated by finding the rate i which yields a uniform annual equivalent, a present worth, or a future worth of zero. This is not to say that there is any flaw in the concept that one of three interrelated returns is the weighted average of the other two. The concept is sound, and we shall make use of it. But, for the reason suggested, we shall not employ it as a basis for rate of return computations.

This brings us to the end of the material which serves as the foundation of the rate of return, or discounted cash flow, method for analyzing a set of mutually exclusive investment alternatives. We shall now go on to the specifics of this technique.

QUESTIONS

6-1 How can the rate of return on the total investment in an alternative be computed with the use of the following:

    a A uniform annual cost expression?
    b A present worth expression?
    c A future worth expression?

6-2 If one of the expressions mentioned in question 6-1 is developed and found to contain only one compound interest factor, how is the unknown rate i ascertained? Under what circumstances would the procedure involved require interpolation?

6-3 If one of the expressions mentioned in question 6-1 is developed and found to contain two or more compound interest factors, how is the unknown rate ascertained? Under what circumstances would the procedure involved require interpolation?

6-4 When the returns on the respective total investments in a number of alternatives are being determined, must equal time periods be taken into consideration? Explain.

6-5 When the rate of return on the extra investment in one alternative as compared with another is being computed, must equal service periods for the two alternatives be considered? Explain.

6-6 One method for determining the return on extra investment begins with a period-by-period comparison of two alternatives' cash-flow patterns. Describe this approach in its entirety. In this description, consider the circumstances under which a trial-and-error procedure is unnecessary, under which a trial-and-error procedure is necessary, under which interpolation is unnecessary, and under which interpolation is necessary.

6-7 Another method for determining the return on extra investment begins with an expression in which the two alternatives' uniform annual costs are shown to be equal. Describe this approach in its entirety. In this description, consider the circumstances under which a trial-and-error procedure is unnecessary, under which a trial-and-error procedure is necessary, under which interpolation is unnecessary, and under which interpolation is necessary.

6-8 Could the determination of the return on extra investment begin with an expression in which the two alternatives' present worths or future worths are shown to be equal? Explain. Ordinarily, is this approach as desirable as the one in which the uniform annual costs are shown to be equal? Explain.

6-9 Does the use of linear interpolation in the process of calculating a rate of return introduce an error in the result? Explain. Is the size of the error likely to be of any significance? Explain.

6-10 What is the relationship among the following rates of return: (1) return on total investment in one alternative, (2) return on total investment in a second alternative, (3) return on extra investment in the one alternative as compared with the other? Under what conditions can this relationship be used as a basis for calculating the value of one of these returns when the other two are known? Under what conditions should this relationship not be used for this purpose?

PROBLEMS

6-1 The board of education of a large city purchased a tract of land for $320,000 with a view to constructing a school on the site at some future time. Twenty-two years later, it became evident that a school would not be needed at that location, and the property was sold. The net receipt was $890,000. No costs were experienced during the period of ownership. What rate of return was realized on the initial investment? Begin the determination in each of the following ways:

    a With an appropriate future worth expression. (Ans. 4.7%)

    b With an appropriate present worth expression.

    c With an appropriate uniform annual cost expression.

6-2 An individual purchased 300 shares of common stock at a total cost of $22 a share. He sold them seven years later and realized net receipts of $24 a share. During the entire period of ownership, he received dividends of $0.39 per share at the end of each quarter. What was his return on total investment? Express this return in the following terms:

    a A rate per quarter.

    b A nominal rate per year.

    c An effective rate per year. (Ans. 8.24%)

6-3 A commissary contractor has paid $20,000 for the right to install and operate food vending machines at a university. This is the only capital investment required of her because she leases the machines from the firm that manufactures them. In any case, she expects average annual receipts from their operation at the university to exceed average annual disbursements by $7,440 during the five-year life of the contract. What return, to the closest whole percent, will she realize on her total investment of $20,000? Arrive at this value with the use of each of the following:

a A uniform annual cost expression.

b A present worth expression.

c A future worth expression.

6-4 A corporation sells a $10,000,000 bond issue to an investment banking concern for $9,000,000. In the course of preparing the issue, the corporation spent $80,000 for such things as engraving costs, registration expenses, and legal fees.

Because the bonds call for an effective annual interest payment of 7.5 percent, the investors in the bonds will receive interest payments which are equivalent to $10,000,000 times 7.5 percent, or $750,000, at the end of each year. The expenses which the corporation will incur in connection with making these interest payments will be $16,000 a year; this will cover such things as clerical costs, postage, and administrative expenses.

If the corporation is going to redeem the bonds at a cost of $10,000,000 at the end of a 20-year period, what will the cost have been, in terms of a rate per year, of the $9,000,000 it received? Begin your determination in each of the following ways:

a With an appropriate present worth expression. (Ans.   8.9%)

b With an appropriate future worth expression.

c With an appropriate uniform annual cost expression.

6-5 A sporting goods store is for sale for $85,000. Another $10,000 would be needed for working capital. A potential buyer estimates that he would operate the store for 10 years and that he could recover his total investment at the end of that period. Meanwhile, annual receipts would be $210,000 the first year and would then increase at a rate of $2,000 a year. Annual disbursements would be $195,000 the first year and would then increase at a rate of $1,500 a year. What is the prospective rate of return on total investment. Compute this with the use of each of the following expressions:

a Future worth.

b Uniform annual cost.

c Present worth.

6-6 A salesman financed the purchase of a new automobile by borrowing $3,000. The repayment plan called for 12 uniform end-of-month payments. The first of these was made one month after the money had been borrowed. The finance corporation's loan officer ascertained the size of the monthly payments on the basis of the institution's "15% plan." The computations involved were as follows:

Amount of loan = $3,000
Interest at 15% = $3,000(0.15) = $450
Total amount owed = $3,000 + $450 = $3,450
Monthly payment = $3,450/12 = $287.50

How much did the money cost the salesman in terms of an interest rate per month? A nominal interest rate per year? An effective interest rate per year? (Ans.   2.2%, 26.4%, 30.2%)

6-7 A manufacturer had been granted a government contract to produce an item of a certain kind for a period of 3 years. The activity necessitated an investment in working capital and in special-purpose equipment which was sold at the end of the third year because it was of no further use to the company.

The total required investment in the project proved to be $517,000. The sum of the recovered working capital and the proceeds from the sale of the equipment was $152,000. During the three-year period, the annual revenues and incremental recurring costs were as follows:

Year	Receipts	Disbursements
1	$363,000	$242,000
2	468,000	338,000
3	405,000	291,000

Ascertain the return that was realized by the manufacturer on his total investment in this activity. Do so with the use of each of the following:

a A present worth expression.
b A future worth expression.
c A uniform annual cost expression.

6-8 A metallurgical laboratory conducts, among other things, mechanical tests for its clients. The manager is giving consideration to making an investment in equipment which will enable the laboratory to carry out tests which it cannot now perform. The equipment would have a first cost of $62,000, a service life of 8 years, and a terminal salvage value of $10,000. There is reason to believe that it would serve to increase average annual revenues by $16,000 and average annual operating costs by $4,000. Calculate the prospective return on total investment with the use of each of the following expressions:

a   Uniform annual cost. (Ans.   12.7%)

 b Present worth.

 c Future worth.

6-9 A stockbroker subscribes to a number of publications prepared by investment advisory services. She has just been notified that one of the subscriptions is expiring and that two renewal plans are available. One calls for a payment of $200 now to renew the subscription for 1 year. The other requires a present payment of $600 to renew the subscription for 4 years. If indications are that the one-year subscription rate will not change in the foreseeable future, what return would the broker realize on her extra investment in the four-year subscription. Determine this in the following ways:

 a By processing the results of a year-by-year comparison of the alternatives' cash flows.

 b By beginning with an expression in which the alternatives' uniform annual costs are shown to be equal.

6-10 A public utility is going to buy one of two pumps. Pump E has a first cost of $10,000, an expected life of 15 years, and a probable salvage value of $1,500. The comparable figures for pump F are $7,500 for its first cost, 10 years for its life, and $1,000 for its salvage value. Annual operating costs will be about $900 with each pump. Calculate the prospective rate of return on the extra investment in pump E. Do so in each of the following ways:

 a By beginning with an expression in which the alternatives' uniform annual costs are shown to be equal. (Ans.   5%)

 b By processing the results of a year-by-year comparison of the alternatives' cash flows.

6-11 A rental service has decided to purchase one of two trucks for leasing purposes. The medium truck costs $25,000, and a heavier truck costs $35,000. Both are expected to have a life of 9 years and a salvage value of $4,000.

 Future revenues from renting the trucks are estimated to be $9,000 a year for the medium truck and $11,300 a year for the heavy truck. Annual recurring costs, for which the lessor will be responsible, are expected to be $2,800 for the medium truck and $3,600 for the heavy truck.

 Compute the value of the indicated return on the extra investment required by the heavy truck. Obtain this value in each of the following ways:

 a By beginning with an expression in which the alternatives' present worths are shown to be equal. (Ans.   6.5%)

 b By processing the results of a year-by-year comparison of the alternatives' cash flows.

6-12 A bank intends to make an additional service available to its customers. The result will be an increase in revenues to the bank. However, a capital investment will have to be made in new equipment.

Equipment of type M requires a total investment of $79,000 and will have a life of 5 years and a terminal salvage value of $8,200. Its operating costs will be $41,000 the first year and will increase at a rate of $700 a year.

Equipment of type R requires a total investment of $93,000 and will have a life of 7 years and a terminal salvage value of $9,000. Its operating costs will be $38,000 the first year and will increase at a rate of $600 a year.

Management estimates that the revenues generated by the service will be unaffected by the choice of equipment and will average $70,000 a year.

What will be the rate of return on the extra investment in equipment R? (Ans. 41.6%)

6-13 The owner of a bookstore believes that she could increase her sales and profits if she were able to increase her stock of books. This would necessitate additional working capital which she does not have. Consequently, she approaches a business acquaintance who might be willing to lend her the necessary funds. She explains to the acquaintance that she has developed two plans for increasing her inventory of books. The first would require that she borrow $14,000. For the use of this money, she would pay the lender $1,820 at the end of each year for 3 years and would also return the $14,000 at the end of the third year. The second plan would require that she borrow $19,000 for a period of 5 years. At the end of each of those years, she would make a payment of $3,040 to the lender and an additional payment of $19,000 at the end of the fifth year.

    a What return on total investment would a lender of $14,000 experience?

    b What return on total investment would a lender of $19,000 realize?

    c What return on extra investment is the bookstore owner offering to someone who will lend her the larger amount?

6-14 In the preceding problem, a lender of $19,000 could think of his return on this amount as being the weighted average of the return he could have obtained on a loan of $14,000 and the return he will realize on his additional loan of $5,000. With the cash-flow patterns involved in this case, it so happens that the appropriate weights are constant throughout the life of each plan. Given this, demonstrate that the return on the $19,000 investment is the weighted average of the respective returns on the $14,000 and the $5,000 investments. Why do the weights remain constant in this case?

6-15 A metal stamping firm owns a punch press which has a market value of $3,400, a remaining economic service life of 5 years, and a terminal salvage value of $800. Future annual operating costs will average $27,000.

A proposed replacement has a first cost of $12,000, an expected life of 10 years, and a terminal salvage value of $2,500. Its future operating costs will average $24,000 a year. There will also be an installation expense of $600.

What is the prospective rate of return on the extra investment in the new press? Determine this by beginning in each of the following ways:

a   With an expression in which the alternatives' future worths are shown to be equal.

b   With an expression in which the alternatives' present worths are shown to be equal.

c   With an expression in which the alternatives' uniform annual costs are shown to be equal.

d   With an expression in which the year-by-year differences between the alternatives are processed.

6-16 There are two mutually exclusive alternatives for carrying out an income-producing activity. A description of the assets required with each is as follows:

	Alternative Y	Alternative Z
First cost	$20,000	$50,000
Economic life	2 years	2 years
Salvage value	$0	$0

Alternative Y will yield net receipts of $13,000 the first year and $11,500 the second. Alternative Z will yield net receipts of $31,000 the first year and $28,000 the second. Ascertain the following rates of return:

a   On the extra investment in alternative Z. (Ans.   10%)

b   On the total investment in alternative Z. (Ans.   12%)

c   On the total investment in alternative Y. (Ans.   15%)

6-17 The cash-flow patterns in the preceding problem are such that the *relative* amount of money invested at a given rate of return is constant from year to year. Accepting this as being true, show that the 12 percent return on the total investment in alternative Z is equal to the weighted average of the 15 percent return on the total investment in alternative Y and the 10 percent return on the extra investment in alternative Z.

7

The Rate of Return or Discounted Cash Flow Method

It has been mentioned that the rate of return method is sometimes called the discounted cash flow method. We shall adopt the first of these names in our discussion of the technique because it is more descriptive than is the other.

With this approach, the potential investor begins by describing each of a set of mutually exclusive investment alternatives in terms of the cash flows it is expected to generate during its service life. If at all possible, this description should be a complete statement of the expenses and receipts which will be experienced with the respective alternatives, so as to permit the analyst to ascertain quantitatively whether a given alternative will yield a satisfactory return on the total investment it requires. As we know, in the event that consideration is given only to those costs and revenues affected by the choice of alternative, judgment must be substituted for a quantitative approach when answering the question of whether a proposed investment is capable of satisfying an established minimum rate of return requirement. While this may be necessary on occasion, it should be avoided if it is at all possible to do so. For the time being, we shall assume that it is possible to do so.

The study proceeds with a calculation of the rates of return on *total* investment that will be realized with the respective alternatives. These prospective returns are compared with the investor's minimum rate-of-return requirement, and, in the absence of irreducible factors, those alternatives which fail to satisfy the requirement are rejected. If no

207

alternatives remain, then no investment is made in the activity involved. Otherwise, the most economical of the remaining alternatives is determined by a process in which a determination and evaluation are made of the returns that will be realized on the *extra* investments required by these remaining alternatives. Why and how this is done can be more easily demonstrated than explained, and, therefore, we must end this general description of the rate of return method with this observation.

The foregoing description, in spite of its generality, suffices to reveal that this technique, like the others we have already considered, is designed to disclose whether any investment at all should be made in a certain activity and, if so, which of the available ways of carrying out the activity is the most economical. The description also serves to bring out the fact that the rate of return method is not a cost comparison method in the strict sense of the term. This is to say that, with this approach, the dollar cost of a proposed course of action is never ascertained. However, as we shall see, an analysis of the prospective returns on the total investments and on the extra investments required by alternative courses of action will enable the investor to identify that alternative which will yield the minimum cost. Hence, the rate of return method proves to be the equivalent of a cost comparison method.

The details of the method will be explained with the use of typical problems. These problems will be selected from those employed in the presentation of the uniform annual cost, present worth, and future worth methods to permit a comparison of the results obtained with the respective methods. It will be recalled that, in the earlier analyses, income tax considerations were taken into account by means of an appropriate adjustment in the investor's minimum rate-of-return requirement, and the same will be true of the analyses to be made at this time. However, the explicit tax consequences of capital investment alternatives will not be disregarded much longer, as indicated by the fact that they will be treated in the next chapter.

THE NEW PRODUCT PROBLEM

The first of the examples presented earlier was one in which a firm was giving consideration to the production and marketing of a new product. The first alternative, K, for doing so necessitated an investment of $84,000 in assets with a four-year life and no salvage value, and an investment of $5,000 in working capital which would not decrease in value; furthermore, annual operating costs would be $30,000, and annual revenues would be $67,000. The second alternative, L, required an investment of $125,000 in assets with a six-year life and a $20,000 salvage value, and an investment of $5,000 in working capital which would not decrease in value; also, annual revenues would be $67,000, and annual operating costs would be $24,000 the first year but would increase thereafter at a rate of $1,000. And, of course, there was the remaining alternative, J, of not producing and marketing the product. Finally, the alternatives were to be compared on a before-tax basis, and the company's minimum rate-of-return requirement before taxes was 20 percent. The latter was arrived at by taking into consideration that 1/4 of the financing would be by debt at a cost of 8 percent, and 3/4 by equity at a before-tax cost of 24 percent.

First Pair of Alternatives. The rate of return analysis begins with a listing of the alternatives in the order of the total investment they require, starting with the lowest. In our example, this enumeration would be as follows:

Alternative	Total investment
J	$ 0
K	89,000
L	130,000

Then, the first two alternatives in such a list are paired and studied to determine which is the more economical. In our example, these are alternatives J and K. A comparison of the two reveals the somewhat obvious fact that the company is going to invest at least $0 in the activity. The question, at this point, is: Can the $89,000 additional investment required by alternative K, as compared with alternative J, be justified? This question is answered by calculating, first, the prospective return on the total investment in alternative K and, second, the prospective return on the extra investment in the same alternative. If *both* of these returns are satisfactory, it will be concluded that alternative K is more economical than alternative J. But if *either* or *both* are unsatisfactory, it will be concluded that alternative K is less economical than alternative J, that is, that it would be more economical not to produce and market the product than to do so with alternative K. As before, a satisfactory return is defined as one which satisfies the company's minimum rate-of-return requirement.

The determination of the return on the total investment of $89,000 in alternative K calls for taking cognizance of the resultant cash flows. These are as follows:

```
84,000
 5,000                                        (5,000)
        30,000      30,000      30,000      30,000
        (67,000)    (67,000)    (67,000)    (67,000)
  ├──────────┼──────────┼──────────┼──────────┤
  0          1          2          3          4
```

Combining certain amounts that appear on this time line, we obtain the following:

```
89,000                                       (5,000)
        (37,000)    (37,000)    (37,000)    (37,000)
  ├──────────┼──────────┼──────────┼──────────┤
  0          1          2          3          4
```

The return on the total investment can be ascertained with the use of the following uniform annual cost expression:

Annual cost $= \$89,000(A\,/\,P)_{n=4}^{i=?} - \$5,000(A\,/\,F)_{n=4}^{i=?} - \$37,000 = 0$

By means of a trial-and-error approach, the following would be found to be true:

i	Annual cost
25%	(−)$ 184
30	(+) 3,274

Interpolating, we obtain a return of 25.3 percent. Because this exceeds the 20 percent minimum rate-of-return requirement, the return on total investment is said to be satisfactory.

To continue, we now go on to determine the return on the extra investment required by alternative K, as compared with alternative J. Actually, no additional computations need be made to arrive at this value. Given that alternative J entails no investment, the extra investment in alternative K will be its total investment of $89,000. Further, since alternative J generates no receipts or operating costs, the consequences of the $89,000 extra investment in alternative K will coincide with the consequences of the $89,000 total investment. Therefore, the return on the extra investment will be equal to the return on the total investment, or to 25.3 percent. Because this exceeds the 20 percent cost of money, it is considered to be satisfactory.

In summary, alternative K yields a satisfactory return on total investment and on extra investment. As a consequence, the total investment can be justified, and alternative K is said to be more attractive than alternative J. Therefore, the latter is dropped from further consideration.

Second Pair of Alternatives. Having rejected alternative J, the company has decided, in effect, to invest at least $89,000 in the activity. The question now becomes: Can the additional investment required by the next alternative on the list be justified? This is answered by comparing this alternative, which is L, with alternative K. The comparison necessitates the determination of the return on the total investment in alternative L and of the return on the extra investment it requires as compared with alternative K. If *both* returns are satisfactory, alternative L will be said to be the more economical of this second pair of alternatives. But if *either* or *both* of the returns are unsatisfactory, the opposite decision will be reached. So let us calculate the return on the $130,000 total investment in alternative L by processing the consequences of this investment, which are as follows:

125,000						(20,000)
5,000						(5,000)
	24,000	25,000	26,000	27,000	28,000	29,000
	(67,000)	(67,000)	(67,000)	(67,000)	(67,000)	(67,000)
0	1	2	3	4	5	6

Combining some of the amounts that appear in this description, we obtain the following:

130,000						(25,000)
	(43,000)	(42,000)	(41,000)	(40,000)	(39,000)	(38,000)
0	1	2	3	4	5	6

One way of calculating the return that will be realized on the $130,000 investment is to begin with the following uniform annual cost expression:

$$\text{Annual cost} = \$130,000(A/P)_{n=6}^{i=?} - \$25,000(A/F)_{n=6}^{i=?} - \$43,000$$

$$+ \$1,000(A/G)_{n=6}^{i=?} = 0$$

A trial-and-error approach must be employed in the solution of this equation, and, when it is, the results are as follows:

i	Annual cost
20%	(−)$4,447
25	(+) 692

The necessary interpolation yields 24.3 percent as the return on the total investment of $130,000. Since this exceeds the 20 percent cost of money, the return is considered to be satisfactory.

The study continues with a comparison of alternatives K and L to determine the return that will be realized on the extra investment required by alternative L. Suppose this will be done by the method in which the year-by-year differences between the alternatives' cash flows are ascertained. This necessitates taking equal time periods into consideration. If the equal time-period requirement is satisfied by assuming that the respective cash-flow patterns will repeat themselves, the resultant service period will be 12 years, and the following cash flows, in thousands of dollars, will be obtained for alternative K:

89   89   89
              (5)   (5)   (5)
    (37) (37) (37) (37) (37) (37) (37) (37) (37) (37) (37) (37)
├─────┼─────┼─────┼─────┼─────┼─────┼─────┼─────┼─────┼─────┼─────┤
0   1   2   3   4   5   6   7   8   9   10   11   12

The comparable cash flows for alternative L will be as follows:

130   130
                (25)   (25)
    (43) (42) (41) (40) (39) (38) (43) (42) (41) (40) (39) (38)
├─────┼─────┼─────┼─────┼─────┼─────┼─────┼─────┼─────┼─────┼─────┤
0   1   2   3   4   5   6   7   8   9   10   11   12

A year-by-year comparison discloses that the consequences of the $41,000 extra investment in alternative L will be as follows:

41   (84)   105   (84)   (20)
      (6)   (5)   (4)   (3)   (2)   (1)   (6)   (5)   (4)   (3)   (2)   (1)
├─────┼─────┼─────┼─────┼─────┼─────┼─────┼─────┼─────┼─────┼─────┤
0   1   2   3   4   5   6   7   8   9   10   11   12

The pattern here is such that it is probably simplest to arrive at the return on the extra investment by setting up the following present worth expression:

$$\text{Present worth} = \$41,000 - \$84,000(P/F)_{n=4}^{i=?} + \$105,000(P/F)_{n=6}^{i=?}$$
$$- \$84,000(P/F)_{n=8}^{i=?} - \$20,000(P/F)_{n=12}^{i=?}$$
$$- \$6,000(P/A)_{n=12}^{i=?} + \$1,000(A/G)_{n=6}^{i=?}(P/A)_{n=12}^{i=?}$$
$$= 0$$

For the rates indicated, the following present worth values would be obtained:

i	Present worth
20%	(−)$3,980
25	(+) 3,253

and, by interpolation, a rate of 22.7 percent would be found to be the return on the extra investment in alternative L. This is greater than the minimum rate-of-return requirement of 20 percent and, therefore, is satisfactory.

As we know, a second method for ascertaining the return on the extra investment in alternative L is to determine the rate i which equates the uniform annual costs of alternatives K and L. If the assumption regarding the nature of future replacements remains unchanged, this method can be applied with the use of the uniform annual cost expressions which we developed in the course of calculating the returns on the total investments in the respective alternatives. The result would be as follows:

$$\$130,000(A/P)_{n=6}^{i=?} - \$25,000(A/F)_{n=6}^{i=?} - \$43,000 + \$1,000(A/G)_{n=6}^{i=?}$$

$$= \$89,000(A/P)_{n=4}^{i=?} - \$5,000(A/F)_{n=4}^{i=?} - \$37,000$$

which yields

$$\$130,000(A/P)_{n=6}^{i=?} - \$25,000(A/F)_{n=6}^{i=?} + \$1,000(A/G)_{n=6}^{i=?}$$

$$- \$89,000(A/P)_{n=4}^{i=?} + \$5,000(A/F)_{n=4}^{i=?} - \$6,000 = 0$$

By trial-and-error, the rate i would be found to be 22.7 percent, just as it was with the first method.

To summarize, alternative L generates a return of 24.3 percent on a total investment of $130,000; therefore, it is satisfactory from that standpoint. Also, the alternative generates a return of 22.7 percent on the extra investment of $41,000 that it requires. Since this too is satisfactory, the extra investment can be justified and, as a consequence, should be made. Hence, alternative L has proved to be more economical than alternative K; so the latter is rejected at this point in the analysis.

It should be stressed that alternative L was compared with alternative K because alternative K had been found to be more economical than the alternative of not producing and marketing the product, that is, alternative J. If alternative K had not proved to be more economical than alternative J, alternative L would have been compared with alternative J; under those circumstances, the required extra investment in alternative L would be the total investment of $130,000, and the return on the extra investment would be the 24.3 percent return on the total investment. In brief, a rejected alternative is never used as a basis for evaluating another course of action. This is because what has been rejected may be so bad that some other alternative, which is also undesirable but to a lesser degree, may erroneously appear to be desirable by comparison with the rejected alternative.

In any event, given that no alternatives remain in our problem, the study has been completed, except for the need to evaluate irreducible factors. But, in the absence of these factors, alternative L is the most attractive alternative, and this coincides with the decision reached when the uniform annual cost, present worth, and future worth techniques were applied.

The Results Explained. The specific results obtained when this problem was analyzed by means of the uniform annual cost, present worth, and future worth methods were as follows:

Alternative	Uniform annual cost	Present worth	Future worth
J	$ 0	$ 0	$ 0
K	(−) 3,551	(−) 15,763	(−) 140,552
L	(−) 4,447	(−) 19,740	(−) 176,017

and the following is a summary of the outcome of the rate of return analysis:

	Alternative		
	J	K	L
Total investment	$0	$89,000	$130,000
Return on total investment	—	25.3%	24.3%
Extra investment	$0	$89,000	$ 41,000
Return on extra investment	—	25.3%	22.7%

As was to be expected, there is no inconsistency in these results. The calculated returns on total investment are greater than the company's 20 percent cost of money, and the negative values of the calculated costs indicated that this would prove to be the case. Also, an analysis of the calculated returns on extra investment served to identify alternative L as being the most economical, and so did an analysis of the calculated costs.

It might be mentioned that, as we know, if alternatives K and L had yielded positive total costs, both would have been rejected in favor of alternative J, that is, the alternative of making no investment in the activity involved. Similarly, if the returns on the respective total investments in these alternatives had been found to be lower than the firm's cost of money, both alternatives would have been rejected in favor of alternative J. Hence, the rate of return method, like the others, enables a potential investor to determine whether an investment of a certain kind should be made and, if so, which is the most economical of a set of mutually exclusive alternatives for carrying out the activity involved.

But let us now return to the actual rates of return obtained in our example. It would not be surprising if someone were troubled by the fact that, although alternative L seems to be more attractive than alternative K, its return of 24.3 percent on total investment is *lower* than the return of 25.3 percent on the total investment in alternative K. This fact, however, is irrelevant. That this is true can be demonstrated with the use of the idea that one of three interrelated rates of return is the weighted average of the other two.

The return of 24.3 percent on the total investment of $130,000 in alternative L can be thought of in the following terms: Of this total amount, $89,000 could be invested in alternative K at 25.3 percent. However, alternative L presents the company with an opportunity to invest an additional $41,000 at 22.7 percent. If advantage is taken of this opportunity, $130,000 will be invested. The return on this total will be the weighted average of the 25.3 percent return on the $89,000 portion and the 22.7 percent return on the $41,000 portion. This average will be equal to

$$\text{Average return} = \frac{\$89,000(25.3\%) + \$41,000(22.7\%)}{\$130,000} \approx 24.3\%$$

As the approximation sign suggests, this expression will not yield a result of exactly 24.3 percent. This is because the appropriate weights will vary from year to year, and, therefore, the constant weights on which the foregoing expression is based will introduce a slight error into the result. Nevertheless, the concept embodied in this expression is correct.

An examination of the expression reveals that the return on total investment decreases from 25.3 percent for alternative K to 24.3 percent for alternative L because the 25.3 percent return is being averaged with the smaller return of 22.7 percent on the extra investment. However, we must now recall that the firm's rate-of-return requirement of 20 percent represents its cost of money. This cost was arrived at, as mentioned earlier, by taking into consideration that 1/4 of any total investment in the activity would be financed by debt funds at a cost of 8 percent, and 3/4 by equity funds at a cost of 24 percent. Consequently, if the company does not invest the extra $41,000 in alternative L, 1/4 of this amount will in effect be used to reduce debt at a saving of 8 percent, and 3/4 of this amount will be invested in other sources at a return of 24 percent. Therefore, the average return on this $41,000 will then be 20 percent. So if the firm were to decide to produce and market the product with alternative K instead of alternative L, it would be deciding to invest only $89,000 in the activity at a return of 25.3 percent and to invest the remaining $41,000 elsewhere at a return of 20 percent. This would serve to generate the following return on the total investment of $130,000:

$$\text{Average return} = \frac{\$89,000(25.3\%) + \$41,000(20.0\%)}{\$130,000} = 23.6\%$$

With the realization that the weights are approximate, we observe that the result of this course of action would be a return of about 23.6 percent on a total investment of $130,000, as compared with the 24.3 percent that could have been realized by investing the entire $130,000 in alternative L. In brief, while it is true that a decision to invest in alternative L will serve to reduce the return that will be realized on the resultant total investment, a decision not to invest in alternative L will bring about an even greater decrease in the return on the resultant total investment. It is for this reason that we say that, in the absence of irreducible factors, an investor should take advantage of every opportunity to invest available additional funds in sources which will yield a return on these funds that is equal to or greater than his cost of money, as represented by his minimum rate-of-return requirement.

The concept of an average return also helps to explain why, in a rate of return study, some analysts compute the returns on the respective extra investments in the alternatives but not on the respective total investments. They then reach a decision by evaluating only the returns on extra investment. In our example, this approach would be applied as follows: To begin with, the return on the *extra* investment in alternative K, as compared with alternative J, would be computed and found to be 25.3 percent. Because the analyst realizes that the extra investment in this case is equal to the total investment, he knows that the return on total investment will also be 25.3 percent, but he does not bother to state this. Instead, it is simply concluded that, given a 20 percent cost of money, the extra investment is justified; so alternative J is rejected. Next, the return on the extra investment in alternative L, as compared with alternative K, is computed and found to be 22.7 percent. This extra investment can also be justified; so now alternative K is rejected. No attempt is made to calculate the return on the total investment in alternative L because of the realization that there is no real need to do so. This stems from the fact that, if the return on the total investment in alternative K exceeds 20 percent and if the return on the extra investment in alternative L exceeds 20 percent, the average of these two returns will also exceed 20 percent. Since this average represents the return on the total investment in alternative L, it follows that the return on total investment will be satisfactory. While there is nothing wrong with this approach, we shall continue to compute returns on both total and extra investments whenever it is possible to do so. The reason for this is that a knowledge of the values of all these returns is often useful in the evaluation of irreducible factors.

A Forecasted Replacement. The equal time-period requirement was satisfied in the preceding analysis by an assumption regarding the nature of future replacements. Given this assumption, we were able to say that, although the 25.3 percent annual return on the total investment in alternative K was computed by processing its cash flows for only 4 years, this return would continue for 12 years because these cash flows would repeat themselves every 4 years. Similarly, although the 24.3 percent annual return on the total investment in alternative L was computed by processing its cash flows for only 6 years, we were able to say that this return would continue for 12 years because these cash flows would repeat themselves every 6 years. And, of course, since the 22.7 percent annual return on the extra investment in alternative L was obtained by comparing cash flows for a 12-year period, that return would be said to prevail for 12 years.

If the firm chooses not to make some such assumption, it must forecast the nature of future replacements. And as we saw in the uniform annual cost, present worth, and future worth analyses of this problem, it *may* be that a forecasted replacement will generate a decision other than the one arrived at on the basis of an assumed replacement. This was demonstrated in those earlier analyses by supposing that alternative K would be replaced by assets which had a first cost of $47,000, a life of 2 years, and a zero salvage value; which would yield annual operating costs of $22,000 and annual revenues of $67,000; and which would continue to require $5,000 in working capital. When these data were added to those applicable to alternative K, the following cash flows were obtained:

84,000				47,000		
5,000						(5,000)
	30,000	30,000	30,000	30,000	22,000	22,000
	(67,000)	(67,000)	(67,000)	(67,000)	(67,000)	(67,000)
0	1	2	3	4	5	6

Because this six-year time period coincided with the six-year life of alternative L, no additional forecasting was required, and the costs of the respective alternatives were calculated for this period and compared. To apply the rate of return method under these same conditions, we should begin by ascertaining the return on the total investment in alternative K. Since it is no longer being assumed that the cash-flow pattern for the first 4 years will repeat itself, it is now necessary to process the cash flows for the six-year service period in the course of calculating this return. By combining some of the values in the preceding time line, we obtain the following description of these cash flows:

```
89,000                                    47,000
      (37,000)   (37,000)   (37,000)   (37,000)   (45,000)   (50,000)
  |_____|_____|_____|_____|_____|_____|
  0        1        2        3        4        5        6
```

The return on the $89,000 total investment can be found by solving the following present worth expression for the unknown rate i:

$$\text{Present worth} = \$89,000 + \$47,000(P/F)_{n=4}^{i=?} - \$37,000(P/A)_{n=4}^{i=?}$$

$$- \$45,000(P/F)_{n=5}^{i=?} - \$50,000(P/F)_{n=6}^{i=?} = 0$$

By trial-and-error, a rate of 28.6 percent would be obtained. This is the return not only on the total investment in alternative K but also on the extra investment it requires as compared with alternative J, that is, with the alternative of not producing the product. Both of these returns exceed the 20 percent requirement, and so they are satisfactory. Therefore, alternative J is rejected at this point, and the study continues with an analysis of alternative L.

The cash flows for alternative L during the six-year period are the same as those considered when the assumption regarding future replacements was made. These were as follows:

```
130,000                                              (25,000)
      (43,000)   (42,000)   (41,000)   (40,000)   (39,000)   (38,000)
  |_____|_____|_____|_____|_____|_____|
  0        1        2        3        4        5        6
```

Although the return on this total investment has already been determined, if it had not been, it could be by solving the following present worth expression for the unknown rate i:

$$\text{Present worth} = \$130,000 - \$25,000(P/F)_{n=6}^{i=?} - \$43,000(P/A)_{n=6}^{i=?}$$

$$+ \$1,000(P/G)_{n=6}^{i=?} = 0$$

By trial-and-error, the return would be found to be, as it was before, 24.3 percent. Since this is satisfactory, the return on the extra investment in alternative L, as compared with alternative K, would now be ascertained. Given that expressions are available for the present worths of these two alternatives, the simplest way to calculate this return is probably by finding the rate i which will make these present worths equal. With the use of the foregoing present worth expressions, we can begin by stating that

$$\$130,000 - \$25,000(P/F)_{n=6}^{i=?} - \$43,000(P/A)_{n=6}^{i=?} + \$1,000(P/G)_{n=6}^{i=?}$$

$$= \$89,000 + \$47,000(P/F)_{n=4}^{i=?} - \$37,000(P/A)_{n=4}^{i=?}$$

$$- \$45,000(P/F)_{n=5}^{i=?} - \$50,000(P/F)_{n=6}^{i=?}$$

If the terms from the right side of the equation are moved to the left side, a value of zero remains on the right. It would then be found, by trial-and-error, that the sum of the terms on the left side is equal to zero for a rate i of 16.5 percent. This return on the extra \$41,000 investment required by alternative L, when compared to the minimum requirement of 20 percent, proves to be unsatisfactory. Consequently, the extra investment in alternative L is not justified, and we conclude that alternative K is the most economical alternative. This decision agrees with the one reached when this set of circumstances was analyzed by the uniform annual cost and present worth techniques. The results of those analyses and those of the rate of return analysis can be summarized as follows:

Alternative	Uniform annual cost	Present worth	Return on total investment	Return on extra investment
J	$ 0	$ 0	— %	— %
K	(−) 5,704	(−) 18,968	28.6	28.6
L	(−) 4,447	(−) 14,791	24.3	16.5

An examination of this summary discloses that the return on total investment decreases from 28.6 percent for alternative K to 24.3 percent for alternative L, because the 28.6 percent is being averaged with the 16.5 percent return on the extra investment in alternative L. However, this 16.5 percent is not sufficiently low to reduce the return on the total investment in alternative L to a value which is obviously unsatisfactory, that is, to a value below 20 percent. As this suggests, an alternative may prove to be uneconomical in spite of the fact that its return on total investment exceeds the established minimum rate-of-return requirement. In this specific case, by investing the extra \$41,000 elsewhere at 20 percent instead of in alternative L at 16.5 percent, the company could increase its return on the total investment of \$130,000 to some value greater than 24.3 percent. Hence, it would be uneconomical to invest the extra \$41,000 in alternative L.

But the primary reason for this analysis of the new product problem on the basis of a forecasted replacement was to demonstrate that the nature of future replacements may have an effect on which of the currently-available alternatives is the most economical. Hence, the characteristics of these future replacements must either be forecasted or assumed. And if they are assumed, the fact that the assumption may not be correct must be treated as an irreducible.

THE REPLACEMENT PROBLEM

At one point in the preceding example, it was stated that, *whenever possible*, returns on total investment would be computed for the respective alternatives even though the most economical alternative can be identified by an analysis of returns on extra investment only. However, before returns on total investment can be ascertained, it is necessary that the respective alternatives be described completely in terms of all the revenues and costs they are expected to generate. If, for example, revenues are not given, there is no way of computing the return on the total investment in some investment alternative.

But as was pointed out when the other analytical techniques were being described, there are circumstances under which it is not possible to obtain the required complete descriptions. In those cases, it is necessary for the investor to decide, on the basis of judgment, whether the return on a total investment will be satisfactory. If he decides that it will be, the analysis can continue with the processing of only those revenues and costs which are affected by the choice of alternative. How this is done with the uniform annual cost, present worth, and future worth methods was explained with the use of a replacement problem, and the same problem will be used to explain the application of the rate of return method under such circumstances.

The Relevant Data. In the replacement example, a building contractor was considering the replacement of a currently-owned unit of construction equipment. One alternative was to keep the old equipment one more year, another was to keep it two more years, and a third was to replace it now. It so happens that, with the rate of return method, such multiple alternative problems must be treated in a special way which it is best to avoid for the moment. Therefore, we shall simplify the problem by recalling that it had been found that the old asset's economic life was 2 years and by assuming that the contractor had succeeded in predicting that this would be the economic life. As a consequence, it will be necessary to compare only the alternative of keeping the old equipment two more years with the alternative of replacing it immediately.

The old equipment had a market value of $3,600, an estimated salvage value of $800 at the end of its two-year life, expected repair and maintenance costs of $960 for the first year and $1,140 for the second, and fuel costs that would exceed those of the new equipment by $190 a year. The new equipment had a first cost of $11,900, a four-year life, a $3,900 salvage value, and annual repair and maintenance costs of $120, $200, $310, and $540, respectively. A before-tax analysis was to be made with the use of a value of 15 percent for the contractor's cost of money, that is, for his minimum rate-of-return requirement.

In the analysis, no consideration was to be given to the alternative of retiring the old equipment and not replacing it because, in the contractor's judgment, the return on the required total investment in the most economical of the remaining alternatives would be satisfactory. It was for this reason that the two alternative courses of action were described in terms of only those costs and revenues that would be affected by the choice of alternative.

The Analysis. The study begins, in this case, with the realization that a decision has already been made to invest a minimum of $3,600 in the activity; this amount is the market value of the old asset. Another way of stating this is to say that it is being assumed that the return on the total investment of $3,600 in the old equipment will be at least 15 percent; incidentally, this will also be the assumed return on the $3,600 extra investment called for by this alternative as compared with the alternative of making no investment in the activity. The only question to be answered is: Can the extra investment called for by the new equipment, as compared with the old equipment, be justified? This question is answered with the rate of return method by calculating the prospective return on this extra investment and comparing it with the established requirement.

To compute this return, we can begin with the following description of the new equipment's cash flows:

```
11,900                                    (3,900)
           120         200        310       540
  |----------+----------+----------+----------|
  0          1          2          3          4
```

These can then be compared with those of the old equipment during the same period. Given the assumption that the old equipment's cost pattern for the first 2 years will repeat itself in the subsequent two-year period, the old equipment's cash flows during the next 4 years would be as follows:

```
3,600                 3,600
                      (800)                (800)
           960        1,140      960       1,140
           190         190       190        190
  |----------+----------+----------+----------|
  0          1          2          3          4
```

A year-by-year comparison of these two cash-flow patterns discloses that the new equipment calls for an extra investment of $8,300 and that the consequences of this extra investment will be as follows:

8,300   (1,030)   (3,930)   (840)   (3,890)
├─────────────┼──────────────┼─────────────┼────────────┤
0   1   2   3   4

The return on this extra investment can be calculated by solving for the unknown rate i in the following present worth expression:

$$\text{Present worth} = \$8,300 - \$1,030(P/F)_{n=1}^{i=?} - \$3,930(P/F)_{n=2}^{i=?}$$

$$- \$840(P/F)_{n=3}^{i=?} - \$3,890(P/F)_{n=4}^{i=?} = 0$$

A trial-and-error approach would yield a return of 5.8 percent. When this is compared with the minimum requirement of 15 percent, it must be concluded that, in the absence of irreducible factors, the extra investment of $8,300 is not warranted. Therefore, the alternative of keeping the old equipment for two more years is more economical than the alternative of replacing it now. This coincides with the decision reached on the basis of the uniform annual cost, present worth, and future worth analyses, which yielded the following results:

Alternative	Uniform annual cost	Present worth	Future worth
Retain old equipment 2 years	$3,076	$ 8,782	$15,359
Replace old equipment now	3,657	10,440	18,260

The fact that we are unable to calculate the return on the total investment in the new equipment is of no consequence. We know, of course, that it is being assumed that this return will be at least 15 percent for the old equipment. Therefore, the return on the total investment in the new equipment will be the weighted average of this rate of at least 15 percent and of the 5.8 percent return on the extra investment in the new equipment. This 5.8 percent may or may not reduce the return on total investment for the new equipment to some value less than 15 percent. But it does not matter whether it does or does not; what does matter is that, instead of investing an extra $8,300 in the new equipment at 5.8 percent, the contractor can invest the $8,300 elsewhere at the more attractive return of 15 percent.

However, had the calculated return on extra investment equaled or exceeded 15 percent, a different decision would have been made. Furthermore, we could take it for granted, in that case, that the return on the total investment in the new equipment would have also been at least 15 percent. Again, this follows from the concept of an average return. If the return on the $3,600 investment in the old equipment is assumed to be at least 15 percent and if it is found that the return on the $8,300 extra investment in the new equipment is at least 15 percent, then the return on the resultant total investment of $11,900 must be at least 15 percent.

To summarize, in this type of problem in which the alternative of making no investment is rejected on the basis of judgment, the rate of return analysis begins with the assumption that the returns on total and extra investments will be satisfactory for that alternative of the remaining two which calls for the lower total investment at this time. Then, the return on extra investment is ascertained for the alternative which calls for an additional investment at this time. If this return is equal to or exceeds the investor's cost of money, the extra investment should be made; otherwise, it should not.

A MULTIPLE-ALTERNATIVE PROBLEM

We shall now consider the application of the rate of return method in a multiple-alternative problem. As we know, this type of problem poses no difficulties when it is to be analyzed by means of either the annual cost, present worth, or future worth methods. The application of any one of these methods simply requires that the total costs of the respective alternatives be calculated and compared. Unfortunately, the application of the rate of return method does not prove to be as straightforward. This is not to say that the procedure involved is particularly complex, but its correct application does require a knowledge and understanding of the specific steps it entails. These steps can be best explained with the use of an example.

The Example. Suppose that a distributor of replacement parts for various types of electronic equipment is confronted by a number of proposals regarding the inventory levels he should maintain. Alternative 1 is to maintain inventories at their current levels; this will require no investment in additional stock. Alternative 2 is to invest $12,000 in additional inventories; this will serve to reduce the cost of lost customer orders and to increase the cost of storage, but the net annual saving will be $1,920. Because the distributor plans to terminate his business activities in 7 years, the estimated net annual saving with this second alternative will continue for only that length of time. Furthermore, the additional stock is not expected to decrease in value, and so the terminal salvage value of the $12,000 investment will be $12,000.

There are five other alternatives, all of which are similar to alternative 2. Each requires some present investment in additional stock; each has a seven-year life; each has a salvage value equal to 100 percent of the amount invested; and each will generate a net annual saving in the cost of lost customer orders. The seven alternatives are also characterized by the fact that the higher the investment in additional stock, the higher will be the corresponding annual saving. Specifically, the alternatives can be described as follows:

| | | Receipts | |
Alternative	Required total investment	End-of-year saving for 7 years	Salvage at end of 7th year
1	$ 0	$ 0	$ 0
2	12,000	1,920	12,000
3	15,000	2,730	15,000
4	20,000	3,000	20,000
5	22,000	3,210	22,000
6	29,000	5,170	29,000
7	33,000	5,780	33,000

The distributor would like to ascertain which of these mutually exclusive alternatives is the most economical by means of a rate of return analysis. The study is to be made on a before-tax basis, and a minimum before-tax rate-of-return requirement of 15 percent has been established.

The Procedure. It might be noted that the cash-flow patterns for the respective alternatives have been developed with a view to minimizing the amount of work which will be required to compute rates of return in this example. This has been done so that we can focus our attention on the elements of the procedure without being distracted by computational details which, hopefully, have been adequately covered in earlier examples.

The first step in the procedure is to list the alternatives in the order of the respective total investments they require, beginning with the lowest. This has been done in the preceding table, and, therefore, we can proceed to the next step. In general, this step calls for breaking down the given multiple-alternative problem into a series of two-alternative problems and arriving at a decision by a process of elimination. More specifically, the initial two-alternative problem in our example would be created by pairing the first two alternatives on our list, that is, alternatives 1 and 2; then, the more economical of these two alternatives is determined by the means applicable to any two-alternative problem. This more economical alternative would then be paired with the next alternative on the list, alternative 3, and the more economical of these two alternatives ascertained. Next, this more economical alternative would be paired with the next alternative on the list, alternative 4, and the more economical of these two alternatives determined. The procedure would continue until all but one of the alternatives had been eliminated.

If the distributor were to apply this approach, he would begin by raising the question of whether alternative 2 is more attractive than the alternative of making no investment in additional inventories, that is, than alternative 1. The answer to this question necessitates the determination of the return on the total investment in alternative 2 and of the return on the extra investment in alternative 2 as compared with alternative 1. In the event that both of these returns satisfy the established requirement of 15 percent, it will be concluded that alternative 2 is preferable to alternative 1. Therefore, the analysis proceeds with the calculation of the return on the total investment in alternative 2, whose cash flows are as follows:

```
12,000                                                            (12,000)
       (1,920)   (1,920)   (1,920)   (1,920)   (1,920)   (1,920)   (1,920)
  |--------+---------+---------+---------+---------+---------+---------|
  0        1         2         3         4         5         6         7
```

The return can be computed with the use of the following expression:

Annual cost $= \$12{,}000(A/P)_{n=7}^{i=?} - \$12{,}000(A/F)_{n=7}^{i=?} - \$1{,}920 = 0$

But it is now helpful to recall that, for a given i and n, the difference between the present-amount annuity factor and the future-amount annuity factor is equal to the rate i. Therefore, the preceding expression will assume the following form:

$\$12{,}000(i) - \$1{,}920 = 0$

from which i is found to be 16 percent.

That this answer is correct becomes apparent when we recognize that the entire \$1,920 annual saving is a dollar return on the \$12,000 investment. In other words, none of it represents a partial recovery of the \$12,000 investment because the \$12,000 is recovered as a single sum at the end of the seventh year. Given that the annual *dollar* return is \$1,920 on an investment of \$12,000 which does not decrease in value, the annual *rate* of return must be \$1,920 divided by \$12,000, or 16 percent. But it is imperative to keep in mind that the return can be obtained this easily only when the salvage value is equal to the initial total investment; in other cases, it might be necessary to solve for the value of an unknown compound interest factor or to employ a trial-and-error approach.

Since all the alternatives in our example have a 100 percent salvage value, the returns on their respective total investments can be found in the same simple way. These returns will not be used at this particular point in the analysis and, therefore, could be computed later, but they will be found to be as shown in Table 7-1.

What is needed at this point is a knowledge of the return on the extra investment of $12,000 required by alternative 2 as compared with alternative 1. Suffice it to say that this return will be equal to the 16.0 percent return on the total investment, because the extra investment is equal to the total investment and its consequences coincide with those of the total investment. Since both returns exceed the minimum requirement of 15 percent, the distributor should conclude that alternative 2 is more economical than alternative 1 and go on to compare alternative 2 with the next alternative on the list, which is alternative 3.

TABLE 7-1   Determination of returns on total investment

Alternative (a)	Total investment (b)	Annual saving (c)	Return on total investment $(d = c \div b)$
1	$ 0	$ 0	— %
2	12,000	1,920	16.0
3	15,000	2,730	18.2
4	20,000	3,000	15.0
5	22,000	3,210	14.6
6	29,000	5,170	17.8
7	33,000	5,780	17.5

As shown in Table 7-1, the return on the total investment in alternative 3 will be 18.2 percent, which is satisfactory. To obtain the return on the extra investment it requires as compared with alternative 2, we begin by examining the given data and find that this extra investment will be $3,000, that the additional annual saving will be $810, and that the additional salvage value will be $3,000. On a time line, all this would appear as follows:

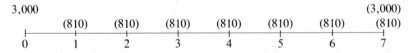

3,000   (3,000)
        (810)   (810)   (810)   (810)   (810)   (810)   (810)
  ├──────────┼──────────┼──────────┼──────────┼──────────┼──────────┼──────────┤
  0   1   2   3   4   5   6   7

Again, the case is a special one in the sense that the investment involved has a 100 percent salvage value. Therefore, the return on the extra investment will be $810 divided by $3,000, or 27.0 percent. This also is satisfactory, with the result that alternative 2 is rejected, and alternative 3 becomes the most attractive alternative of those considered thus far.

Alternative 3 is now compared with alternative 4. From Table 7-1, it is found that the return on the total investment in alternative 4 is 15.0 percent. This just satisfies the minimum rate-of-return requirement. But when the return on the extra investment is calculated as shown in Table 7-2, the result is 5.4 percent. Since the latter is below 15 percent, it is unsatisfactory, and alternative 4 is rejected.

The next alternative on the list is alternative 5. This alternative is not compared with alternative 4, which has just been rejected, but with alternative 3, which was found to be more economical than alternative 4. An examination of Tables 7-1 and 7-2 reveals that the return on the total investment in alternative 5 is 14.6 percent and that the return

TABLE 7-2   Determination of returns on extra investment

Alternative (a)	Alternative with which compared (b)	Extra investment (c)	Additional annual saving (d)	Return on extra investment (e = d ÷ c)
1	—	$ 0	$ 0	— %
2	1	12,000	1,920	16.0
3	2	3,000	810	27.0
4	3	5,000	270	5.4
5	3	7,000	480	6.9
6	3	14,000	2,440	17.4
7	6	4,000	610	15.2

on the extra investment is 6.9 percent. Both are below the required 15 percent, and so alternative 3 remains the most attractive.

Alternative 3 is now paired with alternative 6. In Tables 7-1 and 7-2, the returns for alternative 6 are shown to be 17.8 percent on the total investment and 17.4 percent on the extra investment. Each exceeds the minimum requirement, and so alternative 3 is rejected in favor of alternative 6.

Finally, alternative 6 is compared with alternative 7. The return on the total investment in alternative 7, as computed in Table 7-1, is 17.5 percent, and the return on its extra investment, as computed in Table 7-2, is 15.2 percent. Both of these returns are satisfactory, and, consequently, alternative 7 is accepted. Given that no alternatives remain to be evaluated, the analysis ends with a decision that, in the absence of irreducible factors, alternative 7 represents the most economical course of action.

A Summary. The results of the preceding analysis can be summarized as shown in Table 7-3. A review of this summary reveals that the calculated returns are consistent with those to be expected from an application of the idea that one of three interrelated returns is the weighted average of the other two. To illustrate, let us consider alternatives 2 and 3. Having found that the return on total investment increases from 16.0 percent for alternative 2 to 18.2 percent for alternative 3, we should deduce that the return on the extra investment in alternative 3 exceeds 18.2 percent, since it succeeds in raising the overall return to this level. This deduction proves to be correct, because the return on the extra investment happens to be 27.0 percent.

TABLE 7-3 Summary of calculated returns on total and extra investments

Alternative	Total investment	Return on total investment	Alternative with which compared	Extra investment	Return on extra investment
1	$ 0	— %	—	$ 0	— %
2	12,000	16.0	1	12,000	16.0
3	15,000	18.2	2	3,000	27.0
4	20,000	15.0	3	5,000	5.4
5	22,000	14.6	3	7,000	6.9
6	29,000	17.8	3	14,000	17.4
7	33,000	17.5	6	4,000	15.2

As another example, it was found that the return on total investment decreases from 15.0 percent for alternative 4 to 14.6 percent for alternative 5, and this should permit us to conclude that only a return of less than 14.6 percent on the extra investment in alternative 5 would serve to reduce the overall return to 14.6 percent. Such a conclusion would prove to be correct, because the return on the extra investment is actually 6.9 percent. This example also reveals why an alternative whose return on total investment is unsatisfactory will be an alternative whose return on extra investment is also unsatisfactory. The reason is that only a return on extra investment which is below the required return is able to reduce the return on total investment to a level which is below the required return. Hence, alternative 5 could have been dropped from further consideration as soon as it was determined that the return on its total investment is less than the investor's minimum rate-of-return requirement. However, there is nothing to lose by calculating those returns on extra investment which, theoretically, need not be calculated, and it may be that a knowledge of such returns will prove to be useful in the evaluation of irreducible factors.

Finally, it should be recognized that alternative 7 would also prove to be the most economical on the basis of a uniform annual cost, present worth, or future worth comparison. At a rate of 15 percent, these costs would assume the values contained in the following table, and, as can be seen, the lowest of these values is to be associated with alternative 7:

Alternative	Annual cost	Present worth	Future worth
1	$ 0	$ 0	$ 0
2	(−) 120	(−) 499	(−) 1,328
3	(−) 480	(−) 1,997	(−) 5,312
4	0	0	0
5	(+) 90	(+) 374	(+) 996
6	(−) 820	(−) 3,411	(−) 9,075
7	(−) 830	(−) 3,453	(−) 9,186

ANOTHER MULTIPLE-ALTERNATIVE PROBLEM

The multiple alternative problem just considered was one in which each alternative was described in a way which permitted the determination of the prospective rates of return on the total and on the extra investments in the respective alternatives. These rates enabled the distributor to ascertain not only that alternative 7 was the most economical of the alternatives that called for making some investment in higher inventory levels, but that alternative 7 was also more economical than the alternative of making no investment of the type being proposed.

We shall now consider a multiple-alternative problem in which it is not possible to calculate returns on total investment. This is the case when the alternatives cannot be described completely in terms of all their costs and ievenues, but only in terms of those costs and revenues which will be affected by the choice of alternative. As will be shown with the use of an example, the application of the rate of return method under such circumstances calls for deciding, on the basis of judgment, whether the returns on total investment will be satisfactory and, if it is decided that they will be, going on to compute and evaluate returns on the respective extra investments. In general the procedure is similar to the one employed in a two-alternative problem when returns on total investment cannot be computed.

An Illustration. Suppose that the management of a manufacturing concern finds it necessary to relocate certain work stations in its plant to provide space for the installation of new equipment. The plant layout department has developed four different plans for the relocation. These can be described as follows:

	Plan			
	W	X	Y	Z
Cost of relocation	$6,000	$10,000	$12,000	$15,000
Life of layout	3 years	5 years	5 years	5 years
Annual handling costs	$22,400	$21,000	$19,800	$19,200

The data for plan W are to be interpreted as follows: If $6,000 is spent on relocating facilities at this time, the resultant layout will be satisfactory for 3 years and will result in materials handling costs of $22,400 a year. As the data for the remaining plans suggest, the current layout can be changed to a greater degree by spending more than $6,000 at this time, and the result will be a layout which will be adequate for a longer period of time than 3 years and a layout which will generate annual handling costs of less than $22,400.

The plant layout analyst wants to determine which of these plans is the most economical. He realizes that this necessitates comparing equal time periods and decides to satisfy this requirement by forecasting rather than assuming what will occur 3 years from now in the event that plan W is adopted. His forecast is that $5,000 will be spent at that time to modify the layout in a way which will extend its life for 2 more years, but which will have no effect on the annual materials handling costs of $22,400.

No estimate has been made of the annual revenues to be associated with each plan because it is not possible to ascertain what portion of the firm's total annual revenues is attributable to the arrangement of the production facilities involved. However, there is every reason to believe that these revenues will be unaffected by the plan chosen. Furthermore, on the basis of judgment, management has decided that the revenues will suffice to justify an expenditure of at least $6,000 at this time to provide space for the new equipment; in other words, it is being assumed that the return on the total investment in plan W will satisfy the firm's minimum rate-of-return requirement.

Finally, no salvage value is being assigned to any of the plans because each of the proposed layouts will be obsolete at the end of its life, and, of course, an obsolete layout will have no value.

The four plans are to be compared by the rate of return method on a before-tax basis with the use of a 10 percent minimum rate-of-return requirement.

The Study. Having been told that it is necessary to relocate certain work stations, the analyst has no choice but to begin by rejecting the alternative of making no revision in the current layout. The remaining four plans must then be listed, as they already have been, in the order of the respective total present investments they require, beginning with the lowest. This listing reveals that a decision has been made to invest a minimum of $6,000 in the relayout activity. The question to be answered is: Can any of the extra investments required by the other plans be justified? As in the case of the preceding multiple-alternative problem, this question is answered by breaking down the given problem into a series of two-alternative problems and arriving at the most economical alternative by a process of elimination. However, in this case, the process is based on an analysis of returns on extra investments, and it is assumed that the alternative selected on this basis will yield a satisfactory return on the total investment it requires.

In our example, the first two-alternative problem in the series of such problems will contain plans W and X. Given the assumption that an investment in plan W is justified, we need determine only whether the extra investment required by plan X is warranted. This determination calls for computing and evaluating the return on the extra investment in plan X as compared with plan W.

We know that the cash flows with plan W during the five-year study period will be as follows:

```
6,000                      5,000
        22,400    22,400    22,400    22,400    22,400
  |--------+---------+---------+---------+---------|
  0        1         2         3         4         5
```

and that the cash flows with plan X during the same period will be as follows:

```
10,000
        21,000    21,000    21,000    21,000    21,000
  |--------+---------+---------+---------+---------|
  0        1         2         3         4         5
```

A year-by-year comparison of these two patterns discloses that the consequences of the $4,000 extra investment in plan X can be described in the following manner:

```
4,000                      (5,000)
       (1,400)   (1,400)   (1,400)   (1,400)   (1,400)
  |--------+---------+---------+---------+---------|
  0        1         2         3         4         5
```

To obtain the unknown return on this extra investment, we can start by setting up the following expression:

Present worth = $4,000 - $5,000(P/F)_{n=3}^{i=?} - $1,400(P/A)_{n=5}^{i=?} = 0$

By a trial-and-error method, the return will be found to be 48.8 percent. Since this exceeds the 10 percent requirement, the extra investment can be justified, and plan X is said to be more attractive than plan W. Incidentally, if the assumption was correct that the return on the total investment in plan W will be satisfactory, it is now correct to assume that the return on the total investment in plan X will also be satisfactory. This is because this return will be the average of the return on the total investment in plan W and the return on the extra investment in plan X. Therefore, if each of these two values is equal to or exceeds 10 percent, their average must be at least 10 percent.

The analysis continues with a comparison of plan X and the next alternative on the list, plan Y, whose cash flows were estimated to be as follows:

12,000

	19,800	19,800	19,800	19,800	19,800
0	1	2	3	4	5

When these are compared with those of plan X, the following differences are obtained:

2,000

	(1,200)	(1,200)	(1,200)	(1,200)	(1,200)
0	1	2	3	4	5

The return on the indicated $2,000 extra investment in plan Y as compared with plan X can be determined by first solving the following expression for the value of the compound interest factor it contains:

Annual equivalent = $2,000(A/P)_{n=5}^{i=?} - $1,200 = 0$

The value of this factor proves to be 0.6000, and, from the compound interest tables, the corresponding rate i is found to be 52.8 percent. Because this is greater than the minimum rate-of-return requirement of 10 percent, the conclusion is reached that plan Y is more economical than plan X. And if the return on the total investment in plan X is at least 10 percent, investing an extra $2,000 in plan Y at 52.8 percent will serve to yield a return on the total investment in plan Y which exceeds 10 percent; so the return on the total investment in plan Y must be satisfactory.

Finally, plan Y is paired with plan Z, which is the next alternative on the list. Plan Z is expected to generate the following cash flows:

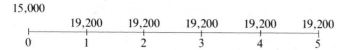

When these are compared with those of plan Y, the following differences are obtained:

The return on this extra investment of $3,000 could be computed by solving for the rate i which will yield a value of zero for the annual equivalent, present worth, or future worth of these amounts. But an examination of this cash-flow pattern reveals that the extra investment of $3,000 is exactly equal to the sum of the future savings of $600 a year for 5 years. Since these savings will permit the firm to recover only its investment of $3,000, the return on this investment must be zero percent. Therefore, given a 10 percent requirement, the analyst should reject the proposal that plan Z be selected and that the required extra investment of $3,000 be made. In this case, it is not possible to say anything specific regarding the return on the total investment in plan Z. We know that the return of zero percent on the extra investment it requires will reduce the return on its total investment to some value which is lower than the return on the total investment in plan Y. But there is no way of ascertaining whether this value will be less than the required 10 percent. However, this is of no consequence because the unsatisfactory return on the extra investment suffices to eliminate the plan. The result is that the study ends with a decision that, in the absence of irreducible factors, plan Y is the most economical of the four alternatives.

Summary of Results. The results of the rate of return analysis of the problem under consideration can be summarized as follows:

Plan	Total investment	Plan with which compared	Extra investment	Return on extra investment
W	$ 6,000	—	$ —	— %
X	10,000	W	4,000	48.8
Y	12,000	X	2,000	52.8
Z	15,000	Y	3,000	0.0

No value is shown in this summary for the extra investment in plan

W because this value did not enter into the computations; however, the extra investment is $6,000 as compared with the alternative of not relocating certain work stations in the plant. Further, no value is shown for the return on this extra investment because the available data did not permit the calculation of this value; but given that the extra investment of $6,000 is equal to the total investment of $6,000 and given the assumption that the return on the total investment will be at least 10 percent, it follows that the return on the extra investment will be at least 10 percent.

The only other thing that might be mentioned is that, had this problem been analyzed by the uniform annual cost, present worth, or future worth method, plan Y would have been found to be the most economical with any one of these methods, just as it was with the rate of return method. At a 10 percent cost of money, these other techniques would have yielded the following results, and, as an examination of these results discloses, the lowest total cost is to be associated with plan Y:

Plan	Annual cost	Present worth	Future worth
W	$24,974	$94,676	$152,466
X	23,638	89,612	144,310
Y	22,966	87,064	140,207
Z	23,157	87,788	141,373

INTERNAL VERSUS EXTERNAL RETURNS

This example brings us to the end of our discussion of the way in which the rate of return method is applied in the analysis of a set of mutually exclusive investment alternatives. As we saw, this method, like the ones described earlier, is capable not only of identifying the most economical of such a set of alternatives, but also of revealing whether this alternative is more attractive than the alternative of making no investment of the type being proposed. But before going on to consider why some investors prefer the rate of return method to the other analytical techniques, let us pause to examine an important assumption which underlies this method.

In an earlier chapter, it was pointed out that, in the uniform annual cost, present worth, and future worth methods, the realistic assumption is made that any net receipts generated by an alternative during its life will be reinvested elsewhere at a rate i equal to the rate used in the determination of the total cost of the alternative. This rate was referred to as the "external rate." As opposed to this, in the rate of return method, the assumption is made that such net receipts will be reinvested elsewhere at a rate i equal to the calculated rate of return. This rate is referred to as the "internal rate." However, this assumption happens to be somewhat less realistic than the preceding one. Why this is so and the consequences of its being so can be seen best with the use of an example. In this example, we shall deal with a calculated return on extra investment only, because, as stated at an earlier point, a rate of return analysis can be based solely on an evaluation of returns on extra investment.

A Repayment Problem. Let us suppose that an individual has an opportunity to lend someone an extra $10,000 for a period of 2 years. At the end of that period, the borrower will repay $12,544. All this would appear as follows on a time line:

```
10,000          (12,544)
├───────────┼───────────┤
0           1           2
```

The question is: If the investor's minimum rate-of-return requirement is 6 percent, should he lend the additional $10,000? To arrive at an answer, we can calculate the prospective return on the $10,000 and compare it with the 6 percent requirement. If this were done, a return of 12 percent would be obtained, and the proposed extra investment would be said to be justified.

It so happens that, in this case, the cash flows are such that the reinvestment rate assumption, which underlies the rate of return method, is correct. At a rate of 12 percent, the lender will have earned $1,200 in interest at the end of the first year. Since this is not withdrawn, he is, in effect, reinvesting the $1,200 in the same loan with the result that, during the second year, he will earn 12 percent on this $1,200 and on the original $10,000, or on a total of $11,200. As a consequence, by the end of the second year, the value of his investment will have grown to $11,200 times 1.12, or $12,544.

But we shall now assume a different repayment plan. This is not to say that the investor has a choice of plans but simply that he is offered a single plan and that it now is as follows: At the end of each year for two years, the borrower will make an interest payment of $1,200, and, at the end of the second year, he will also return the principal of $10,000. On a time line, this repayment plan can be described in the following manner:

```
10,000          (10,000)
       (1,200)  (1,200)
├───────────┼───────────┤
0           1           2
```

This cash-flow pattern will also yield a value of 12 percent for the return on the lender's $10,000 extra investment. However, in this case as opposed to the first one, the 12 percent value will be an overstatement. Let us consider why this is so.

Because the investor will receive $1,200 at the end of year 1, this amount will be available for investment elsewhere. His established minimum rate-of-return requirement of 6 percent tells us that he is able to invest funds elsewhere at 6 percent. Therefore, the $1,200 will be reinvested at 6 percent and will grow to $1,200 times 1.06, or $1,272, by the end of year 2. When this amount is added to the $11,200 that will be received at that point from the original investment, the investor will have a total of $12,472 on hand. In brief, the end result of this second repayment plan will be as follows:

```
10,000            (12,472)
├─────────┼─────────┤
0         1         2
```

The important thing is that this $12,472 is less than the $12,544 generated by the first repayment plan. And, if we were to calculate the return on an extra investment of $10,000 which yields $12,472 in 2 years, we should obtain a value of 11.7 percent. This is less than 12 percent because, while the $10,000 earns 12 percent per year for 2 years, the $1,200 which is reinvested at the end of the first year earns 6 percent for 1 year. The result is that the average return decreases to 11.7 percent per year for 2 years on what is really a combination of two different investments. By comparison, with the first repayment plan, the $10,000 earns 12 percent per year for 2 years, and the $1,200 which is reinvested at the end of the first year earns 12 percent for 1 year; therefore, the average return remains at 12 percent for 2 years.

The issue here is not whether one of these repayment plans is more advantageous to the lender than is the other. Obviously, the first one is, and a proper rate of return analysis would succeed in disclosing this to an investor who must choose between the two plans. In an analysis of this kind, the investor would recognize that, in the first plan as compared with the second, he will receive $1,200 less at point 1 and $1,344 more at point 2. On a time line, this would appear as follows:

```
        1,200   (1,344)
├─────────┼─────────┤
0         1         2
```

In effect, the first plan calls for an extra investment of $1,200 at the end of the first year, as a result of which an additional $1,344 will be received at the end of the second year. To determine whether this extra investment is worthwhile, the lender can calculate the prospective return on the \$1,200 with the use of the following expression:

Present worth $= \$1,200(P/F)_{n=1}^{i=?} - \$1,344(P/F)_{n=2}^{i=?} = 0$

A trial-and-error approach would yield a return of 12 percent. Since this exceeds the 6 percent requirement, the extra investment at the end of the first year would be justified, and the first plan emerges as the more attractive of the two. This is as was to be expected because the first plan provides the investor with an opportunity to reinvest \$1,200 at 12 percent, whereas the second plan provides the investor with an opportunity to reinvest that amount at only 6 percent.

But, in our example, the situation was not one in which the potential lender had to choose between these plans, but one in which a single specific repayment plan was being offered. And it was found that a rate of return analysis will result in an overstatement of the actual return on the extra investment of \$10,000 if the repayment plan being offered happens to be the following one:

```
10,000           (10,000)
        (1,200)   (1,200)
├───────────┼───────────┤
0           1           2
```

Specifically, in this case, the calculated return was 12 percent, but the actual return proved to be only 11.7 percent. Therefore, the question is whether this characteristic of the rate of return method will ever result in its indicating that an extra investment should be made at this time when such an investment would be uneconomical. The answer to this question is that it will not. This will be explained with the use of the foregoing cash-flow pattern which, for purposes of discussion, we shall suppose is the only repayment plan being offered to a potential lender of an extra \$10,000.

What must be recognized is that, for the repayment plan under consideration, the calculated return of 12 percent does represent the return that will be realized on some portion of the money invested during the study period involved. Admittedly, the return that will be realized on the portion represented by the reinvested funds will be equal to only the investor's 6 percent minimum rate-of-return requirement. However, the lender's alternative is to reject the proposal to invest an extra \$10,000 at this time at a return which is the weighted average of 12 percent and 6 percent and, instead, to invest the entire \$10,000 in some other source at 6 percent. Obviously, a combination of 12 percent and 6 percent is more attractive than just 6 percent. From this, it follows that, at worst, the rate of return method may serve to mislead an investor with regard to what portion of his initial investment will be earning the calculated return during the entire study period; but so long as what remains of the initial investment continues to earn a return which equals or exceeds the rate which that balance could be earning elsewhere, the initial investment should be made.

To put all this differently, it is true that, in the rate of return method, the somewhat unrealistic assumption is made that net receipts realized during an alternative's life will be reinvested at a rate equal to the calculated return which, in our example, is 12 percent. Consequently, the lender in our example is led to believe that the result of his investing $10,000 at this time will be that he will accumulate $12,544 in 2 years even if he is paid the 12 percent interest on this $10,000 at the end of each year. But, actually, it is more likely that the return on his reinvested funds will be equal to his cost of money, that is, to 6 percent. Therefore, he will have, as we found earlier, only $12,472 in 2 years. However, his alternative is to invest the entire $10,000 elsewhere at 6 percent, and it can be shown that doing so would yield $11,236 in 2 years. In brief, although $12,472 is less than the expected $12,544, it is more than the $11,236.

Let us now turn our attention to the fact that the calculated return may, on occasion, understate the actual return. To illustrate, the repayment plan offered to the potential lender of an extra $10,000 may be as follows:

```
10,000   (5,000)   (5,000)
 |_____|_____|
 0          1         2
```

Because the two $5,000 payments suffice to repay only the $10,000 principal of the additional loan, the calculated return on the extra investment will be zero percent. Hence, given a return requirement of 6 percent, the extra investment should not be made. But, in this case, the actual return per year for 2 years would prove to be more than zero percent. If the $5,000 received at the end of the first year is reinvested elsewhere at 6 percent, it will increase to $5,300 by the end of the second year. When this is added to the second payment of $5,000 that will be received at that point, the investor will have $10,300 at the end of 2 years as a result of a present extra investment of $10,000, and the corresponding return would prove to be almost 1.5 percent. Yet, the fact remains that a portion of the $10,000 will be earning zero percent during the two-year period, and, therefore, the extra investment should not be made because this portion could be invested in some other source at 6 percent. Again, the result of the rate of return analysis might mislead the investor into believing that the entire $10,000 will be earning no return during the two-year period, but it does not mislead him regarding the best course of action.

To summarize, if applied correctly, the rate of return method is just as capable of identifying the most economical of a set of mutually exclusive alternatives as are the other analytical techniques, in spite of what may be an erroneous assumption with respect to the return that can be realized on reinvested funds. But it is true that, because the calculated return may overstate or understate the actual return, investment alternatives that are *not* mutually exclusive cannot be ranked in the order of their attractiveness on the basis of such calculated returns. However, as will be explained later, uniform annual costs, present worths, and future worths of such alternatives are also unsuitable for this purpose. Fortunately, this is of no consequence for reasons that will be presented when this matter of ranking alternatives that are *not* mutually exclusive is considered in the last chapter of this presentation.

DISADVANTAGES OF THE METHOD

While it is true that all the analytical techniques considered thus far will lead to the same decision in a given problem, it is also true that the rate of return method is, more often than not, the most difficult to apply. The examples presented suffice to demonstrate that the mechanics of computing returns are certainly more tedious and time consuming than those of computing, at some stipulated cost of money, the uniform annual costs, present worths, or future worths of a set of mutually exclusive investment alternatives. However, it might be noted that computer programs have been developed for calculating rates of return, and, therefore, if automatic data processing equipment is available, these computational difficulties can be avoided. But the fact remains that not all analysts have access to such equipment.

Also, the procedure for handling multiple-alternative problems by means of the rate of return method is a cumbersome one as compared with the procedure involved in the annual cost, present worth, or future worth approach. And care must be exercised when applying the rate of return procedure in such problems to ensure that the alternatives are evaluated in the correct order; otherwise, serious errors can result.

Another disadvantage is that the results of a rate of return analysis are more likely to be misinterpreted than are those obtained with the use of one of the other methods. To illustrate, it is not unusual for an investor to conclude that the most attractive alternative is the one with the highest return on total investment when, in reality, an analysis of returns on extra investment may reveal that this is not the case.

Then, there are those situations in which the rate of return approach does not lend itself for use because of the nature of the alternatives involved. In this method, the total investment in an alternative is defined as being a *single* sum of money which will be spent at a *present* point in time. But this is not the form that a total investment always assumes. For example, a company might be evaluating various proposals for constructing a new plant. Each of these is likely to require a *series* of capital expenditures over a period of two or three years for such things as the acquisition of land, the construction of a building, and the procurement and installation of equipment. In this instance, unless these costs are first converted to a single payment equivalent at some rate *i*, it becomes difficult to apply the concept of a return on total investment.

A similar difficulty may arise when an attempt is made to compute the return on an extra investment. In the rate of return method, the extra investment in an alternative is represented by the *single* additional sum of money that must be invested at a *present* point in time in the event that one alternative is selected instead of another. But if two alternatives are being compared whose respective total investments consist of a series of capital expenditures during, say, the first two or three years of their lives, the difference between these total investments will yield an extra investment which also consists of a *series* of amounts. And it now becomes difficult to apply the concept of a return on extra investment. Or, in another case, two alternatives may require the same total investment at the present time, with the result that, strictly speaking, no extra investment is necessary in the one as compared with the other. As was shown in the repayment-plan example considered in the discussion of internal versus external returns, it may still be possible to evaluate such alternatives by the rate of return method, but the best way of doing so might not be apparent, and the result may be difficult to interpret.

Finally, the rate of return method will occasionally yield more than one value for the return on a given investment, and, as might be expected, this can prove to be troublesome. But let us consider this point in more detail.

Multiple Returns. Suppose that an individual has an opportunity to invest $5,000 in an activity which will yield a net receipt of $11,500 at the end of the first year of its two-year life and a net expense of $6,600 at the end of the second year. On a time line, this would appear as follows:

```
5,000   (11,500)   6,600
├──────────┼──────────┤
0          1          2
```

The only other alternative is not to make the investment, and so

$5,000 represents the total investment and the extra investment in the alternative under consideration. The return on these investments can be obtained with the use of the following future worth expression:

$$\text{Future worth} = \$5,000(F/P)_{n=2}^{i=?} - \$11,500(F/P)_{n=1}^{i=?} + \$6,600 = 0$$

By trial and error, it would be found that two rates will yield a future worth of zero. These are 10 and 20 percent, and, therefore, the indicated rate of return is equal to each of these values.

To gain an appreciation of the question this kind of result can raise, let us now suppose that the investor's minimum rate-of-return requirement is 16 percent. Given this requirement, it is not clear whether the requirement is being met by the alternative. The calculated return of 20 percent suggests that it is, but the calculated return of 10 percent suggests that it is not. However, the matter can be clarified by computing the total cost of this alternative at various rates i. This cost can assume the form of an annual equivalent, present worth, or future worth. If the last of these is arbitrarily selected for purposes of illustration, the future worths of the involved cash flows at various rates will be found to be as follows:

Rate	Future worth	Rate	Future worth	Rate	Future worth
5%	(+)$38	12%	(−)$ 8	19%	(−)$ 4
6	(+) 28	13	(−) 10	20	0
7	(+) 20	14	(−) 12	21	(+) 4
8	(+) 12	15	(−) 13	22	(+) 12
9	(+) 4	16	(−) 12	23	(+) 20
10	0	17	(−) 10	24	(+) 28
11	(−) 4	18	(−) 8	25	(+) 38

Since the future worth of the alternative of not investing in the activity is zero dollars, it follows from an examination of the signs of these results that the $5,000 investment is warranted if the minimum rate-of-return requirement is any value from 10 to 20 percent, but not if it is either less than 10 percent or more than 20 percent. And, of course, had uniform annual costs or present worths been calculated, the same conclusion would have been reached because the sign of a calculated uniform annual equivalent or present worth will be the same as the sign of the corresponding future worth. In any event, what has been accomplished by this determination of the total cost of the alternative at various rates i is that we now know how the result of the rate of return analysis is to be interpreted. Namely, if the investor's minimum rate-of-return requirement is any value between the calculated returns of 10 and 20 percent, the $5,000 investment should be made; otherwise, it should not.

Admittedly, this kind of recommendation may not appear to make sense under certain circumstances. More specifically, a potential investor would find it difficult to understand why an investment opportunity which is attractive when his cost of money is 16 percent would be unattractive if his cost of money were only 5 percent. Unfortunately, there is no way of explaining this on an intuitive basis. About all that can be said is that, with certain cash-flow patterns, this proves to be the case.

But it is important to recognize that anomalies of this type stem from the cash-flow pattern that happens to exist and not from the method by means of which the cash flows are analyzed. Therefore, although the potential investor in our example would find it difficult to understand why two different rates of return were obtained, it is likely that he would also find it difficult to understand why the calculated future worths changed from positive values to negative values and then back to positive values. From this, it follows that the rate of return analysis does not create such situations but simply serves to reveal their existence. In other words, had the investor in our example applied the uniform annual cost, present worth, or future worth method using his 16 percent cost of money, he would have obtained a negative value for the calculated cost and, in the absence of irreducible factors, would have simply decided that the investment was justified. But having applied the rate of return method, he obtained a result which, although correct, created a problem of interpretation whose solution disclosed the presence of a somewhat confusing set of circumstances.

Nevertheless, the fact remains that, in these cases, the rate of return approach does create a problem of interpretation which can be avoided with any one of the other analytical techniques. And it might be mentioned that this problem of interpretation can be even greater than it was in our example. This is because it is possible that a given cash-flow pattern may be such that it will yield more than two rates of return. Also, not all the multiple returns that may be found to exist will necessarily be positive; some may prove to be negative or even imaginary numbers.

Yet, care must be taken not to exaggerate the practical implications of this disadvantage of the rate of return method. Cash-flow combinations which yield multiple returns are rarely encountered. For them to occur, it is necessary that the cumulative value of the annual cash flows change sign more than once. To illustrate, these cumulative values in our example are as follows:

End of year	Cash flow	Cumulative cash flow
0	(+)$ 5,000	(+)$5,000
1	(−) 11,500	(−) 6,500
2	(+) 6,600	(+) 100

As can be seen in the last column, the sign of the cumulative cash flow changed twice. Since this is more than once, a multiple-rate solution becomes a possibility. This is not to say that more than one rate *will* be obtained whenever the sign of the cumulative cash flow changes more than once, but only that more than one rate *might* be obtained. Nevertheless, anyone engaged in a rate of return analysis is advised to check the signs of the cumulative cash-flow values to ascertain whether a multiple-rate solution is possible. Unless this is done, an analyst may stop as soon as one rate is found and fail to discover that other rates exist. And it might be that this single rate will lead to an incorrect decision. For example, had the investor in our illustration terminated the analysis when he obtained a value of 10 percent for the return, he would have erroneously concluded that, given a 16 percent cost of money, the investment could not be justified. But having gone on to obtain 20 percent as the second value for the return, he was eventually able to reach the correct conclusion that the investment will satisfy a 16 percent rate-of-return requirement.

It should also be mentioned that, when the sign of the cumulative cash flow changes in the described manner, it is also possible that no rate can be found which will yield a value of zero for the uniform annual equivalent, present worth, or future worth of the involved series of annual cash flows. This would be true in the case of an alternative which generates, for example, the following combination of revenues and expenses:

(1,000) 2,000 (1,500)
|———+———|
0   1   2

If, say, the present worth of these amounts were computed at various rates, it would be found, first, that no rate will yield a present worth of zero and, second, that every rate will yield a negative present worth. More specifically, the present worth gets closest to zero at a rate of 50 percent but never reaches it. This is suggested by the following partial description of the results that a present worth determination at various rates would yield:

Rate	Present worth
48%	(−)$333.45
49	(−) 333.36
50	(−) 333.34
51	(−) 333.36
52	(−) 333.45

Obviously, a rate of return analysis would not enable an investor to evaluate such an alternative for the simple reason that it is not possible to obtain a value for the rate of return. And, yet, each of the other analytical techniques could be applied with no difficulty in this case and would reveal that this specific alternative will satisfy any established rate-of-return requirement. Incidentally, it would also have been impossible to calculate a rate of return if the signs of the three amounts in this cash-flow pattern were the opposite of those given. But, in that event, the present worth of the alternative would prove to be positive at all rates, and, therefore, the investment could not be justified regardless of what value the minimum rate-of-return requirement assumed.

However, the typical investment alternative is one in which an initial expenditure is followed by a combination of revenues and expenses such that the sign of the cumulative cash flow changes only once, that is, from positive to negative. Hence, the occurrence of a situation in which no rate can be obtained or in which multiple rates are obtained is the exception rather than the rule. But when the situation does occur, the investment analyst will find it either necessary or convenient to abandon the rate of return approach in that particular case and adopt one of the other analytical techniques.

ADVANTAGES OF THE METHOD

To summarize, the typical set of mutually exclusive investment alternatives lends itself to analysis by means of the rate of return method, as well as by means of the uniform annual cost, present worth, and future worth methods. In such cases, a need arises for deciding whether the rate of return or some other approach should be employed. Those who select the rate of return method frequently do so for a reason which stems from a feature which the method possesses. This is that a potential investor can calculate the value of a prospective return without first having established a minimum rate-of-return requirement. As opposed to this, a uniform annual cost, present worth, or future worth can be calculated only after such a requirement has been established.

Let us consider why this may be an advantage of the rate of return method.

We know that, when a potential investor is ascertaining his cost of money, he must consider the proportion and cost of debt financing and the proportion and cost of equity financing. The cost of each of these types of financing will be a function of such things as the administrative expenses that might be incurred, anticipated changes in the purchasing power of money, the risks involved, and the tax aspects of a given situation. The nature of these factors is such that the determination of the cost of money is no simple task. In fact, it may prove to be so difficult that an investor might, in an extreme case, maintain that he is unable to estimate this cost for a given combination of circumstances. And, yet, this very same investor, in spite of his inability to establish a minimum rate-of-return requirement, may be capable of responding to the value of an indicated rate of return. This is to say that, although he does not have a specific requirement in mind, he is able to decide whether a calculated prospective return on a certain kind of total or extra investment is satisfactory.

When this condition prevails, it is clear that a comparison of uniform annual costs, present worths, or future worths is not feasible due to the unavailability of the rate i which must enter into the determination of such costs. As a consequence, the rate of return method emerges as the only possible approach despite the fact that, theoretically, the calculated returns cannot be evaluated in the absence of a stipulated minimum required rate i. But, in practice, this evaluation can be made on the basis of judgment.

The rate of return method will also be preferred by those investors who find it easier to evaluate irreducible factors by studying the differences among prospective returns than by studying the differences among uniform annual costs, present worths, or future worths. Therefore, when irreducible factors assume an important role in the decision-making process, such investors would favor the rate of return method in spite of some of its disadvantages.

Of course, even those individuals, who prefer the rate of return approach for one or both of the aforementioned reasons, may find it expedient to select some other technique in situations in which multiple returns occur or no return can be computed or the initial investment assumes the form of a series of expenditures or no extra investment is required. But these situations arise infrequently, and, hence, ample opportunities exist for taking advantage of the possible benefits to be associated with a rate of return analysis. Whether these benefits are more than offset by the disadvantages must be determined on the basis of personal judgment. And this judgment may dictate that, in a given organization, certain kinds of investment problems should be subjected to a rate of return analysis and that others should be analyzed by means of one or more of the other available methods.

QUESTIONS

7-1 How must an investment alternative be described before the return on the total investment it requires can be calculated?

7-2 Must all the expenses and receipts generated by two alternatives be known before the return on the extra investment required by one of them can be calculated? Explain.

7-3 Describe the procedure for applying the rate of return, or discounted cash flow, method when two alternatives are being compared which are described in terms of all the expenses and receipts they are expected to generate.

7-4 Even in those cases in which it is possible to ascertain returns on total investment, can the most economical alternative be identified by an analysis of only the returns on extra investment? Explain.

7-5 Under what circumstances can the costs and revenues, which are unaffected by the choice of alternative, be ignored when comparing investment alternatives by the rate of return method?

7-6 How is the rate of return method applied in a two-alternative problem when it is possible to describe the alternatives only in terms of the differences between them?

7-7 What is the procedure for analyzing a multiple-alternative problem by the rate of return method when a complete description of the alternatives' cash flows has been provided?

7-8 How is the rate of return method applied in a multiple-alternative problem when it is possible to describe the alternatives only in terms of the differences among them?

7-9 Why must investment alternatives be compared for equal time periods with the rate of return method? How can this requirement be satisfied?

7-10 After an alternative is rejected, should it ever be used as a basis for evaluating another alternative? Explain.

7-11 When mutually exclusive investment alternatives are being compared, will the one that yields the largest return on total investment always prove to be the most economical? Explain.

7-12 Can an alternative which yields a satisfactory return on total investment ever yield an unsatisfactory return on the extra investment it requires? Explain.

7-13 Can an alternative which yields an unsatisfactory return on total investment ever yield a satisfactory return on the extra investment it requires? Explain.

7-14 What is the difference between an internal return and an external return?

7-15 What assumption, regarding the reinvestment rate, underlies the discounted cash flow method?

7-16 Why is it said that the calculated rate of return might either overstate or understate the actual return? Under what condition will this prove not to be the case?

7-17 In the event that the calculated return does overstate or understate the actual return, does this occurrence interfere with the rate of return method's ability to identify the most economical of a set of mutually exclusive investment alternatives? Explain.

7-18 What type of cash-flow pattern might yield either multiple returns or no value for the return?

7-19 Are there any circumstances under which the rate of return method cannot be used to analyze a set of mutually exclusive investment alternatives?

7-20 What are the disadvantages of the rate of return, or discounted cash flow, method as compared with the uniform annual cost, present worth, and future worth methods? The advantages?

PROBLEMS

7-1 The owner of a machine shop has been losing certain orders because of his inability to promise satisfactory delivery dates. The difficulty stems from the limited output capacity of one of his departments in which boring operations are performed. To increase this capacity, he is thinking of buying another boring machine.

A machine with the required features is available from two different sources. Each of these units of equipment has the following characteristics:

	Machine E	Machine F
First cost	$72,000	$96,000
Life	9 years	12 years
Salvage value	$14,000	$18,000
Annual disbursements	$63,000	$60,000

Either unit is expected to generate additional revenues of $81,000 a year and will necessitate raising funds at a cost of 15 percent.

Should an investment be made in new equipment of this type? If so, which of the two alternatives is the more economical? Answer these questions on the basis of the results of the following analyses:

a Rate of return. (Ans.   21.3%, 19.8%; 21.3%, 15.7%)
b Uniform annual cost. (Ans.   −$3,743, −$3,909)
c Present worth. (Ans.   −$24,786, −$25,885)
d Future worth. (Ans.   −$3,970,402, −$4,146,487)

7-2 A chemical analyzer is going to be purchased for use in a laboratory. A new unit is available for $97,500. About 5 percent of this amount can be expected to be recovered in the form of a salvage value at the end of the equipment's estimated 14-year service life. The average annual cost of a maintenance contract during this life will be approximately $5,000.

A used analyzer is available at a cost of $54,000. Its economic life is estimated to be 7 years, and its terminal salvage value to be $2,000. The cost of a maintenance contract for this equipment during its life will be about $6,000 a year. All other cash flows will be unaffected by the choice of equipment.

Which of these alternatives is the more economical, given a 25 percent minimum rate-of-return requirement? Answer this question on the basis of each of the following:

a A rate of return analysis. (Ans.   6.5%)
b A uniform annual cost analysis. (Ans. $30,440, $22,953)
c A future worth analysis. (Ans. $2,646,728, $1,995,740)
d A present worth analysis. (Ans. $116,403, $87,772)

7-3 Among the annuities which can be purchased from an insurance company are the following two: Under the first plan, an individual is required to invest $20,000 at the present time; he then receives $2,980 at the end of each year for the next 10 years. Under the second plan, an individual is required to invest $25,000 at the present time; he then receives $4,070 at the end of each year for the next 10 years.

Should someone whose minimum rate-of-return requirement is 6 percent invest in either of these plans? If so, which one? Make your decision after having ascertained the following for the respective plans:

a Relevant rates of return.
b Present worths.
c Uniform annual costs.
d Future worths.

7-4 A series of transmission-line towers is to be constructed. The question to be answered is whether the towers should be built of steel or aluminum. The cost of a steel tower will be $9,675, which is lower than the $11,110 first cost of an aluminum tower. However, annual maintenance expenses for each steel tower are expected to be $200 higher than for an aluminum tower. The estimated service life with either material is 50 years, and there will be no difference between the respective terminal salvage values.

Can the extra investment required by an aluminum tower be justified if the stipulated rate-of-return requirement is 12 percent? Determine this with the use of each of the following:

a Rate of return method.
b Future worth method.
c Present worth method.

d Uniform annual cost method.

7-5 An individual is interested in purchasing and operating an established currency exchange. After a thorough investigation, she has developed a list of six such businesses that are for sale and appear to be attractive investment opportunities. The total investment and the average annual net receipts to be associated with each are as follows:

Location	Required investment	Annual net receipts
1	$45,000	$ 7,300
2	50,000	8,250
3	60,000	11,200
4	75,000	13,400
5	52,000	10,800
6	66,000	13,000

It is estimated that whichever of these is purchased will be sold in 10 years for an amount equal to the initial investment. In each case, 40 percent of the total investment would be financed by borrowing at an interest rate of 12 percent, and the balance by equity funds which could be invested elsewhere in situations of comparable risk and tax status at a return of 17 percent.

Which, if any, of these alternatives would you recommend on the basis of each of the following approaches:

a A rate of return comparison?
b A future worth comparison?
c A present worth comparison?
d A uniform annual cost comparison?

7-6 A railroad is going to make an investment in covered hopper cars which will be used to transport grain. One alternative is to buy six cars of 100-ton capacity each. The other is to buy eight cars of 75-ton capacity each.

The cost of the 100-ton units is $30,000 per car. Their resale value at the end of their 15-year service lives will be $1,500 per car. Maintenance costs per car are estimated to be $3,200 the first year and are expected to increase at an annual rate of $100.

As compared with this, the first cost of the 75-ton cars is $26,000 per unit, the service life is 17 years, and the salvage value is $1,300 per unit. Maintenance expenses will be $2,200 per car in the first year and will then increase at a rate of $50 per year.

If the cost of money is 15 percent, will it be more economical to invest in the 100-ton cars or the 75-ton cars? Determine this with the use of each of the following analytical techniques:

a Rate of return method. (Ans. 10.5%)

   b   Uniform annual cost method. (Ans. $52,530, $53,813)
   c   Present worth method assuming an infinite series of replacements with each alternative. (Ans. $350,200, $358,753)

7-7 The administrators of a hospital have decided to procure a body scanner. The equipment can be either purchased or leased. A decision to purchase will necessitate a total expenditure of $555,000 at this time. The economic life of the equipment is 10 years. Any salvage value at the end of that period would be negligible.

Various leasing arrangements are available, but the one being considered is as follows: The hospital would rent the equipment for 5 years. The rental payments would be made monthly; however, these are equivalent to a series of beginning-of-year payments of $132,000 each. At the end of the fifth year, the hospital would purchase the unit from the lessor for $60,000. It would then operate the equipment for 5 more years and finally dispose of it for a negligible amount.

Under either arrangement, there would be recurring expenditures for maintenance, power, insurance, and operating personnel. But these would be the same regardless of whether the equipment is owned or leased.

Given that the hospital has no equity funds available and borrows money at 12 percent to finance its activities, should the scanner be purchased or rented? Base your recommendation on each of the following:

   a   A rate of return comparison.
   b   A present worth comparison.
   c   A future worth comparison.
   d   A uniform annual cost comparison.

7-8 The management of a shopping center which is under construction must decide what kind of carpeting should be installed in certain areas of the center. The higher the cost of the carpeting, the longer will be its expected life. The final choice is to be made from among the following:

Type	First cost	Life, years
I	$75,000	10
II	72,000	8
III	64,000	7
IV	59,000	5
V	50,000	4

None of the carpeting will have any terminal salvage value, and maintenance costs will be the same with each type.

If the annual cost of money is 30 percent, which carpeting is the most economical? Base your decision on the results obtained with each of the following:

a A rate of return comparison. (Ans.   18.8%, 3.3%, 31.6%, 13.6%)
b A uniform annual cost comparison. (Ans. $24,263, $24,617, $22,842, $24,225, $23,080)
c A present worth comparison assuming an infinite series of replacements with each alternative. (Ans. $80,877, $82,057, $76,140, $80,750, $76,933)

7-9 A retired couple is giving consideration to buying one of two card and gift shops which are for sale. Either of these shops, if purchased, would be operated for 4 years.

The first shop requires a total capital investment of $37,000; this is the sum of the purchase price and the necessary working capital. It is expected that, in 4 years, the sale of the shop and the recovery of working capital will yield $39,500. Insofar as the second shop is concerned, it calls for a total present investment of $44,000, and its terminal value in 4 years is likely to be $47,500.

Additional estimates are made of the annual revenues and recurring expenses that will be experienced with the respective shops. When combined, these yield the following values for the expected net annual receipts:

	Net annual receipts	
Year	First shop	Second shop
1	$2,800	$3,300
2	3,000	3,450
3	3,250	3,700
4	3,700	4,000

Either shop would be purchased with equity funds which could be invested elsewhere in situations of comparable risk and tax status at 10 percent per year. What would you advise the couple to do? Justify your recommendation by means of each of the following:

a A rate of return determination.
b A future worth determination.
c A uniform annual cost determination.
d A present worth determination.

7-10 Two alternative schedules are being evaluated for the production of a part which is a component of a number of different assemblies. The demand for the part is expected to last 9 years.

The schedule selected will affect the choice of production facilities, the annual operating expenses, and the annual revenues. More specifically, these things will be affected as follows:

	Schedule 1	Schedule 2
Required investment	$270,000	$330,000
Life	7 years	9 years
Salvage value	$55,000	$50,000
Annual disbursements	$105,000	$98,000
Additional annual revenues	—	$2,000

If schedule 1 is selected, the equipment involved will not be replaced at the end of its life. Instead, the production of the part will be subcontracted for 2 years at an estimated annual cost of $160,000.

The schedule selected will also have an effect on the resultant average inventory of the part being carried. With schedule 1 and the subcontracting that follows, this average will be about 2,700 units. With schedule 2, it will be about 2,100 units. Annual inventory carrying costs will be approximately $7 per unit.

If the firm's before-tax rate-of-return requirement is 30 percent, which of the schedules is the more attractive? Determine this with the application of each of the following analytical techniques:

a Rate of return method. (Ans.   24.1%)
b Uniform annual cost method. (Ans. $214,359, $218,436)
c Present worth method. (Ans. $647,150, $659,458)
d Future worth method. (Ans. $6,862,703, $6,993,229)

7-11 In a period of rising interest rates, a free lance writer finds that corporate bonds which were issued some time ago are selling at relatively large discounts. She decides to consider this type of investment as a way of obtaining $10,000 which she will require 3 years from now to finance a research activity that she plans to begin at that point.

With the assistance of a securities salesman, she develops a list of four different bonds which will be redeemed in 3 years by the companies which issued them. The companies will, of course, also pay interest on the bonds during the three-year period. Although the interest payments will be made semiannually, the total interest for any one year will be treated as an end-of-year payment in order to simplify the analysis.

The total cost of purchasing bonds which will be redeemed for $10,000 in 3 years and the interest each will yield in the meantime are as follows for the four different bonds being considered:

Bond	Purchase cost	Annual interest payment
A	$9,000	$400
B	8,700	350
C	9,200	575
D	9,300	615

Given that the writer's minimum rate-of-return requirement is 8 percent, which of these bonds represents the most attractive investment alternative? Answer this question by means of each of the following methods:

a   A rate of return analysis. (Ans.   7.9%, 8.6%, 8.9%, 8.9%; <0%, 8.6%, 16.7%, 9.7%)
b   A present worth analysis. (Ans. $31, −$140, −$220, −$223)
c   A uniform annual cost analysis. (Ans. $12, −$54, −$85, −$87)
d   A future worth analysis. (Ans. $39, −$176, −$277, −$281)

7-12 A company in the food industry is designing a system for the processing of a new product. One section of the system consists of a combination of pipes and pumping equipment, and two possible combinations have been developed. The first of these can be described as follows:

Required investment in pipe	$20,000
Life of pipe	24 years
Required investment in pumping equipment	$16,000
Life of pumping equipment	12 years

Pumping costs with this installation will be $3,500 the first year and will then increase at a rate of $270 a year for a period of 12 years. If it becomes necessary to consider future replacements in the cost comparison study, it will be assumed that this initial pattern of pumping costs will repeat itself every 12 years and that replacement costs will be equal to the original costs. Finally, none of the assets is expected to have any salvage value.

By comparison, the alternate installation is estimated to have the following characteristics:

Required investment in pipe	$15,000
Life of pipe	12 years
Required investment in pumping equipment	$12,000
Life of pumping equipment	8 years

With this combination, pumping costs will be $4,000 the first year and will then increase at a rate of $300 for 8 years. Again, if there is a need for taking future replacements into account in the study, it will be assumed that this initial pattern of pumping costs will repeat itself every 8 years and that replacement costs will be equal to the original costs. And, as in the case of the other alternative, none of the assets is expected to have any salvage value.

At a cost of money of 20 percent, which installation is the more economical? Determine this with each of the following methods of analysis:

a   Rate of return.
b   Uniform annual cost.

    c Future worth.
    d Present worth.

7-13 A utility must decide whether to make major repairs on an existing gas main at this time or to replace it at this time. The main has a scrap value of $500, and this is not expected to change in the future. Required repairs will cost $14,000 and will serve to defer the need for the installation of a new main for 3 years. This is to say that, if the main is repaired at this time, it will be replaced by a new one in 3 years instead of now.

    A new distribution main will cost $36,000 and have a life of 30 years and a terminal salvage value of $500. All future replacements will be assumed to have the same characteristics. Also, there is reason to believe that maintenance expenses will be unaffected by the choice of alternative.

    When comparing the alternatives, the analyst will suppose that, if the old main is repaired, it will be replaced in 3 years by an infinite series of new mains. Similarly, if a new main is installed now, she will assume that it will be replaced in 30 years by an infinite series of new mains.

    If the company's minimum rate-of-return requirement is 15 percent, will the analyst find that the existing main should be replaced now or in 3 years? Answer this question by determining what results she will obtain with each of the following:

    a A rate of return approach. (Ans. 17.7%)
    b A uniform annual cost analysis. (Ans. $5,730, $5,482)
    c A present worth comparison. (Ans. $38,200, $36,547)

7-14 One of his milling machines is breaking down with such frequency that a manufacturer of machine tools decides that the equipment must be either overhauled or replaced. The cost of overhauling the unit would be $7,000. In its present condition, it can be sold for $4,000. If overhauled, it could probably be used for another 2 years, at the end of which time its salvage value would be about $3,000. During the two-year period, relevant operating costs would average $48,000 a year.

    Insofar as a replacement is concerned, a choice would be made between two alternatives. These can be described as follows:

	Replacement X	*Replacement Y*
Installed cost	$82,000	$115,000
Economic life	16 years	16 years
Terminal salvage value	$9,000	$14,000
Annual operating costs	$34,000	$28,000

    If the manufacturer's minimum rate-of-return requirement is 20 percent, what course of action would appear to be the most economical after each of the following analyses had been carried out:

a   Rate of return?
b   Uniform annual cost?
c   Present worth?
d   Future worth?

7-15   In the preceding problem, suppose that the manufacturer chooses not to accept our standard assumption regarding the nature of future replacements. Instead, he estimates the following: If the old milling machine is overhauled and retained, it will be replaced in 2 years by new equipment which will have a first cost of $93,000, a life of 14 years, a salvage value of $10,000, and annual operating costs of $32,000. What effect will this have on the calculated values of the following:

a   Rates of return? (Ans.   26.9%, 16.9%)
b   Uniform annual costs? (Ans. $52,590, $51,232, $52,151)
c   Present worths? (Ans. $248,751, $242,327, $246,674)
d   Future worths? (Ans. $4,598,575, $4,479,829, $4,560,188)

Which alternative is now the most economical?

7-16   The problems in this chapter involved *before-tax* analyses to be carried out on the basis of rate of return, uniform annual cost, present worth, and future worth comparisons. Problems to be analyzed on an *after-tax* basis with the use of these four techniques appear at the end of chapter 8. Analyze those for which you choose to or are asked to provide solutions.

8

Tax Determination and After-Tax Evaluations

Income taxes will ordinarily be one of the cash flows experienced with an investment alternative. Furthermore, the value of this cost element is likely to be affected by the choice of alternative. Therefore, taxes are said to be a relevant factor in the analysis of a set of mutually exclusive investment alternatives.

Heretofore, we have taken cognizance of the relevancy of this factor by having the investors in our examples select a minimum rate-of-return requirement which represented their cost of money *before* taxes. This return requirement was greater than what it would have been on an after-tax basis to allow for the fact that the tax expenses were ignored when the cash-flow patterns to be associated with the respective alternatives were being developed. It so happens that, if all the alternatives in a given situation are subject to the same kind of tax treatment, this indirect method for providing for the impact of taxes will usually suffice for purposes of identifying the most economical alternative. But, on occasion, it will not, and the chances that it will not increase significantly when the alternatives being compared are not treated identically for tax purposes. In brief, there is a risk that the alternative which proves to be the most economical before taxes may occasionally not be the one which would prove to be the most economical after taxes. And, since taxes will, as a rule, be incurred, a potential investor should, of course, be governed by the results of an after-tax analysis rather than by the results of a before-tax analysis.

In this chapter, we shall concern ourselves with a second method for evaluating the impact of income taxes on capital investment decisions. This method would be adopted by an investor who decides not to assume the risk of error inherent in the approach in which the rate-of-return requirement is increased to compensate for disregarded tax expenses.

The method to be considered calls for the explicit determination of the income taxes which will be experienced with each of a given set of mutually exclusive investment alternatives. Once this determination has been made, the tax expenses are processed in the same way that any other costs generated by an investment alternative are. However, in the course of finding the uniform annual equivalent, present worth, or future worth of these tax expenses and of the other cash flows, an analyst would use a rate for the time value of money which is equal to the investor's cost of money *after* taxes. In other words, the minimum rate-of-return requirement with this method is an after-tax requirement and, hence, is lower than what the corresponding rate would be in the before-tax approach which we have employed thus far.

As all this suggests, once the tax element of a cash-flow pattern has been determined, the procedures with which we already are familiar would be applied to express this after-tax pattern in terms of an equivalent uniform annual cost, present worth, future worth, or rate of return. Therefore, the major portion of this presentation will deal with the manner in which income taxes are calculated, and the balance with the manner in which this cash-flow element is processed.

SCOPE OF PRESENTATION

The task of income tax determination can be an extremely difficult one because of the complexity of federal, state, and city tax laws. Furthermore, one set of rules may apply when an investment has been made by an individual, another when it has been made by a partnership, and still another when it has been made by a corporation. And finally, tax laws will vary from country to country, from state to state, and from city to city.

The result of all this is that the field of tax accounting has evolved as one which requires years of training and experience on the part of anyone who intends to function effectively in this area. And it is not unusual for even such specialists to have different opinions regarding the tax effects of a specific transaction.

Obviously, a thorough investigation of such an involved topic is beyond the scope of this presentation. Some indication that this is true is that a typical handbook, dealing with only United States federal tax laws in digest form, exceeds 600 pages in length. And, incidentally, such handbooks are published annually to reflect the frequent changes which are made in the tax laws.

Given that the nature of the subject precludes our treating it in detail, we shall limit ourselves to a study of the fundamentals of tax determination. These fundamentals will be presented with the use of a number of examples, each of which will be designed to bring out a different basic aspect of existing tax laws. However, as the opportunity to do so presents itself, reference will be made to complicating circumstances that have intentionally been avoided.

In spite of its limitations, this approach will provide us with the means for ascertaining the tax expenses for most types of investment alternatives. And just as important, it will enable us to recognize those alternatives whose nature is such that the assistance of tax specialists is required in the course of carrying out an after-tax analysis.

THE GENERAL APPROACH

The general procedure for determining an annual tax expense was presented in one of the introductory chapters. We shall review the steps in this procedure before applying it in the first of our illustrations.

One begins with the realization that the tax for any one year is obtained by multiplying the taxable income for that period by the tax rate. The taxable income is equal to the revenues minus the expenses which the tax law allows as deductions. These "tax-deductible" expenses include operating costs, the interest expense, and the depreciation expense. Operating costs comprise such things as manufacturing expenses, administrative expenses, selling expenses, insurance, and property taxes. The interest expense is the cost of *borrowed* money and is a function of the amount of debt and the interest rate. The depreciation expense is affected by the choice of depreciation method for tax purposes; as mentioned earlier, the major methods are straight-line, sum-of-the-years-digits, and double-rate declining-balance.

Effective Tax Rate. Insofar as the tax rate which is applied to the taxable income is concerned, it is customary to employ an *effective* rate when an after-tax investment analysis is being made. This effective rate is a single rate which is a composite of the individual tax rates to which the taxable income is subject. For example, a given organization may have to pay a federal income tax, a state income tax, and a city income tax. Three different rates would probably be involved, and it may be that the state and city income taxes can be treated as deductible expenses for federal tax purposes. The effective rate would be a single rate which would reflect not only the three individual rates but also their interrelationship. To demonstrate how this single rate is obtained, let us consider the most common case, that is, one in which taxable income is subject to a federal tax and a state tax and in which the state tax can be shown as a deductible expense in the course of computing the federal tax.

Suppose that an investment is expected to yield a taxable income of $1,000 per year. This income is subject to a federal tax rate of, say, 40 percent and a state tax rate of, say, 6 percent. However, when computing his annual federal tax, the investor is allowed to reduce the $1,000 taxable income by the annual state tax. Therefore, the effective tax rate would be less than the sum of the 40 percent and 6 percent rates. Specifically, it would prove to be the value obtained by means of the following series of steps:

Net income before taxes = $1,000
State tax = $1,000(6%) = $60
Income subject to federal tax = $1,000 − $60 = $940
Federal tax = $940(40%) = $376
Total state and federal tax = $60 + $376 = $436
Effective tax rate = $436/$1,000 = 43.6%

When these steps are combined into a single expression, the following is obtained:

$$\text{Effective rate} = \frac{\$1,000(6\%) + [\$1,000 - \$1,000(6\%)](40\%)}{\$1,000}$$

$$= 6\% + (1 - 6\%)(40\%) = 43.6\%$$

If the effective tax rate is represented by T_e, the state tax rate by T_s, and the federal tax rate by T_f, the preceding expression will assume the following form:

$$T_e = T_s + (1 - T_s)(T_f) \qquad\qquad (8\text{-}1)$$

Of course, under a different set of circumstances, the expression for the effective rate would differ from Eq. (8-1). These different circumstances might be that a city income tax is involved or that the federal tax is deductible for state tax purposes. But in any case, an approach such as the one employed in our example can be employed to ascertain the effective rate. This is to say that an arbitrary value can be selected for the net income before taxes and processed, as the $1,000 value was in this example, to arrive at the effective rate under the existing circumstances.

Having outlined the general procedure for determining the taxable income and having explained what is meant by an effective tax rate, we shall now go on to ascertain the tax expenses in a given problem. As might have been expected, the problem to be considered is the one considered earlier in which a company was evaluating two proposals for producing and marketing a new product. Once the tax expenses have been determined, we shall be able to make an after-tax analysis of the alternatives and compare the results obtained with those obtained in the before-tax analysis which was made earlier.

THE NEW PRODUCT PROBLEM

The first of the two proposals in the example under consideration was that the firm invest in alternative K. The equipment involved had a first cost of $84,000, an estimated life of 4 years, and an expected salvage value of zero. Furthermore, $5,000 would have to be invested in working capital which would be recovered in its entirety in 4 years. Also, annual operating costs and revenues were given as $30,000 and $67,000, respectively. Finally, the proportion of debt financing would be 0.25 at a cost of 8 percent per year, which is to say that 25 percent, or $22,250, of the required $89,000 total investment would be borrowed at an interest rate of 8 percent.

Because the determination of the income tax expenses for this alternative creates a need for additional information, suppose that we are told the following: (1) the company's effective tax rate is 50 percent, (2) the straight-line method of depreciation will be adhered to for tax purposes, and (3) the terms of the $22,250 loan call for the payment of the 8 percent interest charge at the end of each year and for returning $5,250 of the principal at the end of each year for three years and the balance of $6,500 at the end of the fourth year.

The First Tax Computation. To ascertain the annual income taxes for this alternative, the firm would begin by reporting revenues of $67,000 for each of the 4 years. This $67,000 would then be reduced by the deductible expenses to obtain the taxable income. One of these expenses would be the operating costs of $30,000. Another would be the depreciation expense. To calculate the latter, we begin by noting that the $5,000 investment in working capital will not decrease in value and, in any case, is not a depreciable investment. But the $84,000 investment in equipment is expected to decrease to a value of zero during the four-year period. Hence, the depreciation, as calculated by means of the straight-line method, would be as follows:

Depreciation expense = ($84,000 − $0)/4 = $21,000 per year

The last of the deductible items would be the annual interest expense. With the given interest rate, size of loan, and repayment plan, these expenses would be found to be as follows:

Year (a)	Money owed during year (b)	Payment at end of year (c)	Amount owed at end of year (d = b − c)	Interest expense for year (e = 0.08 × b)
1	$22,250	$5,250	$17,000	$1,780
2	17,000	5,250	11,750	1,360
3	11,750	5,250	6,500	940
4	6,500	6,500	0	520

Having calculated the values of the last of the deductible expenses and knowing that the effective tax rate is 50 percent, we should compute the annual income taxes with alternative K in the manner indicated in Table 8-1.

TABLE 8-1   The tax computation for alternative K

	Year 1	Year 2	Year 3	Year 4
Revenues	$67,000	$67,000	$67,000	$67,000
Less:				
Operating costs	30,000	30,000	30,000	30,000
Depreciation	21,000	21,000	21,000	21,000
Interest	1,780	1,360	940	520
Taxable income	$14,220	$14,640	$15,060	$15,480
Tax at 50%	$ 7,110	$ 7,320	$ 7,530	$ 7,740

The Second Tax Computation. The second proposed method for producing and marketing the product was alternative L. This alternative involved equipment which would have a first cost of $125,000, a service life of 6 years, and a salvage value of $20,000. Working capital of $5,000 would be required, but this investment would not decrease in value and, in any case, is not depreciable. Operating costs were estimated to be $24,000 for the first year and were expected to increase at a rate of $1,000 a year. Annual revenues were estimated to be $67,000. The proportion of debt financing would be 0.25 at an annual cost of 8 percent; this means that 25 percent, or $32,500, of the required $130,000 total investment would be borrowed at an interest rate of 8 percent.

For purposes of tax determination, let us again suppose that the effective tax rate is 50 percent, that the equipment will be depreciated by the straight-line method, and that the annual interest charge will be paid at the end of each year. Insofar as the debt repayment plan is concerned, we shall assume that the company intends to make payments of $4,375 at the end of each year for five years and a final payment of $10,625 at the end of the sixth year; this yields a total of $32,500, which is equal to the amount borrowed.

The annual depreciation expense in this case would be obtained by dividing the expected decrease in the equipment's value by its service life. Doing so, we find that

Depreciation expense = ($125,000 − $20,000)/6 = $17,500 per year

With the given amount of debt financing, the given repayment plan, and the given interest rate, the annual interest expenses would be obtained as follows:

Year (a)	Amount owed during year (b)	Payment at end of year (c)	Amount owed at end of year (d = b − c)	Interest expense for year (e = 0.08 × b)
1	$32,500	$ 4,375	$28,125	$2,600
2	28,125	4,375	23,750	2,250
3	23,750	4,375	19,375	1,900
4	19,375	4,375	15,000	1,550
5	15,000	4,375	10,625	1,200
6	10,625	10,625	0	850

Since the depreciation expenses and the interest expenses are now known and the revenues and operating costs were already known, the firm can ascertain the tax consequences of this alternative in the manner shown in Table 8-2.

A knowledge of the annual tax expenses for the respective alternatives enables the firm to go on to compare them on an after-tax basis. But before we consider how this would be done, let us pause to note some of the assumptions on which the foregoing tax computations were based. To begin with, it was assumed that the service lives adopted for cost

TABLE 8-2   The tax computation for alternative L

	Year 1	Year 2	Year 3	Year 4	Year 5	Year 6
Revenues	$67,000	$67,000	$67,000	$67,000	$67,000	$67,000
Less:						
Operating costs	24,000	25,000	26,000	27,000	28,000	29,000
Depreciation	17,500	17,500	17,500	17,500	17,500	17,500
Interest	2,600	2,250	1,900	1,550	1,200	850
Taxable income	$22,900	$22,250	$21,600	$20,950	$20,300	$19,650
Tax at 50%	$11,450	$11,125	$10,800	$10,475	$10,150	$ 9,825

comparison purposes would coincide with those used for tax depreciation purposes; but, in some cases, the company may choose to take advantage of an opportunity to use a shorter life for tax purposes or may be compelled to use a longer life. Also, it was assumed that there would be no gain or loss experienced upon the disposal of the assets at some future point. Next, it was assumed that the company would not experience losses in its other activities which could be used to reduce the taxable income generated by the new product. Further, it was assumed that there was no investment tax credit provision in the tax law. In addition, it was assumed that the calculated taxes for the time period considered would be unaffected by clauses in the tax law which may permit the carryback or carryover of net operating losses experienced during some other time period. And, finally, it was assumed that the taxes would be unaffected by income averaging which may be permitted under existing tax laws.

Some of these assumptions will be dropped when problems of a different type are considered at a later point, but others will not because doing so would take us beyond the scope of this presentation.

The After-Tax Comparison.   Once the tax consequences of an investment alternative are determined, these additional costs are simply included in the alternative's cash-flow pattern if an after-tax analysis is to be made. As in the case of operating costs and revenues, to reduce the problem of estimation, it is customary to treat income taxes as if they were incurred at the end of each year, in spite of the fact that portions of an annual tax may be paid during the year or some time after the year has ended. Therefore, alternative K would now be described as follows:

84,000				
5,000			(5,000)	
	7,110	7,320	7,530	7,740
	30,000	30,000	30,000	30,000
	(67,000)	(67,000)	(67,000)	(67,000)
0	1	2	3	4

And the following would be a comparable description of alternative L:

125,000						(20,000)
5,000						(5,000)
	11,450	11,125	10,800	10,475	10,150	9,825
	24,000	25,000	26,000	27,000	28,000	29,000
	(67,000)	(67,000)	(67,000)	(67,000)	(67,000)	(67,000)
0	1	2	3	4	5	6

These respective cash-flow patterns can now be processed to obtain *after-tax* uniform annual costs, present worths, future worths, or rates of return. However, as mentioned earlier, an after-tax analysis calls for the establishment of a minimum rate-of-return requirement which reflects the company's cost of money after taxes. As opposed to this, the minimum rate-of-return requirement selected for use in a before-tax comparison of alternatives represents an investor's cost of money before taxes. Let us elaborate upon this by continuing to work with our example.

The new-product problem was introduced when the uniform annual cost method was being presented. At that time, it was stated that 25 percent of any investment in the activity would be financed by debt funds and 75 percent by equity funds. The cost of borrowed money was expected to be 8 percent, and the cost of equity capital, expressed as an opportunity cost before taxes, was estimated to be 24 percent. Consequently, the overall cost of money before taxes was obtained by calculating the average of the 8 percent debt cost and the 24 percent opportunity cost, but this average was weighted to reflect the proportion of the total investment which would be financed at each of these costs. This average proved to be as follows:

Average cost of money = 0.25(8%) + 0.75(24%) = 20%

And it will be recalled that this rate was then used to evaluate calculated before-tax rates of return and to compute before-tax uniform annual costs, present worths, and future worths.

If the alternatives are to be compared on an after-tax basis, the firm's minimum rate-of-return requirement must be described in terms of a requirement after taxes. This value can be obtained by computing the weighted average of the after-tax interest expense and the after-tax opportunity cost.

Insofar as the interest expense is concerned, if this is 8 percent before taxes, it will also be 8 percent after taxes. The reasons for this were given in chapter 2, but we shall now treat them more fully. Let us do so by considering only the $22,250 which would be borrowed at 8 percent to finance alternative K during the first year of its life. At the end of that year, the lenders of this amount will charge $22,250 times 8 percent, or $1,780, for the use of their money. Therefore, the company which borrows the $22,250 will incur a cost of money equal to 8 percent, or $1,780, on this portion of its total investment. To cover this interest expense, the company must earn 8 percent, or $1,780, on the debt portion of its total investment. Consequently, insofar as this portion of its total investment is concerned, the company's minimum rate-of-return requirement will be 8 percent, which is synonymous with a return requirement of $1,780.

This rate-of-return requirement will be the same after taxes as it is before taxes, because the cost of debt capital is the same after taxes as it is before taxes. To return to our example, the after-tax cost of debt would be equal to the before-tax cost for the simple reason that the company must pay the lenders 8 percent of $22,250, or $1,780, at the end of the first year regardless of what the tax consequences of the total investment are. To cover this cost either before or after taxes, the company must earn a minimum of $1,780, or 8 percent, on its $22,250 investment of debt capital. If it does, none of this $1,780 will be subject to a tax because, although the entire $1,780 must be reported as income, an equal amount will be reported as a deductible interest expense. Hence, before-tax earnings of $1,780, or 8 percent, on invested debt capital will yield after-tax earnings of $1,780, or 8 percent, on invested debt capital. From this, it follows that the minimum after-tax rate-of-return requirement on debt capital will be equal to the minimum before-tax requirement.

But the same cannot be said of the return required to cover the cost of equity capital. In the new-product problem, this cost was given as 24 percent before taxes, and this rate represented the return the firm could realize by investing equity funds elsewhere in sources of similar risk and tax status. But if these other investments were made, the dollar return they would provide would be subject to an income tax because there is no deductible expense, comparable to an interest payment, that would serve to eliminate the need to pay a tax on this return on equity capital. Therefore, the opportunity cost to be associated with an equity investment is lower after taxes than it is before taxes. How much lower depends, of course, on the tax treatment to which the returns that could be realized from other sources are subject. If the firm in our example concludes that this tax treatment is such that a before-tax return of 24 percent is equivalent to an after-tax return of, say, 13-1/3 percent on investments whose risk and tax status approximate those of the new-product proposal, the latter percentage would be used to represent the after-tax cost of equity funds.

So let us continue by assuming that the firm does estimate the after-tax cost of equity funds to be 13-1/3 percent. Given that these funds will account for 75 percent of the total investment and that the remaining 25 percent will be accounted for by debt funds whose after-tax cost remains at 8 percent, the average cost of money, after taxes, becomes

Average cost of money = 0.25(8%) + 0.75(13-1/3%) = 12%

Therefore, the company's minimum rate-of-return requirement after taxes is now 12 percent, and this rate would be used to compare the after-tax cash flows of alternatives K and L. To illustrate this, we shall compute the uniform annual equivalents of the cash flows depicted on the preceding time lines. For alternative K, the following would be obtained:

$$\text{Annual cost} = \$89,000(A/P)_{n=4}^{i=12} - \$5,000(A/F)_{n=4}^{i=12} + \$7,110$$
$$+ \$210(A/G)_{n=4}^{i=12} + \$30,000 - \$67,000$$
$$= (-)\$1,350$$

Similarly, the uniform annual cost of alternative L would be found in the following manner:

$$\text{Annual cost} = \$130,000(A/P)_{n=6}^{i=12} - \$25,000(A/F)_{n=6}^{i=12} + \$11,450$$
$$- \$325(A/G)_{n=6}^{i=12} + \$24,000 + \$1,000(A/G)_{n=6}^{i=12}$$
$$- \$67,000$$
$$= (-)\$1,545$$

The fact that each of these costs is negative reveals that both alternatives will yield an after-tax return on total investment greater than the firm's rate-of-return requirement of 12 percent. As a result, in the absence of irreducible factors, either would be preferable to the alternative of not producing and marketing the product, which was alternative J and whose annual cost would be $0. But because the annual cost of alternative L is lower than that of K, it emerges as the most economical course of action. This coincides with the conclusion reached on the basis of a before-tax comparison, which is not surprising given that neither alternative qualifies for preferential tax treatment as compared with the other.

It might also be noted that the assumption has been made that the respective after-tax cash-flow patterns will repeat themselves until a 12-year service period is attained for each alternative. Otherwise, the calculated uniform annual equivalents could not have been compared directly. In the event that the firm chooses not to make some such assumption, it becomes necessary to forecast the nature of future replacements until equal time periods are obtained, ascertain the tax expenses for these replacements, and process the resultant cash flows accordingly.

Finally, although the after-tax comparison of the alternatives was demonstrated with the use of the uniform annual cost method, the cash-flow patterns could have been subjected to a present worth, future worth, or rate of return analysis. Had this been done for a 12-year period, alternative L would again have emerged as the most economical alternative. This can be seen in the following table in which the results that would have been obtained with these approaches are shown:

Alter-native	Uniform annual cost	Present worth	Future worth	Return on total invest-ment	Return on extra invest-ment
J	$ 0	$ 0	$ 0	— %	— %
K	(−) 1,350	(−) 8,362	(−) 32,580	14.1	14.1
L	(−) 1,545	(−) 9,570	(−) 37,285	13.6	12.6

The expressions which underlie these results are not being presented because they are similar to those constructed in the course of making a before-tax analysis of the alternatives. The only differences are that each of these expressions would contain an additional term to account for the presence of a series of income tax expenses and that 12 percent would be used for the company's minimum rate-of-return requirement.

THE CASH-FLOW DESCRIPTION

This is probably an appropriate point at which to introduce a word of caution. In the course of making an after-tax analysis, it becomes necessary to calculate the values of the depreciation expense, the debt repayment expense, and the interest expense. Having done so, an analyst may be inclined to include these values in the cash-flow line. However, this inclination must be overcome for reasons that will be presented with the use of alternative K in the new-product problem.

The Depreciation Expense. The depreciation expenses, debt repayment expenses, interest expenses, and tax expenses for alternative K were either given or found to be as shown in Table 8-3. But, then, only the tax expenses were added to the before-tax cash flows to obtain the following after-tax cash-flow pattern:

```
84,000
 5,000                                          (5,000)
            7,110      7,320      7,530      7,740
           30,000     30,000     30,000     30,000
          (67,000)   (67,000)   (67,000)   (67,000)
   |_____|_____|_____|_____|
   0          1          2          3          4
```

The $21,000 series of depreciation expenses generated by the $84,000 capital investment in equipment was not shown on the time line for the simple reason that the depreciation expenses are not cash flows. Instead, they are a series of values which is *substituted* for the $84,000 value when the tax is being computed. To enter the series on the cash-flow

TABLE 8-3 A partial description of alternative K

Year	Depreciation expense	Debt repayment expense	Interest expense	Tax expense
1	$21,000	$ 5,250	$1,780	$7,110
2	21,000	5,250	1,360	7,320
3	21,000	5,250	940	7,530
4	21,000	6,500	520	7,740
Total	$84,000	$22,250		

line would be to maintain that, in addition to spending $84,000 for equipment at the beginning of the first year, the firm will also spend $21,000 for equipment at the end of each year for 4 years. This, obviously, is not the case, and to treat it as if it were would be to count the $84,000 cost twice. In brief, the $84,000 is spent once, at the beginning of the service period, and the cash-flow line should reflect this fact.

A related observation is that, when the uniform annual equivalent of the $84,000 expenditure is found for the four-year period at a cost of money of 12 percent, the following is obtained:

$$\$84,000(A/P)_{n=4}^{i=12} = \$27,653$$

We know that a part of this annual cost is the average amount by which the asset decreases in value during its life, that is, the devaluation expense. This expense is equal to the total decrease in value of $84,000 divided by 4 years, or $21,000 per year. Therefore, the application of the present-amount annuity factor yields an annual equivalent which reflects the fact that a $21,000 devaluation expense will be incurred. If the $21,000 depreciation expense reported for tax purposes were also included in the cash-flow line, the effect would be to count this average decrease in value twice which, of course, would result in an overstatement of this expense.

The Debt Repayment Expense. Table 8-3 also contains a series of values which describes the manner in which the $22,250 of debt is repaid. As opposed to the depreciation expenses, these debt repayment expenses are cash outflows. Consequently, there is an even stronger inclination to include these amounts as a part of the cash-flow pattern than there is to include the depreciation expenses. But, again, it is incorrect to do so for the following reason:

It is helpful to begin by recognizing that there will be two classes of investors in the activity under consideration. One class will contain the suppliers of the $22,250 of debt funds, and the other will contain the suppliers of the $66,750 of equity funds. In combination, these individuals will supply the required total investment of $89,000.

We have been told by means of what kind of series of payments the debt investors will recover their $22,250. It was possible to obtain this information because the repayment plan was apparently agreed upon at the time the loan was being negotiated. Furthermore, it was necessary to obtain this information because it had an effect on the tax consequences of the investment.

But we must not overlook the fact that the investors of the $66,750 of equity funds will also expect to have their money returned to them eventually, and, therefore, there will also be a series of equity repayment expenses. However, we were not provided with a description of this series for two reasons. First, the information would have been of no relevance in the after-tax analysis, and, second, the exact nature of such a series cannot be predicted. Nevertheless, we know that the alternative is expected to be capable of yielding a series of net receipts which will permit the recovery of the $66,750 equity investment.

The reason for the foregoing reference to the presence of an equity repayment series is that we shall expand our discussion of why the debt repayment series should not be incorporated in the cash-flow pattern to include an explanation of why the same can be said of the equity repayment series.

The most straightforward explanation for not including these repayment series in the cash-flow pattern is that these series of cash outflows are not generated by this alternative for producing and marketing the product. This becomes apparent when we consider those cash flows which are. To begin with, the alternative creates a need for spending $89,000 for equipment and working capital. It continues by creating a need for spending $30,000 each year for operating costs and by creating revenues of $67,000 each year. It concludes by creating a revenue of $5,000 in the form of recovered working capital. As compared with this, the two series of repayments to the debt and equity investors of the $89,000 in capital which they supplied are simply a *distribution* of the net receipts generated by the alternative. Given that these repayment expenses, which total $89,000, are not expenses being generated by the alternative but a distribution of net receipts, it would be incorrect to include them in the alternative's cash-flow pattern. To do so would be to maintain that the alternative requires an expenditure of $89,000 in the form of a single amount at the beginning of the service period and another expenditure of $89,000 in the form of two repayment series during the service period. There is no question but that the alternative requires only the single expenditure of $89,000, and the cash-flow pattern should be described accordingly.

The Interest Expense.   It has also been stated that the interest expenses should not be included in an alternative's cash-flow pattern in the course of ascertaining the most economical of a set of mutually exclusive investment alternatives. But before going on to explain this position, let us note that, in addition to incurring an interest expense which is the cost of borrowed money, the investor will incur an opportunity cost which is the cost of equity funds. And just as it would be incorrect to incorporate the series of interest expenses in the description of an alternative's cash flows, it would be incorrect to incorporate a series of opportunity costs in this description.

Returning to alternative K for purposes of explanation, we begin by noting that the required total investment is $89,000, of which $5,000 will be recovered at the end of 4 years because the $5,000 investment in working capital will not decrease in value. Therefore, the uniform annual capital cost will be

$$\$89,000(A/P)_{n=4}^{i=12} - \$5,000(A/F)_{n=4}^{i=12} = \$28,253$$

It was mentioned earlier that $21,000 of this amount is the devaluation expense generated by the $84,000 investment in equipment. Hence, the balance of $7,253 must be the average annual cost of money at the given rate of 12 percent. But this 12 percent was obtained by taking into account that 1/4 of the total investment would be financed by debt funds at a cost of 8 percent and that 3/4 of the total investment would be financed by equity funds at a cost of 13-1/3 percent. From this, it follows that, when the 12 percent is used in the computation of the uniform annual capital cost by applying the corresponding compound interest factors to the $89,000 total investment and the $5,000 salvage value, the $7,253 which evolves as the average annual cost of money is the *total* cost of money. One part of this total is the interest expense on debt, and the other part is the opportunity cost on equity. Therefore, if the analyst were to include the calculated interest payments of $1,780, $1,360, $940, and $520 in the cash-flow pattern, he would be counting the interest cost twice. Similarly, if he were to include the annual opportunity costs in the cash-flow pattern, he would be counting the opportunity cost twice.

Return on Equity Investment.   There is one occasion on which an investor will enter the series of debt repayment expenses and the series of interest expenses as cash flows on a time line. This is when he is interested in ascertaining the return on only the equity portion of his investment. As we shall see, such a return is a correct but somewhat inconvenient basis for evaluating the alternative, but, for now, we shall not concern ourselves with this fact. Suffice it to say that, if an investor is concerned with the return on equity, he will find it necessary to treat the debt repayment expenses and the interest expenses as cash flows when computing this return. Let us see why with the use of alternative K.

The after-tax consequences of investing a total of $89,000 in alternative K were found to be as follows:

```
89,000                                       (5,000)
          7,110      7,320      7,530        7,740
          30,000     30,000     30,000       30,000
          (67,000)   (67,000)   (67,000)     (67,000)
  |----------|----------|----------|----------|
  0          1          2          3          4
```

which can be simplified to assume the following form:

```
89,000                                       (5,000)
          (29,890)   (29,680)   (29,470)     (29,260)
  |----------|----------|----------|----------|
  0          1          2          3          4
```

The after-tax return on the total investment can be determined by solving the following expression for the unknown rate i:

$$\text{Annual cost} = \$89,000(A/P)_{n=4}^{i=?} - \$5,000(A/F)_{n=4}^{i=?} - \$29,890$$
$$+ \$210(A/G)_{n=4}^{i=?} = 0$$

With a trial-and-error approach, the return would be found to be 14.1 percent.

Let us now suppose that a question is raised with regard to the return that will be realized on the equity capital invested in this alternative, which is 75 percent of $89,000, or $66,750. This return is found by taking into consideration the cash flows the equity investors will experience as a consequence of having invested $66,750. These cash flows will depend on the way in which the annual net receipts generated by the alternative, as shown on the preceding time line, are distributed. More exactly, the relevant cash flows will be equal to the share of the annual net receipts that the equity investors will receive.

To ascertain what this share is, we simply take the difference between the respective total annual net receipts and the amount of these receipts that will be claimed by the investors of debt capital. The amount claimed by the debt investors in any one year will be the sum of (1) the interest which they are to receive that year and (2) the partial repayment of their investment which they are to receive that year. In Table 8-3, the series of interest payments is given as $1,780, $1,360, $940, $520, and the series of debt repayments is given as $5,250, $5,250, $5,250, $6,500.

When these amounts are subtracted from the total annual net receipts shown on the preceding time line, the consequences of the $66,750 equity investment prove to be as follows:

66,750				(5,000)
	(29,890)	(29,680)	(29,470)	(29,260)
	1,780	1,360	940	520
	5,250	5,250	5,250	6,500
66,750	(22,860)	(23,070)	(23,280)	(27,240)
0	1	2	3	4

To calculate the return that the remaining receipts will yield to the equity investors on their $66,750 investment, the analyst can begin by setting up the following expression:

$$\text{Present worth} = \$66,750 - \$22,860(P/F)_{n=1}^{i=?} - \$23,070(P/F)_{n=2}^{i=?}$$
$$- \$23,280(P/F)_{n=3}^{i=?} - \$27,240(P/F)_{n=4}^{i=?} = 0$$

By trial and error, the after-tax return i on the equity investment will be found to be 16.1 percent.

Incidentally, it might be noted that the return to the investors of the $22,250 debt capital can be determined by taking into consideration the portion of the total annual net receipts which they will receive. This portion will be the sum of the amounts of interest and debt repayment which they will receive in any one year. These amounts appear in the preceding time line, and they serve to yield the following cash flows for the investors of debt funds:

22,250				
	(1,780)	(1,360)	(940)	(520)
	(5,250)	(5,250)	(5,250)	(6,500)
22,250	(7,030)	(6,610)	(6,190)	(7,020)
0	1	2	3	4

If a future worth expression were used to find the return which the resultant annual receipts will yield on the debt investment of $22,250, the following would be obtained:

$$\text{Future worth} = \$22,250(F/P)_{n=4}^{i=?} - \$7,030(F/P)_{n=3}^{i=?} - \$6,610(F/P)_{n=2}^{i=?}$$
$$- \$6,190(F/P)_{n=1}^{i=?} - \$7,020 = 0$$

Knowing that an interest rate of 8 percent was used to calculate the values of the interest payments to the debt investors, we should expect to obtain, by trial and error, a value of 8 percent for the return on debt, and this proves to be the case.

In summary, then, it has been found that the after-tax return for alternative K is (a) 14.1 percent on the total investment of $89,000, (b) 16.1 percent on the equity investment of $66,750, and (c) 8.0 percent on the debt investment of $22,250. Because of the interrelationship that exists among these three returns, the return on the total investment should be equal to the weighted average of the returns on the equity and debt investments. This weighted average can be calculated as follows:

$$\text{Weighted average return} = \frac{\$66,750(16.1\%) + \$22,250(8.0\%)}{\$89,000}$$

$$= 0.75(16.1\%) + 0.25(8.0\%)$$

$$= 14.1\%$$

This value coincides with the 14.1 percent we obtained by another method. But it should be noted that the weighted-average approach to the determination of an unknown rate, when two of three interrelated rates are known, should be considered only when the respective weights remain constant throughout the study period. The reason for this is that, as explained in an earlier chapter when the concept of a weighted average return was being discussed, it becomes extremely difficult to apply this method when the weights change from year to year. And suffice it to say that, with a given alternative, the debt repayment plan may be such that the debt ratio and, therefore, the equity ratio change with each passing year. When this is true, the statement that the return on total investment is the weighted average of the returns on equity and debt investments is still true, but it is simpler to solve for any one of these three returns by finding the rate i which yields a value of zero for the annual equivalent, present worth, or future worth of the cash-flow pattern involved. Incidentally, the annual debt and equity ratios did remain constant in the case of alternative K, and, hence, we were able to verify the interrelationship among the three returns by means of the indicated weighted-average approach.

But to conclude, we have seen that, although the way in which the total net receipts generated by an alternative are distributed between the two classes of investors has no effect on the return on the total investment in the alternative, it does have an effect on the returns on the equity investment and the debt investment in the alternative. This is because the latter returns will depend on the share of the total net receipts which each class of investor will receive. Therefore, when computing these respective returns, it becomes necessary to incorporate the interest amounts and the debt repayment amounts in the respective cash-flow patterns. But it would have been incorrect to incorporate these amounts in the cash-flow pattern generated by the total investment for purposes of computing the return on that investment.

The Return-on-Equity Criterion. It was stated that the return on the equity investment in an alternative is not the most convenient criterion for passing judgment on the alternative. This is true because the computational procedure for ascertaining such a return is much more laborious than is the one for ascertaining the return on the total investment. To obtain the latter, one need process only the total net receipts generated by the alternative. But to obtain the return on equity, it becomes necessary to go through the additional step of determining what portion of those receipts belongs to the investors of equity capital. Naturally, if it were essential that the return on equity be known before judgment could be passed on a proposed capital expenditure, there would be no choice but to proceed with the determination of this return in spite of the complexity of the procedure involved. But it so happens that, if the return on total investment is satisfactory, the return on equity investment will also be satisfactory and that, if the return on total investment is unsatisfactory, the return on equity investment will also be unsatisfactory. Hence, there is no real need for a return-on-equity calculation. To demonstrate that this is true, let us return to the preceding analysis of alternative K.

It was stated that one-fourth of the total investment in that alternative would be financed by debt at a cost of 8 percent and that three-fourths of the total investment would be financed by equity at a cost of 13-1/3 percent after taxes. On the basis of these data, the firm went on to establish its after-tax minimum rate-of-return requirement in the following manner:

After-tax return requirement = 0.25(8%) + 0.75(13-1/3%) = 12%

There is no question but that an investment in this alternative is justified only if the resultant net receipts are capable of yielding a return of 8 percent to the investors of debt capital and a return of at least 13-1/3 percent to the investors of equity capital. As this suggests, the actual return on debt and the actual return on equity are anything but irrelevant. But insofar as the return on the debt investment in alternative K is concerned, we know that this return will be exactly 8 percent because the firm has assumed a financial obligation to provide the investors of this capital with a return of exactly 8 percent. So the only question which remains to be answered is whether the return on the equity investment will be at least 13-1/3 percent. To answer this question, one need only examine the value of the calculated return on total investment. If this return satisfies the firm's established 12 percent requirement, the return on equity will be satisfactory; otherwise it will not. This becomes evident from an examination of the terms in the preceding equation with the use of which the after-tax rate-of-return requirement was determined.

The terms in this equation reveal that, given a return on debt of 8 percent, only a return on equity equal to or greater than the required 13-1/3 percent will yield a weighted average return, that is, a return on total investment, equal to or greater than the required 12 percent. To illustrate, the return on the total investment in alternative K was found to be 14.1 percent. But only a return on equity greater than the required 13-1/3 percent would succeed in raising the weighted average return on total investment from the required 12 percent to the actual 14.1 percent; and if we return to the results of our analysis of alternative K, we find that the return on equity proved to be 16.1 percent, which exceeds the required 13-1/3 percent. Obviously, if the return on equity had been exactly 13-1/3 percent, the weighted average return, that is, the return on total investment, would have been equal to the required 12 percent. And if the return on equity had been less than the required 13-1/3 percent, the weighted average return, that is, the return on total investment, would have been less than the required 12 percent.

To summarize, if the return on total investment is found to be satisfactory, there is no doubt that the return on equity will also be satisfactory; this is because, given a specified return on debt, only a return on equity which is equal to or greater than the investor's opportunity cost is capable of yielding an average return which equals or exceeds the investor's cost of money, that is, his minimum rate-of-return requirement. Conversely, if the return on total investment is found to be unsatisfactory, there is no doubt that the return on equity will also be unsatisfactory; this is because, given a specified return on debt, only a return on equity which is below the investor's opportunity cost is capable of yielding an average return which is below the investor's cost of money, that is, below his minimum rate-of-return requirement. In brief, the return on total investment always reflects the return on equity. Therefore, there is no real need for ascertaining the return on equity.

Of course, if a firm chooses to compare mutually exclusive alternatives on the basis of returns on equity, it is free and correct to do so. Just as a return on total investment reflects the return on the equity portion of that investment, the return on the equity portion of a total investment reflects the return on the total investment. Consequently, the alternative which will emerge as the most economical on the basis of an analysis of returns on total investment will emerge as the most economical on the basis of an analysis of returns on equity investment. It might be mentioned, however, that a complete analysis of investment alternatives on the basis of returns on equity will necessitate the determination and evaluation not only of returns on the equity portion of the total investments, but also of the returns on the equity portion of the extra investments in the respective alternatives. Needless to say, this contributes to the computational difficulties to be associated with this approach.

Incidentally, although the mechanics of calculating returns on equity had been demonstrated with the use of an after-tax example, it might be that a firm wants to determine a before-tax return of this type. In that event, consideration is given to the *before-tax* net receipts which the equity investors will experience. To illustrate, let us suppose that the company in our problem is interested in the before-tax return on the $66,750 equity investment in alternative K. The *before-tax* cash flows to be associated with the $89,000 total investment in this alternative were given to be as follows:

```
89,000                                      (5,000)
         30,000     30,000     30,000     30,000
         (67,000)   (67,000)   (67,000)   (67,000)
 |_____|_____|_____|_____|
 0          1          2          3          4
```

Furthermore, it had been found that the cash flows which would be experienced by the investors of $22,250 in debt funds would be as follows:

```
22,250    (7,030)    (6,610)    (6,190)    (7,020)
 |_____|_____|_____|_____|
 0          1          2          3          4
```

When the amounts which appear on this time line are subtracted from those which appear on the preceding time line, the consequences of the $66,750 equity investment are found to be as follows:

```
66,750    (29,970)   (30,390)   (30,810)   (34,980)
 |_____|_____|_____|_____|
 0          1          2          3          4
```

To obtain the before-tax return on the equity investment, it becomes necessary to find the rate which will yield a value of zero for the uniform annual equivalent, present worth, or future worth of this cash-flow pattern. The appropriate present worth expression would be

$$\text{Present worth} = \$66,750 - \$29,970(P/F)_{n=1}^{i=?} - \$30,390(P/F)_{n=2}^{i=?}$$
$$- \$30,810(P/F)_{n=3}^{i=?} - \$34,980(P/F)_{n=4}^{i=?} = 0$$

and, by trial and error, the before-tax return i on equity investment would be found to be about 31 percent.

But whether an after-tax or a before-tax return on equity is being computed, the procedure for doing so is somewhat more troublesome than the one for computing a return on total investment. And since the determination of a return on equity is not essential to an evaluation of an investment alternative, the return on total investment is said to be the more convenient criterion.

THE REPLACEMENT PROBLEM

One of the characteristics of the new-product problem, which has just been analyzed on an after-tax basis, was that all the revenues and costs to be associated with the alternatives were known. This permitted the determination of the annual taxable income and, hence, the annual taxes for each of the alternatives. But, as we know, there are cases in which, for certain reasons, the analyst will be provided only with information regarding those revenues and costs that are affected by the choice of alternative. Under such circumstances, there is no way of calculating the tax expenses for each alternative. However, it is possible to ascertain the differences in annual taxes for two such alternatives, and it is these differences that are then used in an after-tax comparison of the alternatives.

We shall return to the replacement problem, which was analyzed in earlier chapters on a before-tax basis, to demonstrate how such income tax differences are ascertained and employed in an after-tax analysis. At the same time, we shall introduce conditions which will necessitate taking into consideration certain aspects of the tax law that have not been considered thus far; among these will be the investment tax credit provision and the provision for handling gains or losses on disposal of assets.

The New Equipment. The replacement problem was one in which a contractor was giving consideration to the replacement of a unit of construction equipment. The proposed new equipment had a first cost of $11,900, an estimated salvage value of $3,900 at the end of an expected four-year life, and annual repair and maintenance costs of $120, $200, $310, and $540, respectively. There would also be a saving in fuel costs, but this was treated as an additional expense that would be experienced with the old equipment. No specific information was provided with regard to annual revenues, but it was stated that they would be unaffected by the choice of alternative and that they would exceed the costs; as a consequence, the alternative of disposing of the old equipment and not replacing it was rejected on the basis of judgment.

Because the alternative of purchasing the new equipment is to be evaluated on an after-tax basis, let us now suppose that the analyst is also told that (1) the new equipment will be depreciated for tax purposes by the sum-of-the-years-digits method, (2) the $11,900 first cost of the equipment will be financed by borrowing 20 percent, or $2,380, of this amount at an interest rate of 6 percent per year, (3) the debt will be repaid at a rate of $595 at the end of each year for 4 years, (4) the annual interest charge will be paid at the end of each year, and (5) the effective tax rate is 40 percent.

As we shall see, although revenue data have not been provided, it will be possible to determine the differences in annual taxes between this alternative and the one of retaining the old equipment by comparing the deductible expenses that can be reported with the new equipment with those that can be reported with the old equipment. So let us now determine what these deductible expenses will be for the new asset by beginning with the depreciation expense.

The total depreciation expense for the new equipment will be equal to its first cost of $11,900 minus its salvage value of $3,900, or $8,000. A service life of 4 years yields a sum-of-the-years-digits value of 10. Therefore, the annual depreciation expenses for tax purposes will be as follows:

Year	Depreciation expense
1	(4/10)($8,000) = $3,200
2	(3/10)(8,000) = 2,400
3	(2/10)(8,000) = 1,600
4	(1/10)(8,000) = 800

Another deductible expense will be the interest paid on borrowed funds. With the given data regarding debt, the annual interest expenses, to the closest whole dollar, would be found in the following manner:

Year	Amount owed during year	Interest expense
1	$2,380	0.06($2,380) = $143
2	$2,380 − $595 = 1,785	0.06(1,785) = 107
3	1,785 − 595 = 1,190	0.06(1,190) = 71
4	1,190 − 595 = 595	0.06(595) = 35

The last of the deductible expenses will be the annual repair and maintenance costs. When the values given for this expense are added to the calculated depreciation and interest expenses, the following total deductible expenses are obtained:

Year	Total deductible expense
1	$120 + $3,200 + $143 = $3,463
2	200 + 2,400 + 107 = 2,707
3	310 + 1,600 + 71 = 1,981
4	540 + 800 + 35 = 1,375

Because these totals will have to be compared with similar deductions for the old equipment, let us now consider that alternative.

The Old Equipment. The replacement problem, when presented originally, called for determining whether the old equipment's economic life would be 1 year or 2 years. But to avoid, for the time being, the difficulties of a multiple-alternative after-tax analysis, we shall assume that the economic life of the old equipment was correctly estimated to be 2 years.

To continue, we were told that the equipment's present market value was $3,600 and that this was expected to decrease to $800 in 2 years. During this two-year period, annual fuel costs would exceed those of the new equipment by $190, and repair and maintenance costs would be $960 the first year and $1,140 the second.

Suppose we are now told that the contractor adheres to single-asset accounting and that the asset's current book value is equal to the equipment's expected salvage value of $800 two years from now; therefore, if the equipment is retained for two more years, no additional depreciation expenses will be reported. Also, since the debt ratio for new capital expenditures is about 20 percent, the contractor decides to treat the required investment in the old equipment, which is its $3,600 market value, as if 20 percent, or $720, of this amount were debt capital obtained at a cost of 6 percent; for purposes of calculating the interest expenses, he selects a repayment plan which calls for repaying $360 of this $720 at the end of each year and for paying the 6 percent interest charge at the end of each year during the next two years. Finally, to permit a comparison of the two alternatives for the same service period, the simplifying assumption will be made that, at the end of two years, the old equipment will be replaced by an asset that will generate the same pattern of cash flows and tax-deductible expenses as the one that will be generated by the currently-owned equipment.

The determination of the total deductible expenses for this alternative begins with a recognition of the fact that the depreciation expense will be $0 per year for 2 years. Howeve.·, it is to be assumed that a future replacement will yield the same expense for another 2 years, and, as a consequence, this deduction will continue for 4 years, which coincides with the life of the currently-available new equipment.

Insofar as the interest expenses are concerned, these can be determined for the first 2 years and then assumed to repeat themselves during the subsequent two-year period. With the given data regarding debt, the result would be as follows:

Year	Amount owed during year	Interest expense
1	$720	0.06($720) = $43
2	$720 − $360 = 360	0.06(360) = 22
3	720	43
4	360	22

Next, the deductible recurring expenses would simply be the sum of the additional fuel cost and the cost of repairs and maintenance. The estimated values of these costs for the first 2 years and the assumption that they will be repeated during a second two-year period yield the following:

Year	Recurring expenses
1	$190 + $ 960 = $1,150
2	190 + 1,140 = 1,330
3	1,150
4	1,330

In total, then, the annual tax-deductible expenses that will be experienced with the old equipment are the respective sums of the annual depreciation, interest, and recurring expenses. These are shown in the following table:

Year	Total deductible expense
1	$0 + $43 + $1,150 = $1,193
2	0 + 22 + 1,330 = 1,352
3	0 + 43 + 1,150 = 1,193
4	0 + 22 + 1,330 = 1,352

We shall now consider how these total deductible expenses are compared with those for the new equipment to arrive at the tax expenses for the one alternative as compared with the other.

The Tax Difference. When annual revenues are not affected by the choice of alternative, which is to say that they are the same for both, the alternative that has the lower total tax-deductible expense for a given year will have the higher taxable income for that year. To illustrate, the total deductible expense for the first year was found to be $3,463 for the new asset and $1,193 for the old. Because the old asset's deductible expense is $2,270 lower than that of the new, its taxable income will be $2,270 higher than that of the new. Consequently, at the given 40 percent tax rate, the *additional* tax with the old asset will be 40 percent times $2,270, or $908.

If the calculated total deductible expenses for the remaining 3 years are treated in the same manner, the annual tax expenses with the old equipment, as compared with the new equipment, are found to be as follows:

	Total deductible expense		Old asset	
Year (a)	New asset (b)	Old asset (c)	Additional taxable income (d = b − c)	Additional tax expense (e = 0.40 × d)
1	$3,463	$1,193	$2,270	$908
2	2,707	1,352	1,355	542
3	1,981	1,193	788	315
4	1,375	1,352	23	9

Once these tax differences have been ascertained, they can be incorporated as costs in the cash-flow pattern for the old equipment and processed accordingly. Or they can be incorporated as tax savings in the cash-flow pattern for the new equipment and processed accordingly. As this suggests, differences in tax expenses are treated just as differences in, say, fuel costs are treated.

Investment Tax Credit.   It was stated that this example would also be used to introduce aspects of the tax law that have not, as yet, been considered. One of these is the *investment tax credit* provision.

An investment tax credit provision is designed to encourage capital investment in production facilities that are not currently owned. In essence, it allows for an immediate reduction in taxes equal to some percent of the amount invested. For example, if the investment tax credit rate is 5 percent, an organization that purchases an asset for $200,000 would be allowed a tax credit of 5 percent of that amount, or $10,000; if its income taxes for the year under consideration would otherwise be $94,000, they can be reduced by the amount of the credit to $84,000. Furthermore, the $10,000 credit would have no effect on the total depreciation expense that can be reported for tax purposes during the life of the asset; so, if the $200,000 asset had an estimated salvage value of zero at the end of its life, annual depreciation expenses totaling $200,000 could be reported.

The specifics of an investment tax credit provision are changed from time to time, and, in fact, there may be periods during which no such credits are allowed. Furthermore, many of these specifics are somewhat technical and involved. Consequently, one can only make the following general observations with respect to what might be true at a given moment in time: (1) the credit may not apply to certain assets, such as land and buildings, (2) the rate may not be the same for every industry, (3) the credit may not be allowed for assets whose life is less than some stipulated number of years, (4) the effective tax credit rate may vary with the life of the qualified property or with the type of institution making the investment, (5) all or a portion of the credit may have to be returned in the event that the asset is disposed of within a shorter time period than was originally anticipated, (6) there may be a dollar limit on the size of the tax credit that can be claimed in any one year, and (7) the amount by which the calculated value of the credit exceeds an established limit may be carried back or forward to years in which the limit exceeded the amount claimed.

These general observations will suffice for our purposes, and so let us return to the replacement problem and suppose that, if the contractor procures the new equipment, he can take advantage of an available investment tax credit rate which is equivalent to 8 percent of the asset's first cost of $11,900. The old equipment will not qualify for the credit because it is already owned. Therefore, if the new asset is purchased, there will be a reduction in taxes equal to $11,900 times 8 percent, or $952. It is customary to show this as a tax reduction to be associated with the equipment at the time it is purchased, which is at the *beginning* of the first year, in spite of the fact that the actual saving may be experienced some weeks or months later. We shall adhere to this custom, although there is no reason why the tax credit cannot be shown as being realized at the end of the year if a given investor prefers to treat it in that manner.

It might also be noted that our method of computing and handling the credit in this example is based on the assumption that the procedure is consistent with the specifics, such as those outlined earlier, of an existing investment tax credit provision in the tax law. Also, it is being assumed that the investor will have a tax liability at the time he is permitted to take the tax credit, with the result that the credit will actually serve to reduce his tax at that time.

Gains and Losses on Disposal.   Another provision in the tax law deals with gains or losses that might be experienced upon the disposal of a currently-owned asset. A gain is said to occur when the realized value, as represented by the market value, exceeds the asset's book value, and a loss is said to occur when the realized value is less than the book value. Since the book value of a given asset is known only when the firm maintains single-asset accounts, it follows that, ordinarily, the question of whether a gain or loss has been experienced does not arise under a system of multiple-asset accounting.

Current tax laws call for distinguishing between a *capital* gain or loss and an *ordinary* gain or loss, because each may be treated differently for tax purposes. With some exceptions, a *capital* gain or loss is usually experienced with assets which are not depreciated for tax purposes, such as land, stocks, and bonds. Assets of this type have a book value equal to their first cost, and a capital gain or loss occurs when the asset is sold at a price which differs from its book value, that is, from its first cost. For example, if land were purchased for $140,000 and subsequently sold for $216,000, a capital gain of $76,000 would be reported; or, if bonds were purchased for $98,000 and subsequently sold for $60,000, a capital loss of $38,000 would be reported.

A capital gain or loss may be either *long term* or *short term*. It is considered to be a long-term capital gain or loss if the asset involved had been owned for more than some specified period, and a short-term capital gain or loss if the asset involved had been owned for that period or less; at the time this is being written, the specified period is one year, but, in the past, it has been six months and also nine months. In any case, the distinction between long term and short term is necessary because the applicable tax rate may be affected by whether the capital gain or loss is long or short term.

Since the effective tax rate which applies to a capital gain may be lower than the rate which applies to ordinary income, that is, to taxable income generated by a firm's regular operations, fairly complex rules have been developed for combining the capital gains and losses that may have been experienced during a given year. The application of these rules yields a *net* capital gain or loss. A description of these rules and the method for processing the result they yield is beyond the scope of this presentation. Suffice it to say that the rules are changed from time to time. Furthermore, the tax treatment of the value they generate for the *net* capital gain or loss is also subject to change and may depend on whether the investor is an individual or a corporation, may be affected by whether a long-term or short-term value is involved, may call for taking cognizance of an established limit on the loss that can be claimed in any one year, and may necessitate taking carryback and carryover provisions into consideration.

We shall now consider *ordinary* gains and losses. An ordinary gain or loss differs from a capital gain or loss in that it would be subject to the same tax rate that is applicable to ordinary income, whereas a capital gain or loss may be subject to a lower tax rate. As a rule, an ordinary gain or loss is experienced with an asset which is depreciated for tax purposes. In such cases, the difference between the asset's book value and the realized value can usually be attributed to the fact that past depreciation charges either overstated or understated the amount by which the asset actually decreased in value. To illustrate, a machine tool might have been purchased for $23,000 and then sold for $11,000 at a time when its book value was $7,000. Under current tax laws, it is likely that the $4,000 difference between the $11,000 realized value and the $7,000 book value would be defined as an ordinary gain, because it is attributable to the fact that the actual depreciation expense was apparently overstated by $4,000 during the asset's life. On the other hand, if the asset were sold for only $3,000, the $4,000 difference between this $3,000 realized value and the $7,000 book value would be defined as an ordinary loss, because it is attributable to the fact that the actual depreciation expense was apparently understated by $4,000 during the asset's life.

To continue, an earlier overstatement of the depreciation expense would have resulted in an understatement of the ordinary income subject to tax, and an earlier understatement of the depreciation expense would have resulted in an overstatement of the ordinary income subject to tax. Therefore, it is reasonable to demand that a corresponding adjustment be made in the calculated value of the taxable ordinary income for the year in which the asset is sold and in which the size of the past "error" in reported taxable ordinary income becomes known. Hence, in our machine-tool example, if the firm involved experienced taxable income of, say, $99,000 from its ordinary operations during the year in which the machine tool was sold, this $99,000 of taxable ordinary income would be increased to $103,000 if a $4,000 ordinary gain had been realized, or reduced to $95,000 if a $4,000 ordinary loss had been experienced.

The foregoing can be summarized by stating that an ordinary gain or loss is customarily treated as ordinary income and taxed accordingly. But it should be noted that the tax effects of an ordinary gain or loss are deferred if the currently-owned asset is accepted as a trade-in by the supplier of the new asset. To illustrate, let us suppose that, in our machine-tool example, the old asset is replaced by new equipment, which has a first cost of $50,000, and that the manufacturer of this equipment accepts, as payment, the old equipment and the balance in cash. If the old equipment has a market value of $11,000, the cash payment would be $39,000. But, as we saw, a market value of $11,000 at the time of disposal creates an ordinary gain of $4,000. Now, instead of paying a tax at that time on this $4,000, the buyer of the new equipment would enter the equipment into his books at a value equal to its first cost of $50,000 minus the ordinary gain of $4,000, or $46,000, and depreciate it accordingly during its estimated life. If this life is 10 years and the expected salvage value is zero and the straight-line method is to be used, a depreciation expense of $4,600 would be reported each year instead of the $5,000 that would have been reported had no ordinary gain occurred or had the old equipment been sold and a tax paid on the ordinary gain. Similarly, if the market and trade-in value created a $4,000 ordinary loss, the new equipment would have been entered into the books at a value of $50,000 plus $4,000, or $54,000, and then depreciated at a rate of $5,400 per year.

Finally, it should be mentioned that the resultant gain on disposal of an asset might, in part, be a capital gain and, in part, an ordinary gain. For example, a structure might have been purchased for $200,000 and sold for $235,000 at a time when its book value was $110,000. The total gain would be the difference between the realized value of $235,000 and the book value of $110,000, or $125,000. Of this $125,000 total gain, $35,000 would be a capital gain, as determined by taking the difference between the realized value of $235,000 and the first cost of $200,000. The balance of $90,000 would be an ordinary gain; this figure can also be obtained by taking the difference between the structure's $200,000 first cost and its book value of $110,000 to arrive at $90,000 as the amount by which the depreciation expense had been overstated and the taxable ordinary income understated in prior years.

Obviously, all this has been a very general description of a fairly complicated topic. Furthermore, we shall introduce only one aspect of it into the replacement problem being analyzed. Let us begin by recalling that the construction equipment currently owned by the contractor had a present market value of $3,600 and that this was expected to decrease to $800 in two years. It was also stated that the asset's book value is $800. Since this coincides with what the market value is expected to be two years from now, no gain or loss will be experienced at that time. But if the old equipment is replaced now, a gain will occur at this time because the asset's present market value of $3,600 exceeds its book value of $800 by $2,800.

Next, we shall suppose that the equipment had been purchased originally at a cost of $3,000. Therefore, $600 of the total gain of $2,800 will be a capital gain; this is the difference between the present market value of $3,600 and the original cost of $3,000. The balance of $2,200 will be an ordinary gain; the tax effect of this gain cannot be deferred because the old equipment will not be disposed of as a trade-in but will be sold if replaced.

Finally, let us assume that the contractor's capital-gain tax rate is 25 percent, as opposed to the 40 percent rate to which his ordinary income and, therefore, ordinary gains are subjected.

The effect of all this on the alternative of retaining the old equipment is that, if the asset is kept, a tax on the total gain of $2,800 will be avoided. One part of this tax saving will be equal to the capital gain of $600 times the capital-gain tax rate of 25 percent, or $150. The other part will be equal to the ordinary gain of $2,200 times the ordinary-gain tax rate of 40 percent, or $880. Consequently, the total saving will be $150 plus $880, or $1,030.

As in the case of an investment tax credit, it is customary to show such an amount as occurring at the beginning of the first year, and this is what we shall do. But if there is reason to believe that, in a specific situation, the end of the first year is closer to the point at which the tax would have to have been paid, the saving can be shown as taking place at that point. And, of course, regardless of the point selected, it is being assumed that the consequences of the investor's other activities will have no effect on our calculated value of this particular tax.

This brings us to the end of our determination of the impact of tax rules concerning gains and losses on the alternatives under consideration. Only the alternative of keeping the old equipment was affected by these rules because there is no indication that a gain or loss would be experienced with the proposed replacement at the end of its four-year life.

The After-Tax Comparison. There is nothing in the description of the two alternatives to suggest that any taxes, other than those which have already been ascertained, will be incurred. So the respective after-tax cash-flow patterns can be described as follows:

The new equipment requires an initial investment of $11,900; yields an investment tax credit of $952 at the beginning of its four-year life and a terminal salvage value of $3,900; and generates annual recurring costs of $120, $200, $310, and $540. On a time line, this can be shown in the following manner:

```
11,900                                    (3,900)
(952)        120        200        310      540
|-----------+----------+----------+----------|
0            1          2          3          4
```

Retention of the old equipment calls for a present investment of $3,600 in an asset whose salvage value will be $800 in two years, which will generate higher fuel costs of $190 a year, and whose repair and maintenance costs will be $960 the first year and $1,140 the second; it will be assumed that this before-tax cash-flow pattern will repeat itself during the succeeding two-year period. As determined earlier, this alternative will also result in higher annual income taxes of $908, $542, $315, and $9 during the four-year study period generated by the assumption regarding future replacements. Finally, retention of the old equipment will serve to eliminate a gains tax of $1,030 at the present time; the assumption regarding future replacements also necessitates treating this present saving of $1,030 in the gains tax as if it will reoccur at the beginning of the second two-year period. On a time line, all this would appear as follows:

```
3,600                    3,600
                         (800)                      (800)
(1,030)                  (1,030)
              190          190          190          190
              960        1,140          960        1,140
              908          542          315            9
   |-----------+------------+------------+------------|
   0           1            2            3            4
```

The alternatives can now be compared on an after-tax basis by processing the cash flows involved. The contractor's cost of money was given as 15 percent before taxes, but we shall suppose that he estimates that it will be 10 percent after taxes. If he wants to employ the future worth method, he can begin by combining the values which appear on the new equipment's cash-flow line to obtain the following:

```
10,948      120         200         310        (3,360)
   |---------+-----------+-----------+-----------|
   0         1           2           3           4
```

The future worth of these amounts is as follows:

$$\text{Future worth} = \$10{,}948(F/P)_{n=4}^{i=10} + \$120(F/P)_{n=3}^{i=10} + \$200(F/P)_{n=2}^{i=10}$$
$$+ \$310(F/P)_{n=1}^{i=10} - \$3{,}360$$
$$= \$13{,}412$$

If the values which appear on the old equipment's cash-flow line were combined, the following would be obtained:

```
2,570      2,058       3,642       1,465        539
   |---------+-----------+-----------+-----------|
   0         1           2           3           4
```

These amounts yield the following future worth:

$$\text{Future worth} = \$2,570(F/P)_{n=4}^{i=10} + \$2,058(F/P)_{n=3}^{i=10} + \$3,642(F/P)_{n=2}^{i=10}$$

$$+ \$1,465(F/P)_{n=1}^{i=10} + \$539$$

$$= \$13,060$$

These results and those which would have been obtained had the other analytical techniques been employed are shown in the following table:

Alternative	Future worth	Uniform annual cost	Present worth	Return on extra investment
New equipment	$13,412	$2,890	$9,160	8.8%
Old equipment	13,060	2,814	8,920	—

It should be noted that, because a complete description of each alternative's cash flows has not been provided, a return on total investment could not be computed; furthermore, the fact that the calculated costs are positive is of no significance. In any event, on the basis of any one of these comparisons, it would be concluded that, in the absence of irreducible factors, the old equipment should be retained. This was the same decision reached when a before-tax analysis was made; at that time, the uniform annual cost method, for example, yielded a cost of $3,657 for the new equipment and $3,076 for the old, which provided the old equipment with an annual advantage of $581 before taxes. Incidentally, a comparison of the after-tax annual costs reveals that the old equipment's advantage drops to only $76 a year after taxes. And it may be that the nature of the irreducible factors is such that, on a before-tax basis, the contractor would have decided to retain the old equipment, whereas on an after-tax basis, he might decide to replace it. One of these irreducible factors will, of course, be the assumption regarding the nature of the old equipment's future replacement. But it should be stressed that this particular assumption need not be made. Instead, the nature of future replacements can be forecast, or it can be assumed that all future replacements will be like the currently-available new equipment. With either of these alternate approaches, the method for ascertaining the tax differences between the alternatives would be the same as the one employed in this illustration, but the values of the cash flows and tax-deductible expenses being compared would differ.

THE MULTIPLE-ALTERNATIVE INVENTORY PROBLEM

An after-tax analysis will now be made of a multiple-alternative problem in which each of the alternatives is described in terms of all the costs and revenues it is expected to generate. The approach employed under such circumstances is similar to the one employed in a problem of this kind which involves two alternatives. The only difference is that the income tax expenses must be ascertained for a larger number of alternatives. The resultant after-tax cash-flow patterns can then be processed to obtain uniform annual costs, present worths, future worths, or rates of return. The procedures for obtaining these values are the same as those used to obtain them when multiple alternatives are being evaluated on a before-tax basis.

The problem we shall consider for purposes of illustration is the multiple-alternative problem of this kind which we already subjected to a before-tax analysis. This was the one in which a distributor was evaluating seven alternative inventory levels. Each of these called for some dollar investment in stock at this time, and this investment would not decrease in value. Furthermore, each alternative would yield a uniform annual saving attributable to reduced stockout costs. And, finally, the life of each alternative was 7 years. Specifically, the before-tax cash flows during this seven-year period for the various alternatives were given as shown in Table 8-4.

TABLE 8-4   A description of cash flows before taxes

		Before-tax receipts	
Alternative	Required total investment	End-of-year saving for 7 years	Salvage at end of 7th year
1	$ 0	$ 0	$ 0
2	12,000	1,920	12,000
3	15,000	2,730	15,000
4	20,000	3,000	20,000
5	22,000	3,210	22,000
6	29,000	5,170	29,000
7	33,000	5,780	33,000

Since an after-tax analysis is now desired, the analyst is provided with the following additional information: (1) No depreciation expense will be reported for tax purposes because the inventories are not a depreciable asset and, in any case, are not expected to decrease in value, (2) the entire total investment in whichever alternative is selected will be financed by borrowing money at an annual interest rate of 15 percent, (3) the principal of the loan will be repaid in a single sum at the end of the seventh year, but the annual interest charge will be paid at the end of each year, (4) the effective tax rate is 30 percent per year, and (5) the minimum rate-of-return requirement is 15 percent after taxes. With reference to the last item, it might be noted that the 15 percent is the cost of borrowed money. Given that no equity financing is involved, the cost of money to the distributor will simply be his cost of debt financing. The latter is 15 percent before taxes, and, for reasons presented at an earlier point in this chapter, it will also be 15 percent after taxes. Therefore, the before-tax and after-tax minimum rate-of-return requirements are the same because of the method of financing.

The Comparison. The analyst would begin by recognizing that, if an investment is made in inventories, the distributor's annual taxable income will be greater than it otherwise would be because of the reduction in stockout costs which will be experienced. However, for a given alternative, the increase in annual taxable income will be less than the saving in stockout costs because the annual interest expense to be associated with the alternative is a tax-deductible expense. With the repayment plan involved, this annual interest expense will be equal to the amount of the loan times the interest rate. In brief, in the absence of a deductible depreciation expense, the annual taxable income for a given alternative will be simply the difference between the annual saving it yields and the annual interest expense it produces.

The tax, of course, will be obtained by multiplying this taxable income by the 30 percent tax rate. And the after-tax saving in stockout costs will be equal to the before-tax saving minus the income tax.

By proceeding in accordance with these observations, the analyst would obtain the results shown in Table 8-5, in which a calculated negative tax is treated as a tax reduction because it is being assumed that the

TABLE 8-5 Determination of annual taxes

Alternative (a)	Before-tax annual saving (b)	Total investment (c)	Annual interest expense $(d = 0.15 \times c)$	Annual taxable income $(e = b - d)$	Annual tax $(f = 0.30 \times e)$	After-tax annual saving $(g = b - f)$
1	$ 0	$ 0	$ 0	$ 0	$ 0	$ 0
2	1,920	12,000	1,800	120	36	1,884
3	2,730	15,000	2,250	480	144	2,586
4	3,000	20,000	3,000	0	0	3,000
5	3,210	22,000	3,300	(−) 90	(−) 27	3,237
6	5,170	29,000	4,350	820	246	4,924
7	5,780	33,000	4,950	830	249	5,531

distributor's other activities are generating a tax expense in the year under consideration.

When the annual after-tax savings which appear in Table 8-5 are combined with the corresponding values of the required total investment and the expected salvage value, the after-tax cash-flow patterns for the alternatives prove to be as shown in Table 8-6.

TABLE 8-6   A description of cash flows after taxes

		After-tax receipts	
Alternative	Required total investment	End-of-year saving for 7 years	Salvage at end of 7th year
1	$ 0	$ 0	$ 0
2	12,000	1,884	12,000
3	15,000	2,586	15,000
4	20,000	3,000	20,000
5	22,000	3,237	22,000
6	29,000	4,924	29,000
7	33,000	5,531	33,000

At this point, using a rate of 15 percent, the analyst could compute seven after-tax uniform annual costs or seven after-tax present worths or seven after-tax future worths and compare the values obtained with any one of these methods to determine which of the alternatives is the most economical. The following expression for the present worth of alternative 7 is representative of those that would be developed in the course of making such a comparison:

Present worth $= \$33,000 - \$5,531(P/A)_{n=7}^{i=15} - \$33,000(P/F)_{n=7}^{i=15}$

With a rate of return approach, it would be necessary to list the alternatives in the order of the size of the total investment each requires, and this has already been done. The problem would then be broken down into a series of two-alternative problems and solved by a process of elimination, just as it was on a before-tax basis. But in this case, after-tax, instead of before-tax, cash flows would be processed to obtain after-tax returns on total and extra investments for each alternative.

Other than the one that has already been given, the expressions which would have to be developed in the course of applying any one of the four available methods of analysis will not be presented because they differ from those developed for the before-tax analysis only in that an after-tax series of values would be used for the end-of-year savings. Therefore, suffice it to say that the results obtained with these methods,

TABLE 8-7   The results of an after-tax analysis

Alter-native	Uniform annual cost	Present worth	Future worth	Return on total invest-ment	Return on extra invest-ment
1	$ 0	$ 0	$ 0	— %	— %
2	(−) 84	(−) 349	(−) 930	15.7	15.7
3	(−) 336	(−) 1,398	(−) 3,719	17.2	23.4
4	0	0	0	15.0	8.3
5	(+) 63	(+) 262	(+) 697	14.7	9.3
6	(−) 574	(−) 2,388	(−) 6,352	17.0	16.7
7	(−) 581	(−) 2,417	(−) 6,430	16.8	15.2

on an after-tax basis, would be as shown in Table 8-7. A study of these results reveals that, as in the case of the before-tax analysis, alternative 7 evolves as the most economical course of action in the absence of irreducible factors.

THE MULTIPLE-ALTERNATIVE LAYOUT PROBLEM

The next type of problem to be considered in this discussion of after-tax analyses is one in which multiple alternatives are involved but in which the revenues and costs unaffected by the choice of alternative are not given. For purposes of illustration, we shall return to an earlier example in which a manufacturer was confronted by the need to select one of four proposed plans for relocating certain work stations in his plant.

Plan W required an expenditure of $6,000 at this time and $5,000 for a "replacement" in 3 years to provide a layout which would be satisfactory for a total of 5 years and which would yield annual materials handling costs of $22,400. Plan X required only a present expenditure of $10,000 to obtain a layout which would yield annual handling costs of $21,000 for 5 years. Plan Y required a present expenditure of $12,000 for a layout which would yield annual handling costs of $19,800 for 5 years. And plan Z required a present expenditure of $15,000 for a layout which would yield annual handling costs of $19,200 for 5 years.

Suppose that the analyst is now told that the manufacturer believes that, for tax purposes, the cost of relocating facilities can be reported as an operating expense rather than as a capital expenditure. Therefore, if we take plan W as an example, the initial cost of $6,000 will not be depreciated but will be reported as a deductible expense at the beginning of year 1, and, similarly, the $5,000 expenditure for modifying the layout at the end of the third year will be reported as a deductible expense at that point; in addition, the annual handling cost of $22,400 will, of course, be reported as a deductible expense at the end of each year during the five-year study period. As a consequence, no depreciation expenses need be computed for tax purposes.

The analyst is also told that all expenditures to be associated with any one of these plans will be financed with equity funds, and, therefore, there will be no interest expenses reportable for tax purposes. Next, the effective tax rate is given as 52 percent. And, last, the after-tax rate-of-return requirement is said to be 6 percent because this is the after-tax return the manufacturer estimates he could realize by investing equity funds in other sources of comparable risk and tax status.

Ascertaining Tax Differences. As we know, in problems of this type, the assumption is made that the returns on total investment will be satisfactory. Therefore, the analyst begins with the understanding that at least $6,000 will be invested in the relocation activity at this time; this is the total investment required by plan W which requires a lower initial investment than does any one of the other plans. The question to be answered is whether the additional investments called for by the other plans can be justified, and this question can be answered by taking into consideration only the differences among the alternatives. The differences in relocation and handling costs are already known, and so, given that an after-tax analysis is to be made, a need exists for ascertaining only the differences in income taxes. These tax differences cannot be determined by calculating and comparing the total taxes for each alternative because the data required to do so are not available. Hence, some other approach must be employed.

For a reason that will become apparent, the other approach calls for comparing each of the remaining alternatives with the one which requires the minimum total investment at the present time. In this comparison, a determination is made of what the tax expenses will be with each of the remaining alternatives relative to what the tax expenses will be with the alternative which calls for the minimum total investment at the present time. More specifically, in the problem under consideration, the following must be computed: (1) the tax expenses with plan X, as compared with plan W, (2) the tax expenses with plan Y, as compared with plan W, and (3) the tax expenses with plan Z, as compared with plan W.

The effect of this is to break down what began as a four-alternative problem into a series of three two-alternative problems. The differences in taxes between any one of these pairs of alternatives are found in the manner described when the two-alternative replacement example was considered at an earlier point. This is to say that the analyst must begin by determining and comparing the respective tax-deductible expenses for the two alternatives in a given set of two alternatives.

The first of these sets contains plans W and X. Given that the relocation costs will be treated as tax-deductible expenses at the points at which they occur and that the handling costs will be reported as tax-deductible expenses at the end of the respective years, the tax differences for these two plans would be found as shown in Table 8-8. As an example,

TABLE 8-8   Tax differences between plans W and X

End-of- year (a)	Tax-deductible expenses		Plan W vs Plan X (d = b − c)	Additional tax with plan X as compared with plan W (e = 0.52 × d)
	Plan W (b)	Plan X (c)		
0	$ 6,000	$10,000	(−)$4,000	(−)$2,080
1	22,400	21,000	(+) 1,400	(+) 728
2	22,400	21,000	(+) 1,400	(+) 728
3	27,400	21,000	(+) 6,400	(+) 3,328
4	22,400	21,000	(+) 1,400	(+) 728
5	22,400	21,000	(+) 1,400	(+) 728

it will be noted in this table that, at the beginning of the first year, the deductible expenses with plan X are $4,000 *more* than with plan W. Consequently, since revenues are not expected to be affected by the choice of alternative, the taxable income with plan X will be $4,000 *less* than with plan W. At a 52 percent tax rate, the result is that the tax with plan X will be $2,080 *less* than with plan W. This is shown as a saving at that point because it is being assumed, as it has been and will be in this entire presentation, that such a tax advantage can be used to reduce the tax expense being generated at that point by an investor's other activities; otherwise, carryback and carryover provisions in the tax law would have to be considered, and this would introduce a complication we want to avoid. Also, it is worth repeating that relocation costs are shown to be generating deductible expenses at the points at which they occur; if there is reason to believe that it would be more realistic to assume that the resultant deductible expenses will be reported one year later, the analyst is certainly free to do so, and the tax differences would be computed accordingly.

But, to continue, the second pair of alternatives, for which tax differences must be calculated, consists of plans W and Y. Proceeding as he did with the first pair of alternatives, the analyst would obtain the results shown in Table 8-9.

TABLE 8-9   Tax differences between plans W and Y

End-of-year (a)	Tax-deductible expenses		Plan W vs Plan Y (d = b − c)	Additional tax with plan Y as compared with plan W (e = 0.52 × d)
	Plan W (b)	Plan Y (c)		
0	$ 6,000	$12,000	(−)$6,000	(−)$3,120
1	22,400	19,800	(+) 2,600	(+) 1,352
2	22,400	19,800	(+) 2,600	(+) 1,352
3	27,400	19,800	(+) 7,600	(+) 3,952
4	22,400	19,800	(+) 2,600	(+) 1,352
5	22,400	19,800	(+) 2,600	(+) 1,352

The third and last set of alternatives, for which the same type of comparison must be carried out, contains plans W and Z. The results of this comparison are as shown in Table 8-10.

Having ascertained the respective tax differences between the two plans contained in each set of alternatives, the analyst can go on to evaluate the four plans on an after-tax basis. Let us assume that he chooses to do so with the rate of return, or discounted cash flow, method.

The Comparison.   In a problem of this kind, the rate of return method requires that only returns on extra investment be computed and evaluated. Returns on total investment cannot be ascertained because all the costs and revenues for the alternatives involved are not given, and, in any event, these returns are assumed to be satisfactory.

The first step in the procedure is to list the alternatives in ascending order of the total present investment each requires, and this has already been done. Then, the first two plans on this list are compared on an

TABLE 8-10   Tax differences between plans W and Z

End-of-year (a)	Tax-deductible expenses		Plan W vs Plan Z (d = b − c)	Additional tax with plan Z as compared with plan W (e = 0.52 × d)
	Plan W (b)	Plan Z (c)		
0	$ 6,000	$15,000	(−)$9,000	(−)$4,680
1	22,400	19,200	(+) 3,200	(+) 1,664
2	22,400	19,200	(+) 3,200	(+) 1,664
3	27,400	19,200	(+) 8,200	(+) 4,264
4	22,400	19,200	(+) 3,200	(+) 1,664
5	22,400	19,200	(+) 3,200	(+) 1,664

after-tax basis. In our problem, these are plans W and X. The cash-flow pattern for plan W is as follows:

```
6,000                          5,000
       22,400    22,400    22,400    22,400    22,400
├──────────┼──────────┼──────────┼──────────┼──────────┤
0          1          2          3          4          5
```

For plan X, the cash-flow pattern will contain the relocation cost, the handling costs, and the tax expenses with this plan relative to plan W. As shown in Table 8-8, these values are as follows:

```
10,000     21,000    21,000    21,000    21,000    21,000
(2,080)      728       728      3,328       728       728
├──────────┼──────────┼──────────┼──────────┼──────────┤
0          1          2          3          4          5
```

The consequences of the $4,000 extra investment in plan X are found by calculating the differences between its cash flows and those of plan W. When the values contained in the first of the two preceding time lines are subtracted from those contained in the second, the following is obtained:

```
4,000
(2,080)    (672)     (672)    (3,072)     (672)     (672)
├──────────┼──────────┼──────────┼──────────┼──────────┤
0          1          2          3          4          5
```

By trial and error, it would be found that, at a rate i of 48.8 percent, the uniform annual equivalent or present worth or future worth of these values is equal to zero. Therefore, the after-tax return on the extra investment of $4,000 in Plan X is 48.8 percent, and since this exceeds the minimum rate-of-return requirement of 6 percent after taxes, the extra investment can be justified. This is to say that, in the absence of irreducible factors, plan W would be rejected in favor of plan X.

The next step in the analysis calls for comparing plan X with the next alternative on the list, that is, with plan Y. The after-tax cash-flow pattern for plan X was already given to be as follows:

```
10,000     21,000    21,000    21,000    21,000    21,000
(2,080)      728       728      3,328       728       728
├──────────┼──────────┼──────────┼──────────┼──────────┤
0          1          2          3          4          5
```

The first series of figures in this time line contains the relocation and handling expenses, and the second series contains the taxes for plan X as compared with those for plan W. The comparable values for plan Y, as shown in Table 8-9, are as follows:

12,000	19,800	19,800	19,800	19,800	19,800
(3,120)	1,352	1,352	3,952	1,352	1,352
├───────	─┼─────	─┼─────	─┼─────	─┼─────	─────┤
0	1	2	3	4	5

The differences between the second and the first of the two preceding cash-flow patterns yield a description of the consequences of the $2,000 extra investment in plan Y. These differences are as follows:

2,000	(1,200)	(1,200)	(1,200)	(1,200)	(1,200)
(1,040)	624	624	624	624	624
├───────	─┼─────	─┼─────	─┼─────	─┼─────	─────┤
0	1	2	3	4	5

The second series in this pattern of differences reflects the differences in taxes between the two plans. These tax differences have been presented as a separate series to bring out the following fact: If the taxes with plan X relative to plan W and the taxes with plan Y relative to plan W are known, the differences between these relative values are the taxes with plan Y relative to plan X. That this is true can be demonstrated by returning to the preceding time line and noting that the relocation cost with plan Y will be $2,000 higher than with plan X; since this results in an additional $2,000 deductible expense at that point, the tax saving with plan Y, as compared with plan X, will be 52 percent of $2,000, or the indicated $1,040. Next, the annual handling costs with plan Y will be $1,200 lower than with plan X; since there are no revenue differences, the annual taxable income will be $1,200 higher with plan Y than with plan X, and the additional annual tax with plan Y, as compared with plan X, will be 52 percent of this $1,200, or the indicated $624. A simpler explanation of the same point might be that, if the cost of item 2 exceeds that of item 1 by, say, $10 and if the cost of item 3 exceeds that of item 1 by, say, $15, then the cost of item 3 exceeds that of item 2 by $15 minus $10, or $5.

In any case, the analyst would find, by processing the values contained in the preceding time line, that the after-tax return on the $2,000 extra investment in plan Y is 52.8 percent. This exceeds the required 6 percent, and, consequently, the extra investment in plan Y can be justified.

Having eliminated plan X, the analyst goes on to compare plan Y with the next alternative on the list, which is plan Z. The relevant cash flows with plan Y are known to be as follows:

12,000	19,800	19,800	19,800	19,800	19,800
(3,120)	1,352	1,352	3,952	1,352	1,352
├───────	─┼─────	─┼─────	─┼─────	─┼─────	─────┤
0	1	2	3	4	5

For plan Z, the relocation cost, the handling costs, and the tax expenses relative to plan W are as shown in Table 8-10, and they yield the following cash-flow pattern:

15,000	19,200	19,200	19,200	19,200	19,200
(4,680)	1,664	1,664	4,264	1,664	1,664
0	1	2	3	4	5

A comparison of the preceding two patterns reveals that the results of an extra investment of $3,000 in plan Z are as follows:

3,000	(600)	(600)	(600)	(600)	(600)
(1,560)	312	312	312	312	312
0	1	2	3	4	5

The uniform annual equivalent or present worth or future worth of these amounts would be found to be zero at a rate i of zero percent. This after-tax return of zero percent on the $3,000 extra investment in alternative Z is, of course, unsatisfactory because it is less than the manufacturer's 6 percent cost of money; therefore, the proposal that plan Z be adopted would be rejected. Since plan Y is the only remaining alternative, it emerges as the most economical course of action.

Results with Other Techniques. This problem was analyzed by the rate of return method to demonstrate that, once the tax differences are ascertained, the mechanics of an after-tax rate of return analysis are the same as those employed when a multiple-alternative problem of this type is subjected to a before-tax rate of return analysis. However, one of the other three available analytical techniques would probably have been easier to apply in this case. With each of these other methods, it would also be necessary to begin by determining the taxes for plans X, Y, and Z, relative to plan W. Furthermore, the after-tax cash-flow pattern for each of the four plans would have to be described. But, then, it would suffice to compute and compare, at a rate of 6 percent, the uniform annual equivalents or present worths or future worths of these patterns. Naturally, plan Y would again have proved to be the most economical had any one of these other techniques been adopted. That this is true can be seen in the following table, which contains the results that were obtained with the rate of return method and that would have been obtained with each of the other methods:

Plan	Return on extra investment	Annual cost	Present worth	Future worth
W	– %	$24,819	$104,547	$139,905
X	48.8	24,125	101,621	135,989
Y	52.8	23,777	100,155	134,027
Z	0	23,831	100,382	134,331

It might be recalled that plan Y was also found to be the most economical alternative before taxes. And, incidentally, the calculated after-tax returns on extra investment happen to be equal to the before-tax returns. This stems from the fact that, in this problem, the pattern of tax-deductible expenses coincides with the pattern of cash flows for each alternative. As a consequence, each before-tax expenditure is reduced by the tax rate of 52 percent to obtain the equivalent after-tax expenditure. Hence, the amounts which serve to describe the respective cash-flow patterns of a given pair of alternatives are of the same *relative* size after taxes as they were before taxes. Therefore, the return on the extra investment in one of these alternatives, as compared with the other, is the same after taxes as it was before taxes.

The primary purpose of presenting a problem of this kind was to demonstrate how an after-tax analysis is conducted when multiple alternatives are involved and when only an incomplete description of these alternatives is available. However, it also provided us with an opportunity to show that a depreciation expense and an interest expense will not necessarily be among the tax-deductible expenses. And, finally, it enabled us to see how an after-tax analysis is conducted when the investor chooses to forecast the nature of a future replacement, as the manufacturer did with plan W, rather than to make a simplifying assumption regarding this nature.

A FINAL OBSERVATION

This brings us to the close of our presentation of the ways in which the tax consequences of an investment alternative are ascertained and processed. For reasons already given, no attempt was made to describe and apply every provision in the tax law which might affect a capital investment decision, and some of these provisions were described but not applied in the examples. Also, the values selected for such things as tax rates on ordinary income, tax rates on capital gains, and investment tax credit rates were not intended to represent the values these rates will actually assume. And, of course, those aspects of the tax law chosen for purposes of illustration may not prove to be relevant in all countries or during all periods.

None of this is intended to minimize the significance of what has been presented. After-tax analyses were made of situations involving two alternatives for which the respective tax expenses could be computed, two alternatives for which only the differences in the tax expenses could be ascertained, multiple alternatives for which the respective tax expenses could be calculated, and multiple alternatives for which only the differences in the tax expenses could be determined. In the course of these analyses, we encountered cases of 100 percent equity financing, 100 percent debt financing, and combinations of equity and debt financing. We considered cases involving no depreciation, straight-line depreciation, and sum-of-the-years-digits depreciation. We dealt with equal service lives and unequal service lives. And we were confronted by the need to calculate investment tax credits, taxes on ordinary income, taxes on capital gains, and taxes on ordinary gains. Having determined the tax expenses under these various conditions, we went on to process the results by means of the uniform annual cost, present worth, future worth, and rate of return methods.

To summarize, although complexities which would take us beyond the scope of this presentation were avoided, the basic principles of tax determination were described, and the procedures for processing the results were explained. This should suffice to enable an analyst to make an after-tax evaluation under ordinary circumstances and to recognize those circumstances which call for the assistance of tax specialists.

QUESTIONS

8-1 In what way is the fact that income tax expenses will be incurred accounted for in a before-tax analysis of investment alternatives?

8-2 Describe the general procedure for determining an income tax expense.

8-3 What are the basic types of tax-deductible expenses?

8-4 What is meant by the "effective" tax rate?

8-5 What must an investor take into consideration in the course of ascertaining an after-tax minimum rate-of-return requirement?

8-6 Is the return required on debt capital after taxes equal to the return required before taxes? Explain. Is the same true for equity capital? Explain.

8-7 What must be known before the deductible depreciation expenses can be determined? The deductible interest expenses?

8-8 Are any of the following included in an alternative's after-tax cash-flow pattern for the purpose of ascertaining that alternative's total cost or the return it will yield on total investment? Explain your answer for each of the listed items.

    a Depreciation expenses.
    b Debt repayment expenses.
    c Equity repayment expenses.
    d Interest expenses on debt.
    e Opportunity costs of equity.

8-9 What is the procedure for calculating the rate of return on equity investment? On debt investment? Answer each of these questions on a before-tax basis and then on an after-tax basis.

8-10 For a given alternative, what is the relationship among the return on equity investment, return on debt investment, and return on total investment?

8-11 Is the return on equity investment a better basis for evaluating an alternative than is the return on total investment? Explain.

8-12 Can an alternative which yields a satisfactory return on total investment yield an unsatisfactory return on equity investment? Explain.

8-13 Can an alternative which yields an unsatisfactory return on total investment yield a satisfactory return on equity investment? Explain.

8-14 When revenues are not given but it is known that they will be the same for each alternative, how can the differences in taxes for the alternatives be found?

8-15 What is an investment tax credit?

8-16 What is meant by a gain or loss on disposal of an asset? An *ordinary* gain or loss? A *capital* gain or loss? A *long-term* gain or loss? A *short-term* gain or loss? Why is it necessary to distinguish among these?

8-17 Under what condition can the tax effect of an ordinary gain or loss be deferred? By what means is it deferred?

8-18 Summarize the procedure for making an after-tax analysis of each of the following types of problems:

    a Two alternatives are involved and each is described completely in terms of the revenues and costs it is expected to generate.
    b Two alternatives are involved and each is described only in terms of the revenues and costs affected by the choice of alternative.
    c Three or more alternatives are involved and each is described completely in terms of the revenues and costs it is expected to generate.
    d Three or more alternatives are involved and each is described only in terms of the revenues and costs affected by the choice of alternative.

PROBLEMS

8-1 If the state income tax can be claimed as a deductible expense when determining the federal income tax, what will each of the following be:

  a The effective tax rate, given that the federal rate is 44 percent and that the state rate is 4 percent? (Ans. 46.24%)

  b The state tax rate, given that the effective rate is 49.56 percent and that the federal rate is 48 percent? (Ans. 3%)

  c The federal tax rate, given that the effective rate is 26.5 percent and that the state rate is 2 percent? (Ans. 25%)

  d The effective tax rate, given that the state rate is 10 percent and that the federal rate is 38 percent?

  e The state tax rate, given that the federal rate is 28 percent and that the effective rate is 33.4 percent?

  f The federal tax rate, given that the state rate is 6 percent and that the effective rate is 34.2 percent?

8-2 What should an investor's minimum before-tax rate-of-return requirement and the corresponding minimum after-tax rate-of-return requirement be under each of the following conditions?

  a The debt ratio is 0.30. The cost of borrowed money is 10 percent. Equity funds could be invested elsewhere in similar activities at a return of 18 percent before taxes and 12 percent after taxes. (Ans. 15.6%, 11.4%)

  b The entire investment will be financed with equity funds. This money could be invested in alternatives of comparable risk and tax status at an after-tax return of 9 percent and a before-tax return of 15 percent. If money were borrowed, the interest rate would be 6 percent.

  c Eighty percent of the financing will be with equity money. The opportunity cost to be associated with these funds is 32 percent before taxes and 21 percent after taxes. The debt portion of the investment will be raised at a cost of 11 percent.

  d The entire total investment will consist of borrowed money. The cost of debt is 8 percent. Opportunities exist to invest funds in other alternatives at a before-tax return of 20 percent and an after-tax return of 13 percent; however, additional amounts can be borrowed at 8 percent to take advantage of these other investment opportunities.

8-3 The owner of a number of laundromats is thinking of installing additional washers and dryers at some of those locations where space is available for that purpose. If an investment of this kind is made, the equipment will be purchased from one of two manufacturers. A partial description of the cash-flow pattern to be associated with each of these alternatives is as follows:

	Equipment F	Equipment G
Installed cost	$23,000	$31,000
Service life	5 years	5 years
Terminal salvage value	$500	$1,000
First-year operating costs	$15,000	$12,000
Annual increase in operating costs	$750	$600

Installation of either type of equipment will serve to increase receipts by $25,000 the first year, and these will then increase at a rate of $500 a year thereafter.

Because the alternatives are to be compared on an after-tax basis, the owner of the laundromats also takes cognizance of the fact that 100 percent equity financing will be involved, that the assets will be depreciated by the straight-line method, and that the effective tax rate is 42 percent.

With an after-tax rate-of-return requirement of 12 percent, which course of action will evolve as being the most economical on the basis of a rate of return analysis? (Ans.   19.1%, 18.9%; 19.1%, 18.5%)

8-4   Suppose that the relevant tax data in the preceding problem were said to be as follows: The effective tax rate remains at 42 percent, and financing continues to be with only equity funds. However, the tax depreciation method will be double-rate declining-balance. Furthermore, any difference between the terminal salvage value and the book value at the end of an asset's life will be treated and reported as an ordinary gain or loss on disposal.

Compare the alternatives under this set of circumstances by means of the future worth method. (Ans.   -$8,237, -$11,081)

8-5   Returning to problem 8-3, suppose that the relevant tax data had been as follows: The effective tax rate remains at 42 percent, and financing continues to be with only equity funds. But sum-of-the-years-digits depreciation will be adopted for tax purposes. Also, with either alternative, a 7 percent investment tax credit can be claimed at the point at which the equipment is purchased.

Under these conditions, what is the after-tax uniform annual cost of each alternative? (Ans.   -$1,720, -$2,306)

8-6   Let us suppose that the relevant tax data in problem 8-3 were given to be as follows: As stated originally, the straight-line method of depreciation will be adopted, the effective tax rate will be 42 percent, and no investment credit is available. However, there will be a change in the method of financing. Specifically, if a decision is made to buy equipment F, $10,000 will be borrowed at an interest rate of 8 percent; at the end of each year for 5 years, the interest charge for the year and $2,000 of the principal will be paid to the lending institution. But if equipment G is purchased, $15,000 will be borrowed at an interest rate of 8 percent; at the end of each year for 5 years, the interest charge for the year and $3,000 of the principal will be paid to the lending institution.

Given this change in the method of financing, what would be the result of a present worth analysis of the alternatives on an after-tax basis? For purposes of simplicity, assume that a change will also occur in the cost of equity funds such that the change in the method of financing will have no effect on the established after-tax minimum rate-of-return requirement of 12 percent. (Ans. −$4,862, −$6,633)

8-7 A savings institution makes various savings plans available to its depositors. One of these calls for a minimum deposit of $10,000 and requires that this amount be kept in the account for 4 years. But during the four-year period, the depositor of $10,000 is mailed an interest payment of $800 at the end of each year.

The individual who is giving consideration to investing $10,000 in such an account pays a tax of 25 percent on her taxable income. In the event that a part of the $10,000 total investment is borrowed, the cost will be 6 percent per year. Furthermore, any accrued interest on the debt portion of the investment would be paid at the end of each year, but the principal of the loan would be repaid in a single sum at the end of the fourth year.

a If $10,000 of equity funds are invested in such an account, what will be the *before-tax* rate of return on total investment? On equity investment?

b If $2,500 of the total investment consists of borrowed money, what will be the *before-tax* return on total investment? On debt investment? On equity investment? (Ans. 8%, 6%, 8.7%)

c If $7,000 of the total investment consists of borrowed money, what will be the *before-tax* return on total investment? On debt investment? On equity investment?

d If all of the total investment consists of borrowed money, what will be the *before-tax* return on total investment? On debt investment? On equity investment?

e If the entire total investment consists of equity funds, what will be the *after-tax* return on total investment? On equity investment? (Ans. 6%, 6%)

f If $2,500 of the total investment consists of borrowed money, what will be the *after-tax* return on total investment? On debt investment? On equity investment? (Ans. 6.38%, 6%, 6.5%)

g If $7,000 of the total investment consists of borrowed money, what will be the *after-tax* return on total investment? On debt investment? On equity investment?

h If all of the total investment consists of borrowed money, what will be the *after-tax* return on total investment? On debt investment? On equity investment?

8-8 A management consulting firm has been renting a copier. The current lease will soon expire, and the manufacturer of the equipment suggests that the firm may find it more economical to purchase a new copying machine instead of continuing to rent one.

A new unit would have a first cost of $35,500, an economic service life of about 6 years, and a terminal salvage value of approximately $1,900. Maintenance and repair costs, for which the consulting firm would be responsible, are likely to average $4,800 a year.

The same unit can be rented for $12,000 a year; for purposes of analysis, the consulting firm will treat this as an end-of-year expense in spite of the fact that rental payments would have to be made monthly. To continue, at this price, the manufacturer is willing to offer only a two-year lease. He estimates that, during the following two-year period, the annual rental charge will be $13,000 and that, during the third two-year period, the annual rental charge will be $14,000.

Under the rental arrangement, the lessor will assume responsibility for all necessary maintenance and repairs. However, the consulting firm would have to pay for the cost of such things as paper, toner, and power; no attempt is made to estimate these costs because the same expenses would be experienced in the event that the copier is purchased.

For tax purposes, the rental charges will be reported as deductible expenses in the years in which they are incurred. But if the equipment is purchased, it will be depreciated by means of the sum-of-the-years-digits method. No debt financing would be involved if a decision is made to buy. The firm's effective tax rate is 30 percent. Its after-tax minimum rate-of-return requirement is equal to its opportunity cost of 10 percent.

You are asked to ascertain, on the basis of an after-tax uniform annual cost comparison, whether it is more economical to purchase the copier or to rent it for six more years. (Ans. $12,705, $12,264)

8-9 In the preceding problem, assume that the relevant tax data were given to be as follows: If the copier is purchased, $20,000 will be borrowed at 10 percent, which happens to coincide with the firm's opportunity cost, to finance the required capital investment; the interest charge would be paid at the end of each year, but the $20,000 would not be repaid until the end of the sixth year. The tax depreciation method continues to be sum-of-the-years-digits, the effective tax rate remains at 30 percent, and the annual rental costs will be reported as deductible expenses in the years in which they occur.

Make a present worth comparison of the alternatives under these circumstances to determine which is the more economical, given that the after-tax cost of money remains at 10 percent. How does the result of this analysis compare with the one obtained in the preceding problem? (Ans. $55,330, $56,027)

8-10 Continuing to work with an after-tax minimum rate-of-return requirement of 10 percent, compare the alternatives described in problem 8-8 by means of the rate of return method. When doing so, suppose that the relevant tax data were presented as follows: If the copier is purchased, financing will be entirely with equity funds, there will be a 5 percent investment tax credit, and double-rate declining-balance depreciation will be adopted. Any difference between the end-of-life book value and the estimated salvage value will be treated as an ordinary gain or loss for tax purposes. If the copier is leased, annual rental costs will continue to be reported as deductible expenses in the years in which they occur. The effective tax rate remains at 30 percent. (Ans. 9.96%)

8-11 Let us return to problem 8-8 and suppose that the relevant tax data had been as follows: The effective tax rate is 30 percent, and rental charges will be treated as operating expenses for tax purposes. However, in the event that the equipment is bought, the firm will adhere to the straight-line method of depreciation. Also, there will be an investment tax credit of 5 percent. Finally, the purchase would be partially financed by borrowing $9,000 at 10 percent, which happens to coincide with the firm's opportunity cost; at the end of each year for the first three years, the accrued interest plus $3,000 of the principal would be paid to the lending organization.

Given that the rate-of-return requirement remains at 10 percent, which alternative will appear as the more attractive on the basis of a future worth comparison? (Ans. $94,884, $94,421)

8-12 A steel company is going to buy a 6-axle locomotive for switching purposes. The question to be answered is whether the unit purchased should be a new one or a rebuilt used one. The two alternatives can be described as follows:

	New	Used
First cost	$375,000	$150,000
Life	12 years	6 years
Salvage value	$27,000	$6,000
Annual maintenance costs	$6,000	$9,000
Annual fuel costs	$4,000	$5,000

It would be necessary to borrow, at an interest rate of 6 percent, $100,000 to finance the purchase of the new locomotive and $40,000 to finance the purchase of the used one. In each case, the total amount borrowed and all the accrued interest would be repaid in a single sum at the end of the life of the locomotive under consideration.

For tax purposes, each locomotive would be depreciated by the straight-line method. Also, with either alternative, the company would take advantage of an available investment tax credit of 10 percent. The effective tax rate is 40 percent, and the minimum after-tax rate-of-return requirement is 8 percent.

Determine which of the alternatives is the more economical with the use of the uniform annual cost method.

8-13 A firm owns a unit of equipment which it uses to produce cellulose insulation. The equipment was purchased five years ago at a cost of $30,000. At that time, it was assumed that the asset would have a ten-year life and no terminal salvage value; the unit has been depreciated accordingly with the use of the straight-line method.

A new machine of this type has been designed and is being considered as a replacement for the old unit. The new equipment has an installed first cost of $55,000, an estimated service life of 10 years, and an expected salvage value of zero. It would be depreciated by the sum-of-the-years-digits method. Procurement of this equipment would serve to reduce annual operating costs by approximately $4,000.

If the old machine is replaced, it will be sold to a used equipment dealer for $20,000. But if it is retained, it will probably be operated for another 5 years, at the end of which time its market value will be negligible. Meanwhile, tax depreciation by the straight-line method would continue.

With either alternative, a debt ratio of 0.40 is to be assumed. More specifically, $8,000 of the $20,000 present investment in the old equipment and $22,000 of the $55,000 required investment in the new equipment are to be treated as borrowed funds. The $8,000 would be repaid at an end-of-year rate of $1,600 for 5 years, and the $22,000 at an end-of-year rate of $2,200 for 10 years. In addition to these uniform repayments of principal, a payment equal to the annual interest charge would be made at the end of each year.

The cost of borrowed money to the firm is 6 percent, its minimum after-tax rate-of-return requirement is 12 percent, and the effective tax rate is 50 percent.

Will a present worth analysis indicate that the extra investment required by the new machine can be justified? (Ans. $55,000, $49,897)

8-14 The owner of an automobile service station wants to determine whether an investment in wheel balancing equipment should be made. A description of the two types of equipment he is investigating is as follows:

	Type P	Type Q
First cost	$1,000	$4,000
Service life	2 years	4 years
Salvage value	$200	$600
Net annual receipts	$475	$1,100

It will be noted that type Q has the advantage of a longer life. Also, it will serve to increase net annual receipts because it is known to result in more accurate balancing and, as a consequence, will enable the station owner to receive more work of this type and to charge more for this work.

Equipment P would be financed with equity funds. But the selection of equipment Q would necessitate borrowing $2,000 at 8 percent; the entire loan plus the accrued interest would be repaid in one year. The after-tax cost of equity funds is also 8 percent, and so the station owner has established a minimum after-tax rate-of-return requirement of 8 percent.

Either asset would be depreciated by means of the straight-line method, and the effective tax rate is 28 percent.

Should he make an investment in equipment of this kind? If so, which type is the more economical? Base your answers to these questions on a uniform annual cost comparison of the alternatives.

8-15 One of the alternatives considered in the preceding problem was equipment of type Q. If this equipment were purchased, what would the following be:

a The before-tax return on total investment? (Ans.   8.9%)
b The before-tax return on debt investment?
c The before-tax return on equity investment? (Ans.   9.1%)
d The after-tax return on total investment? (Ans.   6.9%)
e The after-tax return on debt investment?
f The after-tax return on equity investment? (Ans.   6.6%)

8-16 A binding machine which is in use in a carpet manufacturer's plant is breaking down quite frequently. Consequently, maintenance and repair costs have risen to a level such that the replacement of the equipment has been proposed.

A new binding machine will cost $2,200, have a service life of 9 years, and yield a negligible terminal salvage value. Maintenance and repair costs will be about $50 in the first year of its life and increase thereafter at an annual rate of $25. The asset would be depreciated by the straight-line method, but the company would take advantage of an opportunity to use a six-year life with a zero salvage value for tax depreciation purposes.

The currently-owned unit has a book value of zero and a market value of $400. If it is replaced, the supplier of the new machine will accept the old one as a trade-in and, hence, give the carpet manufacturer a credit of $400 against the $2,200 price of the new machine. Consequently, the manufacturer would not incur a tax on his ordinary gain at this time but would reduce the initial book value of the new binding machine by the amount of the gain and depreciate it accordingly.

Recent maintenance and repair costs with the old equipment have been averaging $350 a year. It is estimated that they can be maintained at this level for an indefinite time period. As a result, the firm decides to adopt a remaining life for the machine equal to that of the new one, which is 9 years. The unit is not expected to have any value at the end of that life.

The alternatives are to be compared on a future worth basis. The effective tax rate is 36 percent, all financing will be with equity funds, and the after-tax cost of these funds is 6 percent. What course of action will be suggested by the results of the comparison? (Ans. $5,330, $4,727)

8-17 An operator of a retail food store is thinking of increasing the selection of frozen foods which she carries. If she does, an investment will have to be made in additional fixtures, but the result will be an increase in the sales of frozen foods.

Two alternatives are being considered. One is to buy and install a refrigerated display case of a given storage capacity, and the other is to buy and install a case with a larger capacity. A description of the probable consequences is as follows:

	Case I	Case II
Installed cost	$6,000	$8,000
Service life	8 years	8 years
Salvage value	$600	$800
Increase in net annual receipts	$1,300	$2,000

The retailer's effective tax rate is 44 percent, she can claim an 8 percent investment tax credit with either alternative, she would depreciate the assets with the use of the sum-of-the-years-digits method, and her after-tax rate-of-return requirement is 15 percent.

Insofar as financing is concerned, $2,400 would be borrowed if case I is purchased, and $3,200 if case II is. The $2,400 would be repaid at a uniform end-of-year rate of $300, and the $3,200 at a uniform end-of-year rate of $400. In addition to these payments, 12 percent interest would be paid at the end of each year for 8 years.

You are asked to evaluate the alternatives. Do so by means of the rate of return method. (Ans. 14.2%, 17%; 14.2%, 17%)

8-18 Returning to problem 8-17, determine the following:

a The after-tax return on the debt investment in case I.
b The after-tax return on the equity investment in case I.
c The after-tax return on the debt investment in case II.
d The after-tax return on the equity investment in case II.

8-19 Over a period of time, an investor has acquired five tracts of land. The last of these was purchased about two years ago. In each case, the investment was made because there was an opportunity to rent the property to farmers who owned adjoining acreage and because there was a chance that the property would increase in value.

To raise capital which she requires at this time, the investor has decided to sell four of these tracts. Therefore, she wants to ascertain which of the five represents the most economical investment on an after-tax basis and, consequently, should be retained. In her analysis, she will take into consideration, among other things, the initial cost of each property, its present market value, the average net annual rental receipts it will generate, and its future market value. This future market value is estimated in terms of what it will be 7 years from now because she expects that, in every case, the value will reach a maximum at that point. In any event, these data are as follows:

Tract	First cost	Present value	Expected annual net receipts	Future value
1	$47,000	$44,000	$4,800	$46,000
2	29,000	40,000	1,100	43,000
3	42,000	49,000	5,100	50,000
4	33,000	41,000	900	60,000
5	61,000	55,000	6,400	63,000

Land is not depreciated, and, therefore, there will be no tax depreciation expenses during the assumed seven-year life of the alternatives. Also, given that no debt financing is or will be involved, there will be no deductible interest expenses. Ordinary income will be taxed at an effective rate of 46 percent, but the rate applicable to long-term capital gains or losses will be equal to 23 percent.

If the established after-tax minimum rate-of-return requirement is 6 percent, which of the alternatives will appear as being the most economical on the basis of a present worth comparison? (Ans.   −$527, $7,696, −$14, $671, −$4,506)

8-20 A utility is comparing three mutually exclusive alternatives. Plan A calls for replacing an existing regenerator with a new unit to be supplied by a certain manufacturer. Plan B calls for replacing the existing regenerator with one to be supplied by another manufacturer. And plan C calls for eliminating the need for a regenerator by making modifications in the gas turbine. A partial description of these possible courses of action is as follows:

	Plan A	Plan B	Plan C
First cost	$750,000	$500,000	$180,000
Economic life	15 years	15 years	15 years
Salvage value	$30,000	$20,000	$0

The plan selected will determine what additional fuel costs will be incurred in the operation of the turbine. It is estimated that these amounts will be as follows:

	Plan A	Plan B	Plan C
First-year additional fuel cost	$0	$20,000	$40,000
Annual rate of increase	$0	$2,000	$4,000

While other recurring costs will vary slightly from plan to plan, the differences are small enough to be ignored.

Each of the plans will require some amount of debt financing at a cost of 10 percent. The terms of the loan in every case will be such that only the interest need be paid each year; the principal as such will be repaid at the end of the fifteenth year. The exact amounts to be borrowed with the respective alternatives and the resultant end-of-year interest payments will be as follows:

	Plan A	Plan B	Plan C
Amount of debt	$187,500	$125,000	$45,000
Annual interest payment	$18,750	$12,500	$4,500

Finally, if either plan A or B is selected, a 6 percent investment tax credit will be received. None will be available with plan C.

The analyst is going to make a rate of return analysis of the alternatives. When doing so, she will take into consideration that the tax depreciation method will be sum-of-the-years-digits, that the utility's effective tax rate is 52 percent, and that the minimum rate-of-return requirement is 13 percent. Which of the alternatives will she find to be the most attractive? (Ans. 7.1%, 7.8%)

8-21 A printing establishment wants to ascertain whether it is economical to make a capital investment in a kind of press which it does not currently have in its plant. A press of this kind would enable the firm to obtain jobs which it currently is incapable of processing. As a consequence, an increase would be likely to occur in its net annual receipts.

After some study, the company has found that three presses of the kind being considered are available. They differ from each other from the standpoint of installed cost, service life, salvage value, and operating characteristics; the operating characteristics will affect recurring costs and, more importantly, the amount of additional business the firm can obtain. Specifically, the three alternatives have been described as follows:

	Press X	Press Y	Press Z
Installed cost	$400,000	$480,000	$590,000
Service life	10 years	12 years	14 years
Salvage value	$24,000	$27,000	$30,000
First-year additional net receipts	$57,000	$68,000	$74,000
Annual increase in net receipts	$1,000	$1,500	$2,000

Regardless of which press is purchased, the company is entitled to an investment tax credit of 9 percent. The tax depreciation method will be straight-line. The effective tax rate will be 45 percent.

A severe shortage of equity funds would force management to finance any one of the alternatives by borrowing an amount equal to the entire installed first cost of the alternative. The terms of any such loan would call for the following: (1) the payment of the annual interest charge at the end of each year, (2) repayment of one-half of the principal of the loan at the midpoint of the asset's expected life, and (3) repayment of the remaining one-half of the principal at the end of the asset's expected life. Interest would be computed at a rate of 10 percent.

Given the proportion of debt financing and the cost of debt, the firm establishes a rate-of-return requirement of 10 percent for purposes of analysis. At this rate, which of the three presses will yield the minimum uniform annual cost after taxes? Can an investment in this press be justified? Explain.

8-22 A cab company is going to order 100 replacement batteries for its taxis. Until now, it has been the firm's policy to purchase batteries with an expected life of one year. But the battery supplier is suggesting that consideration be given to the procurement of batteries which have a higher first cost but a significantly longer life. More exactly, he recommends that longer-lived batteries be purchased for the 100 vehicles involved; the cab company intends to operate these vehicles for four more years. When asked to describe the possible alternatives, the supplier submits the following:

Battery type	First cost	Estimated life, months
R	$2,000	12
S	2,700	24
T	3,500	36
U	4,400	48

None of the batteries will have a salvage value, and no expense other than the first cost of the 100 batteries will be affected by the choice of alternative.

A decision regarding which of the batteries is the most economical will be based on an after-tax future worth comparison of the alternatives for a period of 4 years. This study period has been selected because it is equal to the remaining service life of the vehicles involved.

Insofar as future replacements are concerned, it will be assumed that battery R will be replaced by a series of three batteries of the same kind, that battery S will be replaced by one battery of the same kind, but that battery T will be replaced by a battery of type R.

For tax purposes, the first costs of the batteries will be reported as maintenance expenses at the points at which the expenditures are made. There will be no deductible interest expenses because all the financing will be with equity funds.

What will be the outcome of the future worth analysis, if the firm's effective tax rate is 48 percent and its after-tax opportunity cost is 12 percent?

8-23 Additional problems to be solved on an after-tax basis by another analytical technique appear at the end of chapter 9. Analyze those for which you choose to or are asked to provide solutions.

9

The Revenue
Requirement Approach

The concepts underlying after-tax analyses of alternative investment opportunities are not particularly difficult. But, as some of the examples in the preceding chapter revealed, the arithmetical steps involved in the application of these concepts may prove to be tedious and time consuming. However, care must be taken not to exaggerate the significance of these computational difficulties. At worst, they may succeed in lengthening the duration of the study by a few days. As a rule, this is of no consequence, given that weeks or months may have been spent in the process of ascertaining the available alternatives and in the course of developing the data required to evaluate these alternatives.

Nevertheless, attempts have been made to simplify the mechanics of after-tax analyses. These attempts have manifested themselves in the development of special analytical approaches. Each of these special approaches stems from one or some combination of the four basic methods of analysis we have considered, but each differs from the underlying basic methods in one important respect. This is that it is characterized by a unique set of assumptions. If these assumed conditions coincide with or approximate actual conditions, the special technique involved can be adopted as a means of simplifying the after-tax analysis of investment alternatives. Otherwise, it cannot.

We shall concern ourselves with only one of these special analytical techniques. The one to be described and explained is the *revenue requirement method*. It has been selected for presentation because there is reason to believe that its underlying assumptions are such that they do not serve to limit its area of application too severely. Furthermore, its nature is such that it is as representative of this class of analytical techniques as is any other special method of analysis.

A GENERAL DESCRIPTION

The revenue requirement method can be most easily described with the use of a certain type of capital investment problem. This is one in which the revenues are the same for each of a set of mutually exclusive alternatives and in which these revenues are large enough to ensure a satisfactory return on the total investments in the respective alternatives. None of this is intended to suggest that the revenue requirement method can be applied only under the foregoing circumstances. But under such conditions, the method calls for describing each alternative in terms of the *positive* costs it is expected to generate; these would include the capital cost, recurring expenses other than income taxes, and income taxes. Then, by means to be presented, a determination is made for each alternative of the uniform annual revenues which would have to be experienced with that alternative if the investor is to realize an after-tax return on the total investment in that alternative just equal to his established minimum rate-of-return requirement. After this has been done, the required revenues for the respective alternatives are compared, and the alternative with the minimum revenue requirement is identified. In the absence of irreducible factors, this alternative is considered to represent the most economical course of action.

We shall now go on to consider the specifics of this method. This will be done with the use of examples of representative types of problems. These examples will be the same as those employed in the preceding chapter so as to permit a comparison of the results of a revenue requirement approach with the results of an after-tax uniform annual cost, present worth, future worth, or rate of return approach. The first of these examples was one in which two proposals for producing and marketing a new product were to be evaluated.

THE NEW PRODUCT PROBLEM

One of the proposals in the new product problem was identified as alternative K. It required an investment of $84,000 in equipment and $5,000 in working capital. The equipment would have no value at the end of its four-year life, but the working capital would be recovered in its entirety at that point. Annual operating costs were given as $30,000, and the firm's after-tax rate-of-return requirement was said to be 12 percent. Finally, annual revenues were expected to be $67,000, but this datum will be ignored for the time being because of the way in which the firm now chooses to evaluate this alternative. Specifically, it wants to begin by determining what the uniform annual revenues would have to be if an after-tax return of exactly 12 percent is to be realized on the total investment of $89,000.

This determination can start with the following description of the alternative's relevant cash flows:

```
89,000                                        (5,000)
          30,000      30,000      30,000      30,000
   ├──────────┼───────────┼───────────┼───────────┤
   0          1           2           3           4
```

It would then continue with the realization that a return of exactly 12 percent will be experienced if the annual revenues are just equal to the sum of (1) the uniform annual capital cost, which includes the devaluation expense and the 12 percent cost of money, (2) the uniform annual equivalent of the operating costs, and (3) the uniform annual equivalent of the income tax expenses.

To ascertain the revenues required to cover the annual capital cost, we simply calculate the value of this cost just as we did in the uniform annual cost method. Doing so, we obtain the following:

$$\text{Annual capital cost} = \$89,000(A/P)_{n=4}^{i=12} - \$5,000(A/F)_{n=4}^{i=12} = \$28,255$$

The revenues required to cover the operating costs are, of course, equal to the annual equivalent of these expenses which is as follows:

$$\text{Annual operating costs} = \$30,000$$

Finally, there is a need to determine the revenues required to cover the uniform annual equivalent of the income tax expenses. It is at this point that a difficulty is encountered because the unknown income tax expenses will be a function of, among other things, the annual revenues. But these revenues are also unknown as indicated by the fact that an attempt is being made to find out what they must be to cover, among other things, income taxes. In brief, the analyst is confronted by two interacting unknowns. Fortunately, the problem this poses has been solved, and it is this solution, which is an integral part of the revenue requirement method, that serves to distinguish it from the uniform annual cost method.

Income Tax Determination. The uniform annual equivalent of the income taxes for which revenues will have to be provided is found with the use of two formulas. The derivations of these formulas are given in Appendix B. Therefore, at this point, we shall only present the formulas, consider the assumptions which underlie them, and explain the manner in which they are applied. The assumptions are as follows:

(1) The total investment in an asset during any one year will be equal

to its book value during that year, as determined by the method of depreciation used for tax purposes.

(2) The amount of debt to be associated with the asset during any one year will be a stated fraction of its book value during that year, and this fraction will remain constant throughout the asset's life.

On the basis of these assumptions, an expression was developed which is designed to yield a value of a so-called tax factor. This expression is as follows:

$$\phi = \left(\frac{t}{1-t} \right) \left(1 - \frac{dr}{i} \right) \qquad (9\text{-}1)$$

where

$\phi (phi)$ = tax factor
t = effective income tax rate
d = proportion of debt financing
r = cost of debt in terms of an interest rate
i = after-tax return requirement on total investment

The value of this tax factor is then substituted in the following formula to find the uniform annual equivalent of the income taxes:

Annual income taxes = $\phi (UACC - UADE)$ \qquad (9-2)

where

$UACC$ = uniform annual capital cost
$UADE$ = uniform annual equivalent of the depreciation expenses reported for tax purposes

We shall now demonstrate the use of these two equations by returning to alternative K for producing and marketing a new product. Let us begin by recalling that (1) the firm's effective tax rate was 50 percent, (2) the proportion of debt financing was 0.25, (3) the cost of debt was 8 percent, and (4) the after-tax return requirement was 12 percent. Substitution of these values in Eq. (9-1) yields the following:

$$\phi = \left(\frac{0.50}{1.00 - 0.50} \right) \left[1 - \frac{0.25(0.08)}{0.12} \right] = 0.833$$

Knowing the value of this factor and having found earlier that the uniform annual capital cost is $28,255, we need calculate only the value of the uniform annual equivalent of the tax depreciation expenses to determine, with the use of Eq. (9-2), the uniform annual equivalent of the income tax expenses. The total depreciation expense in the case under consideration will be the difference between the equipment's first cost of $84,000 and its terminal salvage value of $0, or $84,000. The firm adheres to the straight-line method of depreciation for tax purposes, and, therefore, the annual depreciation expense will be this $84,000 divided by the four-year service life, or $21,000. Since this is a uniform annual amount, it can be substituted directly in 'Eq. (9-2). When this and the other necessary substitutions are made, the following is obtained:

Annual income taxes = 0.833($28,255 − $21,000) = $6,045

This means that, in addition to the revenues required to cover the capital and operating costs, the company will require revenues equal to $6,045 per year to cover the income tax expenses.

Total Revenue Requirement. In summary, if the firm is to realize an after-tax return of exactly 12 percent on the total investment of $89,000 in alternative K, the alternative must be capable of generating the following uniform annual revenues:

Type of cost	Uniform annual equivalent	
Capital:		
Devaluation expense	$21,000	
Cost of money	7,255	$28,255
Operating expenses		30,000
Income taxes		6,045
Total (Revenue requirement)		$64,300

It might be noted that, in this summation, the capital cost has been broken down into its two elements. The first of these is the average annual decrease in the assets' market value, that is, the devaluation expense, which we know to be $21,000. The second element is the 12 percent cost of money, which can be found by taking the difference between the total capital cost of $28,255 and the devaluation expense of $21,000 to obtain $7,255.

In any case, the total revenue requirement proves to be $64,300. This result is to be interpreted as follows: With this alternative, to realize a return of exactly 12 percent after taxes on the total investment of $89,000, the company requires revenues whose annual equivalent is $64,300. If revenues of exactly this amount are realized, the uniform annual equivalent of the resultant income taxes will be $6,045.

The information in the preceding table also reveals the following: With annual revenues of $64,300, the firm will be able to cover the resultant taxes of $6,045, the operating costs of $30,000, and the average annual decrease of $21,000 in the assets' value. Having done so, it will have remaining revenues of $7,255 per year. But this $7,255 is equal to the cost of money at 12 percent per year, and, hence, these remaining revenues represent an after-tax return of 12 percent on total investment. Tangentially, it might be mentioned that this dollar return of $7,255 will be shared by the two classes of investors in the assets, namely, the investors of equity capital and the investors of debt capital. The latter's share will be equal to whatever amount is generated by the 8 percent interest they are to be paid for the use of their capital.

A Check. At this point, the firm would continue the study by determining the revenue requirement for the other alternative in the case under consideration. But it might be interesting to check whether the average annual income taxes will be $6,045 with alternative K if average annual revenues are $64,300. Doing so will also serve to demonstrate the effect of the two assumptions which underlie the revenue requirement method.

We know that the income tax for a given year will be equal to the taxable income for that year times the effective tax rate. The taxable income for the year will be equal to the revenues less the expenses reported for tax purposes. These deductible expenses will consist of depreciation, the operating costs, and the interest paid on borrowed funds. At this point in our example, the only unknown in the foregoing items is the amount of interest paid on borrowed funds. So before we can proceed, these amounts must be determined.

At the time this problem was presented, it was stated that 25 percent of the total investment would be financed with borrowed funds at a cost of 8 percent per year. In the revenue requirement approach, the assumption is made that the dollar amount of debt during any one year will be equal to this debt ratio of 25 percent times the assets' book value during that year. Keeping this in mind, we should find the tax-deductible interest expenses for alternative K in the manner indicated in Table 9-1.

It will be noted that no interest expenses are shown after the fourth year. This is because the book value of the assets will drop to zero when they are disposed of at the end of year 4. Given the assumption that the debt is a stated fraction of the assets' book value, the debt at that point will also drop to zero. In other words, it is being assumed that the remaining debt will be repaid at the end of the fourth year, and, hence, no interest expenses will be incurred after that point.

As can be seen in Table 9-1, the interest expenses are affected by the amounts owed, and these amounts are a function of the method of depreciation adhered to for tax purposes. This is to say that the

TABLE 9-1 Determination of annual interest expenses for alternative K

Year	Depreciation expense	Assets' book value during year	Debt during year	Interest for year
1	$21,000	$89,000 − $ 0 = $89,000	$89,000(0.25) = $22,250	$22,250(0.08) = $1,780
2	21,000	89,000 − 21,000 = 68,000	68,000(0.25) = 17,000	17,000(0.08) = 1,360
3	21,000	68,000 − 21,000 = 47,000	47,000(0.25) = 11,750	11,750(0.08) = 940
4	21,000	47,000 − 21,000 = 26,000	26,000(0.25) = 6,500	6,500(0.08) = 520

adopted depreciation method gives rise to a specific assumed debt repayment pattern. Had the company used, say, sum-of-the-years-digits depreciation for tax purposes, a different pattern of debt repayments and interest expenses would have been generated. And, incidentally, it might be mentioned that the values of the interest expense shown in Table 9-1 are equal to those generated by the actual debt repayment plan which was described in the preceding chapter. This is because, in this case, the assumed debt repayment plan happens to coincide with the actual plan.

But to continue, having determined the tax-deductible interest expenses and knowing the other deductible expenses, we can go on to calculate the annual taxes that will be incurred if revenues are equal to the revenue requirement of $64,300. This is done in Table 9-2.

When the calculated tax amounts which appear in Table 9-2 are treated as end-of-year expenses, their uniform annual equivalent proves to be as follows:

$$\text{Annual income taxes} = \$5,760 + \$210(A/G)_{n=4}^{i=12} = \$6,045$$

This coincides with the amount obtained with the use of Eqs. (9-1) and (9-2) and, thus, verifies the accuracy of the result obtained with those formulas. Furthermore, the process of verification served to reveal the effect of the assumptions which underlie the formulas.

Relevancy of Formula Factors. A return to the computations in Table 9-2 provides us with a means for obtaining an intuitive understanding

TABLE 9-2 Calculation of annual income taxes for alternative K

	Year 1	Year 2	Year 3	Year 4
Revenues	$64,300	$64,300	$64,300	$64,300
Less:				
Operating costs	30,000	30,000	30,000	30,000
Depreciation	21,000	21,000	21,000	21,000
Interest expense	1,780	1,360	940	520
Taxable income	$11,520	$11,940	$12,360	$12,780
Tax at 50%	$ 5,760	$ 5,970	$ 6,180	$ 6,390

of why the two formulas contain the factors they do. To begin with, the computations demonstrate that taxable income and, hence, taxes are affected by the depreciation expenses reported for tax purposes which, in turn, are affected by the depreciation method employed. Therefore, if the company in our example adhered to, say, the sum-of-the-years-digits method instead of the straight-line method, the reported depreciation expenses would no longer be a uniform $21,000 a year, and the taxes would have been computed accordingly, and a different series of taxes would have been obtained. It is for this reason that the tax formula, Eq. (9-2), takes into account the method of depreciation employed. It does this by calling for the substitution of the uniform annual equivalent of whatever pattern of depreciation charges is experienced with the adopted method.

Table 9-2 also demonstrates the significance of interest on borrowed funds and of the tax rate in the tax computation. It is because of the relevancy of these items that the proportion of debt financing, the cost of debt, and the tax rate appear in Eq. (9-1), the expression for the tax factor ϕ.

Of course, there is the question of why this factor is applied to the difference between the annual capital cost and the annual depreciation expense to obtain the annual tax. The answer to this question is suggested by the fact that, as pointed out earlier, this difference is the firm's annual dollar return on total investment. And, in general, it is this dollar return which is subject to an income tax. More specifically, only that portion of the dollar return is taxed which remains for the equity investors after the investors of debt capital have claimed their share; however, this is taken into account in the derivation of the tax factor ϕ. The annual revenues that serve to recover the interest expense, which represents the return to debt investors, are not taxable because they are offset by the deductible interest expense. Similarly, the annual revenues which serve to recover the operating costs and the devaluation expense are not taxable because these revenues are offset by the deductible operating costs and the deductible depreciation expense.

The Other Alternative. It was mentioned that the firm would continue the study by determining the revenue requirement for the other alternative in the case under consideration. This is alternative L. Alternative L required an initial investment of $130,000 in equipment and working capital whose combined salvage value would be $25,000 at the end of the assets' six-year life. Operating costs were estimated to be $24,000 for the first year but were expected to increase at a rate of $1,000 a year. Annual revenues were given as $67,000, but these will be ignored for now because the firm simply wants to ascertain what revenues will suffice to generate an after-tax return of 12 percent on the total investment in this alternative. Consequently, the relevant cash flows for this purpose are as follows:

130,000						(25,000)
	24,000	25,000	26,000	27,000	28,000	29,000
0	1	2	3	4	5	6

The determination can begin with a calculation of the uniform annual revenues needed to cover the capital cost which is

$$\text{Annual capital cost} = \$130,000(A/P)_{n=6}^{i=12} - \$25,000(A/F)_{n=6}^{i=12}$$

$$= \$28,539$$

The revenue requirement created by the operating costs will be equal to the uniform annual equivalent of these costs which is

$$\text{Annual operating costs} = \$24,000 + \$1,000(A/G)_{n=6}^{i=12} = \$26,172$$

Finally, the revenues required to recover the annual income taxes are found with the use of Eqs. (9-1) and (9-2). The value of the tax factor ϕ with this alternative will be 0.833, just as it was for alternative K, because both alternatives have the same tax rate, debt ratio, cost of debt, and rate-of-return requirement. Since the assets in both alternatives are subject to straight-line depreciation, the annual depreciation expense for alternative L will be equal to its total depreciation expense, which is the $105,000 by which the equipment will decrease in value, divided by the six-year service life. The result is a depreciation expense of $17,500 a year. Having already calculated the annual capital cost to be $28,539, we can now make the necessary substitutions in Eq. (9-2) to obtain the following:

$$\text{Annual income taxes} = 0.833(\$28,539 - \$17,500) = \$9,199$$

Therefore, the total revenue requirement for alternative L is as follows:

Item	Annual revenue requirement
Capital cost	$28,539
Operating costs	26,172
Income taxes	9,199
Total	$63,910

As the foregoing computations reveal, the revenue requirement determination becomes simple and straightforward when there is no need to explain each step in the procedure. In any event, the result obtained tells us that, with the second alternative, the firm requires annual revenues equivalent to $63,910 during the alternative's six-year life to realize an after-tax return of 12 percent on the total investment of $130,000. And, incidentally, revenues of this amount will generate average annual income taxes of $9,199.

The Comparison and Interpretation. The revenue requirement was found to be $64,300 per year for alternative K and $63,910 per year for alternative L. The next step in the analysis calls for giving consideration to the question of whether the respective alternatives are capable of satisfying these requirements because, if neither is, the company should make no investment in the activity. This question can be answered on the basis of either judgment or estimates. The latter can be used in this particular case because the firm did estimate annual revenues to be $67,000 for each of the alternatives. These estimated revenues can be combined with the required revenues to obtain the following:

	Alternative K	Alternative L
Estimated revenues	$67,000	$67,000
Required revenues	64,300	63,910
Surplus revenues	$ 2,700	$ 3,090

The "surplus revenues" represent the amount by which the estimated revenues exceed the required revenues. Since this surplus is a maximum with alternative L, this alternative would be considered to be the more economical of the two in the absence of irreducible factors; furthermore, it is more economical than the alternative of not producing the product because that alternative would yield no surplus revenues. It will be recalled that this same decision was reached when the other methods of analysis were applied to this problem on an after-tax basis.

It should be noted that the calculated surplus revenues were compared directly in spite of the fact that the two alternatives have different service lives. As this suggests, it is being assumed, just as it was with the other methods of analysis, that the nature of future replacements will be such that the respective surplus revenues will continue until equal time periods are obtained.

After-Tax Surplus Revenues. The revenue requirement analysis of this problem has been completed. However, certain additional observations can be made which will contribute to one's understanding of the method.

It was stated that, when an after-tax study was made of the two alternatives by means of the basic analytical techniques, alternative L was also found to be the more economical of the two. But let us now compare the specific results obtained by means of one of those techniques with the specific results obtained by means of the revenue requirement method. The comparison will prove to be more meaningful if we compare calculated uniform annual costs with the outcome of the revenue requirement approach, because all the values involved will then be expressed in terms of a uniform annual equivalent. The result of such a comparison is as follows:

Alternative	Surplus revenues	After-tax uniform annual cost
K	$2,700	(−)$1,350
L	3,090	(−) 1,545

Although alternative L has the advantage in both cases, this advantage is equal to $390 a year with the revenue requirement method but only $195 a year with the uniform annual cost method. As a rule, some such discrepancy is to be expected, because the debt repayment pattern generated by the assumptions underlying the revenue requirement method will ordinarily differ to some degree from the actual debt repayment plan which is taken into consideration in the uniform annual cost method. Consequently, the interest expenses and, therefore, the resultant income taxes will differ with the two methods. But it so happens that, in this case, the assumed debt repayment plan coincides with the actual debt repayment plan. That this is true for alternative K was already pointed out, and suffice it to say that a check would prove that it is also true for alternative L. Hence, there must be some other explanation for the discrepancy. This explanation is as follows:

The surplus revenues for alternatives K and L represent the *before-tax* excess of estimated revenues over required revenues. And, strictly speaking, an after-tax analysis requires that these surplus revenues be compared on an *after-tax* basis. To do so, we can begin with alternative K. We had found that, with this alternative, annual income taxes would be $6,045 if revenues were equal to the required $64,300. But the estimated revenues of $67,000 exceed the required revenues of $64,300 by $2,700. This entire $2,700 will be subject to the 50 percent tax rate because there are no offsetting additional tax-deductible expenses. Therefore, an *additional* annual tax of 50 percent times $2,700, or $1,350, will be experienced with this alternative. When this is added to the $6,045 tax with revenues of $64,300, the total tax becomes $7,395 with revenues of $67,000. Given that the assumptions which underlie the revenue requirement method are correct in this problem, the total tax of $7,395 should be equal to the uniform annual equivalent of the taxes obtained for this alternative in Table 8-1 of the preceding chapter, and it is.

Insofar as alternative L is concerned, annual income taxes were computed to be $9,199 with the required revenues of $63,910. But since the expected revenues of $67,000 exceed the required revenues of $63,910 by $3,090, an *additional* annual income tax expense will be incurred. Given that there are no offsetting additional deductible expenses, this additional tax will be 50 percent of $3,090, or $1,545. When this is added to the $9,199 tax with revenues of $63,910, the total tax becomes $10,744 with revenues of $67,000. For the reason given with reference to alternative K, this total of $10,744 should be equal to the uniform annual equivalent of the taxes obtained for this alternative in Table 8-2 of the preceding chapter, and it is.

To summarize, the before-tax surplus revenues generate the additional income taxes and the resultant after-tax surplus revenues shown in the following table:

	Alternative K	Alternative L
Before-tax surplus revenues	$2,700	$3,090
Less: Tax at 50%	1,350	1,545
After-tax surplus revenues	$1,350	$1,545

Because the same tax rate is applied to each of the before-tax amounts, alternative L continues to have the advantage. But this advantage has decreased from $390 a year to $195. And this $195 advantage now coincides with the $195 advantage obtained in the earlier comparison of after-tax uniform annual costs.

Since the tax rate in a given problem is a constant, the alternative which yields the highest before-tax surplus revenues will also yield the highest after-tax surplus revenues, and, as a result, it is common practice to base the investment decision on a comparison of the calculated before-tax values. But it can be argued that every step in an after-tax analysis should reflect the impact of taxes and, therefore, that after-tax surplus revenues should be ascertained when the revenue requirement method is being applied.

The Effect of Revenues.   We shall now return to the way in which the results of a revenue requirement analysis of this problem would ordinarily be presented. This is as follows:

	Alternative K	Alternative L
Estimated revenues	$67,000	$67,000
Required revenues	64,300	63,910
Surplus revenues	$ 2,700	$ 3,090

An examination of these results reveals that the alternative which minimizes the revenue requirement maximizes the revenue surplus. But this may not be true if the estimated revenues are affected by the choice of alternative. To illustrate, it may be that alternatives K and L are expected to yield annual revenues of $69,000 and $67,000, respectively. The outcome of a revenue requirement analysis would then be as follows:

	Alternative K	Alternative L
Estimated revenues	$69,000	$67,000
Required revenues	64,300	63,910
Surplus revenues	$ 4,700	$ 3,090

Alternative K now proves to be the more economical of the two because its higher revenue requirement is more than offset by the larger revenues it will generate.

And, of course, it could be that the most economical course of action would be not to produce and market the new product; this was identified in preceding chapters as alternative J. Alternative J would have a revenue requirement of zero because it would have no costs. Furthermore, it would yield no revenues. Therefore, if alternatives K and L were expected to yield annual revenues of only $61,000, the results of the analysis would be as follows:

	Alternative J	Alternative K	Alternative L
Estimated revenues	$0	$61,000	$61,000
Required revenues	0	64,300	63,910
Surplus revenues	$0	(−)$ 3,300	(−)$ 2,910

Under such circumstances, the alternative of making no investment in the activity yields the highest revenue surplus.

Finally, it should be noted that there might be cases in which it will be assumed that each alternative will yield revenues equal to its required revenues. An example would be the case of a public utility whose rates are under the control of a regulatory commission. Such commissions expect the regulated firm to conduct its affairs in a manner which will enable it to minimize the cost of its products and services to its customers, while realizing an authorized after-tax return on total investment; the authorized return is intended to enable the firm to attract and retain the capital it requires to operate. As a consequence, the management of such a firm, when confronted by mutually exclusive alternatives, is expected to select the alternative which minimizes the revenues required to yield the authorized return on total investment. By doing so, management will be able to minimize the cost of the firm's products and services to its customers.

In instances such as this, actual revenues with each alternative are expected to be equal to the required revenues because, at least theoretically, the firm has the authority and ability to establish and maintain a price that will generate actual revenues which are equal to required revenues. Therefore, if the company in our new product example were, say, a public utility, it would probably have developed the following comparison:

	Alternative K	Alternative L
Required revenues	$64,300	$63,910
Estimated revenues	64,300	63,910
Surplus revenues	$ 0	$ 0

These results would then be interpreted as follows: Since revenues with either alternative can be expected to yield a satisfactory return of 12 percent on total investment, the alternative of making no investment is rejected. Of the remaining alternatives, alternative L minimizes the revenues required to realize this satisfactory return and, hence, will minimize the unit price at which the product would have to be sold to the public. Therefore, it would be considered to be more attractive than alternative K. But a question may now be raised regarding whether the utility's return on the extra investment required by alternative L will also be satisfactory. The answer is that it will be. Let us consider why this is so. For each of the alternatives, the annual revenue requirement is equal to the sum of the alternative's positive costs at a rate of 12 percent. Furthermore, in this case, each alternative's annual revenues will be equal to this sum of its positive costs. Therefore, the total uniform annual cost of each alternative will be zero at a rate of 12 percent. As we know, the rate which equates the total uniform annual costs of two alternatives represents the return on the extra investment required by one of those alternatives. Hence, the return on the extra investment in alternative L will be 12 percent, which is considered to be satisfactory.

This last example and all the others presented in this section were designed to demonstrate the relevancy of expected revenues in a revenue requirement analysis. However, the fact remains that, for reasons considered in earlier chapters, an investor may not be able to estimate what these revenues will be. But if he has reason to believe that they will exceed the calculated values of the revenue requirement, he can begin by rejecting, on the basis of judgment, the alternative of making no investment. And if he has reason to believe that the revenues will be the same for the remaining alternatives, he can assume that the most economical of these alternatives is the one with the minimum revenue requirement.

We shall now go on to apply the revenue requirement method to other types of problems. Before we do, it might be mentioned that some firms prefer to express the revenue requirement as a present worth rather than as a uniform annual equivalent. This can be done by multiplying a calculated uniform annual revenue requirement by an appropriate uniform-series present worth factor. But care must be taken to obtain the present worth of the revenue requirement for the same number of years for each alternative. In the new-product problem, this number of years would be 12, given the respective service life estimates of 4 and 6 years and given the assumption regarding the nature of future replacements. Consequently, a uniform-series present worth factor for 12 years would be applied to each of the annual revenue requirements to arrive at the present worths of these requirements. And, of course, if someone prefers to express the revenue requirements in terms of equivalent future worths, he can do so by applying an appropriate uniform-series future worth factor to the calculated annual requirements.

THE MULTIPLE-ALTERNATIVE INVENTORY PROBLEM

We shall now consider a problem which differs from the preceding one in that it involves multiple alternatives and no tax depreciation expense. The problem will be the earlier one in which a distributor of replacement parts for electronic equipment had to evaluate seven proposals regarding the amount of money to be invested in inventories. In general, each of the alternatives had a seven-year life, required an initial investment which would not decrease in value, and would yield a uniform annual reduction in stockout costs. More specifically, the before-tax cash flows were as shown in Table 9-3.

It was also stated that the after-tax rate-of-return requirement was 15 percent, the tax rate was 30 percent, the entire investment would be financed by debt at a cost of 15 percent, and no depreciation expenses would be reported for tax purposes because none would occur and, in any case, inventories are not a depreciable asset.

A revenue requirement analysis of this problem begins with a recognition of the fact that each alternative is described completely in terms of the revenues and costs it is expected to generate. The revenues assume the form of a net annual saving in stockout costs, and the costs will assume the form of an annual capital cost and an annual income tax expense. Therefore, it becomes possible to ascertain the surplus revenues to be associated with the respective alternatives. Because there are seven

TABLE 9-3   A description of cash flows before taxes

| Alternative | Required total investment | Before-tax receipts | |
		End-of-year saving for 7 years	Salvage at end of 7th year
1	$ 0	$ 0	$ 0
2	12,000	1,920	12,000
3	15,000	2,730	15,000
4	20,000	3,000	20,000
5	22,000	3,210	22,000
6	29,000	5,170	29,000
7	33,000	5,780	33,000

alternatives, seven such values will have to be calculated and compared. In the absence of irreducible factors, the most economical alternative will be the one with the maximum surplus revenues.

Taking alternative 7 for purposes of illustration, we can start by determining the revenues required to cover its capital cost which is

$$\text{Annual capital cost} = \$33,000(A/P)_{n=7}^{i=15} - \$33,000(A/F)_{n=7}^{i=15}$$

$$= \$33,000(0.15) = \$4,950$$

No need exists to consider the revenues required to cover operating costs because the expected annual saving in stockout costs was reduced to reflect these costs. Therefore, we can go on to the determination of the revenues required to cover income taxes.

The appropriate substitutions in Eq. (9-1) will yield the following value for the tax factor:

$$\phi = \left(\frac{0.30}{1.00 - 0.30}\right)\left[1 - \frac{1.0(0.15)}{0.15}\right] = 0$$

This value of the tax factor, the $4,950 value of the capital cost, and the $0 value of the tax depreciation expense yield the following annual taxes when substituted in Eq. (9-2):

$$\text{Annual income taxes} = 0(\$4,950 - \$0) = \$0$$

The uniform annual revenue requirement for the alternative will be the sum of its annual capital cost and these annual taxes which is

$$\text{Annual revenue requirement} = \$4,950 + \$0 = \$4,950$$

The before-tax surplus revenues can be ascertained by taking the difference between the estimated saving in stockout costs of $5,780 a year and the revenue requirement of $4,950 a year. This difference is equal to

Before-tax annual surplus revenues = $5,780 − $4,950 = $830

The revenue requirement analysis of this alternative can end at this point, but it might be pointed out that these surplus revenues will be subject to the 30 percent tax rate because they will not be offset by any additional tax-deductible expenses. As a result, only 100 percent minus 30 percent, or 70 percent, of this surplus will remain after taxes. Hence, the surplus revenues after taxes will be as follows:

After-tax annual surplus revenues = $830 − 0.30($830)

$$= 0.70(\$830) = \$581$$

When the foregoing approach is applied to each of the remaining six alternatives, the results obtained are as shown in Table 9-4.

The Comparison. An examination of Table 9-4 reveals that alternative 7 has the highest surplus revenues before the taxes on such revenues are taken into consideration. Similarly, it has the highest surplus revenues after the taxes on such revenues are taken into consideration. But this consistency in ranking was to be expected because the before-tax surplus revenues for each alternative are reduced by the same percent to obtain its after-tax surplus revenues. Therefore, the revenue requirement analysis could have ended with a determination of surplus revenues before taxes, since these suffice to identify alternative 7 as being the most economical of the alternatives. And as stated in the new-product problem, the analysis ordinarily is terminated at that point so as to eliminate an additional computation for which there is no real need.

The reason the additional computation was made in this case is to enable us to compare the results of this analysis with those obtained when the uniform annual cost method was applied in the preceding

TABLE 9-4   The results of a revenue requirement analysis of an inventory problem

Alter-native (a)	Annual revenue requirement — Capital cost (b)	Income taxes (c)	Total (d = b + c)	Annual estimated revenues (e)	Before taxes (f = e − d)	Taxes (g = 0.30 × f)	After taxes (h = f − g)
1	$ 0	$0	$ 0	$ 0	$ 0	$ 0	$ 0
2	1,800	0	1,800	1,920	120	36	84
3	2,250	0	2,250	2,730	480	144	336
4	3,000	0	3,000	3,000	0	0	0
5	3,300	0	3,300	3,210	(−) 90	(−) 27	(−) 63
6	4,350	0	4,350	5,170	820	246	574
7	4,950	0	4,950	5,780	830	249	581

chapter. It was pointed out in that chapter that the distributor would repay borrowed funds in a single sum at the end of the seventh year. This repayment plan happens to coincide with the repayment plan generated in this problem by the assumptions which underlie the revenue requirement method. Let us see why with the use of alternative 7 for purposes of illustration.

Given 100 percent debt financing, alternative 7 calls for borrowing the entire $33,000 investment it requires. Because the inventories involved are not expected to decrease in value, their book value and, hence, the assumed debt will remain at $33,000 during the entire seven-year period. At the end of that period, the inventories will be liquidated. As a result, their book value will drop to zero and so will the assumed value of the debt. But the debt can drop to zero only if it is repaid in its entirety at that point. Thus, we find that the assumed debt repayment plan is the same as the actual plan.

It follows that, since the assumptions which underlie the revenue requirement method are correct in this problem, the method should yield uniform annual equivalents which reflect those obtained with the uniform annual cost method. However, the calculated uniform annual costs include *total* income taxes, and, for purposes of comparison, the results of a revenue requirement analysis must do the same. In other words, a comparison must be made of after-tax surplus revenues and after-tax uniform annual costs. Such a comparison is made for the problem under consideration in Table 9-5, and it serves to demonstrate that the outcome of the one method of analysis is equivalent to the outcome of the other. More specifically, it reveals that the attractiveness of alternative 7, relative to any of the other alternatives, proves to be the same with either approach.

The primary reason for applying the revenue requirement method to a problem of this type was to demonstrate that, when multiple

TABLE 9-5   The results of an after-tax analysis by two different methods

Alternative	Annual after-tax surplus revenues	After-tax uniform annual cost
1	$ 0	$ 0
2	(+) 84	(−) 84
3	(+) 336	(−) 336
4	0	0
5	(−) 63	(+) 63
6	(+) 574	(−) 574
7	(+) 581	(−) 581

alternatives are involved, the required revenues must simply be ascertained for each of the alternatives and combined with the estimated revenues to determine which is the most economical course of action. But it also served to demonstrate that the method can be applied whether depreciable or nondepreciable assets are involved. Finally, it provided us with another indication of the fact that, when the underlying assumptions are correct, the method yields results which are identical to those obtained with the basic analytical techniques.

THE LAYOUT PROBLEM

The alternatives in the new-product problem and the inventory problem were each described completely in terms of the costs and revenues which they would generate. We shall now make a revenue requirement analysis of a situation in which a revenue estimate is not possible but in which the alternative of making no investment has been rejected on the basis of judgment and in which there is reason to believe that revenues will be the same for each of the remaining alternatives.

The specific problem to be considered is the multiple-alternative layout problem which has already been analyzed by the basic techniques. In that problem, a manufacturer was confronted by four proposals for relocating certain work stations in his plant. The cost of relocation would be completely financed by equity funds, which is to say that the debt ratio would be zero. The after-tax return requirement was 6 percent. And the effective income tax rate was 52 percent. Therefore, if the revenue requirement analysis were to begin with a determination of the value of the tax factor, the result would be as follows:

$$\phi = \left(\frac{0.52}{1.00 - 0.52} \right) \left[1 - \frac{0(r)}{0.06} \right] = 1.083(1 - 0) = 1.083$$

Turning to the four alternatives that were to be compared, we might recall that plan Z required the highest immediate expenditure. This was $15,000. The resultant layout would be satisfactory for 5 years, would have no salvage value, and would yield annual handling costs of $19,200. With this alternative, revenues would be required to recover the annual handling costs of $19,200 and the following capital cost:

Annual capital cost $= \$15,000(A/P)_{n=5}^{i=6} = \$3,561$

The revenues required to cover the income taxes will be a function of this capital cost, of the tax factor, and of the uniform annual equivalent of the tax depreciation expenses. With reference to the last of these items, it had been stated that the $15,000 capital investment would be reported as a tax-deductible expense at the time it was made. This is tantamount to a reported depreciation expense of $15,000 at that point, and the uniform annual equivalent of this amount during the five-year service period would be

Equivalent annual depreciation expense $= \$15{,}000(A/P)_{n=5}^{i=6} = \$3{,}561$

As a result, the revenues required to cover the income taxes would be as follows:

Annual income taxes $= 1.083(\$3{,}561 - \$3{,}561) = \$0$

When the revenue requirements generated by this tax expense of $0, the handling costs of $19,200, and the capital cost of $3,561 are totaled, the following is obtained:

Annual revenue requirement $= \$3{,}561 + \$19{,}200 + \$0 = \$22{,}761$

A second alternative, plan Y, required an immediate investment of $12,000, would have a service life of 5 years, would have no salvage value, and would yield annual handling costs of $19,800. For tax purposes, this total investment of $12,000 would also be depreciated completely at the beginning of the five-year service period. To determine the revenue requirement for this alternative, we can combine the steps involved in this determination and, by doing so, obtain the following:

$$\text{Annual revenue requirement} = \$12{,}000(A/P)_{n=5}^{i=6} + \$19{,}800$$

$$+ 1.083\,[\$12{,}000(A/P)_{n=5}^{i=6}$$

$$- \$12{,}000(A/P)_{n=5}^{i=6}]$$

$$= \$2{,}849 + \$19{,}800 + \$0 = \$22{,}649$$

Before going on to the remaining two alternatives, we might pause to comment on what has been ascertained thus far. With respect to alternative Z, the calculated income tax of $0 means that the tax will be $0 if the actual revenues are equal to the calculated required value of $22,761. Similarly, with respect to alternative Y, the calculated income tax of $0 means that the tax will be $0 if the actual revenues are equal to the calculated required value of $22,649. But the fact that the calculated tax is $0 in each case does not mean that this method of analysis fails to discover the tax difference that was found in the preceding chapter to exist between the alternatives. The revenue requirement of $22,649 for alternative Y is $112 less than the revenue requirement of $22,761 for alternative Z. Therefore, because the actual revenues are expected to be the same for both alternatives, the annual before-tax surplus revenues will be $112 more with alternative Y than with alternative

Z. These surplus revenues will be subject to a 52 percent tax rate, and, consequently, alternative Y will generate a higher annual tax of 52 percent times $112, or $58. And, incidentally, this amount is equal to the uniform annual equivalent of the tax differences between these alternatives as ascertained in the preceding chapter. This was to be expected because the actual debt in this case is equal to the debt generated by the assumptions underlying the revenue requirement method. Specifically, the actual debt is zero at all times, and so is the assumed debt. The assumed debt proves to be zero for the following reason: Any one layout's book value is always zero because the layout is immediately charged with a depreciation expense equal to the expenditure it requires. To continue, the revenue requirement method assumes that the debt is a stated fraction of an asset's book value. But any fraction of a zero book value is zero. From this, it follows that the assumed debt is always zero.

Let us now go on to the third alternative, plan X. This plan called for an expenditure of $10,000 to realize a layout which would have a five-year life and no salvage value and which would yield annual handling costs of $21,000. Given that the entire $10,000 capital expenditure would be reported as a tax-deductible expense at the beginning of the first year, the revenue requirement for plan X would be found in the following manner:

$$\text{Annual revenue requirement} = \$10,000(A/P)_{n=5}^{i=6} + \$21,000$$
$$+ 1.083\,[\$10,000(A/P)_{n=5}^{i=6}$$
$$- \$10,000(A/P)_{n=5}^{i=6}]$$
$$= \$23,374$$

The last alternative was plan W. This plan required an initial investment of $6,000 in a layout which would have no salvage value and would yield annual handling costs of $22,400. However, it would be satisfactory for only 3 years. But instead of making the simplifying assumption, regarding the nature of future replacements, to satisfy the equal time-period requirement, the manufacturer chose to estimate that, at the end of the third year, another $5,000 would be invested in a revised layout which would be satisfactory for 2 years, would have no salvage value, and would continue to yield annual handling costs of $22,400. All this would appear on a time line as follows:

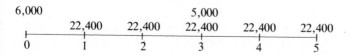

A cash-flow combination of this type introduces a slight complication in a revenue requirement analysis because the initial pattern of costs does not repeat itself. In this case, the simplest way to handle the situation is, first, to determine the revenue requirement for the first three years and, then, to determine the revenue requirement for the next two years. These will not be the same, and, therefore, the overall uniform annual equivalent of the three-year series and the two-year series will have to be ascertained for the entire five-year period.

Beginning with the initial three-year period, we take into consideration the following cash flows:

```
6,000
        22,400     22,400     22,400
 |----------|----------|----------|
 0          1          2          3
```

As with the other alternatives, the initial capital investment will be reported as a deductible expense at its point of occurrence, and, consequently, the annual revenue requirement for the three-year period will be computed in the following manner:

$$\text{Annual revenue requirement} = \$6,000(A/P)_{n=3}^{i=6} + \$22,400$$

$$+ 1.083\,[\$6,000(A/P)_{n=3}^{i=6}$$

$$- \$6,000(A/P)_{n=3}^{i=6}]$$

$$= \$24,645$$

For the succeeding two-year period, we take into consideration the following cash flows:

```
5,000
        22,400     22,400
 |----------|----------|
 3          4          5
```

The $5,000 capital expenditure will be reported as a deductible expense at the beginning of the two-year period, and, hence, the revenue requirement for this period will be as follows:

$$\text{Annual revenue requirement} = \$5,000(A/P)_{n=2}^{i=6} + \$22,400$$

$$+ 1.083\,[\$5,000(A/P)_{n=2}^{i=6}$$

$$- \$5,000(A/P)_{n=2}^{i=6}]$$

$$= \$25,127$$

When the two calculated values of the revenue requirement are combined, the following is obtained:

24,645	24,645	24,645	25,127	25,127
0 1	2	3	4	5

The annual revenue requirement for this plan would be equal to the uniform annual equivalent of the foregoing nonuniform series which is equal to

$$\text{Annual revenue requirement} = [\$24{,}645(P/A)_{n=3}^{i=6}$$
$$+ \$25{,}127(P/F)_{n=4}^{i=6}$$
$$+ \$25{,}127(P/F)_{n=5}^{i=6}](A/P)_{n=5}^{i=6}$$
$$= \$24{,}819$$

No alternatives remain to be evaluated, and so we can go on to compare the revenue requirements for the various plans.

The Comparison. The results of the preceding computations can be summarized as follows:

Plan	Annual revenue requirement
W	$24,819
X	23,374
Y	22,649
Z	22,761

An examination of these results reveals that plan Y has the minimum revenue requirement. Therefore, in the absence of irreducible factors, the manufacturer would consider this alternative to be the most economical in spite of the fact that no revenue estimates are available. This is because it is being assumed that the actual revenues will be the same for each of the four alternatives and that they will suffice to satisfy the revenue requirements. Under such circumstances, the alternative which minimizes the revenue requirement will maximize the revenue surplus.

It should also be noted that alternative Y was found to be the most economical when the other methods of analysis were applied. For example, the outcome of the after-tax analysis of this problem by means of the uniform annual cost method is shown in the following table:

Plan	After-tax uniform annual cost	Annual revenue requirement
W	$24,819	$24,819
X	24,125	23,374
Y	23,777	22,649
Z	23,831	22,761

The annual revenue requirements have also been shown to permit a comparison with the uniform annual costs. It will be noted that the annual cost of plan W is equal to its revenue requirement. But this is not true for the other plans. The reason for this was suggested earlier when the computed taxes for plans Y and Z were being discussed. As compared with plan W, each of the other plans will have higher annual before-tax surplus revenues. These higher before-tax surplus revenues will be subject to the 52 percent tax rate, but the resultant additional taxes are not included in the calculated values of the revenue requirement. If they were, the revenue requirement for each alternative would be exactly equal to its uniform annual cost, which does include these additional taxes, because the assumed and actual debt repayment plans are the same. But as explained in the analysis of the new-product and the inventory problems, failure to consider explicitly the income taxes on before-tax surplus revenues is of no consequence, since each of these revenues is subject to the same tax rate. Hence, the alternative which generates the highest before-tax surplus revenues will generate the highest after-tax surplus revenues.

This brings us to the end of the analysis of this problem. The problem was introduced as one which would serve to demonstrate how the revenue requirement method is applied when the expected revenues for the alternatives are not available. But it also permitted us to see how the method is applied when the investor chooses to forecast the nature of future replacements and when an investor is, in effect, able to report a capital expenditure as a depreciation expense at the point at which it occurs.

THE REPLACEMENT PROBLEM

The next example of an application of the revenue requirement method involves the replacement problem which had been solved earlier by the basic methods of analysis. Unlike the cases which have already been considered in this chapter, this one contains an actual debt repayment plan which differs from the one generated by the assumptions which underlie the revenue requirement method. The problem also differs from the others in that it involves an investment tax credit, a gain on disposal, sum-of-the-years-digits depreciation, and an incomplete description of annual operating costs. Our purpose is to ascertain how all this affects the revenue requirement determination.

The Tax Factor. It will be recalled that, in this problem, a contractor wanted to determine whether it would be economical to replace a unit of construction equipment. The required total investments in the currently-owned equipment and its proposed replacement would both be financed by a combination of 20 percent debt and 80 percent equity capital. The cost of debt was given as 6 percent per year. We were also told that the minimum after-tax rate-of-return requirement on total investment was 10 percent and that the effective tax rate was 40 percent. These data suffice for the purpose of calculating the value of the tax factor which will be used to ascertain the revenues required to cover the annual income taxes with each alternative. So we shall begin by making the necessary substitutions in Eq. (9-1) to obtain the following:

$$\phi = \left(\frac{0.40}{1.00 - 0.40} \right) \left[1 - \frac{0.20(0.06)}{0.10} \right] = 0.587$$

The New Equipment. The proposed replacement required an investment of $11,900 in equipment whose salvage value at the end of its estimated four-year life was expected to be $3,900. Therefore, its uniform annual capital cost would be equal to

$$\text{Annual capital cost} = \$11,900(A/P)_{n=4}^{i=10} - \$3,900(A/F)_{n=4}^{i=10} = \$2,914$$

and revenues of this amount would be required to recover this cost which consists of the devaluation expense and the 10 percent cost of money.

For tax purposes, the equipment would be depreciated by the sum-of-the-years-digits method, and, as we found in the preceding chapter, the result would be the following series of annual depreciation expenses: $3,200, $2,400, $1,600, $800. The uniform annual equivalent of these charges can be found as follows:

$$\text{Equivalent annual depreciation} = \$3,200 - \$800(A/G)_{n=4}^{i=10} = \$2,095$$

This value and the values of the uniform annual capital cost and of the tax factor would be substituted in Eq. (9-2) to obtain the following revenues as being required to recover the income tax expenses:

$$\text{Annual income taxes} = 0.587(\$2,914 - \$2,095) = \$481$$

To continue, it was stated that the annual repair and maintenance costs with this equipment would be $120, $200, $310, and $540, respectively. The revenue requirement produced by these costs is the uniform annual equivalent of the amounts involved which is equal to

$$\text{Recurring costs} = [\$120(P/F)_{n=1}^{i=10} + \$200(P/F)_{n=2}^{i=10}$$
$$+ \$310(P/F)_{n=3}^{i=10} + \$540(P/F)_{n=4}^{i=10}](A/P)_{n=4}^{i=10}$$
$$= \$276$$

In summary, the revenues required to cover the costs generated by this alternative are as follows:

Item	Annual revenue requirement
Capital cost	$2,914
Income taxes	481
Recurring costs	276
Total	$3,671

However, one more relevant factor remains to be taken into consideration. This is that the contractor will realize an investment tax credit of $952 at the beginning of the first year if he purchases the new equipment. The uniform annual equivalent of this credit is as follows:

$$\text{Equivalent annual tax credit} = \$952(A/P)_{n=4}^{i=10} = \$300$$

This suggests, and correctly so, that the receipt of the $952 investment credit is equivalent to a tax saving of $300 a year for four years and that this will serve to reduce the value of the alternative's revenue requirement by some amount. To arrive at this amount, we begin by noting that the $300 saving is not subject to an income tax. Therefore, it is equivalent to some larger taxable revenue. The size of the annual taxable revenue which is equivalent to the annual tax credit can be ascertained by recognizing that the difference between this revenue and the tax on this revenue must be equal to the tax credit. This is to say that

$$\text{Tax credit} = (\text{equivalent revenue}) - (\text{tax rate})(\text{equivalent revenue})$$

which yields

$$\text{Equivalent revenue} = \frac{\text{tax credit}}{1 - \text{tax rate}} \tag{9-3}$$

When the data from our problem are substituted in Eq. (9-3), the result is as follows:

$$\text{Equivalent revenue} = \frac{\$300}{1.00 - 0.40} = \$500$$

To explain, if the contractor were to receive annual revenues of $500, these would be subject to a 40 percent tax rate because there are no offsetting deductible expenses. Therefore, an annual tax of $200 would be incurred, and the after-tax receipt to the investor would be $300. But this is equal to the annual tax credit of $300, and, hence, we conclude that the realization of a credit of $300 is equivalent to the realization of taxable revenues of $500.

Another way of checking the accuracy of the result is to begin by noting that, when the tax rate is 40 percent, the after-tax revenues will be equal to 100 percent minus 40 percent, or 60 percent, of the before-tax revenues. When the 60 percent is applied to the $500, an after-tax amount of $300 is obtained.

From this, it follows that the revenue requirement for the alternative will be $500 less than it would be in the absence of the investment tax credit. When the revenue requirement of $3,671, which was generated by the costs of the alternative, is reduced by this $500, the following is obtained:

	Amount per year
Revenue requirement to recover costs	$3,671
Less:	
Revenue equivalent of investment tax credit	500
Net revenue requirement	$3,171

This $3,171 represents the equivalent annual revenues required if an after-tax return of 10 percent is to be realized on the total investment of $11,900 in the new equipment.

The Result Examined. The analysis would continue with a determination of the revenue requirement for the alternative of retaining the old equipment. But we shall interrupt the study, at this point, for a number of reasons. One is to demonstrate that, in this case, the assumed debt repayment plan differs from the actual repayment plan described in the preceding chapter.

To obtain the assumed repayment plan and the resultant interest expenses, we begin by noting that the specific assumption in this problem is that the debt during any one year will be equal to 20 percent of the asset's book value during that year. Next, we take into consideration that the asset's book value during the first year will be equal to its initial cost of $11,900 and that this value will be reduced in succeeding years by the amounts generated by the sum-of-the-years-digits method of depreciation. Finally, we recall that the interest expense for a given year will be 6 percent of the debt during that year. Proceeding accordingly, we should obtain the interest expenses shown in Table 9-6.

TABLE 9-6   An assumed debt repayment plan and the resultant interest expenses

	Year 1	Year 2	Year 3	Year 4
Depreciation at end of year	$ 3,200	$2,400	$1,600	$ 800
Book value during year	11,900	8,700	6,300	4,700
Debt = 20% × book value	2,380	1,740	1,260	940
Interest = 6% × debt	143	104	76	56

But if we were to return to the preceding chapter, we should find that the contractor intended to repay the $2,380 of borrowed funds at a uniform rate of $595 a year for four years. The resultant actual series of annual interest expenses proved to be $143, $107, $71, and $35. As compared with this, Table 9-6 reveals that the assumed series is $143, $104, $76, and $56. Admittedly, the difference between the two series is not significant, but it does exist. And it could be that, in a given situation, the actual debt repayment plan is such that the difference will not be as insignificant as it is in this case.

To continue, since the interest expenses affect the income taxes, the average annual income taxes obtained with the revenue requirement approach may differ from what would have been obtained had the actual interest expenses been taken into consideration. In our example, it had been found with the revenue requirement approach that annual income taxes for the new equipment would be $481 with annual revenues of $3,671 and that a reduction of $500 in these revenues would serve to reduce these annual taxes by 40 percent of this $500, or by $200. In summary, average annual taxes would be $481 minus $200, or $281, with average annual revenues of $3,171. That this is so can be demonstrated with the results obtained in Table 9-7.

Table 9-7 shows what the respective annual taxes will be with annual revenues of $3,171, with the actual recurring costs and depreciation expenses, and with the assumed interest expenses. The uniform annual equivalent of these taxes is

TABLE 9-7   Calculation of income taxes with an assumed series of interest expenses

	Year 1	Year 2	Year 3	Year 4
Revenues	$3,171	$3,171	$3,171	$3,171
Less:				
Recurring costs	120	200	310	540
Depreciation	3,200	2,400	1,600	800
Interest expense	143	104	76	56
Taxable income	(−)$ 292	$ 467	$1,185	$1,775
Tax at 40%	(−)$ 117	$ 187	$ 474	$ 710

$$\text{Annual income taxes} = [(-)\$117(P/F)_{n=1}^{i=10} + \$187(P/F)_{n=2}^{i=10}$$
$$+ \$474(P/F)_{n=3}^{i=10} + \$710(P/F)_{n=4}^{i=10}](A/P)_{n=4}^{i=10}$$
$$= \$281$$

This agrees with the $281 obtained by the application of the revenue requirement approach. But it is important to take cognizance of the fact that this value was obtained with the use of the interest expenses generated by the assumptions underlying the approach. Because the actual interest expenses differ from the assumed ones, the actual income taxes will not be exactly $281. Hence, the revenue requirement of $281 for taxes and the resultant total revenue requirement of $3,171 contain some error.

The Old Equipment. Insofar as the alternative of retaining the currently-owned equipment is concerned, the value of the tax factor ϕ for this alternative will remain at 0.587 because the values of the items that affect this factor remain unchanged.

To continue, we had been told that the equipment's market value is $3,600 and that this is expected to decrease to $800 by the end of its estimated economic remaining service life of 2 years. The revenues needed to recover the resultant capital cost will be as follows:

$$\text{Annual capital cost} = \$3,600(A/P)_{n=2}^{i=10} - \$800(A/F)_{n=2}^{i=10} = \$1,693$$

Then, it was stated that the relevant recurring expenses will be $1,150 in the first year of the equipment's life and $1,330 in the second. The uniform annual equivalent of these costs is

$$\text{Annual recurring costs} = \$1,150 + \$180(A/G)_{n=2}^{i=10} = \$1,236$$

and revenues equal to this amount will be required to recover these costs.

Next, the revenues needed to recover the annual equivalent of the income taxes must be calculated. A difficulty will be encountered at this point because, although the asset is expected to decrease in value from \$3,600 to \$800, or by \$2,800, during the next two years, it was mentioned that no further depreciation expenses would be reported for tax purposes because the equipment's current book value is also \$800. A situation such as this is handled in the following manner:

For the moment, the taxes are computed as if the \$2,800 devaluation expense were going to be reported as a tax-deductible depreciation expense. The respective annual deductions are determined on the basis of the sum-of-the-years-digits method of depreciation to which the company adheres. The sum of the digits is 3 with a two-year service life, and, therefore, the assumed annual depreciation expenses become

Year	Depreciation expense
1	(2/3) (\$3,600 − \$800) = \$1,867
2	(1/3) (\$3,600 − \$800) = \$ 933

The uniform annual equivalent of these amounts is as follows:

Equivalent annual depreciation $= \$1,867 - \$934(A/G)_{n=2}^{i=10} = \$1,422$

A tax factor of 0.587, an annual capital cost of \$1,693, and the assumed equivalent annual depreciation expense of \$1,422 yield the following revenue requirement for income taxes:

Annual income taxes $= 0.587(\$1,693 - \$1,422) = \$159$

But, now, an adjustment is required. At the time the tax formula, Eq. (9-2), was introduced, it was pointed out that the difference between the uniform annual capital cost and the uniform annual equivalent of the depreciation expenses represents the dollar return on total investment and that, in general, it is this amount which is subject to an income tax. More specifically, only that portion of this dollar return claimed by the equity investors is taxed, but the tax factor ϕ takes this into account. Therefore, the \$159 tax expense which has just been calculated is the tax on the dollar return on equity capital.

In this case, however, the \$1,422 annual equivalent of the depreciation expenses cannot be reported as a deductible expense, and, hence, there will also be an income tax on the revenues which serve to recover this cost. To determine the value of this additional tax, we can begin with the following expression which describes the way in which income taxes are computed:

Taxes = (tax rate) (revenues − deductible expenses)   (9-4)

In the revenue requirement method, the tax is ascertained for revenues which are equal to the required revenues. These required revenues are equal to the sum of the capital cost, operating costs, and taxes. Therefore, Eq. (9-4) can be expressed in the following form:

Taxes = (tax rate) (capital cost + operating costs

+ taxes − deductible expenses)   (9-5)

The term "taxes" appears on both sides of this equation, and when the equation is solved for "taxes", the result is as follows:

$$\text{Taxes} = \left(\frac{\text{tax rate}}{1 - \text{tax rate}}\right)(\text{capital cost} + \text{operating costs})$$

$$-\left(\frac{\text{tax rate}}{1 - \text{tax rate}}\right)(\text{deductible expenses}) \qquad (9\text{-}6)$$

The last term in this equation reveals that every deductible expense reduces taxes by the following amount:

$$\text{Tax reduction} = \frac{(\text{tax rate})(\text{deductible expense})}{1 - \text{tax rate}} \qquad (9\text{-}7)$$

To return to the initial tax calculation for the old equipment, it had been assumed in that calculation that there would be a tax-deductible depreciation expense of $1,422. But this is not true, and, as a consequence, total income taxes will be the calculated $159 plus some additional amount. The additional amount will be equal to the tax reduction which had been generated by the assumed deductible expense of $1,422. With the use of Eq. (9-7), this is found to be

$$\text{Additional income taxes} = \frac{0.40(\$1,422)}{1.00 - 0.40} = \$948$$

When this is added to the taxes of $159 computed earlier, the following is obtained for the revenues required to recover annual income taxes:

Total annual income taxes = $159 + $948 = $1,107

Finally, one more factor remains to be taken into consideration. It will be recalled that, if the old equipment is retained, the contractor will avoid a gains tax of $1,030 at the present time. The uniform annual equivalent of this tax saving is equal to

Equivalent annual tax saving = $1,030(A/P)$_{n=2}^{i=10}$ = $593

In principle, there is no difference between a reduction in taxes attributable to the elimination of a gains tax and a reduction in taxes attributable to an investment tax credit. Therefore, like a tax credit, a gains-tax saving will serve to reduce an alternative's revenue requirement by an amount equal to the revenue equivalent of the saving. This revenue equivalent would be ascertained just as it was for the tax credit, which is to say that use would be made of the following variation of Eq. (9-3):

$$\text{Equivalent revenue} = \frac{\text{tax saving}}{1 - \text{tax rate}} \qquad (9\text{-}8)$$

In the problem under consideration, appropriate substitutions in this equation yield the following:

$$\text{Equivalent revenue} = \frac{\$593}{1.00 - 0.40} = \$988$$

This tells us that the annual gains-tax saving of $593 is equivalent to the investor's receiving annual revenues of $988. Since there are no offsetting deductible expenses, this $988 will be subject to a 40 percent tax rate, and the investor will retain the remaining 60 percent. And 60 percent of $988 proves to be $593.

No other data remain to be processed, and so our findings can be summarized as follows:

	Amount per year	
Capital cost	$1,693	
Recurring costs	1,236	
Income taxes	1,107	$4,036
Less:		
Gains-tax revenue equivalent		988
Total revenue requirement		$3,048

In brief, revenues of $3,048 a year will be required if the contractor is to realize an after-tax return of 10 percent on the total investment of $3,600 in the old equipment. With these revenues, annual income taxes will be the indicated $1,107 minus 40 percent of the indicated $988 revenue reduction; this is $1,107 minus $395, or $712. Although this will not be done, a check, such as the one made in Tables 9-6 and 9-7 for the proposed new equipment, would verify the accuracy of the preceding statement and would also reveal a slight discrepancy between the assumed interest expenses for this alternative and the actual interest expenses given in the preceding chapter.

The Comparison. When the respective revenue requirements for the two alternatives are compared with their after-tax uniform annual costs, as computed in the preceding chapter, the following is obtained:

Alternative	Annual revenue requirement	After-tax uniform annual cost
New equipment	$3,171	$2,890
Old equipment	3,048	2,814
Difference	$ 123	$ 76

The first thing to be noted is that, in the absence of irreducible factors, retaining the old equipment proves to be the more economical alternative with either method of analysis. However, its annual advantage is $123 in the one case and only $76 in the other. This is easily explained. The actual annual revenues, although not estimated, are expected to be the same for both alternatives and are expected to exceed those required to realize a satisfactory return on total investment. Therefore, as suggested by the calculated values of the revenue requirement, the old equipment will yield surplus revenues which will be $123 greater before taxes than those generated by the new equipment. But at a tax rate of 40 percent, the after-tax surplus revenue advantage will be only 60 percent of this $123, or $74. The $2 difference between this amount and the $76 obtained with the uniform annual cost method is attributable to the difference between the assumed debt repayment plans and the actual debt repayment plans.

It might also be noted that the calculated revenue requirement for each alternative exceeds its calculated uniform annual cost by what appears to be a significant amount. The reason for this will be explained with reference to the new equipment. In the uniform annual cost analysis, the income taxes for the new equipment were shown to be $0 and then the *additional* taxes for the old equipment were ascertained. But the revenue requirement analysis yielded annual income taxes of $281 for the new equipment and some larger amount for the old. Therefore, a somewhat more meaningful comparison of the results can be made if each of the calculated uniform annual costs is increased by $281. When this is done, the uniform annual cost of the new equipment becomes $3,171, and this coincides with that alternative's revenue requirement. With the $281 adjustment, the old equipment's annual cost becomes $3,095, and it continues to have an after-tax advantage of $76.

This concludes our analysis of the replacement problem by the revenue requirement method. We saw that, although the assumption regarding the debt repayment pattern was not correct in this case, the results of the analysis differed by an insignificant amount from those obtained with the actual repayment pattern. Next, the presence of sum-of-the-years-digits depreciation simply served to emphasize that the method requires only that the uniform annual equivalent be found of whatever pattern of tax depreciation charges is involved. But complications arose because of the availability of an investment tax credit and the fact that market values and book values did not always coincide; the method is capable of coping with such complications, but the means for doing so might not always be obvious or easily understood. And, finally, the fact that only the differences in operating costs were given created no difficulties, because the disregarded additional operating costs would have increased each of the calculated revenue requirements by the same amount; however, costs which are unaffected by the choice of alternative cannot be ignored if the results of a revenue requirement determination are to be used, for example, as a basis for determining required unit selling prices.

AN EVALUATION

Additional applications of the revenue requirement method could be presented, but those considered suffice to demonstrate how the method is applied and provide us with a basis for evaluating the approach. It is with an evaluation that we shall now concern ourselves.

A given analytical technique has advantages and disadvantages only in relation to other available methods of analysis. The other available methods which have been described are the uniform annual cost, present worth, future worth, and rate of return approaches. As compared with those basic approaches, the revenue requirement method was developed for the specific purpose of simplifying after-tax analyses. This is not to say that the method cannot be applied on a before-tax basis. To do so, one would employ a before-tax rate-of-return requirement and give no consideration to the revenues required to recover income taxes. But if this is done, the calculated value of an alternative's revenue requirement or of an alternative's revenue surplus is nothing more than the alternative's uniform annual cost before taxes. As this suggests, under such circumstances, the revenue requirement method is simply the uniform annual cost method by another name.

In brief, what is unique about the revenue requirement method is the manner in which it enables an investor to ascertain the income tax consequences of a proposed course of action. Hence, it becomes an optional approach in the strict sense of the term only when an after-tax analysis is to be made. And as we have seen, the required steps in this type of analysis can ordinarily be more easily carried out with the revenue requirement method than with the others. Of course, there will be situations in which this will not be the case. The kinds of difficulties that may be encountered were suggested in the illustration in which it was necessary to alter the basic procedure in order to provide for the occurrence of an investment tax credit, a gains tax, and a devaluation expense which was not tax deductible. In the presence of such complicating factors, the analyst may correctly conclude that one of the basic analytical techniques will prove to be more straightforward.

One may also be well advised to reject the revenue requirement method on occasion because of its underlying assumptions. When these assumptions generate a debt repayment plan and corresponding interest expenses which are totally unlike those that will occur, simplicity may have to be forsaken for the sake of accuracy. This is not to say that the application of the method is warranted only when assumed and actual conditions are alike in every respect. It has been shown that an assumed debt repayment plan which approximates the actual plan suffices to yield a result which enables the analyst to identify the most economical alternative. However, if the assumed and actual debt repayment plans differ significantly, what proves to be the most economical alternative on the basis of, say, a uniform annual cost approach may not appear to be the most economical alternative on the basis of a revenue requirement approach. Now, it might be argued that this is likely to happen only when one alternative does not have a decided advantage over the other with the result that, with either approach, the final decision will be based on irreducible factors. But this cannot be said with certainty.

Of course, there will be times when the actual debt repayment plan is unknown. This stems from the fact that, very often, capital is not raised to finance a specific investment. Instead, the firm simply draws funds for this purpose from its pool of available capital. Therefore, while it is possible for the firm to determine what proportion of its total available capital represents debt, it may not be possible for the firm to determine what proportion of a single capital expenditure will consist of borrowed funds. Consequently, it is not unusual for such a firm simply to assume that the debt ratio for a single proposed investment will be equal to its overall ratio of debt financing. Also, such a firm will not be repaying all of its borrowed funds in exactly the same way. And since the exact source of the borrowed funds to be associated with a specific investment is not known, there is no way of determining what the specific repayment plan will be. As a result, a repayment plan, which may be a composite of those that exist, will be assumed even when an after-tax analysis of investment alternatives is made by means of one of the basic analytical techniques. Under these circumstances, those techniques no longer have the advantage of being based on an actual debt repayment plan. And it may be that concerned individuals will conclude that the repayment plan generated by the assumptions underlying the revenue requirement method is as representative of what will occur as is any repayment plan they may choose to assume on the basis of judgment.

Another feature of the revenue requirement method becomes apparent when we consider a situation in which an investor is unable to estimate the revenues that will be generated by an alternative. Unless these revenues are known, there is no way of ascertaining quantitatively whether the after-tax return on total investment in the alternative will be satisfactory. Instead, judgment must be substituted for a quantitative approach. But the results of a revenue requirement determination can aid the investor when a need for exercising such judgment arises. For a given alternative, if all its costs are taken into consideration, the revenue requirement technique will reveal what the minimum revenues must be if a satisfactory after-tax return is to be realized. And it may be that, although a meaningful revenue estimate cannot be made, it is possible to judge with a high degree of accuracy whether a proposed course of action is capable of yielding the minimum revenues that are now known to be needed to satisfy an established return requirement.

A knowledge of the value of the revenue requirement may be useful for another reason. The company engaged in an analysis of investment alternatives might be subject to government control with respect to the prices it can charge for its products and services. Theoretically, it will be allowed to charge prices which suffice to generate the minimum revenues required by the firm to cover its capital costs, operating expenses, and income taxes. But any request to a regulatory commission that specific prices be authorized must be supported by evidence that the requested prices are necessary if a satisfactory after-tax return on total investment is to be realized. The results of revenue requirement analyses can serve as a basis for determining what the requested prices should be and for demonstrating that these prices are necessary.

To summarize, the revenue requirement method, like any of the other analytical techniques, has its advantages and disadvantages. In some cases, the disadvantages may preclude its use, and, in others, the advantages may dictate its use. But, more often than not, whether this method of analysis or some other should be employed will be a matter of personal preference. And, as mentioned when the basic analytical techniques were being compared, there is no reason why one approach cannot be adopted under one set of circumstances and some other approach under another set.

To conclude, it will be recalled that the revenue requirement method was introduced as an example of the *special* methods of analysis that have been developed for use in the evaluation of capital investment opportunities. It is the only such technique we shall consider. The others, like this one, involve certain assumptions, but all are based on concepts and principles which are common to the four basic methods of analysis. Hence, a knowledge and understanding of those concepts and principles should enable one to comprehend any of those other approaches with little, if any, difficulty.

QUESTIONS

9-1 In what general way do special methods for analyzing investment alternatives differ from the basic methods considered in earlier chapters?

9-2 Describe, in general terms, the revenue requirement approach to the determination of the most economical investment alternative.

9-3 What does an alternative's revenue requirement represent?

9-4 What assumptions underlie the revenue requirement method?

9-5 What are the elements of an alternative's total revenue requirement?

9-6 How can the revenues, which are required to recover each of the following, be ascertained:

   a The capital cost?
   b The operating expenses?
   c The income taxes?

9-7 If the revenues which an alternative is expected to yield are estimated, how does this information enter into the revenue requirement analysis?

9-8 Under what conditions can actual revenues be ignored in a revenue requirement study?

9-9 Describe the relationship among an alternative's required revenues, its actual revenues, and the after-tax return on the total investment in the alternative.

9-10 What are before-tax surplus revenues? After-tax surplus revenues? How is each computed?

9-11 When the available data permit the determination of surplus revenues for each of a set of mutually exclusive alternatives, must taxes on these surplus revenues be considered in the identification of the most economical alternative? Explain.

9-12 Suppose that one alternative's actual revenues are equal to its required revenues and that a second alternative's actual revenues are equal to its required revenues. What can be said about the prospective rate of return on the extra investment called for by the one alternative as compared with the other?

9-13 Can a revenue requirement be expressed as a present worth? A future worth? If so, how is each of these obtained?

9-14 In what respect does a revenue requirement analysis of a multiple-alternative problem differ from a revenue requirement analysis of a two-alternative problem?

9-15 What is the procedure for ascertaining the revenue requirement for an alternative, which consists of a currently-available asset and its future replacement, when the cash-flow pattern generated by the currently-available asset differs from the cash-flow pattern its future replacement is expected to generate?

9-16 How is each of the following processed in a revenue requirement determination:

    a An investment tax credit?

    b The tax effect of a gain or loss on disposal?

    c A devaluation expense which is not a tax-deductible depreciation expense?

9-17 Is it necessary to consider those recurring costs, which are not affected by the choice of alternative, in a revenue requirement study? Explain.

9-18 What are the advantages and disadvantages of the revenue requirement method?

PROBLEMS

9-1 Consideration is being given to the purchase of a truck by a parcel delivery service. The proposed truck has a first cost of $12,000, a four-year economic life, and an estimated $750 terminal salvage value. Annual recurring expenses are expected to assume the form of the following series: $18,000, $19,000, $21,000, $24,000.

The double-rate declining-balance method would be adopted for tax depreciation purposes. Seventy percent of the financing would be with debt funds which would be obtained at a cost of 6 percent. The firm's effective tax rate is 40 percent, and its after-tax rate-of-return requirement is 8 percent.

    a What is this investment alternative's uniform annual revenue requirement?

    b In the preceding part of this problem, annual taxes should have been found to be $152, and the annual revenue requirement to be $23,916. Accepting the assumptions which underlie the revenue requirement method, demonstrate that the uniform annual equivalent of the income taxes will be $152 if the truck is capable of generating revenues whose uniform annual equivalent is $23,916.

    c Suppose that the manager of the delivery service has reason to believe that, if the truck is purchased, the firm will be able to increase its revenues by $26,000 a year. In that event, what total uniform annual income taxes would be experienced with this alternative? (Ans. $986)

9-2 A corporate bond can be purchased at this time for $1,000. This coincides with the amount for which the bond will be redeemed in 14 years by the issuing corporation.

A private investor is thinking of buying the bond with equity funds. If she does, she will retain ownership of the security for 14 years. Her effective tax rate is 25 percent, and her after-tax rate-of-return requirement is 6 percent.

a What is the revenue requirement for this investment alternative?

b In the course of ascertaining the revenue requirement, you should have found the annual taxes to be $20. Show that average annual income taxes will be equal to this amount if the bondholder receives interest payments equal to the calculated value of the revenue requirement.

c Suppose that the actual interest payments to the bondholder are equivalent to a uniform series of $90 end-of-year amounts. What will be the resultant total annual income tax expense?

9-3 A salesman of amusement games is encouraging the manager of a bus depot to purchase and install a new game in the passenger waiting area. The unit has a first cost of $1,300, a probable life of 3 years, and a terminal salvage value of $100. Annual operating costs would average $400. The manufacturer of the equipment is willing to finance the entire purchase at an interest rate of 12 percent.

The bus company, whose effective tax rate is 52 percent, would depreciate the asset by means of the sum-of-the-years-digits method. Because no equity funds need be invested, the minimum rate-of-return requirement would be equal to the 12 percent cost of debt.

a What is the uniform annual equivalent of the game's revenue requirement? (Ans. $911)

b Assume that the amusement game is capable of yielding revenues equal to the revenue requirement. Then, working with the assumptions on which the revenue requirement method is based, go on to show that the annual income taxes will be equal to the value of $0 which had been obtained in the preceding part of this problem.

c What would the annual income taxes be if the game were purchased and succeeded in generating average annual revenues of $1,400? (Ans. $254)

9-4 Two condensate pumps are to be compared by the revenue requirement method to determine which is the more economical. Pump A will have an installed first cost of $10,000, a service life of 12 years, and a negligible terminal salvage value. During its twelve-year life, it will have to be rehabilitated at the end of the second, fourth, sixth, eighth, and tenth years at a cost of $800 each time.

Pump B will have an installed first cost of $12,000, a service life of 15 years, and a negligible salvage value. During its fifteen-year life, it will have to be rehabilitated at the end of the third, sixth, ninth, and twelfth years at a cost of $900 each time. Annual power and routine maintenance costs with this pump will be about equal to those of the other one.

The initial investment in each pump will be depreciated by the straight-line method. However, the rehabilitation costs will be reported as operating expenses at the points at which they occur. Financing in each case will be entirely with equity funds.

If the effective tax rate is 45 percent and the after-tax rate-of-return requirement is 10 percent, which of the pumps will prove to be the more attractive alternative? (Ans. $2,331, $2,458)

9-5 In the preceding problem, the pumps' estimated service lives were given as 12 and 15 years, respectively. Suppose that these estimates remain unchanged but that the firm is able to depreciate either pump over a period of 8 years for tax purposes. When doing so, it would continue to depreciate the asset involved by the straight-line method but on the basis of an assumed salvage value of zero at the end of the asset's eight-year tax life. Evaluate the alternatives under this revised set of circumstances by means of the revenue requirement method.

9-6 An individual is in the process of deciding whether to begin a self-service dry cleaning business at a location which is available for rent. If she decides to do so, she will have to make an investment in dry cleaners, steam cabinets, and ventilators. Some minimum number of units of each type would, of course, be required. But space is available for the installation of a larger number of units, and, if this additional capacity is provided, the result will be a corresponding increase in revenues. Suffice it to say that the potential investor is considering three alternatives, in addition to the one of making no investment in the activity. These three alternatives, each of which represents a different service capacity level, can be described as follows:

	Capacity X	Capacity Y	Capacity Z
Installed cost of assets	$44,500	$64,000	$79,500
Service life	5 years	5 years	5 years
Terminal salvage value	$4,500	$6,000	$7,500
Annual operating costs	$23,000	$28,000	$32,000
Annual revenues	$39,000	$51,000	$58,000

Because the analysis is to be made on an after-tax basis, attention will also be given to the following factors:

Tax depreciation method: Straight-line
Proportion of debt financing: 0.25
Cost of debt: 9%
Effective tax rate: 38%
After-tax return requirement: 15%

The possible courses of action are to be analyzed with the use of the revenue requirement method. More specifically, the alternatives' after-tax surplus revenues will be determined and compared. In the process of this determination, what will the following be found to be:

a   The alternatives' respective revenue requirements?
b   The alternatives' respective before-tax surplus revenues?
c   The alternatives' respective after-tax surplus revenues?

Which set of these results could be used to identify the most economical alternative? Why? (Ans. $38,007, $49,640, $58,877; $993, $1,360, −$877; $616, $843, −$544)

9-7 No mention was made in the preceding problem of an investment tax credit. Therefore, it was to be assumed that none was available. But suppose that you are now told that the investor can claim a 10 percent tax credit of this kind. What effect will this have on the following:

a   The alternatives' respective revenue requirements?
b   The alternatives' respective before-tax surplus revenues?

9-8 At the present time, a manufacturing concern adheres to an inventory control system which is implemented manually. It is estimated that the cost of operating the system during the coming year will be $280,000 and that, thereafter, this cost will increase at an annual rate of $14,000.

The same degree of control can be maintained with the use of an electronic data processing system. The equipment involved will have an installed cost of $1,375,000, a service life of 10 years, and a salvage value equal to 20 percent of the equipment's installed cost. Expenses of a recurring nature would be about $36,000 the first year but would then increase at a rate of $3,000 a year.

For tax purposes, the equipment would be depreciated by the sum-of-the-years-digits method. Other relevant tax information is as follows:

Effective tax rate = 51%
Proportion of debt financing = 0.35
Cost of borrowed money = 10%

Given that the firm's minimum rate-of-return requirement is 12 percent after taxes, make a revenue requirement comparison of the alternatives to determine which is the more economical. Express this requirement in terms of a present worth for a service period of 10 years for each alternative.

9-9 Suppose that the firm referred to in the preceding problem adopted the straight-line method of depreciation rather than the sum-of-the-years-digits method and that it would be entitled to an 8 percent investment tax credit if it installed the electronic data processing system. What effect would this have on the present worths of the alternatives' revenue requirements? Which alternative would then be the more economical? (Ans. $1,865,551, $1,816,272)

9-10 A processor of meat products finds that he is unable to satisfy the entire demand for certain kinds of sausage which he produces. To increase his output capacity, he would have to make a capital investment in a chopper, a mixer, and a stuffer. Either new or rebuilt equipment of this kind can be purchased. These respective types would have the following characteristics:

	New	Rebuilt
Total first cost	$68,000	$52,000
Service life	30 years	20 years
Salvage value	$2,900	$1,600

Annual recurring expenses would include the cost of such things as ingredients, labor, maintenance, and power. With either alternative, these expenses would be $43,000 in the first year and would then increase at an annual rate of $2,000. This rate of increase would continue for 30 years with the new equipment but for only 20 years with the rebuilt equipment.

Both types of equipment would have the same effect on annual revenues. In each case, it is estimated that the additional output would serve to increase revenues by $54,000 in the first year and that these revenues would then increase at a rate of $1,400 per year. This rate of increase would continue for 30 years with the new equipment and for 20 years with the rebuilt equipment.

Because the alternatives are to be evaluated by the revenue requirement method, the following additional data have been compiled:

Tax depreciation method: Sum-of-the-years-digits
Rate-of-return requirement: 10%
Investment tax credit: 5%
Debt ratio: 0.30
Cost of debt: 8%
Effective tax rate: 54%

Should the processor be advised to increase his output capacity? If so, should he do so by buying the new equipment or the rebuilt equipment?

9-11 A furniture manufacturer is making use of a unit of sanding equipment which is so deteriorated that it must be either overhauled or replaced.

The machine's book value and market value are both zero. A thorough overhaul would cost $6,000 and would serve to extend the unit's life by 3 years, at the end of which time the unit would have a negligible salvage value. The $6,000 expenditure would be financed with equity funds whose opportunity cost is 15 percent. For tax purposes, the overhaul cost would be reported as an operating expense at the point at which it occurs.

A new machine would have a first cost of $19,000, an estimated life of 17 years, and a terminal salvage value of $2,000. Fifty percent of this expenditure would be financed with debt funds whose cost is also 15 percent. The tax depreciation method would be straight-line.

Recurring expenses with either alternative would be about the same. The manufacturer's effective tax rate is 43 percent. The minimum after-tax rate-of-return requirement is 15 percent for both alternatives.

By means of the revenue requirement method, ascertain whether the equipment should be overhauled or replaced.

9-12 Let us suppose that the furniture manufacturer referred to in the preceding problem chooses not to accept the implied assumption regarding the nature of future replacements. Instead, he makes the following forecast: If the currently-owned sanding equipment is overhauled, it will be replaced in 3 years by a new unit whose first cost will be $26,000, whose life will be 14 years, whose salvage value will be $5,000, and whose operating costs will be equal to those of the currently-available new equipment. This future replacement will also require 50 percent debt financing at a cost of 15 percent and will be depreciated by the straight-line method.

Continuing to work with a 43 percent tax rate and a 15 percent return requirement for both alternatives, make a revenue requirement comparison of the alternatives under this revised set of circumstances. (Ans. $4,427, $3,908)

9-13 The owner of a fishing-boat charter service is giving consideration to a proposal that he expand his operation by purchasing another boat. If he decides to do so, he will make an investment in a certain type of boat which is available in three sizes. In general, costs will be higher with a larger boat but so will the revenues. The latter is true because there will be space for more fishermen on a larger boat and, also, such a boat may be able to go out under weather conditions which would be unsafe with a smaller boat. In any case, a description of the cash-flow patterns to be associated with the three sizes of boats is as follows:

	Small	*Medium*	*Large*
First cost	$37,000	$49,000	$58,000
Service life	8 years	10 years	12 years
Salvage value	$5,500	$7,750	$9,250
First-year net receipts	$8,000	$10,000	$11,000
Annual increase in net receipts	$500	$600	$700

Unfortunately, the owner of the business is confronted by a serious financing problem which stems from the fact that he has no equity capital available for the proposed investment. Although he can obtain the necessary capital by borrowing, he can do so only by agreeing to pay the relatively high interest rate of 20 percent.

Insofar as tax considerations are concerned, double-rate declining-balance depreciation will be employed, multiple-asset accounting is adhered to, a 7 percent investment tax credit is available, and the effective tax rate is 35 percent.

Make a revenue requirement analysis of the four available alternatives to determine which is the most economical.

9-14 A manufacturer of machine tools is comparing the alternative of retaining a unit of general-purpose equipment with the alternative of replacing it by a unit of special design.

The old equipment has a book value of zero but a market value of $2,100. Therefore, one of the consequences of immediate replacement would be that an ordinary gain of $2,100 would have to be reported for tax purposes; since the firm's effective tax rate is 36 percent, the resultant gains tax would be $756. If the asset is not replaced at this time, it will probably be kept another 3 years and then disposed of for some negligible amount; hence, no gain or loss would be experienced at that point.

The new equipment has an installed first cost of $190,000, an estimated life of 25 years, and a net terminal salvage value equal to 5 percent of the installed first cost. As compared with the old equipment, it has the advantage of being capable of bringing about a significant reduction in the annual cost of labor, defective output, and repairs. This would be offset to some degree by an increase in the annual cost of power and property taxes, but the net saving per year would, nevertheless, amount to $18,000.

Because the two alternatives are to be compared on a revenue requirement basis, the analyst will also take into consideration the following factors when computing the revenue requirement for each alternative:

Tax depreciation method: Straight-line
Proportion of debt financing: 0.20
Cost of borrowed money: 6%
Return requirement: 8%

Will it be found that the extra investment required by the new equipment can be justified? (Ans. $18,806, $22,670)

9-15 A boiler is being designed for use in a generating station. The boiler will contain eight burners. Two alternative designs for these burners have been proposed. Both will have a life of 40 years and a zero salvage value. But the advanced-design burners will each cost $15,000 more than those of simple design. This disadvantage is offset to some degree by the fact that they will reduce fuel costs by $24,000 a year. However, the expected loading pattern of the station is such that this annual saving will be experienced only during the first 20 years; after that, fuel costs with the burners of advanced design will be about equal to the fuel costs with the burners of simple design.

The company depreciates assets of this type by the sum-of-the-years-digits method. Its effective tax rate is 50 percent, its debt ratio is 0.40, its cost of debt is 7.5 percent, its after-tax return requirement is 12 percent, and it can claim a 6 percent investment tax credit.

Will a revenue requirement analysis justify the extra investment called for by the advanced-design burners?

9-16 Packaged items are currently being transported between two areas in a warehouse with the use of a truck, and it has been suggested that the truck be replaced by a conveyor system. This system would cost $25,200 and have a 35-year life and no terminal salvage value. The cost of operating the system would be $2,800 the first year, but this would then increase at a constant annual rate of $150.

The truck has a market value of $500, and this is not expected to decrease during its estimated remaining life of 2 years. Its book value is also $500 and will remain at this level because no depreciation expenses will be claimed during the truck's remaining life. The cost of operating the truck will be $11,000 next year and $12,000 the year after.

In the revenue requirement analysis which is to be made, cognizance will be taken of the fact that (1) 24 percent of the required investment in either alternative will consist of borrowed money whose cost is 13 percent, (2) the conveyor will be depreciated by the sum-of-the-years-digits method and qualifies for a 10 percent investment tax credit, (3) the after-tax rate-of-return requirement is 15 percent, and (4) the effective tax rate is 52 percent. What will be the result of the analysis?

9-17 The management of a corporate farm has decided that a building to be used for storage purposes must be constructed. However, it has yet to decide which of two plans is the more economical.

Plan I calls for constructing a building, whose storage capacity will be adequate for 15 years, at a cost of $240,000. Fifteen years from now, $180,000 would have to be spent for an addition to the building in order to increase the storage capacity to the level that would be required from that point on. Annual maintenance costs and property taxes would average $24,000 during the first 15 years and $42,000 thereafter.

Plan II calls for constructing a larger building at this time and, thereby, eliminating the need for an addition in 15 years. Such a building would cost $300,000. Its annual maintenance costs and property taxes would average $30,000.

It is likely that either building will be razed 50 years from now at a cost which will be equal to the value of the materials which can be salvaged. Meanwhile, the depreciation expenses would be determined by the straight-line method.

The corporation's effective tax rate is 40 percent, and its minimum after-tax rate-of-return requirement is 10 percent. Approximately 55 percent of any capital investment in either building would consist of money borrowed at a cost of 9 percent.

Which of the two plans is the more economical? Determine this by the revenue requirement method. (Ans. $64,362, $68,449)

9-18 A transformer which has been in operation in a steel company for a number of years has failed. Consequently, it must be either replaced or repaired.

The first cost of a new transformer is $46,000. At the end of its probable life of 20 years, it can be expected to yield $4,000 in salvage. If purchased, it will be depreciated by the sum-of-the-years-digits method and will generate an 8 percent investment tax credit.

The cost of repairing the transformer which has failed is $5,000; this would be treated as an operating cost for tax purposes. In its present condition, the unit can be sold for $3,000. If repaired, it will be operated for about 4 more years and will have a $1,000 salvage value at the end of that period.

The current book value of the old transformer is zero. As a result, an ordinary gain of $3,000 will be experienced if the asset is replaced now. If it is repaired, an ordinary gain of $1,000 will be experienced when the asset is disposed of for $1,000 in 4 years. Either gain will be subject to an effective tax rate of 56 percent.

The fact that the failed transformer's book value is zero also means that no depreciation expenses can be claimed for tax purposes in the future. However, if it were possible to report the expected decrease of $2,000 in the unit's market value as a depreciation expense, the respective annual amounts would be ascertained with the use of the sum-of-the-years-digits method.

Other than those described, there are no significant differences between the alternatives. This is to say that the operating costs will be about the same with each. Also, debt financing will account for 10 percent of the present $3,000 investment in the old transformer and for 10 percent of the proposed $46,000 investment in the new one. The cost of borrowed money is 14 percent.

If the rate-of-return requirement is 20 percent and the effective tax rate is 56 percent, what will be the result of a revenue requirement analysis of the two possible courses of action? (Ans. $15,190, $2,867)

10

Break-even, Sensitivity, and Risk Analyses

The assumptions which underlie special analytical techniques, such as the one described in the preceding chapter, are an innate part of those methods of analysis. This is to say that those special approaches cannot be employed unless the investor is willing to accept the assumptions on which they are based. But this is not true of the assumptions which were made in the application of the basic uniform annual cost, present worth, future worth, and rate of return methods. In those cases, assumptions were made and accepted as a matter of convenience rather than of necessity. More specifically, the assumptions involved were designed to simplify the problem of estimation which confronts anyone who is responsible for the analysis of capital investment alternatives. That this is so becomes apparent when the more important of these assumptions are reviewed.

To begin with, it was assumed that annual operating costs, revenues, and income taxes will occur at the end of a given year. However, an analyst who is confident of his ability to forecast the points during the year at which these cash flows will occur is perfectly free to do so and, after having done so, would process the data accordingly. Also, it was assumed that future replacements will reproduce the cash-flow pattern to be associated with a currently-available asset. But, again, an analyst can choose to predict the characteristics of future replacements and work with these rather than with the assumed characteristics. Next, in the rate of return method, it was assumed that the net receipts realized during an alternative's life will be reinvested at a rate equal to the "internal" return, and, in the other basic methods, it was assumed that the reinvestment rate would be equal to the "external" return. However, with any one of these approaches, an analyst can choose to estimate the actual returns that will be realized on specific reinvestments and carry out the study in accordance with these estimates.

Other examples could be given, but these suffice to demonstrate that the assumptions made in the course of applying the basic analytical techniques need not be made. At the same time, they demonstrate that, if the assumptions are made, the problem of estimation is alleviated to some degree.

In this chapter, we shall deal with other means that have been developed in an attempt to reduce the problem of estimation still farther. Unlike the use of assumptions, these means do not serve to eliminate the need for particular estimates. Instead, they are based on the realization that certain kinds of estimates must be made, and they are designed to aid the analyst in his efforts to develop estimates which will serve to reflect the actual consequences of alternative courses of action. Unless such data are available, the most sophisticated analytical technique may prove to be of little value in this area of decision making.

The estimation aids to be considered will be presented with the use of examples. In these examples, we shall limit ourselves to before-tax analyses. Doing so will eliminate the need for tax computations with which we are already acquainted, and, hence, we shall be able to focus our attention on things with which we are unfamiliar. Because the revenue requirement method is an after-tax approach, this means that, in the examples, we shall adopt the before-tax uniform annual cost, present worth, future worth, and rate of return methods for purposes of illustration.

BREAK-EVEN POINT DETERMINATION

There are situations in which an investor has little confidence in his ability to estimate a specific value of some type. And, yet, he may be able to judge quite well whether the value will be greater than or less than a certain amount. To illustrate, an investor may have difficulty ascertaining what his cost of money is, but, nevertheless, he may be able to decide whether an indicated rate of return on investment is satisfactory. Or he may not be able to predict what revenues will be generated by an alternative, but if he knows what minimum revenues are needed to satisfy an established rate-of-return requirement, he may be capable of concluding whether a proposed activity can be expected to yield such revenues.

It will be recognized that these two illustrations contain observations that had been made when the rate of return method and the revenue requirement method were being discussed. But they are now being repeated because they suggest one way in which estimation difficulties can sometimes be alleviated. Specifically, when the value of some characteristic of an investment alternative cannot be estimated, it may be possible to calculate what minimum or maximum value this characteristic must assume before an investment in the alternative can be justified. This value is referred to as the *break-even point.* After such a determination has been made, the investor must decide whether the actual value of the characteristic is likely to be equal to, less than, or greater than the required value. If he concludes that it will be equal to the required value, the investment is only just warranted. Otherwise, it will be either not warranted or more than warranted, depending on the nature of the characteristic involved. Let us now go on to apply this approach.

The Example. Suppose that a company has definitely decided to purchase and install a tank to store a chemical used in one of its processes. The question to be answered is: Should the tank be constructed of material Q or material R? For the moment, we shall assume that all the relevant cash flows for each of these alternatives can be estimated and that these are as follows:

	Tank Q	Tank R
Installed cost	$70,000	$110,000
Life	10 years	20 years
Salvage value	$0	$0
Annual maintenance	$2,000	$1,000

The firm will base its decision on a before-tax uniform annual cost comparison in which it will use 12 percent as its cost of money before taxes.

To satisfy the equal time-period requirement, the assumption will be made that the cash-flow pattern to be associated with tank Q will repeat itself when the tank is replaced at the end of its ten-year life. Therefore, the uniform annual cost of tank Q, during the resultant study period of 20 years, would be found by processing the following cash flows:

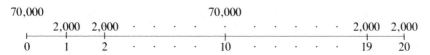

Doing so, we obtain

Annual cost $= \$70,000(A/P)_{n=10}^{i=12} + \$2,000 = \$14,390$

For tank R, the comparable cost for 20 years would be found by processing the following cash flows:

110,000
```
      1,000  1,000  · · · ·    ·    · · · ·  1,000  1,000
 |------+------+--------------+----------------+------|
 0      1      2    · · · ·   10   · · · · ·   19     20
```

Doing so, we obtain

Annual cost $= \$110,000(A/P)_{n=20}^{i=12} + \$1,000 = \$15,729$

A comparison of these results discloses that, in the absence of irreducible factors, tank Q is the more economical of the two alternatives.

The First Variation. We shall now make the first of a series of changes in the statement of the problem. Suppose that the firm is unable to decide what rate should be used to represent its cost of money before taxes. This precludes its being able to compute the alternatives' uniform annual costs, present worths, or future worths. But it does not prevent the company from being able to answer the following question: What rate-of-return requirement would just warrant the extra investment called for by tank R? The question can be answered by calculating the return that will be realized on the extra investment should tank R be selected.

Tank R requires an extra investment of $110,000 minus $70,000, or $40,000. The consequences of this investment will be that there will be an annual reduction of $1,000 in maintenance costs for 20 years and that there will be no need to spend $70,000 for the replacement of tank Q at the end of its ten-year life. On a time line, all this would appear as follows:

40,000   (70,000)
```
    (1,000) (1,000) · · · ·     ·    · · · · (1,000) (1,000)
 |------+------+--------------+----------------+------|
 0      1      2    · · · ·   10   · · · · ·   19     20
```

The return on the $40,000 extra investment can be obtained by finding the rate i which will yield a present worth of zero for this cash-flow pattern. This would be done with the use of the following expression:

Present worth $= \$40,000 - \$1,000(P/A)_{n=20}^{i=?} - \$70,000(P/F)_{n=10}^{i=?} = 0$

By trial and error, the unknown rate would be found to be 8.7 percent.

Ordinarily, the analysis would continue with a comparison of this return with the investor's minimum rate-of-return requirement. But, in this case, the investor maintains that he is unable to determine what this requirement should be. Therefore, the indicated return of 8.7 percent must be looked upon as a break-even point. This is to say that, if the cost of money is 8.7 percent, the extra investment in tank R is just warranted. And, if the cost of money is less than 8.7 percent, the extra investment in tank R is more than justified. But, if the cost of money is greater than 8.7 percent, tank R will be the less attractive of the two alternatives.

From this, it follows that, under the circumstances, the firm must now decide whether its cost of money is equal to, less than, or more than 8.7 percent. As a matter of fact, since the alternatives will be equally attractive at a return requirement of 8.7 percent, it is necessary, for all practical purposes, to decide simply whether the cost of money is less than or more than 8.7 percent. And there is reason to believe that, on many occasions, a potential investor can make this kind of decision even though he may be unable to provide the analyst with a specific value for the rate-of-return requirement.

The Second Variation. We shall now make a different change in the problem. Let us suppose that the company has no difficulty in estimating that its cost of money is 12 percent but that it is very uncertain about the years of service that it can expect from tank R. In the absence of this datum, none of the analytical techniques can be employed to compare the two alternatives. However, it is possible to answer the following question: What service life for tank R would just warrant the extra investment which this tank requires? This question can be answered by determining the service life that will result in the total cost of tank R being equal to the total cost of tank Q.

The respective total costs of alternatives Q and R can be expressed in terms of a uniform annual cost, present worth, or future worth. If the firm chooses to adopt a uniform annual cost approach, it can begin its determination of the service life which equates the annual costs by developing the following expression:

$$\$110,000(A/P)_{n=?}^{i=12} + \$1,000 = \$70,000(A/P)_{n=10}^{i=12} + \$2,000$$

This expression simply states that, for some unknown service life n, the uniform annual cost of alternative R will be equal to that of alternative Q. Similar expressions had been developed in earlier chapters when it was necessary to determine the rate i at which two uniform annual costs would be equal. In those cases, if the expression contained only one unknown compound interest factor, the value of this factor was calculated and the corresponding rate found in the tables in Appendix C. But if the expression contained more than one unknown compound interest factor, a trial-and-error approach had to be employed. The same procedure is followed when the life n is the unknown. The only difference is that the tables in Appendix C are used to find the life which corresponds to a calculated value of a compound interest factor, or that different values are assumed for the life until the one which satisfies the equation is found.

To return to our example, when all the terms in the equation are moved to the left side, the result is as follows:

$$\$110,000(A/P)_{n=?}^{i=12} - \$70,000(A/P)_{n=10}^{i=12} - \$1,000 = 0$$

Only one unknown factor is present, and its value proves to be

$$(A/P)_{n=?}^{i=12} = 0.1217$$

The values of compound interest factors at a rate of 12 percent are contained in Table C-6. That table reveals that, for an n of 35, the value of the present-amount annuity factor is 0.1223 and that, for an n of 40, the value of the factor is 0.1213. Linear interpolation between these two amounts yields a service life of 38 years. In other words, if tank R lasts 38 years, its uniform annual cost will be equal to the uniform annual cost of tank Q, and, therefore, 38 years is the break-even point. At that point, both alternatives are equally attractive. It can also be said that, at that point, the return on the extra investment in tank R will be equal to the firm's 12 percent cost of money. This is because the alternatives' uniform annual costs are equal when the life n of tank R is 38 years and the rate i is 12 percent. And, as we know, the rate at which the uniform annual costs of two alternatives are equal represents the return on the extra investment required by the one alternative as compared with the other.

To continue, the firm must now decide whether tank R is likely to last less than 38 years or more than 38 years. And this kind of decision is more easily made than is one regarding the exact number of years the tank is likely to last. In any event, if the decision is that the tank's life will be less than 38 years, the extra investment should not be made because a life of less than 38 years serves to increase the uniform annual cost of tank R to a level which would be above that of tank Q. But if the decision is that the tank's life will be more than 38 years, the extra investment should be made because a life of more than 38 years serves to decrease the uniform annual cost of tank R to a level which would be below that of tank Q.

Incidentally, it might be noted that, in this example, the break-even point could not have been ascertained on an after-tax basis. This is because the taxes generated by tank R would be affected by the deductible depreciation expenses it will yield, but these expenses will be a function of its service life which is being treated as an unknown in the analysis.

For a similar reason, after-tax analyses may not be possible in some of the examples which follow this one.

The Third Variation. We shall now return to the original set of data provided in this problem and make a different change. In the original description of the cash flows involved, it was stated that tank R was expected to have no salvage value. Let us now suppose that the estimator believes that tank R will have some salvage value but that he is unable to decide upon a specific value. All the other estimates remain the same.

In the absence of a salvage value estimate, a cost comparison of the alternatives cannot be made. However, a decision regarding which of the two alternatives is the more economical can be based on the answer to the following question: What would the minimum salvage value of tank R have to be to justify the higher total investment called for by this tank? The general answer to this question is that the salvage value would have to be an amount which would result in the two alternatives' total costs being equal.

To obtain a specific answer, the firm can develop an expression in which the total cost of tank R is equated to the total cost of tank Q and in which the salvage value of tank R appears as an unknown. If it is decided to express these respective total costs as future worths at the end of the twenty-year study period, the expression would appear as follows:

$$\$110,000(F/P)_{n=20}^{i=12} + \$1,000(F/A)_{n=20}^{i=12} - (\text{salvage value})$$

$$= \$70,000(F/P)_{n=20}^{i=12} + \$70,000(F/P)_{n=10}^{i=12} + \$2,000(F/A)_{n=20}^{i=12}$$

Solving this equation for the salvage value, we obtain

Salvage value = \$96,394

This amount represents a break-even point. At this point, the alternatives' total costs are equal, the return on the \$40,000 extra investment in tank R is 12 percent, and tank R is as economical as tank Q.

To ascertain whether tank R is less economical or more economical than tank Q, the firm must now decide whether the salvage value of tank R will be less than \$96,394 or more than this amount. It is assumed, with this approach, that this kind of decision can be made even though a specific estimate of the salvage value cannot be made. In any event, an expected salvage value of less than \$96,394 would increase the total cost of tank R and make it less economical than tank Q, while an expected salvage value of more than \$96,394 would decrease the total cost of tank R and make it more economical than tank Q.

The Fourth Variation. Let us now suppose that the two alternatives are described as they originally were, but with one exception. This is that the estimator states that he is unable to estimate what the annual maintenance expense will be with tank R.

The effect of this change in the given data is the same as the effect of the changes made earlier. Namely, the alternatives cannot be compared on the basis of either their total costs or a prospective rate of return. But they can be evaluated on the basis of the answer to the following question: What maximum annual maintenance expense for tank R would serve to justify making the required extra investment in this alternative?

The question can be answered by ascertaining what maintenance expense for tank R will generate a total cost for this tank equal to the total cost of tank Q. Should the firm choose to express these total costs as uniform annual equivalents, the unknown maintenance expense can be found with the use of the following expression:

$$\$110,000(A/P)_{n=20}^{i=12} + (\text{maintenance expense})$$

$$= \$70,000(A/P))_{n=10}^{i=12} + \$2,000$$

which yields

Maintenance expense $= (-)\$339$

This is to say that, if the annual maintenance expense with tank R is a negative $339, this tank will be as economical as tank Q. More specifically, at this break-even point, the alternatives' total costs will be equal, which means that the return on the extra investment in tank R will be equal to the company's rate-of-return requirement of 12 percent.

However, if there is reason to believe that the maintenance expense with tank R will exceed minus $339 a year, then the total cost of tank R will exceed that of tank Q, and the latter will be the more economical alternative. As this suggests, tank R will be the more attractive of the two only if its annual maintenance cost will be less than minus $339. This, of course, is impossible; so, in the absence of irreducible factors, the firm should select tank Q.

This example demonstrates that, on occasion, the break-even approach will yield a result whose nature is such that the solution to the problem becomes obvious. In other words, the value of the break-even point might represent a requirement which cannot possibly be satisfied by the affected alternative, and, hence, the alternative can be rejected without further consideration.

The Fifth Variation. A different change will now be made in the data presented originally. From these original data, we learned that the required total investment in tank R is $110,000. Suppose it had also been stated that, of this amount, $85,000 is the purchase cost and $25,000 is the estimated installation cost. But we shall now assume that the firm is very uncertain about the cost of installation. This uncertainty is so great that the individuals involved are reluctant to make a specific estimate of this expense. Instead, they recommend that the most economical tank be identified on the basis of a break-even analysis in which the following question is answered: What installation cost for tank R will make this tank as economical as tank Q?

To answer this question, an analyst must begin by recognizing that the two alternatives will be equally attractive if their total costs are equal. Therefore, there is a need for determining the value of the installation expense for tank R which will yield a total cost for this alternative equal to the total cost for tank Q. Should the analyst choose to express these respective total costs as present worths for the twenty-year service period, he would continue the study by developing the following expression:

$$(\$85,000 + \text{installation cost}) + \$1,000(P/A)_{n=20}^{i=12}$$

$$= \$70,000 + \$70,000(P/F)_{n=10}^{i=12} + \$2,000(P/A)_{n=20}^{i=12}$$

Solving for the unknown installation cost, he would obtain

Installation cost $= \$15,009$

This value is a break-even point in the sense that, if tank R can be installed at a cost of exactly $15,009, its total present worth will be equal to that of tank Q. Also, the return on the extra investment, which it will now require, will be equal to the company's 12 percent cost of money, and, as a consequence, the extra investment can be justified. In brief, the two alternatives will be equally attractive.

The final step in the analysis calls for deciding whether the actual installation expense will be less than or more than $15,009. It may be that this can be done in spite of an inability to estimate the exact expense. A decision that the actual expense will be less than $15,009 would favor tank R because the present worth of all its costs would then be lower than that of tank Q. On the other hand, a decision that the installation expense will be more than $15,009 would favor tank Q because the present worth of all its costs would then be lower than that of tank R.

This is the final variation in the original problem with which we shall concern ourselves. The purpose of a series of variations was to show that the break-even point can be found for any of an alternative's many characteristics. We considered only those related to one of the tanks, but break-even values could have also been computed for the other tank's service life, salvage value, maintenance expense, and so on. But it should be noted that, in each of the examples, the break-even point for only one characteristic of one alternative was being sought. Had additional unknowns been introduced in a given example, the described procedure could not have been applied. This is because there would be more than one combination of values for these unknowns which would serve to equate the alternatives' total costs. Despite this limitation, the approach does represent one possible means for reducing the problem of estimation.

SENSITIVITY ANALYSIS

A break-even analysis can be resorted to when an investor finds it practically impossible to describe some characteristic of an investment alternative in terms of a single specific value. However, the more common situation is one in which some such estimate can be made, but in which there is also a realization that the estimate may prove to be inaccurate. As might be expected, the result is that the investor is not certain that the alternative which appears to be the most economical on the basis of this estimate is truly so.

An approach which often proves to be useful under such circumstances is one in which a determination is made of how sensitive the decision is to changes in estimated values. In brief, the analyst simply revises one or more of the original estimates to obtain what are likely to be extreme values. Then, depending on the analytical technique being employed, he will use these new estimates to recompute total costs or prospective rates of return. In some cases, it will be found that the decision is not sensitive to changes in the estimated values, and, therefore, the investor need not concern himself with the consequences of estimates which may be incorrect to some degree. As opposed to this, there will be instances when the decision is found to be sensitive to revisions in the estimated values, and, consequently, the investor must then decide which set of estimates is most likely to be correct.

The approach which has just been outlined is referred to as *sensitivity analysis*. Its application will now be demonstrated with the use of an example. We shall begin, as we did in the discussion of break-even points, with a given set of data, and the problem will be analyzed accordingly. Then, a series of changes will be made in the original data, and the sensitivity of the decision to each of these changes will be ascertained.

A Rent-or-Buy Example. Let us suppose that a scientist has accepted a position which necessitates his moving to a city in which a certain research project is to be carried out. When the project is completed, he will be transferred to some other location.

The scientist makes a preliminary visit to the area to which he has been assigned to arrange for housing for his family and himself. He finds a suitable house which can be either rented or bought. The annual rental charge is $6,600, payable at the beginning of each year, and the owner is willing to give the scientist a lease for whatever number of years he desires. Furthermore, the owner will assume full responsibility for the cost of maintenance, utilities, insurance, and property taxes.

Insofar as the alternative of buying is concerned, the house can be purchased for $70,000. The scientist estimates that the market value of the house will increase at a rate of $1,000 a year for whatever number of years the property is owned. However, he estimates that the research project will be terminated in 3 years and, therefore, that the house will have a resale value of $73,000 at the time he will find it necessary to relocate once again. Also, he estimates that the cost of maintenance, utilities, insurance, and property taxes will be $3,000 the first year and that these costs will increase at a rate of $500 a year for whatever number of years the house is owned. For purposes of analysis, these recurring expenses will be treated as end-of-year costs.

The scientist has definitely decided to obtain the house, and the only question is whether the house should be rented or bought. The decision is to be based on a before-tax uniform annual cost comparison of the two alternatives in which 8 percent will be used as the cost of money. Therefore, the scientist begins by taking into consideration the cash flows to be associated with the alternative of renting. These are as follows:

```
6,600      6,600      6,600
|----------|----------|----------|
0          1          2          3
```

To convert this beginning-of-year series to an equivalent end-of-year series, it is necessary to move each of the amounts one year into the future, and this is done in the following manner:

Annual cost $= \$6,600(F/P)_{n=1}^{i=8} = \$7,128$

Turning to the alternative of buying, the scientist finds that the cash flows involved are as follows:

```
70,000                    (73,000)
           3,000    3,500    4,000
|----------|----------|----------|
0          1          2          3
```

The uniform annual equivalent of these amounts would be found in the following manner:

$$\text{Annual cost} = \$70,000(A/P)_{n=3}^{i=8} - \$73,000(A/F)_{n=3}^{i=8} + \$3,000$$
$$+ \$500(A/G)_{n=3}^{i=8}$$
$$= \$8,150$$

A comparison of the calculated annual costs discloses that renting the house is the more economical course of action. This, of course, is based on the assumption that the estimated cash flows are correct and that there are no relevant irreducible factors.

The First Revision. Suppose that we are told that the 8 percent cost of money used in the foregoing study is the weighted average of an interest expense on borrowed funds and an opportunity cost on equity funds. Furthermore, the opportunity cost was based on an estimate about which the scientist is very uncertain. In fact, he suspects that the actual opportunity cost may be far enough below his estimate so as to bring the overall cost of money down to 6 percent. However, there is also a chance that the opportunity cost may be far enough above his estimate so as to bring the overall cost of money up to 10 percent. In brief, it would be more correct to say that the actual cost of money will be some value between 6 percent and 10 percent, rather than to say that it will be 8 percent.

Under these circumstances, the scientist cannot help but wonder whether an error in his estimated value is of any consequence. To determine whether it is, he can go on to ascertain how sensitive the decision is to a change in the cost of money. This simply requires that he compare the alternatives on the basis of each of the extreme values which the cost of money might assume. If he begins with the 10 percent value, he would find that the annual cost of renting is now equal to

$$\text{Annual cost} = \$6,600(F/P)_{n=1}^{i=10} = \$7,260$$

and that the annual cost of buying will be as follows:

$$\text{Annual cost} = \$70,000(A/P)_{n=3}^{i=10} - \$73,000(A/F)_{n=3}^{i=10}$$
$$+ \$3,000 + \$500(A/G)_{n=3}^{i=10}$$
$$= \$9,562$$

A comparison of these results reveals that the alternative of renting continues to be the more economical. Hence, the decision is not sensitive to an increase in the cost of money, and the scientist need not be concerned about the possibility of having underestimated this cost.

The sensitivity analysis would continue with a determination of what the uniform annual costs will be should the cost of money assume the other extreme value of 6 percent. At that rate, the annual cost of renting becomes

$$\text{Annual cost} = \$6,600(F/P)_{n=1}^{i=6} = \$6,996$$

and the annual cost of buying is equal to

$$\text{Annual cost} = \$70,000(A/P)_{n=3}^{i=6} - \$73,000(A/F)_{n=3}^{i=6} + \$3,000$$
$$+ \$500(A/G)_{n=3}^{i=6}$$
$$= \$6,738$$

The alternative of buying now becomes the more economical of the two, which is to say that the decision is sensitive to a decrease in the investor's cost of money. Given this, the scientist must conclude, on the basis of judgment, whether or not his actual cost of money is likely to be as low as 6 percent and act accordingly.

To summarize, the sensitivity analysis, in this case, succeeded in demonstrating that an underestimate of the cost of money is of no significance but that an overestimate is. Hence, the area in which judgment must be exercised has been reduced.

The Second Revision.   We shall now return to the original description of the alternatives in which no question was raised regarding the cost of money. From that description, it is evident that the cash-flow pattern of the alternative of renting is known with certainty. But this is not true of the alternative of buying because some of the elements of that cash-flow pattern were estimated. Let us now suppose that, when making those estimates, the scientist was somewhat uncertain about the duration of the research project. More specifically, his estimate of 3 years represents the most likely life, but it may be that the actual life will prove to be as short as 1 year or as long as 5 years. Since the number of years for which he will either rent or own the house will coincide with the life of the project, he wonders about the possible consequences of an error in his three-year life estimate.

Whether or not an error in this estimate is of any consequence can be ascertained by means of a sensitivity analysis. The analysis could begin with a determination of which alternative will prove to be the more economical in the event that the life is equal to the minimum estimated value of 1 year and would then continue with a determination of which alternative will prove to be the more economical in the event that the life is equal to the maximum estimated value of 5 years.

Insofar as the alternative of renting is concerned, the uniform annual cost of this alternative is unaffected by a change in the life estimate because the house can be rented for any length of time at a beginning-of-year annual cost of $6,600. Therefore, at an 8 percent cost of money, the uniform annual cost of this alternative, for a service period of either 1 year or 5 years, will be what it was found to be originally. This is as follows:

Annual cost $= \$6,600(F/P)_{n=1}^{i=8} = \$7,128$

But the uniform annual cost of the alternative of buying will be affected by a revision in the service life estimate. This stems from the fact that the house appreciates in value at a rate of $1,000 a year and that the recurring expenses increase at a rate of $500 a year. As a result, the cash flows for a one-year period would be as follows:

```
70,000    (71,000)
          3,000
├───────────┤
0          1
```

and their uniform annual equivalent would be

Annual cost $= \$70,000(A/P)_{n=1}^{i=8} - \$71,000(A/F)_{n=1}^{i=8} + \$3,000$

$= \$7,600$

However, if the house were owned for 5 years, the resultant cash-flow pattern would be as follows:

```
70,000                                        (75,000)
      3,000    3,500    4,000    4,500    5,000
├────────┼────────┼────────┼────────┼────────┤
0        1        2        3        4        5
```

and the corresponding uniform annual cost would be

Annual cost $= \$70,000(A/P)_{n=5}^{i=8} - \$75,000(A/F)_{n=5}^{i=8} + \$3,000$

$+ \$500(A/G)_{n=5}^{i=8}$

$= \$8,670$

A comparison discloses that both, the average annual cost of owning the house for 1 year and the average annual cost of owning the house for 5 years, exceed the $7,128 annual cost of renting. This was also true of the annual cost of owning the house for 3 years. Therefore, the decision is not sensitive to changes in the life estimate, and there is no reason why the scientist should be concerned about the possibility that the actual service period will be as much as 2 years less or 2 years more than his estimate of 3 years.

The Third Revision. When the alternatives were compared on the basis of the original estimates, it was found that the uniform annual cost of renting would be $7,128 for three years and that the uniform annual cost of buying would be $8,150 for three years. The latter figure was arrived at by taking into consideration, among other things, recurring expenses which would amount to $3,000 the first year and would then increase at an annual rate of $500.

We shall now suppose that the scientist is interested in ascertaining the sensitivity of the decision to changes in the estimated rate at which the recurring expenses of ownership will increase. As this suggests, he is confident that his estimated value of $3,000 for the first-year recurring expenses is accurate, but he questions the accuracy of his estimated value of $500 for the annual rate of increase in these expenses.

It so happens that, in this case, no computations must be made to determine the effect, on the decision, of a gradient which exceeds the estimated value of $500. If the alternative of buying is unattractive when this alternative's recurring expenses increase at an annual rate of $500, it would be even more unattractive if these expenses were to increase at a greater rate. This is because higher recurring expenses will simply serve to increase the total uniform annual cost of buying the house.

As opposed to this, a decrease in these expenses will reduce the total annual cost of buying, and the reduction may be sufficient to make the alternative of buying more attractive than the alternative of renting. Hence, if the rate at which the recurring expenses of ownership will increase has been overstated, the decision based on the original cost comparison may be in error. It follows, therefore, that the scientist should revise his estimate of the gradient to obtain some lower value which he believes is likely to occur. Having done so, he would go on to compute the uniform annual cost of the alternative with the use of this revised estimate and determine how sensitive the decision is to the change.

But let us assume, at this point, that the scientist experiences some difficulty in arriving at a revised estimate of this type. More exactly, although he is certain that the recurring expenses will definitely increase at some rate, he is unable to decide which value between the minimum possible value of $0 and the originally estimated value of $500 should be selected as a revised estimate. Under such circumstances, the difficulty can sometimes be circumvented by selecting, for the moment, the extreme value, which in this case is a gradient of $0, and going on with the analysis. If this were done, the uniform annual cost of owning would be found by processing the following cash flows:

```
70,000                          (73,000)
          3,000      3,000       3,000
    ├────────┼──────────┼──────────┤
    0        1          2          3
```

Doing so would yield

Annual cost = $70,000(A/P)_{n=3}^{i=8} - \$73,000(A/F)_{n=3}^{i=8} + \$3,000$

$= \$7,676$

When this is compared to the $7,128 annual cost of renting, it is found that renting is still the more economical alternative. And if this is true with a gradient of $0, it will also be true with any gradient between $0 and $500. Hence, the selection of an improbably low value has obviated the need for making a more accurate revised estimate. Of course, had the decision proved to be sensitive to what is known to be an imprecise new estimate, the time and effort necessary to arrive at a more accurate figure would have to be expended.

In any event, the decision proves to be insensitive to either an increase or a decrease in the rate at which recurring expenses of ownership will rise. Consequently, the scientist need not concern himself with the fact that the original estimate of this rate might have been in error.

The Fourth Revision. The future resale value of the house is the remaining characteristic of the alternative of buying which the scientist estimated. If he wants to ascertain the sensitivity of the decision to changes in this value, he can proceed as he did when revisions were made in the other estimates.

In the original set of estimates, it was stated that the house was expected to have a resale value, that is, a salvage value, of $73,000 at the end of 3 years. With these original estimates, the uniform annual cost of owning the house was calculated to be $8,150, and this exceeded the $7,128 cost of renting. It should be apparent that, if the actual salvage value happens to be less than the estimated $73,000, the annual cost of owning will be even higher. Therefore, the decision is not affected by any decrease which might occur in the assumed resale value of the house.

But this may not be true if an increase occurs. A higher salvage value will reduce the uniform annual capital cost and, hence, the uniform annual total cost of the alternative. And it may be that a higher resale value will succeed in reducing the total cost of owning the house to a level which falls below the cost of renting. As this suggests, if the scientist believes that he may have underestimated the resale value, he should revise the estimate accordingly and determine what effect this will have on the decision. So let us suppose that, after some deliberation, the scientist concludes that the resale value at the end of 3 years may be as high as $77,500, with the result that the cash flows will be as follows:

```
70,000                    (77,500)
         3,000    3,500    4,000
├─────────┼────────┼────────┤
0         1        2        3
```

Continuing, he would find the uniform annual equivalent of these amounts to be

$$\text{Annual cost} = \$70,000(A/P)_{n=3}^{i=8} - \$77,500(A/F)_{n=3}^{i=8} + \$3,000$$
$$+ \$500(A/G)_{n=3}^{i=8}$$
$$= \$6,764$$

A comparison of this cost with the $7,128 cost of renting discloses that, at the higher salvage value, the alternative of owning becomes the more economical of the two alternatives. Because the decision is sensitive to the change in the expected resale value of the house, the scientist must now reexamine his original estimate and determine, on the basis of judgment, whether this estimate or the revised one is more likely to be correct.

In summary, the sensitivity analysis succeeded in revealing that the decision is not affected by an overestimate in the resale value but may be affected by an underestimate. From this, it follows that there is no reason why the scientist should worry about possibly having overestimated the resale value, but there is some reason for concern about a possible underestimate.

This is the last example of a sensitivity analysis we shall consider. In each of the examples presented, certain things were done for purposes of simplicity. To begin with, estimated cash flows were revised for only one of the alternatives. In an actual study, revisions might be made in estimated cash flows for every alternative. Also, whenever a given estimate was changed to some other specific value, only one or two possible changes were considered. But in an actual study, the analyst may want to ascertain a decision's sensitivity to many more possible changes in a given estimate. Furthermore, it was assumed in every example that the accuracy of only one of the estimates was in doubt. However, in an actual study, the analyst may want to determine a decision's sensitivity to a combination of changes in an alternative's cash-flow pattern.

These more complex situations call for no alteration in the basic approach which has been described. But chances are that the mechanics of applying the procedure will be more troublesome. This is because of the many combinations of estimated values that may have to be processed. To illustrate, if one of the alternatives has three characteristics and four different values are estimated for each, the number of different ways in which these estimates can be combined is 4 times 4 times 4, or 64. Obviously, the resultant number of possible combinations may be so great that a sensitivity analysis is not practicable. This might be because of the cost of such an analysis or because of the amount of judgment that will be required in the interpretation of the results. Nevertheless, the fact remains that there will usually be real opportunities to alleviate the difficulties posed by uncertain estimates by means of a sensitivity analysis, and a knowledge of the approach involved will enable an investor to take advantage of these opportunities.

ANALYSES UNDER THE CONDITION OF RISK

A sensitivity analysis requires that an investor estimate more than one value for a certain variable. Hopefully, he will find that the decision will be unaffected by his choice of value. But if the decision is sensitive to his choice, a need arises for determining which value will be adopted as his final choice. When such a situation arose in our examples of sensitivity analyses, it was simply stated that the investor should select what he believes to be, on the basis of judgment, the value which is most likely to occur.

In this section, we shall consider still another method for evaluating investment alternatives when the analyst is not certain what single value will be assumed by some element of an alternative's cash-flow pattern. This approach calls for estimating the different values the element under consideration might assume and also estimating the probability of occurrence to be associated with each of these values. These probabilities of occurrence then become an integral part of the analysis. When they do, the analysis is said to be carried out under the *condition of risk*. In any event, because the method involved does necessitate the processing of values which represent probabilities, we shall precede our presentation of the details of the method with a brief discussion of probability.

Some Fundamentals of Probability. The topic of probability is a complex one. Fortunately, for our purposes, it will suffice to deal with only a few of the fundamentals of this topic. Furthermore, there will be no need to treat these fundamentals in a rigorous manner. Therefore, we shall employ a somewhat casual approach to acquire an understanding of a few aspects of this subject.

The probability of something happening can be thought of as the relative frequency with which something will occur in the long run. To illustrate, someone may state that the probability is 0.80 that a piece of farm equipment will have a terminal salvage value of $500. In theory, this means that, if an investment were made in an infinite number of units of such equipment, 80 percent of these units would be disposed of for $500 at the time of their retirement. Any one unit, of course, either will or will not yield $500.

In terms of a decimal, the minimum possible value of a probability is 0, and the maximum is 1. The probability would be said to be 0 when something will never happen, and 1 when something will always happen. For example, the probability is likely to be 0 that an investor in real estate will not experience property taxes, and 1 that he will.

It is occasionally necessary to consider the probability of one thing or another occurring. As an illustration, let us suppose that a bureau of the federal government is giving consideration to purchasing a unit of testing equipment of a certain type. The service life of the equipment is not known with certainty. Instead, it is estimated that the life will assume one of the values shown in the following table and that the corresponding probabilities of occurrence are as indicated:

Life in years	Probability of occurrence
5	0.08
6	0.12
7	0.37
8	0.23
9	0.16
10	0.04
Total	1.00

For one reason or another, the bureau may be interested in determining the probability that a unit of this equipment will have a life of 5 years or 7 years or 9 years. Each of these outcomes is considered to be an *event*. Furthermore, the three events are *mutually exclusive*, which is to say that, if one of them occurs, none of the others can occur at the same time.

When events are mutually exclusive, the probability, *Pr*, that one of them will occur can be found with the use of the following rule of addition:

$$Pr(A \text{ or } B \text{ or } \cdots \text{ or } Z) = Pr(A) + Pr(B) + \cdots + Pr(Z) \qquad (10\text{-}1)$$

If the events are not mutually exclusive, the addition rule assumes a more complex form, but we shall not concern ourselves with this because our analyses will be limited to problems involving only mutually exclusive events.

So, to continue, with the use of Eq. (10-1) and the probabilities given in the preceding table, we should find that the probability that the equipment will have a life of 5 or 7 or 9 years is equal to

$$Pr(n = 5 \text{ or } 7 \text{ or } 9) = Pr(n = 5) + Pr(n = 7) + Pr(n = 9)$$

$$= 0.08 + 0.37 + 0.16$$

$$= 0.61$$

It might also be mentioned that a listing of all the events that can possibly occur is said to represent an *exhaustive set of events*. Furthermore, there can be no question but that one of these events will take place. Therefore, the probability is 1 that one of an exhaustive set of events will occur. To relate this to the testing equipment's life, it will be noted that the sum of the individual probabilities shown in the preceding table is equal to 1. This is because it was stated that the equipment's life would assume one of the lives contained in that table. Hence, these lives represent an exhaustive set of events, and it is certain that one of them will occur.

On occasion, there will be a need to ascertain the probability that a number of events will occur. For example, the government bureau might be considering the procurement of four units of the testing equipment over a period of time and would like to determine what the probability is that the first unit will have a life of 6 years *and* that the second unit will have a life of 7 years *and* that the third unit will have a life of 9 years *and* that the fourth unit will have a life of 10 years. These four events are considered to be *independent*. Events are independent when their natures are such that the occurrence of one of the events has no effect on the probability of occurrence to be associated with any of the other events. If events are independent, the probability that they will all occur can be found with the use of a multiplication rule which assumes the following form:

$$Pr(A \text{ and } B \text{ and } \cdots \text{ and } Z) = Pr(A) \times Pr(B) \times \cdots \times Pr(Z) \quad (10\text{-}2)$$

Applying this rule to the problem under consideration, the government bureau would substitute the individual probabilities from the preceding table in Eq. (10-2) and find that

$$Pr(n_1 = 6 \text{ and } n_2 = 7 \text{ and } n_3 = 9 \text{ and } n_4 = 10)$$

$$= Pr(n_1 = 6) \times Pr(n_2 = 7) \times Pr(n_3 = 9) \times Pr(n_4 = 10)$$

$= 0.12 \times 0.37 \times 0.16 \times 0.04$

$= 0.00028$

If the individual events in this example were not independent but dependent, a modified form of the multiplication rule would have to be applied. But we shall not concern ourselves with this modification at this time because, in this chapter, our analyses will be limited to problems which involve only independent events. A problem which involves dependent events is considered in Appendix A.

To continue, a need may arise to apply probability values in the course of determining the *expected value* of a variable. For example, the government bureau might want to ascertain the expected value of the testing equipment's service life. In the field of statistics, the term "expected value" is defined in a way which differs from a layman's definition of the term.

Specifically, the expected value is said to be the average value of a variable in the long run. Therefore, the expected value of the service life of the equipment in our illustration would be the average of the service-life values which appear in the preceding table. But these individual values must be weighted to reflect the relative frequencies with which they will occur in the long run. Hence, the expected service life is the weighted average of the probable service lives, and this is equal to

Expected life $= 0.08(5) + 0.12(6) + 0.37(7) + 0.23(8)$

$+ 0.16(9) + 0.04(10)$

$= 7.39$ years

This brings us to the end of the discussion of those fundamentals of probability which we shall employ in this chapter to analyze investment alternatives under the condition of risk. We shall now go on to apply the concepts involved.

An Expected Value Problem. The first application to be considered is one in which it will be necessary to ascertain an expected value. Let us suppose that a utility provides electricity to a given area by means of overhead lines which are subject to storm damage. The average cost of repairing storm-damaged lines is $1,800 per occurrence.

On the basis of a review of its records, which cover many years, the firm develops estimates of the number of times that storm damage will occur in any one year and of the corresponding probabilities of occurrence. These estimates are as follows:

Annual frequency of storm damage	Probability
0	0.35
1	0.30
2	0.20
3	0.10
4	0.05
Total	1.00

It has been proposed that the overhead lines be placed underground at a cost of $26,000. The resultant installation will have, for all practical purposes, an infinite life and will completely eliminate any chance of storm damage. No other costs will be affected by the installation.

The current overhead installation has a market value of zero. Given the utility's maintenance program, the life of this installation can also be considered to be infinite.

In summary, management is confronted by two alternatives. One is to retain the overhead lines, and the other is to replace them with underground facilities. The underground installation will require an extra investment at this time of $26,000 and will generate an annual saving equal to the annual cost of the storm damage which will be experienced with the overhead installation. To continue the analysis, it becomes necessary to determine what this cost will be. On the basis of the available data, this determination can begin with a calculation of the different values that the annual cost of storm damage can assume. This would be done in the following manner:

Annual frequency of damage (a)	Cost per occurrence (b)	Resultant annual cost $(c = a \times b)$
0	$1,800	$ 0
1	1,800	1,800
2	1,800	3,600
3	1,800	5,400
4	1,800	7,200

Now, if the utility knew exactly how many damaging storms will occur in any one year, it could describe the future pattern of resultant annual costs accordingly. But, unfortunately, it does not possess this knowledge. All it has is an estimate of the probability of occurrence to be associated with each of the possible values this annual cost can assume. Consequently, the most it can do is to compute the expected value of the annual cost of storm damage. Applying the estimated probabilities to the annual costs which appear in the preceding table, it would obtain the following result:

Expected annual cost = 0.35($0) + 0.30($1,800) + 0.20($3,600)

$$+ 0.10(\$5,400) + 0.05(\$7,200)$$

$$= \$2,160$$

This average cost of $2,160 would then be used in lieu of the unavailable exact annual costs. In other words, the consequences of the required extra investment of $26,000 would be said to be a saving in storm damage costs of $2,160 a year for an infinite number of years. This would appear on a time line as follows:

26,000

```
        (2,160)   (2,160)   (2,160)   ·  ·  ·   ·   ·   ·   ·   ·   (2,160)
  |_____|_____|_____|_____|
  0        1         2         3    ·   ·   ·   ·   ·   ·   ·   ·      ∞
```

If the firm wants to analyze the problem by means of the rate of return method, it can go on to calculate the prospective return on the extra investment required by the proposed installation. This could be done by finding the rate i which yields a uniform annual equivalent of zero for the cash flows which appear on the preceding time line. The procedure would begin with the following expression:

$$\$26,000(A/P)_{n=\infty}^{i=?} - \$2,160 = \$26,000(i) - \$2,160 = 0$$

from which it would be found that the return will be 8.3 percent. If the utility's before-tax minimum rate-of-return requirement is equal to or less than this amount, the extra investment called for by the underground installation can be justified. Otherwise it cannot.

But, as always, there might be irreducible factors to be evaluated. And the use of expected values serves to introduce another irreducible into the decision-making process. This is that some of the actual values in a cash-flow pattern will not coincide with the adopted expected values. In our illustration, for example, the comparison of the alternatives was based, in effect, on the assumption that the annual series of storm damage costs with overhead lines would consist of a sequence of $2,160 amounts. But it is known that the actual series will consist of a sequence of amounts other than $2,160. Specifically, in any one year, the actual amount will be $0 or $1,800 or $3,600 or $5,400 or $7,200. It so happens that the order in which these amounts will occur is not known. But if it were and if the resultant series were processed accordingly, the effect of the time value of money might be such that a decision would be reached which differs from the one reached on the basis of the expected value series.

While this deficiency of the expected value approach must be taken into consideration as an irreducible, it does not destroy the usefulness of the approach. When an investor is confronted by a situation in which he simply cannot determine the exact characteristics of an actual cash-fiow pattern, it may be that only a willingness to adopt expected values will enable him to carry out the required analysis.

Risk Analysis with Compound Events. The firm in the preceding example was uncertain about the values that would be assumed by only one of the elements of a cash-flow pattern. The more common situation, however, is one in which this uncertainty exists with reference to a number of elements. For example, a potential investor may be experiencing some difficulty in his attempt to arrive at a single estimate not only of an alternative's recurring costs, but also of its service life and its terminal salvage value. In such cases, a risk analysis requires that an effort be made to estimate, for each such element, the different values that might occur and their corresponding probabilities. These data are then processed to obtain the expected value of the alternative's total cost. This is done for each of a set of mutually exclusive alternatives, and the alternative with the minimum value of the expected total cost is, in the absence of irreducible factors, considered to be the most economical.

The specifics of this procedure will be presented with the use of an illustration that involves a refreshment concession which is available for a period of one year in a sports arena. The concession, which can be operated on a part-time basis, requires only an investment in working capital which will be recovered in its entirety at the end of the year. During the year, revenues will be realized from the sale of food and beverages; the net receipts for the year will be the difference between these revenues and the operating expenses which will include such things as labor, the cost of goods sold, and a concession fee which is equal to a stated percent of sales.

An individual, who is evaluating this investment opportunity, believes that the amount of working capital required will be one of two values and that the net receipts for the year will also be one of two values. He goes on to estimate the relative frequencies of occurrence to be associated with these values and, when doing so, assumes that the required working capital and the net annual receipts are independent of each other. In any event, his estimates can be summarized as follows:

Event	Description	Probability
A	$11,000 capital requirement	0.2
B	$14,000 capital requirement	0.8
C	$2,300 net annual receipts	0.7
D	$2,800 net annual receipts	0.3

The question to be answered is whether an investment should be made in the concession, given that the individual's before-tax rate-of-return requirement is 20 percent and that the other alternative is to make no investment of this type. The more desirable course of action is to be determined by means of a present worth analysis in which expected values will be taken into account.

It is imperative to recognize at the outset of the study that the two possible values of the working capital and the two possible values of the net annual receipts can be combined in 2 times 2, or 4, different ways. The first of these is a combination of $11,000 of working capital and $2,300 of net annual receipts. Keeping in mind that the working capital will be recovered at the end of the year and treating the net receipts as an end-of-year amount, we should describe the cash-flow pattern, which will be generated by this combination, in the following manner:

```
11,000          (11,000)
                (2,300)
├───────────────┤
0               1
```

The probability that this combination will occur can be computed with the use of the multiplication rule. Given a probability of 0.2 that the working capital requirement will be $11,000 and a probability of 0.7 that the net receipts will be $2,300, the probability that both of these events will occur is the product of 0.2 and 0.7, or 0.14. This is also to say that the probability is 0.14 that the present worth of investing in the concession will be as follows:

Present worth = $11,000 - $13,300(P/F)$_{n=1}^{i=20}$ = (-)$83

A second possible combination is $11,000 of working capital and $2,800 of net annual receipts. The consequences of this would be

```
11,000          (11,000)
                (2,800)
├───────────────┤
0               1
```

and the resultant present worth is

Present worth $= \$11{,}000 - \$13{,}800(P/F)_{n=1}^{i=20} = (-)\$500$

Working with the estimated individual probabilities, we should find that the probability of occurrence to be associated with this present worth is 0.2 times 0.3, or 0.06.

The third possible combination is a working capital requirement of $14,000 and net annual receipts of $2,300. This yields the following cash flows:

```
14,000          (14,000)
                 (2,300)
  |-----------------|
  0                 1
```

and these generate the following present worth:

Present worth $= \$14{,}000 - \$16{,}300(P/F)_{n=1}^{i=20} = \$417$

With the approach employed when the other combinations were considered, the probability of this happening would be found to be 0.8 times 0.7, or 0.56.

The fourth possible combination of events is $14,000 of working capital being required and $2,800 of net annual receipts being experienced. This would cause the following cash flows:

```
14,000          (14,000)
                 (2,800)
  |-----------------|
  0                 1
```

whose present worth is equal to

Present worth $= \$14{,}000 - \$16{,}800(P/F)_{n=1}^{i=20} = \$0$

The probability of these two events' occurring at the same time, that is, of this compound event, is 0.8 times 0.3, or 0.24.

Having considered the last possible combination, we can summarize the results obtained thus far in the following manner:

Compound event	Present worth	Probability
A and C	(−)$ 83	0.14
A and D	(−) 500	0.06
B and C	(+) 417	0.56
B and D	0	0.24
Total		1.00

If the potential investor wants to base his decision on an expected value, the next step calls for calculating the expected value of the possible present worth values. This would be done as follows:

Expected present worth = 0.14(−$83) + 0.06(−$500) + 0.56($417)

$$+ 0.24(\$0)$$

$$= \$192$$

If the second alternative in this problem also involved more than one estimated value for some of the elements of its cash-flow pattern, the expected value of its present worth would be calculated just as it has been for the first alternative. But the second alternative is simply to make no investment, and, hence, its present worth is zero. This is less than the expected present worth of $192 for the alternative of investing in the concession, and, therefore, the alternative of making no investment is the more economical of the two. The same conclusion could have been reached by examining the sign of the concession's expected present worth. Because the alternative's cash flows were described completely, the fact that a positive present worth was obtained means that the return on the total investment required by the concession will be less than the 20 percent minimum rate-of-return requirement.

At this point, of course, the potential investor will want to recognize that his estimates may be in error and that, even if they are not, the $192 present worth is an expected value. An expected value of $192 means that, if an infinite number of such investments were made, the average present worth would be $192. However, the summary of our results discloses that any one such investment will have a present worth of minus $83 or minus $500 or plus $417 or $0. And chances are that only one such investment will be made, and it could be that its cash flows will yield a present worth of, say, minus $500. Were this to be the case, the decision based on long term considerations would prove to be incorrect in the short run. The effect of such possibilities on the final decision would have to be evaluated on the basis of judgment.

It should also be stressed that the method of analysis, as applied in this example, can be employed only when the value of one element in a cash-flow pattern is independent of, that is, not affected by, the value of another element. Further, the approach can become cumbersome when many combinations of estimated values are possible. From all this, it follows that, under certain circumstances, the approach will not be a feasible one. But when it is, it will aid the analyst in his efforts to cope with the problem of uncertain estimates.

Another Risk Approach. As has just been pointed out, the expected value approach employed in the preceding illustration may not be a practical one when many combinations of estimated values are possible. This is because of the difficulty of estimating and processing the large number of values and probabilities that would have to be taken into account.

Under such circumstances, an investment analyst may find it useful to simplify the problem by preparing only three sets of estimates for each alternative. The first of these would be a *pessimistic* estimate, the second a *normal* estimate, and the third an *optimistic* estimate. As the term suggests, a pessimistic estimate would be one which contains the highest first cost, the shortest life, the lowest salvage value, the highest recurring costs, the lowest revenues, and the highest cost of money that is likely to be experienced with the alternative; hence, it would serve to generate the highest total cost that the alternative is likely to yield. An optimistic estimate would be at the other extreme; in brief, it would contain a combination of values which would generate the lowest total cost that is likely to be experienced with the alternative. Finally, the normal estimate would represent a point in between the two extremes; the values involved and the resultant total cost would be the ones that are the most likely to occur.

As an example of such estimates, let us consider a case in which a processor of meat products is considering an investment in an automatic wrapping machine which would be used in a packaging operation. The wrapping is now done manually at a cost of $59,000 a year, and this cost is expected to remain at this level in the foreseeable future.

However, the processor experiences some difficulty in his attempt to arrive at the total cost of mechanizing the operation. To begin with, he is uncertain about the size of the total required investment; this is because installation of the equipment will necessitate the rearrangement of other production facilities which will cause disrupted production schedules, and the resultant cost might prove to be any one of a number of possible amounts. Next, he suspects that the equipment's life, terminal salvage value, and operating costs are likely to assume any one of a number of possible values. Also, he cannot arrive at any single value for the cost of money; this is due to the fact that the financing will be with equity funds, and the opportunity cost to be associated with such funds cannot be ascertained with certainty.

If it so happens that each of the aforementioned variables is capable of assuming a large number of different values, the processor might very well balk when it is suggested that each of these values and their probabilities of occurrence be estimated and taken into consideration in the analysis. This is understandable, given the difficulty of describing an exhaustive set of events and of processing the resultant description. But he may be more comfortable with and receptive to the idea of making the three sets of estimates mentioned earlier. So let us suppose that he is and that these estimates are as follows:

	Type of estimate		
	Pessimistic	Normal	Optimistic
Initial investment	$62,000	$60,000	$55,000
Life	3 years	5 years	10 years
Salvage value	$0	$2,000	$3,000
Recurring expenses	$39,000	$37,000	$34,000
Cost of money	15%	12%	8%

After such estimates have been made, the study can continue with a determination of the total cost that each set of estimates will yield. If the processor in our illustration chooses to express the total cost in terms of a uniform annual equivalent, he will find the pessimistic cost to be as follows:

Pessimistic annual cost = $62,000(A/P)$_{n=3}^{i=15}$ + $39,000 = $66,156

In a similar manner, the normal cost would be found to be

Normal annual cost = $60,000(A/P)$_{n=5}^{i=12}$ − $2,000(A/F)$_{n=5}^{i=12}$

$$+ \$37,000$$

$$= \$53,329$$

And the optimistic cost will be equal to

Optimistic annual cost = $55,000(A/P)$_{n=10}^{i=8}$ − $3,000(A/F)$_{n=10}^{i=8}$

$$+ \$34,000$$

$$= \$41,988$$

These results can now be evaluated in one of two basic ways. The first is to proceed as one would in a sensitivity analysis. To do so, the processor would begin by noting that the annual cost of continuing the packaging operation with the manual method was estimated to be $59,000. A comparison of this cost with the annual cost of mechanizing would reveal that, in the absence of irreducible factors, the decision depends on which of the three sets of estimates is accepted. Specifically, the pessimistic estimate encourages the retention of the manual method, and the other two estimates encourage the adoption of the mechanized method. At this point, as in a sensitivity analysis, the processor would simply have to decide, on the basis of judgment, whether to be governed by the pessimistic estimate or by the other two estimates.

But another way of proceeding, after the three annual costs for a given alternative have been computed, is to take into consideration the probabilities of occurrence to be associated with the three sets of estimates. These three sets do not represent an exhaustive set of events. However, to keep the task within manageable proportions, the investor can be asked to treat them as if they were and to estimate the probabilities accordingly. If the processor in our example were to do so, the outcome might be as follows:

Type of estimate	Resultant annual cost	Probability of occurrence
Pessimistic	$66,156	0.4
Normal	53,329	0.5
Optimistic	41,988	0.1
Total		1.0

It now becomes possible to ascertain the expected value of the total cost of the alternative. For the wrapping machine, this value would be as follows:

$$\text{Expected annual cost} = 0.4(\$66,156) + 0.5(\$53,329) + 0.1(\$41,988)$$

$$= \$57,325$$

The decision can now be based on a comparison of this value with a similar value for some other alternative. In our example, the other alternative is the manual method which has an annual cost of $59,000. A comparison of this cost with the expected annual cost of $57,325 for the automatic method suggests that the latter is the more economical alternative.

This might be an appropriate point at which to mention that not all risk analyses need be based on a comparison of expected values. In another approach, the investor might choose to base the decision on a comparison of the total costs which have the highest probability of occurrence. To illustrate, of the three annual costs computed for the automatic wrapping machine, the highest probability, namely, 0.5, is to be associated with the normal cost of $53,329. So, with this approach, it would be this cost that would be compared with the $59,000 cost of the manual operation and a conclusion reached that the alternative of mechanization is the more economical of the two.

With still another approach, the investor might choose to be governed by cumulative probabilities. If the processor in our example adopted this approach, he would note that the alternative of mechanization is the more attractive with either a normal or an optimistic estimate; the probability that one or the other of these sets of values will occur is 0.5 plus 0.1, or 0.6. However, the manual method is the more attractive with the pessimistic estimate; but the probability that this set of values will occur is only 0.4. In brief, the probability is 0.6 that the mechanized method is the more economical of the two, and only 0.4 that it is not. Consequently, the investor who chooses to be governed by these cumulative probabilities would be inclined to select the mechanized method, but with the realization that this might be a mistake because the pessimistic estimate may prove to be the correct one.

It so happens that, in this case, the same decision would be reached with each of the foregoing approaches, but this will not always be true. In any event, these are some additional ways in which capital investment alternatives can be analyzed under the condition of risk. In the example used for purposes of explanation, three sets of estimates were made for the cash-flow pattern of only one of the alternatives. If the need to do so exists, similar estimates can be made for the other alternatives in a given situation. Also, there is no reason, in theory, why more than three sets of estimates cannot be made for each alternative. But, in practice, an attempt to do so may create serious problems of estimation, processing, and interpretation.

This is our last illustration of an investment analysis conducted under the condition of risk. The approaches described involve probabilities and, hence, values which, at best, will be correct in the long run. And, as we know, what may prove to be the best decision if such a decision and its consequences occur an infinite number of times may not prove to be the best decision when such a decision and its consequences occur only once or some other finite number of times. This, together with the chance that the probability estimates might be in error, must be treated as an irreducible in the final step in the decision-making process. Although this serves to reduce the value of these approaches to some degree, the results are still likely to be better than they would be if a potential investor were to rely solely on intuition when he is confronted by a situation in which he is reluctant to assign single values to the respective elements of a future cash-flow pattern.

It should also be mentioned that analytical techniques, other than those which we have considered, have been developed for use under the condition of risk. But their natures are such that their treatment would take us beyond the scope of this presentation. However, an article by John F. Magee, which deals with some of the other aspects of this topic, is reproduced in Appendix A and should prove to be of interest and value to anyone who wishes to pursue this subject further.

ESTIMATION AND INFLATION

Three methods have been presented by means of which an investment analyst might be able to mitigate the problem of estimation which is inherent in any evaluation of alternative capital expenditure proposals. The first of these methods involved the determination of a break-even point, the second required that a decision's sensitivity to changes in estimated values be ascertained, and the third called for taking into consideration the probabilities of occurrence to be associated with various estimated values.

In a given case, the potential investor may have confidence in his ability to develop a fairly accurate estimate of future cash flows and, as a result, will not find it necessary to utilize any one of these methods. At the other extreme, he may use all three in the course of deciding which of a set of mutually exclusive alternatives is the most economical. But it is probably correct to say that, regardless of the approach to estimation adopted, one final question arises. This is the following: What is the best way to account for anticipated changes in the future purchasing power of money when forecasting cash flows? In recent times, this purchasing power has been decreasing, and indications are that this will continue. Therefore, the more specific question deals with the impact of inflation on cash-flow estimates.

Some individuals maintain that future cash flows should be expressed in *constant* dollars, that is, dollars whose purchasing power is equal to the present purchasing power of a dollar; if this is done, the resultant cash-flow pattern assumes the pattern that it would have assumed had no inflation or deflation been expected to occur during the investment alternative's service period. Others, however, maintain that future cash flows should be expressed in *current* dollars, that is, dollars which reflect the purchasing power of a dollar at the time it is being spent or received; if this is done, the resultant cash-flow pattern assumes the pattern generated by, among other things, the inflationary or deflationary forces that are expected to exist during the investment alternative's service period.

Those who favor the use of constant dollars argue that a cash-flow pattern which is described in current dollars consists of a combination of numbers which are not all expressed in the same units. And, if the units vary from one amount to another, the result obtained by subjecting these amounts to various arithmetic operations is meaningless. A somewhat dramatic way of illustrating this point is to suppose that an analyst estimates that the operating costs with a given alternative will be 20,000 American dollars the first year, 800,000 Polish zlotys the second, and 50,000 German marks the third. Obviously, a calculated uniform annual equivalent of these three numbers would be a value which is unintelligible because one dollar does not have the same purchasing power as does one unit of either of the other two currencies. But, in principle, there is no difference between processing a series of three such numbers and processing a series of three numbers expressed in terms of dollars of unequal purchasing power.

The argument for estimates in terms of constant dollars rather than current dollars can also be presented with the use of another example. Suppose that $10,000 can be invested for one year during which the rate of inflation will be 10 percent and that the investment will yield a receipt of $11,000 at the end of the year. The purported rate of return would be the $1,000 return divided by the $10,000 investment, or 10 percent. But since the purchasing power of the dollar will decrease by the same percent in the meantime, the *real* rate of return will be zero. Hence, the indicated return of 10 percent is misleading. To obtain the true rate of return, the analyst should deflate the future receipt of $11,000 to obtain the equivalent amount in constant dollars. If this is done by dividing the $11,000 by a factor of 1.10, which reflects the 10 percent increase in price levels, it will be found that the $11,000 receipt is equal to $10,000 of the kind that were invested. Therefore, no return would be realized on the $10,000 investment.

But many decision makers in the area of capital investment analysis are likely to react to such an example in the following way: They would maintain, and correctly so, that the investor who would describe the cash-flow pattern in the preceding example in terms of constant dollars would, for the sake of consistency, have to establish a minimum rate-of-return requirement equal to what the cost of money would be in the absence of inflation. This requirement might be 5 percent. Consequently, this investor's calculated return of zero percent would prove to be unsatisfactory, and the alternative would be rejected. But an investor who would describe the cash-flow pattern in the preceding example in terms of current dollars would, for the sake of consistency, establish a minimum rate-of-return requirement which takes into account the expected inflation rate. Hence, he would increase the return require- ment from 5 percent, which is what it would be if no inflation were expected, to 15 percent, which is what it will be if the anticipated inflation rate is 10 percent. Thus, when this investor computes the return to be 10 percent, he will compare this result to his required return of 15 percent and also reject the alternative.

More could be said about each side of the argument, but the important thing is that, in practice, there is a natural inclination to express cash flows in current dollars. Furthermore, it is a tendency which is almost impossible to overcome. This being the case, it is prudent to maintain that future cash flows can be estimated in light of what price levels are expected to be when these costs and revenues occur; but, to compensate for the fact that all the dollars involved will not have the same purchasing power, an appropriate adjustment will have to be made in the established minimum rate-of-return requirement. If inflation is anticipated, this rate will be higher than it otherwise would be; if deflation is anticipated, this rate will be lower than it otherwise would be.

This is not to say, however, that estimates must be made in this manner. An investor who is comfortable with the concept of constant dollars is certainly free to express his estimates in terms of dollars of that type. But, of course, his cost of money must then be ascertained on the basis of what it would be under the condition of price stability.

Although no explicit statement was made to this effect, it was taken for granted in all our illustrations that estimates would be expressed in current dollars rather than in constant dollars. For this reason, a statement was made in one of the early chapters that an investor who expects the purchasing power of money to decrease will increase his rate-of-return requirement accordingly. Also, mention was made of the need to take into consideration the fact that future replacement costs may not be equal to the cost of currently-available assets because of price level changes. And, finally, since income taxes must be computed with the use of current dollars, the dollars processed in our determinations of this expense had to be, of necessity, current dollars.

RANKING INVESTMENT ALTERNATIVES

Throughout this discussion of the problems of estimation to be associated with the application of the techniques of investment analysis and throughout the earlier description of the techniques as such, the emphasis was placed on the need for identifying the most economical of a set of mutually exclusive alternatives. Once this has been done for each such set of alternatives, the result is a list of investment opportunities which are *not* mutually exclusive. No consideration was given to ranking such opportunities in the order of their attractiveness for two reasons. One is that there is no practical way of doing so. But the more important reason is that there is no need to do so.

For the moment, we shall ignore the fact that this kind of ranking is not necessary and deal with the fact that this kind of ranking is not feasible. Let us begin by supposing that it is proposed that the investment opportunities involved be ranked on the basis of their respective total annual costs, present worths, or future worths. In such a ranking of investment opportunities which are not mutually exclusive, the one with the lowest total cost would appear as the most attractive, and the one with the highest total cost would appear as the least attractive. But the validity of such a ranking would be questionable. To begin with, the calculated costs may not be comparable because some of them might not really be total costs; as we know, total costs cannot be obtained in those cases in which it is not possible to describe an alternative in terms of all the costs and revenues it will generate. Next, it is unlikely that all the investment opportunities involved will have the same service life; as a consequence, their respective present or future worths cannot be compared and their respective annual costs can be only in the presence of an appropriate assumption regarding future investment opportunities. And, finally, the ranking would not take into account the total investments required by the respective investment opportunities; hence, an alternative, which requires an investment of $200,000 and will make a contribution of $10,000 to a firm's net worth, would appear more attractive than a second alternative which requires an investment of only $60,000, will make a contribution of $9,000 to a firm's net worth, and will enable the firm to invest the remaining $140,000 in a third alternative which will contribute another $8,000 to the firm's net worth.

It might be proposed that this last objection could be overcome by ranking investment opportunities, which are not mutually exclusive, not on the basis of their total costs, but on the basis of the respective returns they will yield on total investment. Doing so would appear to be permissible because the total investment in one of two alternatives that are not mutually exclusive also represents the extra investment which the one alternative requires as compared with the other. Hence, an analysis of returns on total investment becomes equivalent to an analysis of returns on extra investment when such alternatives are being compared. Nevertheless, this method of ranking also poses difficulties. One of these is that it may not be possible to ascertain some of the alternatives' returns on total investment, because it may not be possible to estimate all their costs and revenues. Another is that all the alternatives may not entail the same degree of risk, and, hence, their individual returns do not provide a sound basis for ranking. Still another is that each of the investment opportunities will not necessarily have the same life, and, therefore, the respective returns on total investment are not comparable unless some assumption is made with regard to the nature of future investment opportunities. A final difficulty becomes apparent when we recall something that was explained in the discussion of the rate of return, or discounted cash flow, method. This is that a calculated rate of return might overstate or understate the actual return, because of what may be an incorrect assumption that periodic net receipts will be reinvested elsewhere at a rate equal to the calculated internal return.

For reasons given earlier, this does not interfere with the method's ability to identify the most economical of a set of mutually exclusive alternatives. But it does mean that the calculated return on the total investment in one alternative may be equal to the actual rate, in another it may be more than the actual rate, and in still another it may be less than the actual rate. Obviously, such values for alternatives which are not mutually exclusive do not lend themselves for use in ranking these alternatives in the order of their attractiveness.

Fortunately, these obstacles to ranking are of no consequence because this type of ranking is unnecessary. Let us consider why this is so. The proponents of ranking present it as a means for allocating available funds in an efficient manner among investment opportunities which are not mutually exclusive. Such an allocation becomes a necessity when sufficient funds are not available to finance all the investment proposals that appear to be attractive. Under such circumstances, an appropriate ranking system would permit the identification of the most attractive of those proposals. Admittedly, this is true. But it is also true that the need for this kind of allocation system arises only if a mistake has been made in the selection of the rate used to represent the cost of money when the investment alternatives were being evaluated. If the rate used is such that the investor cannot finance all the proposals which proved to be attractive at that rate, this simply means that his established rate-of-return requirement was too low. The way to eliminate the consequences of this error is not by a ranking process, but by increasing the rate-of-return requirement and reanalyzing each set of mutually exclusive investment alternatives. At the higher rate, it may be found, in some cases, that no investment at all should be made in a certain kind of activity; in other cases, it will be found that a smaller total investment should be made in a certain kind of activity. Consequently, the total demand for capital will be reduced. If it is reduced to an amount which falls below the level of available capital, a slightly upward adjustment in the rate could then be made. This would continue until a rate is found which equates the demand for capital to the supply.

It might be maintained that this is a somewhat troublesome procedure. Actually, the most difficult and time-consuming phases of any investment analysis are those in which the alternatives are being determined, the values of the relevant factors are being ascertained, and the irreducible factors are being evaluated. Once the mechanics of the analytical techniques have been mastered, their application to arrive at an annual cost, present worth, future worth, or rate of return is relatively simple and straightforward. Hence, a need to recalculate total costs or to reevaluate prospective rates of return in light of a revised value for the cost of money is not going to increase the length or the expense of the study by a significant amount.

In brief, then, the appropriate capital rationing device is the established minimum rate-of-return requirement. For the sake of convenience, the foregoing explanation of why this is true was presented as if this rate would assume a single value. But, as mentioned at a much earlier point, a given investor may establish one requirement for one type of investment and another requirement for another type of investment, depending on the risk and tax status of the respective types.

A FINAL OBSERVATION

This brings us to the close of our discussion of the principles of capital expenditure analysis. Four basic analytical techniques and one special method of analysis were described and evaluated, and ways were considered for alleviating the estimation difficulties which will be encountered in the application of these approaches.

The benefits to be realized from the application of these methods were presented, and so were the methods' limitations. Because these limitations do exist, some judgment must continue to be exercised in the final step of the decision-making process. But the approaches do compel the potential investor to take into consideration all the relevant factors, force him to state explicitly what values he believes these factors will assume, and ensure the correct processing of the resultant data. This cannot help but reduce the degree to which the final decision will have to depend on hunch, intuition, and judgment. Hence, there should be a corresponding increase in the quality of the final decisions.

QUESTIONS

10-1 What is meant by a break-even point in a comparison of investment alternatives?

10-2 How is a break-even point ascertained?

10-3 In what way is the value of a break-even point used to determine whether the extra investment called for by a given alternative is justified?

10-4 Give some examples of an alternative's characteristics for which a break-even value can be computed.

10-5 Of what advantage is a break-even approach to the evaluation of an investment alternative? What are the approach's limitations?

10-6 Describe the procedure for carrying out a sensitivity analysis.

10-7 How can a sensitivity analysis aid an investor in his evaluation of investment alternatives?

10-8 What are some of the difficulties that might be experienced when an attempt is made to conduct a sensitivity analysis?

10-9 When is the condition of risk said to exist in a capital investment analysis?

10-10 Define the following terms: (a) probability, (b) relative frequency of occurrence, (c) mutually exclusive events, (d) independent events, (e) dependent events, (f) exhaustive set of events, (g) expected value, and (h) compound event.

10-11 Under what conditions is a probability value found with the use of the addition rule? The multiplication rule?

10-12 How can expected values be used to identify the most economical investment alternative?

10-13 What advantage is to be associated with making a risk analysis of capital expenditure proposals?

10-14 Should future cash flows be expressed in constant or current dollars? Explain.

10-15 Is the value of an investor's minimum rate-of-return requirement affected by whether he chooses to work with constant dollars or current dollars? Explain.

10-16 What difficulties might be encountered when an attempt is made to rank investment opportunities, which are not mutually exclusive, in the order of their attractiveness on the basis of their respective total costs? On the basis of their respective rates of return on total investment?

10-17 Evaluate ranking as a means for allocating available funds among investment opportunities which are not mutually exclusive. Can this allocation be carried out more effectively by means of an appropriate minimum rate-of-return requirement? Explain.

10-18 Does the application of the principles of capital expenditure analysis eliminate the need for judgment on the part of an investment analyst? If not, what does it do?

PROBLEMS

10-1 As a result of a significant increase in the demand for some of its products, a company finds it necessary to purchase another forging hammer. The installed first cost of a new unit of the required type will be $1,200,000, and it is estimated that its service life will be 30 years.

A used equipment dealer happens to have a similar hammer for sale. Its installed cost would be $750,000. As compared with the new unit, its life would be only 15 years, and it would have an operating cost disadvantage of $40,000 a year.

The analyst forecasts that the salvage value of the used hammer will be $90,000 at the end of its 15-year life. But he has little confidence in his ability to predict what the market value of something will be 30 years from now; hence, he is experiencing a great deal of difficulty in his attempt to estimate the new hammer's terminal salvage value. Consequently, he decides to ascertain what the minimum salvage value must be to justify the extra investment required by the new hammer. In the course of doing so, he will take into consideration that the firm's before-tax rate-of-return requirement is 12 percent.

a   What will the necessary salvage prove to be? (Ans. $321,905)
b   Suppose that, after arriving at this value, the analyst is inclined to believe that such an amount cannot possibly be realized. Which alternative should he then recommend?

10-2   For public relations purposes, a large corporation has agreed to finance an exhibit, related to its activities, in a metropolitan museum of science and industry. One of the firm's officers has proposed that the exhibit be expanded, at a cost of $88,000, to include a consumer testing center. She points out that the center would provide the company with a means for obtaining the reaction of the museum's visitors to ideas the company has concerning such things as new products, product modifications, packaging methods, promotional approaches, price changes, and so on.

Currently, the corporation engages marketing research firms to obtain this kind of information. With its own consumer testing center, it could reduce its payments to such firms by $72,000 a year. However, a portion of this saving would be offset by the annual cost of operating the center which is estimated to be $61,000. As a result, the net saving would be $11,000 a year.

On the basis of judgment, management concludes that this net saving will not suffice to justify the proposed expenditure of $88,000. But before rejecting the proposal, it decides to consider the possibility that other companies will be willing to pay the corporation a fee for the use of the center for their own consumer research activities. After some discussion, it is decided that such revenues can be realized. Unfortunately, no one seems to be able to estimate what these revenues might be. Therefore, it is decided to determine what they must be to justify an investment in the center.

In the determination, consideration will be given to the aforementioned data and to the fact that the exhibit will be maintained for 8 years, that there will be no terminal salvage value, and that the corporation's before-tax cost of money is 25 percent.

a   What revenues will suffice to enable the corporation to break even on such an investment?
b   In the event that the consensus is that it is likely that these necessary revenues can be realized, should the investment be made?

10-3   A processor of steel products must choose between an oil-fired furnace and an electric induction furnace. A partial description of the two is as follows:

	Oil	Induction
First cost	$150,000	$975,000
Life	40 years	40 years
Salvage value	$0	$100,000

With one exception, the operating cost advantages and disadvantages of the respective furnaces tend to cancel each other out. The exception is the annual downtime cost. Downtime stems from the occasional need to rebrick the oil-fired furnace and the occasional need to replace coils in the induction furnace. While there is no significant difference between the annual costs of these activities, much more time is required to rebrick the one kind of furnace than to replace coils in the other. Hence, the oil-fired furnace will be out of operation for much longer periods of time than will be the induction furnace, and a corresponding increase will occur in the cost of disrupted production schedules and lost customer orders.

It so happens that the firm is unable to develop an estimate of what the difference will be between the annual downtime costs of the two furnaces. Therefore, it decides to proceed by ascertaining what the reduction in this expense must be to warrant an investment in the electric induction furnace rather than in the oil-fired furnace. What will this value be found to be, given that the established minimum rate-of-return requirement is 10 percent? If, in spite of its inability to make the necessary estimate, management decides that this required cost reduction cannot be realized, which furnace should it select? (Ans. $84,168)

10-4 A utility makes use of safety devices on its distribution circuits to improve service reliability. Device P is constructed in such a way that it can continue to be used after it has been activated. Its installed first cost is $400 per unit, its economic life is 25 years, and its salvage value is zero.

The design of device Q is such that it must be replaced after a single operation. Its installed first cost is $130 per unit, and it has no salvage value. The life of any one unit will, of course, depend on how soon, after its installation, conditions will arise which activate the device. Because the firm cannot estimate what value should be assigned to this time period, it wants to determine what its length must be if device Q is to be as economical as device P. In this determination, 20 percent will be used to represent the cost of money.

a What average life for device Q will result in its generating an annual cost equal to that of device P?

b In the event that management concludes that the actual average life will be longer than the one which represents the break-even point, which device should it adopt?

10-5 A combine has been in use for a number of years, and a point has been reached at which it requires very major repairs. In fact, its present condition is such that it has no market value. Unless the equipment is overhauled, it will have to be replaced.

A new combine will cost $35,000, have an economic life of 10 years, and yield about $3,000 when it is sold at the end of its life.

Before obtaining an estimate of the cost of overhauling the old equipment, its owner wants to ascertain what maximum expenditure of this kind can be justified. In his computations, he will take into consideration that the life of the rebuilt unit will be about 5 years and that it will have a negligible salvage value. Also, he expects average annual maintenance and repair expenses with the overhauled equipment to be approximately $500 a year higher than with the new combine.

If the farm operator places a time value of 30 percent on money, what will be the result of his analysis? Suppose that he subsequently learns that the rehabilitation cost will be $9,000. What should he do? (Ans. $26,186)

10-6 It has become necessary to replace a valve through which a corrosive liquid passes. Because of the nature of the liquid, the question has arisen regarding which of two valves will be the more economical. Valve A has a lower first cost but is made of material such that the valve will have a relatively short life and relatively high repair costs. Valve B is made of material which is not as subject to corrosion; as a result, although the valve's first cost is higher, its life will be longer and its maintenance costs will be lower. In quantitative terms, the characteristics of both valves can be described as follows:

	Valve A	Valve B
First cost	$6,000	$9,000
Salvage value	$100	$150
Economic life	3 years	6 years
Annual maintenance	$500	$200

A present worth comparison of the two valves has been made on the basis of a 15 percent rate-of-return requirement, and valve B has been found to be the more economical. But the individual who must approve the additional investment in this valve believes that the six-year life estimate is too high and that the $200 maintenance cost estimate is too low. He maintains that it would be more realistic to assume a life of only 5 years and an annual maintenance cost of $400 for valve B.

a What were the results of the initial present worth comparison? (Ans. $11,727, $9,691)

b Will it be found in the revised present worth comparison that the decision is sensitive to the suggested changes in the life and maintenance cost estimates for valve B? (Ans. $18,120, $17,909)

10-7 A railroad is going to place an order for 2,000,000 ties. Because of the high cost of maintaining hardwood ties, consideration is being given to ties made of concrete.

The group of engineers, who have been asked to compare the wood ties with the concrete ties on a uniform annual cost basis, agree on the following:

	Wood	Concrete
First cost per tie	$23	$40
Average life	40 years	20 years
Salvage value	none	none

Also, they are willing to assume that, in 20 years, the concrete ties will be replaced by ties which will generate an identical cash-flow pattern. However, there is some disagreement with regard to what the annual cost will be of maintaining the two million ties during the 40-year study period. More specifically, all the engineers believe that, during the first year, maintenance costs will be the same with both kinds of ties and that, from that point on, the cost of maintaining the wood ties will exceed the cost of maintaining the concrete ties. But some of the engineers estimate that the difference between the two series of annual maintenance costs will be a gradient series of 40-years' duration in which the gradient is $500,000, while the remaining engineers estimate that the size of the gradient will be only $300,000.

At an 8 percent cost of money, will they find that their recommendation is sensitive to which of the two estimates they adopt?

10-8 A married couple has learned of some undeveloped lakeshore property which is for sale for $27,000. Although their interests are such that they would make no use of the property, they are thinking of purchasing it as an investment. They estimate that the land will reach its maximum market value of $65,000 in 9 years. Furthermore, they expect that the recurring costs of ownership will be $540 during the first of these 9 years and will then increase at a rate of $30 a year. If the property is purchased, no debt financing will be involved.

Whether or not they should make the investment will be decided upon on the basis of a future worth analysis. The wife believes that their minimum rate-of-return requirement should be 10 percent, because she estimates that their equity funds could be invested at this rate in other investment opportunities of comparable risk and tax status. The husband maintains that the other opportunities are likely to yield an average return of only 6 percent.

Will a sensitivity analysis reveal that this difference of opinion is of any significance? (Ans. $7,370, -$11,932)

10-9 To obtain a certain kind of subcontracting work, the owner of a machine shop finds it necessary to invest in equipment of a type which he does not currently own. The two models which are available can be described as follows:

	Model I	Model II
First cost	$72,000	$96,000
Service life	14 years	14 years
Salvage value	$9,000	$11,000
Annual operating cost advantage		$3,500

In addition to an operating cost advantage, model II has the advantage of a larger output capacity. In spite of the fact that there is no certainty that this additional capacity will be needed in the future, there is no denying that model II does have the potential for providing the owner of the business with additional net annual revenues. At one extreme, a demand will exist for all of this capacity, and the resultant net annual revenue advantage would be $1,600 per year. At the other extreme, no demand will exist for any of this capacity, and there would be no resultant net annual revenue advantage. What is most likely, however, is that the actual net annual revenue advantage will prove to be some value in between these extreme amounts.

Because he is unable to estimate this most likely value, the owner decides to process each of the extreme values in his attempt to ascertain whether the extra investment required by model II should be made. In the course of doing so, he will make a rate of return analysis in which his rate-of-return requirement will be 11 percent. Determine whether he will find that the decision is sensitive to the value placed on the greater output capacity of model II. (Ans.   11.7%, 19.7%)

10-10 A restaurant is under construction, and a choice must be made between an electric and a gas air-conditioning installation. The installed cost of an electric unit will be $10,800, and its average annual operating costs will be $1,640. The installed cost of a gas unit will be $13,200, and its average annual operating costs will be $765. At any point in either unit's life, its net terminal salvage value will be zero because the cost of its removal will about equal its market value.

The gas unit is expected to last 15 years. However, the analyst is uncertain about the life of the electric unit. Nevertheless, he is able to estimate that it will be between 8 and 12 years. As a compromise, he selects a ten-year life and goes on to analyze the alternatives by the uniform annual cost method.

Following this, he continues the study by ascertaining the decision's sensitivity to changes in the life estimate for the electric unit. He does this by adopting, first, the minimum expected life of 8 years and, then, the maximum expected life of 12 years. What will he find, given that the time value of money is 25 percent?

10-11 A mail-order retail chain is going to open a catalog store in a town which, on occasion, is subject to flooding once a year from a nearby river. Two suitable buildings are available for purchase. Their first costs, estimated lives, and expected salvage values are as follows:

	Building X	*Building Y*
First cost	$110,000	$120,000
Service life	50 years	50 years
Salvage value	$60,000	$60,000

Revenues and ordinary operating costs will be unaffected by the choice of building. However, building X is located in a section of the town for which the probability of a damaging flood is higher than it is for the section in which building Y is located.

A study of past records suggests that the probability of a damaging flood in any one year is 0.24 at location X and 0.08 at location Y. When a flood does occur, the damage is likely to be $7,000 at location X and $3,000 at location Y.

Given a rate-of-return requirement of 17 percent, compare the two alternatives, with the use of the rate of return method, to determine which of the buildings should be purchased. (Ans. 14.4%)

10-12 A proposed revenue-producing activity can be carried out by means of either of two processes. Process V requires a present investment of $58,000, and process W requires a present investment of $46,000. The assets involved in each case have a life of 7 years and no terminal salvage value.

With either process, the probability is 0.40 that annual revenues will be $73,000, and 0.60 that they will be $77,000.

Insofar as operating costs are concerned, some will be fixed, and others will be variable. The fixed operating costs will average $17,000 per year with process V and $18,500 per year with process W.

The variable operating costs will be a function of revenues. For process V, it is estimated that the probability is 0.25 that these annual expenses will be equal to 54 percent of revenues, and 0.75 that they will be equal to 59 percent of revenues. For process W, it is estimated that the probability is 0.25 that these annual expenses will be equal to 61 percent of annual revenues, and 0.75 that they will be equal to 66 percent of annual revenues.

The two processes are to be evaluated by calculating and comparing the expected values of their respective future worths. What will these values be if the firm's minimum rate-of-return requirement is 10 percent?

10-13 A private investor has been studying the stocks of two different companies with a view to making an investment of equity funds in the one or the other. In the event that she decides to do so, she will buy 1,000 shares of the selected stock.

The present market value of either stock is, of course, known. It is also known that either stock will be held for 4 years; this is because the investor has certain plans which will necessitate her converting the stock into cash at that time.

What is not known with certainty are the stocks' future market values, the average annual dividends they will yield, and the opportunity cost that will be experienced. Suffice it to say that the investor elects to make three sets of estimates for each of these factors. When these are combined with what is known about the alternatives, the result is as follows for the first stock:

	Type of estimate for first stock		
	Pessimistic	Normal	Optimistic
Present value	$41,000	$41,000	$41,000
Life	4 years	4 years	4 years
Terminal value	$38,000	$46,000	$50,000
Annual dividends	$1,700	$2,400	$2,800
Opportunity cost	10%	8%	6%

and as follows for the second stock:

	Type of estimate for second stock		
	Pessimistic	Normal	Optimistic
Present value	$49,000	$49,000	$49,000
Life	4 years	4 years	4 years
Terminal value	$45,000	$55,000	$57,000
Annual dividends	$3,000	$3,200	$3,300
Opportunity cost	10%	8%	6%

If the decision is going to be based on the results of a present worth analysis, what will this decision be under each of the following circumstances:

a The investor is pessimistic by nature and, consequently, is inclined to be governed by the pessimistic estimates? (Ans. $9,657, $8,755)

b The investor is optimistic by nature and, consequently, is inclined to be governed by the optimistic estimates? (Ans. −$8,307, −$7,585) c The investor is neither pessimistic nor optimistic by nature and, consequently, is inclined to be governed by the normal estimates? (Ans. −$759, −$2,023)

10-14 Suppose that the investor in the preceding problem decides to take into consideration the probability of occurrence to be associated with each type of estimate and that her judgment is that these probabilities are as follows for both alternatives:

Estimate	Probability
Pessimistic	0.15
Normal	0.65
Optimistic	0.20

a Which stock will appear to be the more attractive if she chooses to compute and compare the expected values of the alternatives' present worths? (Ans. −$705, −$1,519)

b Which stock will appear to be the more attractive if she chooses to compare those present worths which have the highest probability of occurrence? (Ans. −$759, −$2,023)

10-15 A system for the production of a chemical compound is to be selected. The compound is produced in batches. If the system malfunctions during any one run, the entire batch is lost at a cost of $45,000.

The probability of some specific number of malfunctions per year depends on the design of the system. These probabilities for two alternative designs which have been developed are as follows:

	Probability of occurrence	
Malfunctions per year	Design R	Design S
0	0.06	0.09
1	0.11	0.28
2	0.42	0.50
3	0.27	0.13
4	0.10	—
5	0.04	—

Other relevant data are as follows:

	Design R	Design S
Required investment	$440,000	$550,000
Service life	13 years	18 years
Terminal salvage value	$22,000	$27,500
Annual maintenance	$11,000	$9,000

The firm uses 12 percent for its cost of money and evaluates capital expenditure proposals by making a uniform annual cost comparison. Which of the two designs will yield the lower annual cost? (Ans. $184,923, $159,503)

10-16 An automatic die sinking machine is either going to be rehabilitated or replaced. The proposed replacement requires an investment of $185,000 and is expected to have a salvage value of $30,000 at the end of its 20-year life. Those operating costs which are going to be affected by its purchase will be $12,000 the first year and will then increase at a rate of $600 a year.

In its present condition, the old equipment has a market value of $19,000. If it is rehabilitated, its market value will be $24,000 in 3 years; thereafter, this value will change by a negligible amount. Also, it is estimated that (1) the probability is 1/2 that the asset's rehabilitation cost will be $32,000, and 1/2 that it will be $38,000, (2) the probability is 1/3 that the asset's remaining life will be 3 years, and 2/3 that it will be 4 years, and (3) the probability is 1/4 that the asset's relevant operating costs will average $20,000 per year, and 3/4 that they will average $25,000 per year.

a If the time value of money is 15 percent, what will be the uniform annual cost of the new machine? (Ans. $44,488)

b If the old machine's rehabilitation cost, remaining life, and future operating costs are independent of each other, what will be the expected value of its uniform annual cost? (Ans. $38,736)

c Should the old machine be rehabilitated or replaced?

10-17 Until now, a sales organization has been purchasing the automobiles which its personnel use. However, consideration is going to be given to the alternative of leasing.

In the course of developing the cash-flow pattern which ownership of a typical automobile can be expected to generate, the analyst prepares the following three sets of estimates:

	Optimistic	Normal	Pessimistic
Purchase price	$5,200	$5,200	$5,200
Economic life	4 years	3 years	2 years
Salvage value	$2,100	$2,600	$3,300
First-year upkeep	$1,800	$2,000	$2,200
Annual increase in upkeep costs	$100	$175	$250
Cost of money	12%	15%	20%
Probability of occurrence	0.23	0.54	0.23

If a comparable automobile is rented, the option selected would be one in which the lessor would assume the cost of maintenance, repairs, licenses, and insurance. Hence, the upkeep expense to the lessee would consist solely of the cost of gasoline and oil, and this expense is estimated to be $950 a year. The only additional cost would be the annual rental charge of $2,800. For purposes of simplicity, the analyst will treat both of these costs as end-of-year costs.

For each of the following conditions, determine which alternative will be found to have the lower uniform annual cost:

a The analyst decides to compare the cost of leasing with the expected value of the cost of ownership.

b The analyst decides to adopt the optimistic estimate when computing the cost of ownership.

c The analyst decides to adopt the normal estimate when computing the cost of ownership.

d The analyst decides to adopt the pessimistic estimate when computing the cost of ownership.

Appendix A

Decision Trees for Decision Making*

John F. Magee

The management of a company that I shall call Stygian Chemical Industries, Ltd., must decide whether to build a small plant or a large one to manufacture a new product with an expected market life of ten years. The decision hinges on what size the market for the product will be.

Possibly demand will be high during the initial two years but, if many initial users find the product unsatisfactory, will fall to a low level thereafter. Or high initial demand might indicate the possibility of a sustained high-volume market. If demand is high and the company does not expand within the first two years, competitive products will surely be introduced.

If the company builds a big plant, it must live with it whatever the size of market demand. If it builds a small plant, management has the option of expanding the plant in two years in the event that demand is high during the introductory period; while in the event that demand is low during the introductory period, the company will maintain operations in the small plant and make a tidy profit on the low volume.

Management is uncertain what to do. The company grew rapidly during the 1950s; it kept pace with the chemical industry generally. The new product, if the market turns out to be large, offers the present management a chance to push the company into a new period of profitable growth. The development department, particularly the development project engineer, is pushing to build the large-scale plant to exploit the first major product development the department has produced in some years.

*Harvard Business Review, July–August 1964, Copyright © 1964 by the President and Fellows of Harvard College; all rights reserved.

The chairman, a principal stockholder, is wary of the possibility of large unneeded plant capacity. He favors a smaller plant commitment, but recognizes that later expansion to meet high-volume demand would require more investment and be less efficient to operate. The chairman also recognizes that unless the company moves promptly to fill the demand which develops, competitors will be tempted to move in with equivalent products.

The Stygian Chemical problem, oversimplified as it is, illustrates the uncertainties and issues that business management must resolve in making investment decisions. (I use the term "investment" in a broad sense, referring to outlays not only for new plants and equipment but also for large, risky orders, special marketing facilities, research programs, and other purposes.) These decisions are growing more important at the same time that they are increasing in complexity. Countless executives want to make them better—but how?

In this article I shall present one recently developed concept called the "decision tree," which has tremendous potential as a decision-making tool. The decision tree can clarify for management, as can no other analytical tool that I know of, the choices, risks, objectives, monetary gains, and information needs involved in an investment problem. We shall be hearing a great deal about decision trees in the years ahead. Although a novelty to most businessmen today, they will surely be in common management parlance before many more years have passed.

Later in this article we shall return to the problem facing Stygian Chemical and see how management can proceed to solve it by using decision trees. First, however, a simpler example will illustrate some characteristics of the decision-tree approach.

DISPLAYING ALTERNATIVES

Let us suppose it is a rather overcast Saturday morning, and you have 75 people coming for cocktails in the afternoon. You have a pleasant garden and your house is not too large; so if the weather permits, you would like to set up the refreshments in the garden and have the party there. It would be more pleasant, and your guests would be more comfortable. On the other hand, if you set up the party for the garden and after all the guests are assembled it begins to rain, the refreshments will be ruined, your guests will get damp, and you will heartily wish you had decided to have the party in the house. (We could complicate this problem by considering the possibility of a partial commitment to one course or another and opportunities to adjust estimates of the weather as the day goes on, but the simple problem is all we need.)

This particular decision can be represented in the form of a "payoff" table:

	Events and Results	
Choices	Rain	No Rain
Outdoors	Disaster	Real comfort
Indoors	Mild discomfort,	Mild discomfort,
	but happy	but regrets

Much more complex decision questions can be portrayed in payoff table form. However, particularly for complex investment decisions, a different representation of the information pertinent to the problem—the decision tree—is useful to show the routes by which the various possible outcomes are achieved. Pierre Massé, Commissioner General of the National Agency for Productivity and Equipment Planning in France, notes:

"The decision problem is not posed in terms of an isolated decision (because today's decision depends on the one we shall make tomorrow) nor yet in terms of a sequence of decisions (because under uncertainty, decisions taken in the future will be influenced by what we have learned in the meanwhile). The problem is posed in terms of a tree of decisions."[1]

Exhibit 1 illustrates a decision tree for the cocktail party problem. This tree is a different way of displaying the same information shown in the payoff table. However, as later examples will show, in complex decisions the decision tree is frequently a much more lucid means of presenting the relevant information than is a payoff table.

The tree is made up of a series of nodes and branches. At the first node on the left, the host has the choice of having the party inside or outside. Each branch represents an alternative course of action or decision. At the end of each branch or alternative course is another node representing a chance event—whether or not it will rain. Each subsequent alternative course to the right represents an alternative outcome of this chance event. Associated with each complete alternative course through the tree is a payoff, shown at the end of the rightmost or terminal branch of the course.

When I am drawing decision trees, I like to indicate the action or decision forks with square nodes and the chance-event forks with round ones. Other symbols may be used instead, such as single-line and double-line branches, special letters, or colors. It does not matter so much which method of distinguishing you use so long as you do employ

---

[1] *Optimal Investment Decisions: Rules for Action and Criteria for Choice* (Englewood Cliffs, N.J., Prentice-Hall, Inc., 1962), p. 250.

EXHIBIT 1   Decision Tree for Cocktail Party

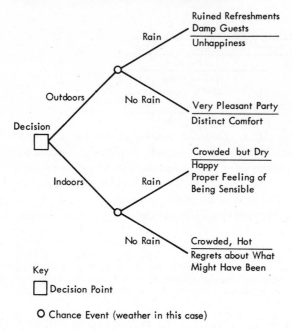

Key

☐ Decision Point

O Chance Event (weather in this case)

one or another. A decision tree of any size will always combine (a) *action* choices with (b) different possible *events* or *results* of action which are partially affected by chance or other uncontrollable circumstances.

Decision-Event Chains.   The previous example, though involving only a single stage of decision, illustrates the elementary principles on which larger, more complex decision trees are built. Let us take a slightly more complicated situation:

You are trying to decide whether to approve a development budget for an improved product. You are urged to do so on the grounds that the development, if successful, will give you a competitive edge, but if you do not develop the product, your competitor may—and may seriously—damage your market share. You sketch out a decision tree that looks something like the one in Exhibit 2.

Your initial decision is shown at the left. Following a decision to proceed with the project, if development is successful, is a second stage of decision at Point A. Assuming no important change in the situation

EXHIBIT 2   Decision Tree with Chains of Actions and Events

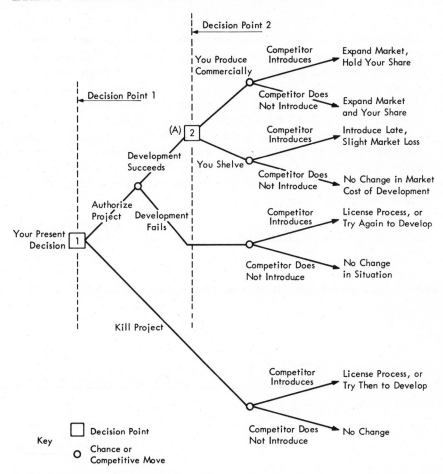

between now and the time of Point A, you decide now what alternatives will be important to you at that time. At the right of the tree are the outcomes of different sequences of decisions and events. These outcomes, too, are based on your present information. In effect you say, "If what I know now is true then, this is what will happen."

Of course, you do not try to identify all the events that can happen or all the decisions you will have to make on a subject under analysis. In the decision tree you lay out only those decisions and events or results that are important to you and have consequences you wish to compare.

ADDING FINANCIAL DATA

Now we can return to the problems faced by the Stygian Chemical management. A decision tree characterizing the investment problem as outlined in the introduction is shown in Exhibit 3. At Decision #1 the company must decide between a large and a small plant. This is all that must be decided *now*. But if the company chooses to build a small plant and then finds demand high during the initial period, it can in two years—at Decision #2—choose to expand its plant.

But let us go beyond a bare outline of alternatives. In making decisions, executives must take account of the probabilities, costs, and returns which appear likely. On the basis of the data now available to them, and assuming no important change in the company's situation, they reason as follows:

• Marketing estimates indicate a 60% chance of a large market in the long run and a 40% chance of a low demand, developing initially as follows:

EXHIBIT 3   Decisions and Events for Stygian Chemical Industries, Ltd.

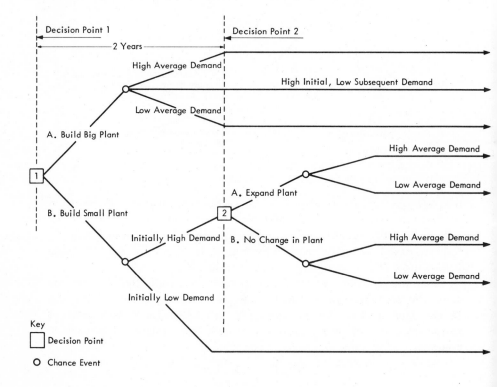

Initially high demand, sustained high 60%
Initially high demand, long-term low . . . . 10%⎫
Initially low and continuing low . . . . 30%⎬ Low = 40%
Initially low and subsequently high . . . . 0%⎭

- Therefore, the chance that demand initially will be high is 70%, (60 + 10). *If* demand is high initially, the company estimates that the chance it will continue at a high level is 86% (60 ÷ 70). Comparing 86% to 60%, it is apparent that a high initial level of sales changes the estimated chance of high sales in the subsequent periods. Similarly, if sales in the initial period are low, the chances are 100% (30 ÷ 30) that sales in the subsequent periods will be low. Thus the level of sales in the initial period is expected to be a rather accurate indicator of the level of sales in the subsequent periods.

- Estimates of annual income are made under the assumption of each alternative outcome:

1. A large plant with high volume would yield $1,000,000 annually in cash flow.
2. A large plant with low volume would yield only $100,000 because of high fixed costs and inefficiencies.
3. A small plant with low demand would be economical and would yield annual cash income of $400,000.
4. A small plant, during an initial period of high demand, would yield $450,000 per year, but this would drop to $300,000 yearly in the long run because of competition. (The market would be larger than under Alternative 3, but would be divided up among more competitors.)
5. If the small plant were expanded to meet sustained high demand, it would yield $700,000 cash flow annually, and so would be less efficient than a large plant built initially.
6. If the small plant were expanded but high demand were not sustained, estimated annual cash flow would be $50,000.

- It is estimated further that a large plant would cost $3 million to put into operation, a small plant would cost $1.3 million, and the expansion of the small plant would cost an additional $2.2 million.

When the foregoing data are incorporated, we have the decision tree shown in Exhibit 4. Bear in mind that nothing is shown here which Stygian Chemical's executives did not know before; no numbers have been pulled out of hats. However, we are beginning to see dramatic evidence of the value of decision trees in *laying out* what management knows in a way that enables more systematic analysis and leads to

EXHIBIT 4   Decision Tree with Financial Data

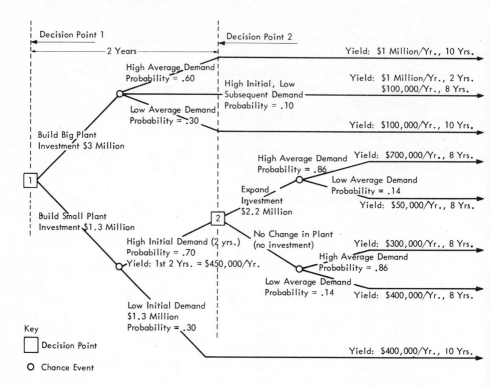

better decisions. To sum up the requirements of making a decision tree, management must:

1. Identify the points of decision and alternatives available at each point.
2. Identify the points of uncertainty and the type or range of alternative outcomes at each point.
3. Estimate the values needed to make the analysis, especially the probabilities of different events or results of action and the costs and gains of various events and actions.
4. Analyze the alternative values to choose a course.

CHOOSING COURSE OF ACTION

We are now ready for the next step in the analysis—to compare the consequences of different courses of action. A decision tree does not give management the answer to an investment problem; rather, it helps management determine which alternative at any particular choice point will yield the greatest expected monetary gain, given the information and alternatives pertinent to the decision.

Of course, the gains must be viewed with the risks. At Stygian Chemical, as at many corporations, managers have different points of view toward risk; hence they will draw different conclusions in the circumstances described by the decision tree shown in Exhibit 4. The many people participating in a decision—those supplying capital, ideas, data, or decisions, and having different values at risk—will see the uncertainty surrounding the decision in different ways. Unless these differences are recognized and dealt with, those who must make the decision, pay for it, supply data and analyses to it, and live with it will judge the issue, relevance of data, need for analysis, and criterion of success in different and conflicting ways.

For example, company stockholders may treat a particular investment as one of a series of possibilities, some of which will work out, others of which will fail. A major investment may pose risks to a middle manager—to his job and career—no matter what decision is made. Another participant may have a lot to gain from success, but little to lose from failure of the project. The nature of the risk—as each individual sees it—will affect not only the assumptions he is willing to make but also the strategy he will follow in dealing with the risk.

The existence of multiple, unstated, and conflicting objectives will certainly contribute to the "politics" of Stygian Chemical's decision, and one can be certain that the political element exists whenever the lives and ambitions of people are affected. Here, as in similar cases, it is not a bad exercise to think through who the parties to an investment decision are and to try to make these assessments:

What is at risk? Is it profit or equity value, survival of the business, maintenance of a job, opportunity for a major career?

Who is bearing the risk? The stockholder is usually bearing risk in one form. Management, employees, the community—all may be bearing different risks.

What is the character of the risk that each person bears? Is it, *in his terms,* unique, once-in-a-lifetime, sequential, insurable? Does it affect the economy, the industry, the company, or a portion of the company?

Considerations such as the foregoing will surely enter into top management's thinking, and the decision tree in Exhibit 4 will not eliminate them. But the tree will show management what decision today will contribute most to its long-term goals. The tool for this next step in the analysis is the concept of "rollback."

"Rollback" Concept. Here is how rollback works in the situation described. At the time of making Decision #1 (see Exhibit 4), management does not have to make Decision #2 and does not even know if it will have the occasion to do so. But if it *were* to have the option at Decision #2, the company would expand the plant, in view of its current knowledge. The analysis is shown in Exhibit 5. (I shall ignore for the moment the question of discounting future profits; that is introduced later.) We see that the total expected value of the expansion alternative is $160,000 greater than the no-expansion alternative, over the eight-year life remaining. Hence that is the alternative management would choose if faced with Decision #2 with its existing information (and thinking only of monetary gain as a standard of choice).

Readers may wonder why we started with Decision #2 when today's problem is Decision #1. The reason is the following: We need to be able to put a monetary value on Decision #2 in order to "roll back" to Decision #1 and compare the gain from taking the lower branch ("Build Small Plant") with the gain from taking the upper branch ("Build Big Plant"). Let us call that monetary value for Decision #2 its *position value*. The position value of a decision is the expected value of the preferred branch (in this case, the plant-expansion fork). The expected value is simply a kind of average of the results you would expect if

EXHIBIT 5 Analysis of Possible Decision #2 (using maximum expected total cash flow as criterion)

Choice	Chance event	Prob-ability (1)	Total yield, 8 Years (thousands of dollars) (2)	Expected value (thousands of dollars) (1) × (2)
Expansion	High average demand	.86	$5,600	$4,816
	Low average demand	.14	400	56
			Total	$4,872
			Less investment	2,200
			Net	$2,672
No expansion	High average demand	.86	$2,400	$2,064
	Low average demand	.14	3,200	448
			Total	$2,512
			Less investment	0
			Net	$2,512

EXHIBIT 6   Cash Flow Analysis for Decision #1

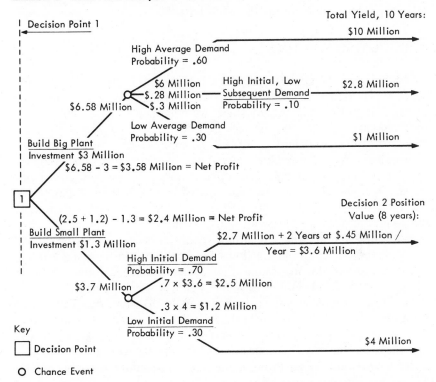

you were to repeat the situation over and over—getting a $5,600 thousand yield 86% of the time and a $400 thousand yield 14% of the time.

Stated in another way, it is worth $2,672 thousand to Stygian Chemical to get to the position where it can make Decision #2. The question is: Given this value and the other data shown in Exhibit 4, what now appears to be the best action at Decision #1?

Turn now to Exhibit 6. At the right of the branches in the top half we see the yields for various events if a big plant is built (these are simply the figures in Exhibit 4 multiplied out). In the bottom half we see the small plant figures, including Decision #2 position value plus the yield for the two years prior to Decision #2. If we reduce all these yields by their probabilities, we get the following comparison:

Build big plant:
    ($10 × .60) + ($2.8 × .10) + ($1 × .30) − $3 = $3,580 thousand
Build small plant:
    ($3.6 × .70) + ($4 × .30) − $1.3 = $2,400 thousand

The choice which maximizes expected total cash yield at Decision #1, therefore, is to build the big plant initially.

ACCOUNTING FOR TIME

What about taking differences in the *time* of future earnings into account? The time between successive decision stages on a decision tree may be substantial. At any stage, we may have to weigh differences in immediate cost or revenue against differences in value at the next stage. Whatever standard of choice is applied, we can put the two alternatives on a comparable basis if we discount the value assigned to the next stage by an appropriate percentage. The discount percentage is, in effect, an allowance for the cost of capital and is similar to the use of a discount rate in the present value or discounted cash flow techniques already well known to businessmen.

When decision trees are used, the discounting procedure can be applied one stage at a time. Both cash flows and position values are discounted.

For simplicity, let us assume that a discount rate of 10% per year for all stages is decided on by Stygian Chemical's management. Applying the rollback principle, we again begin with Decision #2. Taking the same figures used in previous exhibits and discounting the cash flows at 10%, we get the data shown in Part A of Exhibit 7. Note particularly that these are the present values *as of the time Decision #2 is made.*

Now we want to go through the same procedure used in Exhibit 5 when we obtained expected values, only this time using the discounted yield figures and obtaining a discounted expected value. The results are shown in Part B of Exhibit 7. Since the discounted expected value of the no-expansion alternative is higher, *that* figure becomes the position value of Decision #2 this time.

Having done this, we go back to work through Decision #1 again, repeating the same analytical procedure as before only with discounting. The calculations are shown in Exhibit 8. Note that the Decision #2 position value is treated at the time of Decision #1 as if it were a lump sum received at the end of the two years.

The large-plant alternative is again the preferred one on the basis of discounted expected cash flow. But the margin of difference over the small-plant alternative ($290 thousand) is smaller than it was without discounting.

UNCERTAINTY ALTERNATIVES

In illustrating the decision-tree concept, I have treated uncertainty alternatives as if they were discrete, well-defined possibilities. For my

EXHIBIT 7   Analysis of Decision #2 with Discounting

A. *Present Values of Cash Flows*

Choice-outcome	Yield	Present value (in thousands)
Expand-high demand	$700,000/year, 8 years	$4,100
Expand-low demand	50,000/year, 8 years	300
No change-high demand	300,000/year, 8 years	1,800
No change-low demand	400,000/year, 8 years	2,300

B. *Obtaining Discounted Expected Values*

Choice	Chance event	Prob-ability (1)	Present value yield (in thousands) (2)	Discounted expected value (in thousands) (1) × (2)
Expansion	High average demand	.86	$4,100	$3,526
	Low average demand	.14	300	42
		Total		$3,568
		Less investment		2,200
		Net		$1,368
No expansion	High average demand	.86	$1,800	$1,548
	Low average demand	.14	2,300	322
		Total		$1,870
		Less investment		0
		Net		$1,870

Note: For simplicity, the first year cash flow is not discounted, the second year cash flow is discounted one year, and so on.

examples I have made use of uncertain situations depending basically on a single variable, such as the level of demand or the success or failure of a development project. I have sought to avoid unnecessary complication while putting emphasis on the key interrelationships among the present decision, future choices, and the intervening uncertainties.

In many cases, the uncertain elements do take the form of discrete, single-variable alternatives. In others, however, the possibilities for cash flow during a stage may range through a whole spectrum and may depend on a number of independent or partially related variables subject to chance influences—cost, demand, yield, economic climate, and so forth. In these cases, we have found that the range of variability or the likelihood of the cash flow falling in a given range during a stage can be calculated

EXHIBIT 8   Analysis of Decision #1

Choice	Chance event	Probability (1)	Yield (in thousands)	Discounted value of yield (in thousands) (2)	Discounted expected yield (in thousands) (1) × (2)
Build big plant	High average demand	.60	$1,000/year, 10 years	$6,700	$4,020
	High initial, low average demand	.10	1,000/year, 2 years 100/year, 8 years	2,400	240
	Low average demand	.30	100/year, 10 years	700	210
				Total	$4,470
				Less investment	3,000
				Net	$1,470
Build small plant	High initial demand	.70	$ 450/year, 2 years	$ 860	$ 600
			Decision #2 value, $1,870 at end of 2 years	1,530	1,070
	Low initial demand	.30	$ 400/year, 10 years	2,690	810
				Total	$2,480
				Less investment	1,300
				Net	$1,180

readily from knowledge of the key variables and the uncertainties surrounding them. Then the range of cash-flow possibilities during the stage can be broken down into two, three, or more "subsets," which can be used as discrete chance alternatives.

CONCLUSION

Peter F. Drucker has succinctly expressed the relation between present planning and future events: "Long-range planning does not deal with future decisions. It deals with the futurity of present decisions."[2] Today's decision should be made in light of the anticipated effect it and the outcome of uncertain events will have on future values and decisions. Since today's decision sets the stage for tomorrow's decision, today's decision must balance economy with flexibility; it must balance the need to capitalize on profit opportunities that may exist with the capacity to react to future circumstances and needs.

---

[2] "Long-Range Planning," *Management Science*, April 1959, p. 239.

The unique feature of the decision tree is that it allows management to combine analytical techniques such as discounted cash flow and present value methods with a clear portrayal of the impact of future decision alternatives and events. Using the decision tree, management can consider various courses of action with greater ease and clarity. The interactions between present decision alternatives, uncertain events, and future choices and their results become more visible.

Of course, there are many practical aspects of decision trees in addition to those that could be covered in the space of just one article. When these other aspects are discussed in subsequent articles, the whole range of possible gains for management will be seen in greater detail.

Surely the decision-tree concept does not offer final answers to managements making investment decisions in the face of uncertainty. We have not reached that stage, and perhaps we never will. Nevertheless, the concept is valuable for illustrating the structure of investment decisions, and it can likewise provide excellent help in the evaluation of capital investment *opportunities.*

Appendix B
Derivations

Expressions for nine compound interest factors were presented in Chapter 3, and an explanation of how these factors are applied was given. Similarly, in Chapter 9, two formulas used in the revenue requirement method of analysis were presented, and their application was explained. But at neither point was a derivation of the expressions involved provided, because a knowledge of such derivations is not necessary for the acquisition of an understanding of how the expressions are applied and an understanding of the meaning of the results obtained with the use of the expressions. Nevertheless, for those individuals who are interested in the manner in which the nine compound interest factors and the two revenue requirement formulas were developed, the derivations will now be presented in the order in which the resultant expressions appear in the text.

SINGLE-AMOUNT COMPOUND INTEREST FACTORS

The first compound interest factor considered was the single-amount future worth factor, which served to describe the relationship among P, F, n, and i, where

P = present sum of money
F = future sum of money
n = number of interest periods
i = interest rate per interest period

On a time line, the first three of these amounts would appear at the following points:

When P, n, and i are known, the value of F can be obtained as follows: The amount on hand at the beginning of the first period is P. The interest for the period is equal to this amount P times the rate i, or Pi. Therefore, the amount on hand at the end of the first period will be equal to the amount on hand at the beginning of the period plus the interest for the period, that is, to

$$P + Pi = P(1 + i)^1$$

This sequence of steps is summarized in the first line of Table B-1 in which the amount P is expressed as $P(1 + i)^0$; this is permissible because $(1 + i)^0$ is equal to 1.

Table B-1   Determination of amounts on hand at various points in time

Period (a)	Beginning-of-period amount (b)	Interest for the period (c)	End-of-period amount (d = b + c)
1	$P(1 + i)^0$	$P(1 + i)^0(i)$	$P(1 + i)^0 + P(1 + i)^0(i) = P(1 + i)^1$
2	$P(1 + i)^1$	$P(1 + i)^1(i)$	$P(1 + i)^1 + P(1 + i)^1(i) = P(1 + i)^2$
3	$P(1 + i)^2$	$P(1 + i)^2(i)$	$P(1 + i)^2 + P(1 + i)^2(i) = P(1 + i)^3$
.	. . . . . .	. . . . . .	. . . .
$n - 1$	$P(1 + i)^{n-2}$	$P(1 + i)^{n-2}(i)$	$P(1 + i)^{n-2} + P(1 + i)^{n-2}(i) = P(1 + i)^{n-1}$
n	$P(1 + i)^{n-1}$	$P(1 + i)^{n-1}(i)$	$P(1 + i)^{n-1} + P(1 + i)^{n-1}(i) = P(1 + i)^n$

To continue, the amount on hand at the beginning of the second period is equal to the amount on hand at the end of the first period, which is $P(1 + i)^1$. The interest for the period is $P(1 + i)^1 (i)$. Hence, as shown in the second line of Table B-1, the amount on hand at the end of the second period will be equal to

$$P(1 + i)^1 + P(1 + i)^1(i) = P(1 + i)^1(1 + i) = P(1 + i)^2$$

At the beginning of the third period, the amount on hand is this $P(1 + i)^2$, and the interest for the period is $P(1 + i)^2(i)$. As a result, the amount on hand at the end of the third period will be equal to

$$P(1 + i)^2 + P(1 + i)^2(i) = P(1 + i)^2(1 + i) = P(1 + i)^3$$

The way in which this quantity was obtained is described in the third line of Table B-1. An examination of the first three lines in this table reveals that each beginning-of-period amount is equal to P multiplied by the term $(1 + i)$ raised to some power. It so happens that the exponent is always equal to the number of the period involved minus 1. Specifically, for periods 1, 2, and 3, the corresponding values of the exponents are 0, 1, and 2.

This observation permits one to conclude that the amount on hand at the beginning of the last period n will be $P(1 + i)^{n-1}$. Consequently, as indicated in the last line of Table B-1, the interest for the period becomes $P(1 + i)^{n-1}(i)$, and the amount on hand at the end of the period will be

$$P(1 + i)^{n-1} + P(1 + i)^{n-1}(i) = P(1 + i)^{n-1}(1 + i) = P(1 + i)^n$$

An analysis of the last column of Table B-1 discloses that this final value is consistent with the end-of-period values obtained for the earlier periods. For each of those periods, the amount on hand at the end of a given period is equal to P multiplied by the term $(1 + i)$ raised to some power, and the exponent proves to be equal to the number of periods involved. Specifically, for periods 1, 2, and 3, the corresponding values of the exponents are 1, 2, and 3. It follows that the amount F which will be on hand at the end of period n will be equal to

$$F = P(1 + i)^n \tag{B-1}$$

In the event that the unknown is P rather than F, Eq. (B-1) can be solved for P to obtain

$$P = F\left[\frac{1}{(1 + i)^n}\right] \tag{B-2}$$

The multiplier which appears in Eq. (B-1) is referred to as the *single-amount future worth factor*, and the multiplier which appears in Eq. (B-2) is referred to as the *single-amount present worth factor*.

UNIFORM-SERIES COMPOUND INTEREST FACTORS

The next set of compound interest factors contained those which served to describe the relationship among a single amount, a uniform end-of-period series of amounts, the number of interest periods, and the interest rate per period. One of these factors was designed for use when a uniform series of amounts A is to be converted to its single amount equivalent F at the point at which the last amount in the series occurs. On a time line, this condition would appear as follows:

Because the series is uniform, each of the A values is of the same size, and the subscripts simply serve to identify the point at which a specified end-of-period payment or receipt occurs.

If A, n, and i are known, the value of F can be obtained in the following manner: First, each amount in the series is treated as a single amount. Next, the future worth at point n of each of these amounts is calculated with the use of an appropriate single-amount future worth factor. And, last, these individual future worths are summed to arrive at the total future worth of the series. In equation form, this approach can be described as follows:

$$F = A_1(1 + i)^{n-1} + A_2(1 + i)^{n-2} + A_3(1 + i)^{n-3} + \cdots$$
$$\cdots + A_{n-2}(1 + i)^2 + A_{n-1}(1 + i)^1 + A_n(1 + i)^0$$

It will be noted that the power to which each $(1 + i)$ term is raised represents the number of periods during which the corresponding amount A will be earning interest. At one extreme, this number of periods is $n - 1$ for the first amount A_1, and, at the other extreme, it is 0 for the last amount A_n. But, to continue, given that each of the amounts in the series is equal to some uniform amount A, the preceding equation can be expressed in the following form:

$$F = A(1 + i)^{n-1} + A(1 + i)^{n-2} + A(1 + i)^{n-3} + \cdots$$
$$\cdots + A(1 + i)^2 + A(1 + i)^1 + A(1 + i)^0 \qquad \text{(B-3)}$$

For the sake of convenience, the order of the terms on the right side of this expression can be reversed to obtain the following:

$$F = A(1 + i)^0 + A(1 + i)^1 + A(1 + i)^2 + \cdots$$
$$\cdots + A(1 + i)^{n-3} + A(1 + i)^{n-2} + A(1 + i)^{n-1} \qquad \text{(B-4)}$$

The right side of Eq. (B-4) is a geometric progression in which the constant is $(1 + i)$. This is to say that every term in this progression is equal to the preceding term multiplied by $(1 + i)$. Such expressions can be simplified by, first, multiplying both sides of the equation by the constant involved. When Eq. (B-4) is multiplied by $(1 + i)$, the following is obtained:

$$F(1 + i) = A(1 + i)^1 + A(1 + i)^2 + A(1 + i)^3 + \cdots$$
$$\cdots + A(1 + i)^{n-2} + A(1 + i)^{n-1} + A(1 + i)^n \qquad \text{(B-5)}$$

Now, if Eq. (B-4) were to be subtracted from Eq. (B-5), the result would be as follows:

$$Fi = A(1 + i)^n - A(1 + i)^0 = A[(1 + i)^n - 1]$$

which yields

$$F = A \left[\frac{(1 + i)^n - 1}{i} \right] \qquad \text{(B-6)}$$

where n is equal to the number of end-of-period amounts contained in the series.

A comparison of this equation with Eq. (B-3) permits one to state that

$$\frac{(1 + i)^n - 1}{i} = (1 + i)^{n-1} + (1 + i)^{n-2} + (1 + i)^{n-3} + \cdots$$

$$\cdots + (1 + i)^2 + (1 + i)^1 + (1 + i)^0 \qquad \text{(B-7)}$$

In any event, if it so happens that A rather than F is the unknown, Eq. (B-6) can be solved for A to obtain

$$A = F\left[\frac{i}{(1 + i)^n - 1}\right] \qquad \text{(B-8)}$$

The multiplier in Eq. (B-6) is called the *uniform-series future worth factor,* and the multiplier in Eq. (B-8) is called the *future-amount annuity factor.* The algebraic expressions for these factors serve to describe the relationship between a uniform end-of-period series of amounts and a *future* single amount. But, on occasion, there is a need to ascertain a *present* single amount which is equivalent to the series of amounts. If the present single amount P appears at the beginning of the series' first period, the situation can be described on a time line in the following way:

P

	A	A	A	·	·	·	A	A	A
0	1	2	3	·	·	·	$n-2$	$n-1$	n

To calculate the value of P when A, n, and i are known, one can begin with Eq. (B-6) which states that

$$F = A\left[\frac{(1 + i)^n - 1}{i}\right]$$

and go on to Eq. (B-1) which states that

$$F = P(1 + i)^n$$

When the second of these equations is substituted in the first, the following is obtained:

$$P(1 + i)^n = A\left[\frac{(1 + i)^n - 1}{i}\right]$$

and this yields

$$P = A \left[\frac{(1 + i)^n - 1}{i(1 + i)^n} \right] \tag{B-9}$$

in which the multiplier is the *uniform-series present worth factor.*

Should A be the unknown and P the known value, Eq. (B-9) can be solved for A to obtain the following:

$$A = P \left[\frac{i(1 + i)^n}{(1 + i)^n - 1} \right] \tag{B-10}$$

in which the multiplier is the *present-amount annuity factor.*

GRADIENT-SERIES COMPOUND INTEREST FACTORS

The remaining three compound interest factors are used to find the equivalent of an end-of-period gradient series. In one of those cases, the equivalent is a single future amount F that appears at the end of the last period of a series in which the gradient is G and which continues for n periods during which the interest rate per period is i. On a time line, the nature of the series and the location of the equivalent single amount can be presented as follows:

```
                                                         F
        0G      1G      2G    ·   ·   ·  (n−3)G (n−2)G (n−1)G
├───────┼───────┼───────┼──────────────────┼──────┼──────┤
0       1       2       3    ·   ·   ·    n−2    n−1     n
```

One way to compute the value of F, when G, n, and i are given, is to begin by describing the gradient series in the following manner:

```
                                                         1G
                                         1G      1G
                                 1G      1G      1G
                                 ·       ·       ·
                                 ·       ·       ·
                         1G  ·  ·  ·     1G      1G      1G
                 1G      1G  ·  ·  ·     1G      1G      1G
        0G       0G      0G  ·  ·  ·     0G      0G      0G
       ───      ───     ───             ───     ───     ───
        0G       1G      2G  ·  ·  ·  (n−3)G  (n−2)G  (n−1)G
├───────┼───────┼───────┼──────────────────┼──────┼──────┤
0       1       2       3    ·  ·  ·     n−2    n−1     n
```

In this description, the original gradient series has been replaced by a number of uniform end-of-period series which, when combined, yield the gradient series. Therefore, the total future worth at point n of these uniform series will be equal to the future worth at that point of the gradient series.

To obtain the total future worth of these uniform series, one can begin by calculating the future worth of each individual uniform series with the use of an appropriate uniform-series future worth factor. Then, these respective future worths can be summed to obtain their total.

When this approach is applied, the future worth at point n of the first and longest uniform series proves to be

$$F = 0G \left[\frac{(1 + i)^n - 1}{i} \right]$$

because this series contains n end-of-period amounts.

Similarly, the future worth of the next longest uniform series would be found to be

$$F = 1G \left[\frac{(1 + i)^{n-1} - 1}{i} \right]$$

because this series contains $n - 1$ end-of-period amounts.

Continuing in this manner, one would eventually reach the last and shortest uniform series and determine its future worth to be

$$F = 1G \left[\frac{(1 + i)^1 - 1}{i} \right]$$

because this series contains 1 end-of-period amount.

The total future worth would be equal to the sum of these individual future worths which is

$$F = 0G \left[\frac{(1 + i)^n - 1}{i} \right] + 1G \left[\frac{(1 + i)^{n-1} - 1}{i} \right]$$

$$+ 1G \left[\frac{(1 + i)^{n-2} - 1}{i} \right] + \cdots + 1G \left[\frac{(1 + i)^3 - 1}{i} \right]$$

$$+ 1G \left[\frac{(1 + i)^2 - 1}{i} \right] + 1G \left[\frac{(1 + i)^1 - 1}{i} \right]$$

Because the value of the first term on the right side of this expression is zero, the expression becomes

$$F = 1G \left[\frac{(1 + i)^{n-1} - 1}{i} \right] + 1G \left[\frac{(1 + i)^{n-2} - 1}{i} \right] + \cdots$$

$$\cdots + 1G \left[\frac{(1 + i)^3 - 1}{i} \right] + 1G \left[\frac{(1 + i)^2 - 1}{i} \right]$$

$$+ 1G \left[\frac{(1 + i)^1 - 1}{i} \right]$$

which can also assume the following form:

$$F = \frac{G}{i} \{ [(1 + i)^{n-1} - 1] + [(1 + i)^{n-2} - 1] + \cdots$$

$$\cdots + [(1 + i)^3 - 1] + [(1 + i)^2 - 1] + [(1 + i)^1 - 1] \}$$

The braces in this equation enclose $n - 1$ bracketed terms. Therefore, the quantity minus 1 appears $n - 1$ times, and the preceding equation can be expressed as follows:

$$F = \frac{G}{i} [(1 + i)^{n-1} + (1 + i)^{n-2} + \cdots + (1 + i)^3$$

$$+ (1 + i)^2 + (1 + i)^1 - 1(n - 1)]$$

which yields

$$F = \frac{G}{i} [(1 + i)^{n-1} + (1 + i)^{n-2} + \cdots + (1 + i)^3$$

$$+ (1 + i)^2 + (1 + i)^1 + 1 - n]$$

or

$$F = \frac{G}{i} \{ [(1 + i)^{n-1} + (1 + i)^{n-2} + \cdots + (1 + i)^3$$

$$+ (1 + i)^2 + (1 + i)^1 + (1 + i)^0] - n \} \qquad \text{(B-11)}$$

But a return to Eq. (B-7) discloses that the bracketed terms in Eq. (B-11) are equal to

$$\frac{(1 + i)^n - 1}{i}$$

so that Eq. (B-11) becomes

$$F = \frac{G}{i} \left[\frac{(1 + i)^n - 1}{i} - n \right]$$

which yields

$$F = G \left[\frac{(1 + i)^n - 1}{i^2} - \frac{n}{i} \right] \tag{B-12}$$

This multiplier is the *gradient-series future worth factor*.

In another case, there may be a need to convert a gradient series into an equivalent single present amount P that appears at the beginning of the series' first period. This set of circumstances can be described on a time line as follows:

P

	$0G$	$1G$	$2G$	·	·	·	$(n-3)G$	$(n-2)G$	$(n-1)G$
0	1	2	3	·	·	·	$n-2$	$n-1$	n

An expression which describes the relationship among P, G, n, and i can be developed with the use of Eq. (B-12), which has just been derived, and with the use of Eq. (B-1), which had been derived earlier and which assumed the following form:

$$F = P(1 + i)^n$$

When Eqs. (B-1) and (B-12) are combined, the following is obtained:

$$P(1 + i)^n = G \left[\frac{(1 + i)^n - 1}{i^2} - \frac{n}{i} \right]$$

which yields

$$P = G \left[\frac{(1 + i)^n - 1}{i^2(1 + i)^n} - \frac{n}{i(1 + i)^n} \right] \tag{B-13}$$

in which the multiplier is the *gradient-series present worth factor*.

Finally, it may be necessary to determine the end-of-period uniform series that is equivalent to an end-of-period gradient series. On a time line, the values involved would appear as follows:

	A	A	A	·	·	·	A	A	A
	$0G$	$1G$	$2G$	·	·	·	$(n-3)G$	$(n-2)G$	$(n-1)G$
0	1	2	3	·	·	·	$n-2$	$n-1$	n

The relationship among A, G, n, and i can be ascertained with the use of Eqs. (B-13) and (B-9). Eq. (B-13) has just been derived, and it will be recalled that Eq. (B-9) was as follows:

$$P = A \left[\frac{(1 + i)^n - 1}{i(1 + i)^n} \right]$$

Substituting Eq. (B-9) in Eq. (B-13), one would obtain the following:

$$A\left[\frac{(1+i)^n-1}{i(1+i)^n}\right] = G\left[\frac{(1+i)^n-1}{i^2(1+i)^n} - \frac{n}{i(1+i)^n}\right]$$

and this yields

$$A = G\left[\frac{1}{i} - \frac{n}{(1+i)^n-1}\right] \tag{B-14}$$

The multiplier in this case is the *gradient-series annuity factor,* and it is the last of the nine compound interest factors which are used in the analysis of capital investment alternatives.

THE REVENUE REQUIREMENT TAX FORMULAS

Two formulas were presented for use in the determination of the uniform annual revenues required to cover the uniform annual income tax expense to be associated with a proposed investment alternative being analyzed by the revenue requirement method. More exactly, the formulas served to yield the amount of taxes that would be experienced if actual revenues were equal to the total revenues needed to satisfy an established after-tax rate-of-return requirement. Underlying the formulas are the following assumptions:

(1) The total investment in an asset during any one year will be equal to its book value during that year, which is to say that the market value will be equal to the book value.
(2) The amount of debt capital invested in an asset during any one year will be a constant fraction of its book value during that year.

Given these assumptions, one can begin the derivation of the formulas with the basic expression for computing income taxes which is as follows:

Income taxes = (tax rate)(taxable income)   (B-15)

In this and all subsequent expressions, it is to be understood that the factors involved are expressed in terms of some amount *per year.* But to continue, the taxable income which appears in Eq. (B-15) is ascertained in the following manner:

Taxable income = (revenues) − (deductible expenses)   (B-16)

The revenues in this equation will be equal to the total revenue requirement. This requirement will be the sum of the revenues required to offset the following:

Capital cost
Operating costs
Income taxes

However, the capital cost consists of the devaluation expense and the cost of money, and so a more detailed listing would be as follows:

Devaluation expense
Cost of money
Operating costs
Income taxes

But because the cost of money is equal to the required return on equity capital plus the required return on debt capital, a still more detailed listing would be as follows:

Devaluation expense
Required return on equity investment
Required return on debt investment
Operating costs
Income taxes

in which each of these items is expressed in terms of a uniform dollar amout per year.

In brief, then, there is a need for ascertaining what the annual income taxes will be when annual revenues are equal to the sum of the foregoing amounts. To continue the determination, it becomes necessary to consider the deductible expenses by which these revenues will be reduced to arrive at the taxable income. These expenses are as follows:

Depreciation expense
Interest expense on debt
Operating costs

To summarize, the taxable income will be equal to the difference between the revenues and deductible expenses whose respective elements are shown in the following table:

Revenues	Deductible expenses
Devaluation expense	Depreciation expense
Return on equity	—
Return on debt	Interest expense
Operating costs	Operating costs
Income taxes	—

When the difference between these elements is being determined, it will be found that the revenues needed to cover the devaluation expense will be exactly offset by the deductible depreciation expense, because it is assumed in the revenue requirement method that an asset decreases in value by an amount equal to the reported tax depreciation expense. Also, the revenues needed to yield the required return on debt capital will be exactly offset by the deductible interest expense, because the required return on debt will be equal to the cost of debt. And the revenues needed to recover the operating costs will be exactly offset by the deductible operating costs. Consequently, all that remains after the revenues are reduced by the deductible expenses is an amount equal to the sum of the required return on equity and the income taxes; this amount is the taxable income. Hence, it has been found that

Taxable income = (return on equity) + (income taxes)

and, therefore, Eq. (B-15) assumes the following form:

Income taxes = (tax rate) [(return on equity) + (income taxes)]

When this expression is simplified, the following is obtained:

$$\text{Income taxes} = \left(\frac{\text{tax rate}}{1 - \text{tax rate}} \right)(\text{return on equity})$$

$$= \left(\frac{t}{1 - t} \right)(\text{return on equity}) \qquad \text{(B-17)}$$

where t is the effective income tax rate.

A need now arises for determining the value of the "average annual dollar return on equity" term which appears in Eq. (B-17). The dollar return on total investment will, of course, be equal to

Total return = (return on equity) + (return on debt)

which yields

Return on equity = (total return) − (return on debt)

which is equal to

Return on equity = (total return) − (interest expense)   (B-18)

The dollar value of the total return which appears in Eq. (B-18) can be calculated as follows:

Total return = (total investment)(rate-of-return requirement)

$$= (\text{total investment})(i) \qquad \text{(B-19)}$$

where i is the after-tax return requirement on total investment.

The dollar value of the interest expense which appears in Eq. (B-18) can be found in the following manner:

Interest expense = (amount of debt)(interest rate)

$$= \text{(total investment)(debt ratio)(interest rate)} \qquad \text{(B-20)}$$

in which the debt ratio is some constant proportion of the total investment.

When Eqs. (B-19) and (B-20) are substituted in Eq. (B-18), the following is obtained:

Return on equity = (total investment)(rate-of-return requirement)

$$- \text{(total investment)(debt ratio)(interest rate)}$$

$$= \text{(total investment)} \left[\text{(rate-of-return requirement)} \right.$$

$$- \text{(debt ratio)(interest rate)} \right]$$

$$= \text{(total investment)}(i - dr) \qquad \text{(B-21)}$$

where: i = after-tax return requirement on total investment
d = debt ratio = proportion of debt financing
r = cost of debt in terms of an interest rate

This return on equity can be expressed as a fraction of the return on total investment by dividing the equity return by the total return, that is, by dividing Eq. (B-21) by Eq. (B-19). Doing so yields

$$\frac{\text{Equity return}}{\text{Total return}} = \frac{\text{(total investment)}(i - dr)}{\text{(total investment)}(i)} = \frac{i - dr}{i} = 1 - \frac{dr}{i}$$

When this expression is solved for the return on equity, the result is

$$\text{Return on equity} = \left(1 - \frac{dr}{i} \right)(\text{total return}) \qquad \text{(B-22)}$$

If Eq. (B-22) is substituted in Eq. (B-17), the following is obtained:

$$\text{Income taxes} = \left(\frac{t}{1 - t} \right)\left(1 - \frac{dr}{i} \right)(\text{total return}) \qquad \text{(B-23)}$$

At this point, only the value of the total return remains to be ascertained. This is done by recalling that the uniform annual capital cost of an alternative consists of two elements. The first is the devaluation expense, and the second is the cost of money. The total revenue requirement will just suffice to cover, among other things, these two costs. Consequently, with those revenues, the dollar return on total investment will be equal to the cost of money, which is equal to the difference between the uniform annual capital cost and the uniform annual devaluation expense. This is to say that

Total return = cost of money
= (uniform annual capital cost) − (uniform annual devaluation expense)

But, and this is extremely important, it is assumed in the revenue requirement method that the total investment in an asset during any one year is equal to its book value during that year. In other words, it is assumed that the annual devaluation expense is equal to the annual depreciation expense reported for tax purposes. Therefore, the equivalent uniform annual devaluation expense coincides with the equivalent uniform annual depreciation expense, and it can be said that

Total return = (uniform annual capital cost) − (uniform annual depreciation expense)

or, in abbreviated form, that

Total return = $UACC - UADE$

When this expression for the dollar return on total investment is substituted in Eq. (B-23), the result is as follows:

Income taxes = $\left(\dfrac{t}{1-t}\right)\left(1 - \dfrac{dr}{i}\right)(UACC - UADE)$

In the revenue requirement method, the first two terms on the right side of this expression are said to be the tax factor ϕ. As a consequence, the formula for determining the annual revenues required to recover annual income taxes becomes

Annual income taxes = $\phi(UACC - UADE)$ (B-24)

where

$$\phi = \left(\frac{t}{1-t}\right)\left(1 - \frac{dr}{i}\right)$$ (B-25)

Eqs. (B-24) and (B-25) are the two which were presented and applied in Chapter 9.

Appendix C
Interest Tables

FUTURE WORTH FACTORS:

Name	Symbol	Formula
Single-amount future worth factor	F/P	$(1+i)^n$
Uniform-series future worth factor	F/A	$\dfrac{(1+i)^n-1}{i}$
Gradient-series future worth factor	F/G	$\dfrac{(1+i)^n-1}{i^2}-\dfrac{n}{i}$

PRESENT WORTH FACTORS:

Name	Symbol	Formula
Single-amount present worth factor	P/F	$\dfrac{1}{(1+i)^n}$
Uniform-series present worth factor	P/A	$\dfrac{(1+i)^n-1}{i(1+i)^n}$
Gradient-series present worth factor	P/G	$\dfrac{(1+i)^n-1}{i^2(1+i)^n}-\dfrac{n}{i(1+i)^n}$

ANNUITY FACTORS:

Name	Symbol	Formula
Present-amount annuity factor	A/P	$\dfrac{i(1+i)^n}{(1+i)^n-1}$
Future-amount annuity factor	A/F	$\dfrac{i}{(1+i)^n-1}$
Gradient-series annuity factor	A/G	$\dfrac{1}{i}-\dfrac{n}{(1+i)^n-1}$

TABLE C-1   Values of 2% Compound Interest Factors

Number of periods n	Future worth factors			Present worth factors		
	Single-amount F/P	Uniform-series F/A	Gradient-series F/G	Single-amount P/F	Uniform-series P/A	Gradient-series P/G
1	1.0200	1.000	0.00	0.9804	0.980	0.000
2	1.0404	2.020	1.00	0.9612	1.942	0.961
3	1.0612	3.060	3.02	0.9423	2.884	2.846
4	1.0824	4.122	6.08	0.9238	3.808	5.617
5	1.1041	5.204	10.20	0.9057	4.713	9.240
6	1.1262	6.308	15.41	0.8880	5.601	13.680
7	1.1487	7.434	21.71	0.8706	6.472	18.903
8	1.1717	8.583	29.15	0.8535	7.325	24.878
9	1.1951	9.755	37.73	0.8368	8.162	31.572
10	1.2190	10.950	47.49	0.8203	8.983	38.955
11	1.2434	12.169	58.44	0.8043	9.787	46.998
12	1.2682	13.412	70.60	0.7885	10.575	55.671
13	1.2936	14.680	84.02	0.7730	11.348	64.948
14	1.3195	15.974	98.70	0.7579	12.106	74.800
15	1.3459	17.293	114.67	0.7430	12.849	85.202
16	1.3728	18.639	131.96	0.7284	13.578	96.129
17	1.4002	20.012	150.60	0.7142	14.292	107.555
18	1.4282	21.412	170.62	0.7002	14.992	119.458
19	1.4568	22.841	192.03	0.6864	15.678	131.814
20	1.4859	24.297	214.87	0.6730	16.351	144.600
21	1.5157	25.783	239.17	0.6598	17.011	157.796
22	1.5460	27.299	264.95	0.6468	17.658	171.379
23	1.5769	28.845	292.25	0.6342	18.292	185.331
24	1.6084	30.422	321.09	0.6217	18.914	199.630
25	1.6406	32.030	351.51	0.6095	19.523	214.259
26	1.6734	33.671	383.55	0.5976	20.121	229.199
27	1.7069	35.344	417.22	0.5859	20.707	244.431
28	1.7410	37.051	452.56	0.5744	21.281	259.939
29	1.7758	38.792	489.61	0.5631	21.844	275.706
30	1.8114	40.568	528.40	0.5521	22.396	291.716
31	1.8476	42.379	568.97	0.5412	22.938	307.954
32	1.8845	44.227	611.35	0.5306	23.468	324.403
33	1.9222	46.112	655.58	0.5202	23.989	341.051
34	1.9607	48.034	701.69	0.5100	24.499	357.882
35	1.9999	49.994	749.72	0.5000	24.999	374.883
40	2.2080	60.402	1020.10	0.4529	27.355	461.993
45	2.4379	71.893	1344.64	0.4102	29.490	551.565
50	2.6916	84.579	1728.97	0.3715	31.424	642.361
55	2.9717	98.587	2179.33	0.3365	33.175	733.353
60	3.2810	114.052	2702.58	0.3048	34.761	823.698
∞	∞	∞	∞	0.0000	50.000	2500.000

TABLE C-1   Values of 2% Compound Interest Factors (continued)

Number of periods n	Annuity factors		
	Present-amount A/P	Future-amount A/F	Gradient-series A/G
1	1.0200	1.0000	0.0000
2	0.5151	0.4951	0.4951
3	0.3468	0.3268	0.9868
4	0.2626	0.2426	1.4753
5	0.2122	0.1922	1.9604
6	0.1785	0.1585	2.4423
7	0.1545	0.1345	2.9208
8	0.1365	0.1165	3.3961
9	0.1225	0.1025	3.8681
10	0.1113	0.0913	4.3367
11	0.1022	0.0822	4.8021
12	0.0946	0.0746	5.2643
13	0.0881	0.0681	5.7231
14	0.0826	0.0626	6.1786
15	0.0778	0.0578	6.6309
16	0.0737	0.0537	7.0799
17	0.0700	0.0500	7.5256
18	0.0667	0.0467	7.9681
19	0.0638	0.0438	8.4073
20	0.0612	0.0412	8.8433
21	0.0588	0.0388	9.2760
22	0.0566	0.0366	9.7055
23	0.0547	0.0347	10.1317
24	0.0529	0.0329	10.5547
25	0.0512	0.0312	10.9745
26	0.0497	0.0297	11.3910
27	0.0483	0.0283	11.8043
28	0.0470	0.0270	12.2145
29	0.0458	0.0258	12.6214
30	0.0447	0.0247	13.0251
31	0.0436	0.0236	13.4257
32	0.0426	0.0226	13.8230
33	0.0417	0.0217	14.2172
34	0.0408	0.0208	14.6083
35	0.0400	0.0200	14.9961
40	0.0366	0.0166	16.8885
45	0.0339	0.0139	18.7034
50	0.0318	0.0118	20.4420
55	0.0302	0.0102	22.1057
60	0.0288	0.0088	23.6961
∞	0.0200	0.0000	50.0000

TABLE C-2   Values of 4% Compound Interest Factors

Number of periods n	Future worth factors			Present worth factors		
	Single-amount F/P	Uniform-series F/A	Gradient-series F/G	Single-amount P/F	Uniform-series P/A	Gradient-series P/G
1	1.0400	1.000	0.00	0.9615	0.962	0.000
2	1.0816	2.040	1.00	0.9246	1.886	0.925
3	1.1249	3.122	3.04	0.8890	2.775	2.703
4	1.1699	4.246	6.16	0.8548	3.630	5.267
5	1.2167	5.416	10.41	0.8219	4.452	8.555
6	1.2653	6.633	15.82	0.7903	5.242	12.506
7	1.3159	7.898	22.46	0.7599	6.002	17.066
8	1.3686	9.214	30.36	0.7307	6.733	22.181
9	1.4233	10.583	39.57	0.7026	7.435	27.801
10	1.4802	12.006	50.15	0.6756	8.111	33.881
11	1.5395	13.486	62.16	0.6496	8.760	40.377
12	1.6010	15.026	75.65	0.6246	9.385	47.248
13	1.6651	16.627	90.67	0.6006	9.986	54.455
14	1.7317	18.292	107.30	0.5775	10.563	61.962
15	1.8009	20.024	125.59	0.5553	11.118	69.735
16	1.8730	21.825	145.61	0.5339	11.652	77.744
17	1.9479	23.698	167.44	0.5134	12.166	85.958
18	2.0258	25.645	191.14	0.4936	12.659	94.350
19	2.1068	27.671	216.78	0.4746	13.134	102.893
20	2.1911	29.778	244.45	0.4564	13.590	111.565
21	2.2788	31.969	274.23	0.4388	14.029	120.341
22	2.3699	34.248	306.20	0.4220	14.451	129.202
23	2.4647	36.618	340.45	0.4057	14.857	138.128
24	2.5633	39.083	377.07	0.3901	15.247	147.101
25	2.6658	41.646	416.15	0.3751	15.622	156.104
26	2.7725	44.312	457.79	0.3607	15.983	165.121
27	2.8834	47.084	502.11	0.3468	16.330	174.138
28	2.9987	49.968	549.19	0.3335	16.663	183.142
29	3.1187	52.966	599.16	0.3207	16.984	192.121
30	3.2434	56.085	652.12	0.3083	17.292	201.062
31	3.3731	59.328	708.21	0.2965	17.588	209.956
32	3.5081	62.701	767.54	0.2851	17.874	218.792
33	3.6484	66.210	830.24	0.2741	18.148	227.563
34	3.7943	69.858	896.45	0.2636	18.411	236.261
35	3.9461	73.652	966.31	0.2534	18.665	244.877
40	4.8010	95.026	1375.64	0.2083	19.793	286.530
45	5.8412	121.029	1900.73	0.1712	20.720	325.403
50	7.1067	152.667	2566.68	0.1407	21.482	361.164
55	8.6464	191.159	3403.98	0.1157	22.109	393.689
60	10.5196	237.991	4449.77	0.0951	22.623	422.997
∞	∞	∞	∞	0.0000	25.000	625.000

TABLE C-2   Values of 4% Compound Interest Factors (continued)

Number of periods n	Annuity factors		
	Present-amount A/P	Future-amount A/F	Gradient-series A/G
1	1.0400	1.0000	0.0000
2	0.5302	0.4902	0.4902
3	0.3604	0.3204	0.9739
4	0.2755	0.2355	1.4510
5	0.2246	0.1846	1.9216
6	0.1908	0.1508	2.3857
7	0.1666	0.1266	2.8433
8	0.1485	0.1085	3.2944
9	0.1345	0.0945	3.7391
10	0.1233	0.0833	4.1773
11	0.1142	0.0742	4.6090
12	0.1066	0.0666	5.0344
13	0.1002	0.0602	5.4533
14	0.0947	0.0547	5.8659
15	0.0900	0.0500	6.2721
16	0.0858	0.0458	6.6720
17	0.0822	0.0422	7.0656
18	0.0790	0.0390	7.4530
19	0.0761	0.0361	7.8342
20	0.0736	0.0336	8.2091
21	0.0713	0.0313	8.5780
22	0.0692	0.0292	8.9407
23	0.0673	0.0273	9.2973
24	0.0656	0.0256	9.6479
25	0.0640	0.0240	9.9925
26	0.0626	0.0226	10.3312
27	0.0612	0.0212	10.6640
28	0.0600	0.0200	10.9909
29	0.0589	0.0189	11.3121
30	0.0578	0.0178	11.6274
31	0.0569	0.0169	11.9371
32	0.0560	0.0160	12.2411
33	0.0551	0.0151	12.5396
34	0.0543	0.0143	12.8325
35	0.0536	0.0136	13.1199
40	0.0505	0.0105	14.4765
45	0.0483	0.0083	15.7047
50	0.0466	0.0066	16.8123
55	0.0452	0.0052	17.8070
60	0.0442	0.0042	18.6972
∞	0.0400	0.0000	25.0000

TABLE C-3   Values of 6% Compound Interest Factors

Number of periods n	Future worth factors			Present worth factors		
	Single-amount F/P	Uniform-series F/A	Gradient-series F/G	Single-amount P/F	Uniform-series P/A	Gradient-series P/G
1	1.0600	1.000	0.00	0.9434	0.943	0.000
2	1.1236	2.060	1.00	0.8900	1.833	0.890
3	1.1910	3.184	3.06	0.8396	2.673	2.569
4	1.2625	4.375	6.24	0.7921	3.465	4.946
5	1.3382	5.637	10.62	0.7473	4.212	7.935
6	1.4185	6.975	16.26	0.7050	4.917	11.459
7	1.5036	8.394	23.23	0.6651	5.582	15.450
8	1.5938	9.897	31.62	0.6274	6.210	19.842
9	1.6895	11.491	41.52	0.5919	6.802	24.577
10	1.7908	13.181	53.01	0.5584	7.360	29.602
11	1.8983	14.972	66.19	0.5268	7.887	34.870
12	2.0122	16.870	81.17	0.4970	8.384	40.337
13	2.1329	18.882	98.04	0.4688	8.853	45.963
14	2.2609	21.015	116.92	0.4423	9.295	51.713
15	2.3966	23.276	137.93	0.4173	9.712	57.555
16	2.5404	25.673	161.21	0.3936	10.106	63.459
17	2.6928	28.213	186.88	0.3714	10.477	69.401
18	2.8543	30.906	215.09	0.3503	10.828	75.357
19	3.0256	33.760	246.00	0.3305	11.158	81.306
20	3.2071	36.786	279.76	0.3118	11.470	87.230
21	3.3996	39.993	316.55	0.2942	11.764	93.114
22	3.6035	43.392	356.54	0.2775	12.042	98.941
23	3.8197	46.996	399.93	0.2618	12.303	104.701
24	4.0489	50.816	446.93	0.2470	12.550	110.381
25	4.2919	54.865	497.74	0.2330	12.783	115.973
26	4.5494	59.156	552.61	0.2198	13.003	121.468
27	4.8223	63.706	611.76	0.2074	13.211	126.860
28	5.1117	68.528	675.47	0.1956	13.406	132.142
29	5.4184	73.640	744.00	0.1846	13.591	137.310
30	5.7435	79.058	817.64	0.1741	13.765	142.359
31	6.0881	84.802	896.69	0.1643	13.929	147.286
32	6.4534	90.890	981.50	0.1550	14.084	152.090
33	6.8406	97.343	1072.39	0.1462	14.230	156.768
34	7.2510	104.184	1169.73	0.1379	14.368	161.319
35	7.6861	111.435	1273.91	0.1301	14.498	165.743
40	10.2857	154.762	1912.70	0.0972	15.046	185.957
45	13.7646	212.744	2795.73	0.0727	15.456	203.110
50	18.4202	290.336	4005.60	0.0543	15.762	217.457
55	24.6503	394.172	5652.87	0.0406	15.991	229.322
60	32.9877	533.128	7885.47	0.0303	16.161	239.043
∞	∞	∞	∞	0.0000	16.667	277.778

TABLE C-3 Values of 6% Compound Interest Factors (continued)

Number of periods n	Annuity factors		
	Present-amount A/P	Future-amount A/F	Gradient-series A/G
1	1.0600	1.0000	0.0000
2	0.5454	0.4854	0.4854
3	0.3741	0.3141	0.9612
4	0.2886	0.2286	1.4272
5	0.2374	0.1774	1.8836
6	0.2034	0.1434	2.3304
7	0.1791	0.1191	2.7676
8	0.1610	0.1010	3.1952
9	0.1470	0.0870	3.6133
10	0.1359	0.0759	4.0220
11	0.1268	0.0668	4.4213
12	0.1193	0.0593	4.8113
13	0.1130	0.0530	5.1920
14	0.1076	0.0476	5.5635
15	0.1030	0.0430	5.9260
16	0.0990	0.0390	6.2794
17	0.0955	0.0355	6.6240
18	0.0924	0.0324	6.9597
19	0.0896	0.0296	7.2867
20	0.0872	0.0272	7.6052
21	0.0850	0.0250	7.9151
22	0.0831	0.0231	8.2166
23	0.0813	0.0213	8.5099
24	0.0797	0.0197	8.7951
25	0.0782	0.0182	9.0722
26	0.0769	0.0169	9.3415
27	0.0757	0.0157	9.6030
28	0.0746	0.0146	9.8568
29	0.0736	0.0136	10.1032
30	0.0727	0.0127	10.3422
31	0.0718	0.0118	10.5740
32	0.0710	0.0110	10.7988
33	0.0703	0.0103	11.0166
34	0.0696	0.0096	11.2276
35	0.0690	0.0090	11.4319
40	0.0665	0.0065	12.3590
45	0.0647	0.0047	13.1413
50	0.0635	0.0035	13.7964
55	0.0625	0.0025	14.3411
60	0.0619	0.0019	14.7910
∞	0.0600	0.0000	16.6667

TABLE C-4   Values of 8% Compound Interest Factors

Number of periods n	Future worth factors			Present worth factors		
	Single-amount F/P	Uniform-series F/A	Gradient-series F/G	Single-amount P/F	Uniform-series P/A	Gradient-series P/G
1	1.0800	1.000	0.00	0.9259	0.926	0.000
2	1.1664	2.080	1.00	0.8573	1.783	0.857
3	1.2597	3.246	3.08	0.7938	2.577	2.445
4	1.3605	4.506	6.33	0.7350	3.312	4.650
5	1.4693	5.867	10.83	0.6806	3.993	7.372
6	1.5869	7.336	16.70	0.6302	4.623	10.523
7	1.7138	8.923	24.04	0.5835	5.206	14.024
8	1.8509	10.637	32.96	0.5403	5.747	17.806
9	1.9990	12.488	43.59	0.5002	6.247	21.808
10	2.1589	14.487	56.08	0.4632	6.710	25.977
11	2.3316	16.645	70.57	0.4289	7.139	30.266
12	2.5182	18.977	87.21	0.3971	7.536	34.634
13	2.7196	21.495	106.19	0.3677	7.904	39.046
14	2.9372	24.215	127.69	0.3405	8.244	43.472
15	3.1722	27.152	151.90	0.3152	8.559	47.886
16	3.4259	30.324	179.05	0.2919	8.851	52.264
17	3.7000	33.750	209.38	0.2703	9.122	56.588
18	3.9960	37.450	243.13	0.2502	9.372	60.843
19	4.3157	41.446	280.58	0.2317	9.604	65.013
20	4.6610	45.762	322.02	0.2145	9.818	69.090
21	5.0338	50.423	367.79	0.1987	10.017	73.063
22	5.4365	55.457	418.21	0.1839	10.201	76.926
23	5.8715	60.893	473.67	0.1703	10.371	80.673
24	6.3412	66.765	534.56	0.1577	10.529	84.300
25	6.8485	73.106	601.32	0.1460	10.675	87.804
26	7.3964	79.954	674.43	0.1352	10.810	91.184
27	7.9881	87.351	754.38	0.1252	10.935	94.439
28	8.6271	95.339	841.74	0.1159	11.051	97.569
29	9.3173	103.966	937.07	0.1073	11.158	100.574
30	10.0627	113.283	1041.04	0.0994	11.258	103.456
31	10.8677	123.346	1154.32	0.0920	11.350	106.216
32	11.7371	134.214	1277.67	0.0852	11.435	108.857
33	12.6760	145.951	1411.88	0.0789	11.514	111.382
34	13.6901	158.627	1557.83	0.0730	11.587	113.792
35	14.7853	172.317	1716.46	0.0676	11.655	116.092
40	21.7245	259.057	2738.21	0.0460	11.925	126.042
45	31.9204	386.506	4268.82	0.0313	12.108	133.733
50	46.9016	573.770	6547.13	0.0213	12.233	139.593
55	68.9139	848.923	9924.04	0.0145	12.319	144.006
60	101.2571	1253.213	14915.17	0.0099	12.377	147.300
∞	∞	∞	∞	0.0000	12.500	156.250

TABLE C-4   Values of 8% Compound Interest Factors (continued)

Numbers of periods n	Annuity factors		
	Present-amount A/P	Future-amount A/F	Gradient-series A/G
1	1.0800	1.0000	0.0000
2	0.5608	0.4808	0.4808
3	0.3880	0.3080	0.9488
4	0.3019	0.2219	1.4040
5	0.2505	0.1705	1.8465
6	0.2163	0.1363	2.2764
7	0.1921	0.1121	2.6937
8	0.1740	0.0940	3.0985
9	0.1601	0.0801	3.4910
10	0.1490	0.0690	3.8713
11	0.1401	0.0601	4.2395
12	0.1327	0.0527	4.5958
13	0.1265	0.0465	4.9402
14	0.1213	0.0413	5.2731
15	0.1168	0.0368	5.5945
16	0.1130	0.0330	5.9046
17	0.1096	0.0296	6.2038
18	0.1067	0.0267	6.4920
19	0.1041	0.0241	6.7697
20	0.1019	0.0219	7.0370
21	0.0998	0.0198	7.2940
22	0.0980	0.0180	7.5412
23	0.0964	0.0164	7.7786
24	0.0950	0.0150	8.0066
25	0.0937	0.0137	8.2254
26	0.0925	0.0125	8.4352
27	0.0915	0.0115	8.6363
28	0.0905	0.0105	8.8289
29	0.0896	0.0096	9.0133
30	0.0888	0.0088	9.1897
31	0.0881	0.0081	9.3584
32	0.0875	0.0075	9.5197
33	0.0869	0.0069	9.6737
34	0.0863	0.0063	9.8208
35	0.0858	0.0058	9.9611
40	0.0839	0.0039	10.5699
45	0.0826	0.0026	11.0447
50	0.0818	0.0018	11.4107
55	0.0812	0.0012	11.6902
60	0.0808	0.0008	11.9015
∞	0.0800	0.0000	12.5000

TABLE C-5   Values of 10% Compound Interest Factors

Number of periods n	Future worth factors			Present worth factors		
	Single-amount F/P	Uniform-series F/A	Gradient-series F/G	Single-amount P/F	Uniform-series P/A	Gradient-series P/G
1	1.1000	1.000	0.00	0.9091	0.909	0.000
2	1.2100	2.100	1.00	0.8264	1.736	0.826
3	1.3310	3.310	3.10	0.7513	2.487	2.329
4	1.4641	4.641	6.41	0.6830	3.170	4.378
5	1.6105	6.105	11.05	0.6209	3.791	6.862
6	1.7716	7.716	17.16	0.5645	4.355	9.684
7	1.9487	9.487	24.87	0.5132	4.868	12.763
8	2.1436	11.436	34.36	0.4665	5.335	16.029
9	2.3579	13.579	45.79	0.4241	5.759	19.421
10	2.5937	15.937	59.37	0.3855	6.144	22.891
11	2.8531	18.531	75.31	0.3505	6.495	26.396
12	3.1384	21.384	93.84	0.3186	6.814	29.901
13	3.4523	24.523	115.23	0.2897	7.103	33.377
14	3.7975	27.975	139.75	0.2633	7.367	36.800
15	4.1772	31.772	167.72	0.2394	7.606	40.152
16	4.5950	35.950	199.50	0.2176	7.824	43.416
17	5.0545	40.545	235.45	0.1978	8.022	46.582
18	5.5599	45.599	275.99	0.1799	8.201	49.640
19	6.1159	51.159	321.59	0.1635	8.365	52.583
20	6.7275	57.275	372.75	0.1486	8.514	55.407
21	7.4002	64.002	430.02	0.1351	8.649	58.110
22	8.1403	71.403	494.03	0.1228	8.772	60.689
23	8.9543	79.543	565.43	0.1117	8.883	63.146
24	9.8497	88.497	644.97	0.1015	8.985	65.481
25	10.8347	98.347	733.47	0.0923	9.077	67.696
26	11.9182	109.182	831.82	0.0839	9.161	69.794
27	13.1100	121.100	941.00	0.0763	9.237	71.777
28	14.4210	134.210	1062.10	0.0693	9.307	73.650
29	15.8631	148.631	1196.31	0.0630	9.370	75.415
30	17.4494	164.494	1344.94	0.0573	9.427	77.077
31	19.1943	181.943	1509.43	0.0521	9.479	78.640
32	21.1138	201.138	1691.38	0.0474	9.526	80.108
33	23.2252	222.252	1892.52	0.0431	9.569	81.486
34	25.5477	245.477	2114.77	0.0391	9.609	82.777
35	28.1024	271.024	2360.24	0.0356	9.644	83.987
40	45.2593	442.593	4025.93	0.0221	9.779	88.953
45	72.8905	718.905	6739.05	0.0137	9.863	92.454
50	117.3909	1163.909	11139.09	0.0085	9.915	94.889
55	189.0591	1880.591	18255.91	0.0053	9.947	96.562
60	304.4816	3034.816	29748.16	0.0033	9.967	97.701
∞	∞	∞	∞	0.0000	10.000	100.000

TABLE C-5   Values of 10% Compound Interest Factors (continued)

Number of periods n	Annuity factors		
	Present-amount A/P	Future-amount A/F	Gradient-series A/G
1	1.1000	1.0000	0.0000
2	0.5762	0.4762	0.4762
3	0.4021	0.3021	0.9366
4	0.3155	0.2155	1.3812
5	0.2638	0.1638	1.8101
6	0.2296	0.1296	2.2236
7	0.2054	0.1054	2.6216
8	0.1875	0.0875	3.0045
9	0.1737	0.0737	3.3724
10	0.1628	0.0628	3.7255
11	0.1540	0.0540	4.0641
12	0.1468	0.0468	4.3884
13	0.1408	0.0408	4.6988
14	0.1358	0.0358	4.9955
15	0.1315	0.0315	5.2789
16	0.1278	0.0278	5.5493
17	0.1247	0.0247	5.8071
18	0.1219	0.0219	6.0526
19	0.1196	0.0196	6.2861
20	0.1175	0.0175	6.5081
21	0.1156	0.0156	6.7189
22	0.1140	0.0140	6.9189
23	0.1126	0.0126	7.1085
24	0.1113	0.0113	7.2881
25	0.1102	0.0102	7.4580
26	0.1092	0.0092	7.6187
27	0.1083	0.0083	7.7704
28	0.1075	0.0075	7.9137
29	0.1067	0.0067	8.0489
30	0.1061	0.0061	8.1762
31	0.1055	0.0055	8.2962
32	0.1050	0.0050	8.4091
33	0.1045	0.0045	8.5152
34	0.1041	0.0041	8.6149
35	0.1037	0.0037	8.7086
40	0.1023	0.0023	9.0962
45	0.1014	0.0014	9.3741
50	0.1009	0.0009	9.5704
55	0.1005	0.0005	9.7075
60	0.1003	0.0003	9.8023
∞	0.1000	0.0000	10.0000

TABLE C-6   Values of 12% Compound Interest Factors

Number of periods n	Future worth factors			Present worth factors		
	Single-amount F/P	Uniform-series F/A	Gradient-series F/G	Single-amount P/F	Uniform-series P/A	Gradient-series P/G
1	1.1200	1.000	0.00	0.8929	0.893	0.000
2	1.2544	2.120	1.00	0.7972	1.690	0.797
3	1.4049	3.374	3.12	0.7118	2.402	2.221
4	1.5735	4.779	6.49	0.6355	3.037	4.127
5	1.7623	6.353	11.27	0.5674	3.605	6.397
6	1.9738	8.115	17.63	0.5066	4.111	8.930
7	2.2107	10.089	25.74	0.4523	4.564	11.644
8	2.4760	12.300	35.83	0.4039	4.968	14.471
9	2.7731	14.776	48.13	0.3606	5.328	17.356
10	3.1058	17.549	62.91	0.3220	5.650	20.254
11	3.4785	20.655	80.45	0.2875	5.938	23.129
12	3.8960	24.133	101.11	0.2567	6.194	25.952
13	4.3635	28.029	125.24	0.2292	6.424	28.702
14	4.8871	32.393	153.27	0.2046	6.628	31.362
15	5.4736	37.280	185.66	0.1827	6.811	33.920
16	6.1304	42.753	222.94	0.1631	6.974	36.367
17	6.8660	48.884	265.70	0.1456	7.120	38.697
18	7.6900	55.750	314.58	0.1300	7.250	40.908
19	8.6128	63.440	370.33	0.1161	7.366	42.998
20	9.6463	72.052	433.77	0.1037	7.469	44.968
21	10.8038	81.699	505.82	0.0926	7.562	46.819
22	12.1003	92.503	587.52	0.0826	7.645	48.554
23	13.5523	104.603	680.02	0.0738	7.718	50.178
24	15.1786	118.155	784.63	0.0659	7.784	51.693
25	17.0001	133.334	902.78	0.0588	7.843	53.105
26	19.0401	150.334	1036.12	0.0525	7.896	54.418
27	21.3249	169.374	1186.45	0.0469	7.943	55.637
28	23.8839	190.699	1355.82	0.0419	7.984	56.767
29	26.7499	214.583	1546.52	0.0374	8.022	57.814
30	29.9599	241.333	1761.11	0.0334	8.055	58.782
31	33.5551	271.292	2002.44	0.0298	8.085	59.676
32	37.5817	304.847	2273.73	0.0266	8.112	60.501
33	42.0915	342.429	2578.58	0.0238	8.135	61.261
34	47.1425	384.520	2921.01	0.0212	8.157	61.961
35	52.7996	431.663	3305.53	0.0189	8.176	62.605
40	93.0510	767.091	6059.10	0.0107	8.244	65.116
45	163.9876	1358.230	10943.58	0.0061	8.283	66.734
50	289.0022	2400.018	19583.49	0.0035	8.305	67.762
∞	∞	∞	∞	0.0000	8.333	69.444

TABLE C-6 Values of 12% Compound Interest Factors (continued)

Number of periods n	Annuity factors		
	Present-amount A/P	Future-amount A/F	Gradient-series A/G
1	1.1200	1.0000	0.0000
2	0.5917	0.4717	0.4717
3	0.4164	0.2964	0.9246
4	0.3292	0.2092	1.3589
5	0.2774	0.1574	1.7746
6	0.2432	0.1232	2.1721
7	0.2191	0.0991	2.5515
8	0.2013	0.0813	2.9132
9	0.1877	0.0677	3.2574
10	0.1770	0.0570	3.5847
11	0.1684	0.0484	3.8953
12	0.1614	0.0414	4.1897
13	0.1557	0.0357	4.4683
14	0.1509	0.0309	4.7317
15	0.1468	0.0268	4.9803
16	0.1434	0.0234	5.2147
17	0.1405	0.0205	5.4353
18	0.1379	0.0179	5.6427
19	0.1358	0.0158	5.8375
20	0.1339	0.0139	6.0202
21	0.1323	0.0123	6.1913
22	0.1308	0.0108	6.3514
23	0.1296	0.0096	6.5010
24	0.1285	0.0085	6.6407
25	0.1275	0.0075	6.7708
26	0.1267	0.0067	6.8921
27	0.1259	0.0059	7.0049
28	0.1253	0.0053	7.1098
29	0.1247	0.0047	7.2071
30	0.1242	0.0042	7.2974
31	0.1237	0.0037	7.3811
32	0.1233	0.0033	7.4586
33	0.1229	0.0029	7.5303
34	0.1226	0.0026	7.5965
35	0.1223	0.0023	7.6577
40	0.1213	0.0013	7.8988
45	0.1207	0.0007	8.0572
50	0.1204	0.0004	8.1597
∞	0.1200	0.0000	8.3333

TABLE C-7   Values of 15% Compound Interest Factors

Number of periods n	Future worth factors			Present worth factors		
	Single-amount F/P	Uniform-series F/A	Gradient-series F/G	Single-amount P/F	Uniform-series P/A	Gradient-series P/G
1	1.1500	1.000	0.00	0.8696	0.870	0.000
2	1.3225	2.150	1.00	0.7561	1.626	0.756
3	1.5209	3.472	3.15	0.6575	2.283	2.071
4	1.7490	4.993	6.62	0.5718	2.855	3.786
5	2.0114	6.742	11.62	0.4972	3.352	5.775
6	2.3131	8.754	18.36	0.4323	3.784	7.937
7	2.6600	11.067	27.11	0.3759	4.160	10.192
8	3.0590	13.727	38.18	0.3269	4.487	12.481
9	3.5179	16.786	51.91	0.2843	4.772	14.755
10	4.0456	20.304	68.69	0.2472	5.019	16.979
11	4.6524	24.349	89.00	0.2149	5.234	19.129
12	5.3503	29.002	113.34	0.1869	5.421	21.185
13	6.1528	34.352	142.35	0.1625	5.583	23.135
14	7.0757	40.505	176.70	0.1413	5.724	24.972
15	8.1371	47.580	217.20	0.1229	5.847	26.693
16	9.3576	55.717	264.78	0.1069	5.954	28.296
17	10.7613	65.075	320.50	0.0929	6.047	29.783
18	12.3755	75.836	385.58	0.0808	6.128	31.156
19	14.2318	88.212	461.41	0.0703	6.198	32.421
20	16.3665	102.444	549.62	0.0611	6.259	33.582
21	18.8215	118.810	652.07	0.0531	6.312	34.645
22	21.6447	137.632	770.88	0.0462	6.359	35.615
23	24.8915	159.276	908.51	0.0402	6.399	36.499
24	28.6252	184.168	1067.79	0.0349	6.434	37.302
25	32.9190	212.793	1251.95	0.0304	6.464	38.031
26	37.8568	245.712	1464.75	0.0264	6.491	38.692
27	43.5353	283.569	1710.46	0.0230	6.514	39.289
28	50.0656	327.104	1994.03	0.0200	6.534	39.828
29	57.5755	377.170	2321.13	0.0174	6.551	40.315
30	66.2118	434.745	2698.30	0.0151	6.566	40.753
31	76.1435	500.957	3133.05	0.0131	6.579	41.147
32	87.5651	577.100	3634.00	0.0114	6.591	41.501
33	100.6998	664.666	4211.10	0.0099	6.600	41.818
34	115.8048	765.365	4875.77	0.0086	6.609	42.103
35	133.1755	881.170	5641.13	0.0075	6.617	42.359
40	267.8635	1779.090	11593.94	0.0037	6.642	43.283
45	538.7693	3585.128	23600.86	0.0019	6.654	43.805
50	1083.6574	7217.716	47784.78	0.0009	6.661	44.096
∞	∞	∞	∞	0.0000	6.667	44.444

TABLE C-7 Values of 15% Compound Interest Factors (continued)

Number of periods n	Annuity factors		
	Present-amount A/P	Future-amount A/F	Gradient-series A/G
1	1.1500	1.0000	0.0000
2	0.6151	0.4651	0.4651
3	0.4380	0.2880	0.9071
4	0.3503	0.2003	1.3263
5	0.2983	0.1483	1.7228
6	0.2642	0.1142	2.0972
7	0.2404	0.0904	2.4499
8	0.2229	0.0729	2.7813
9	0.2096	0.0596	3.0922
10	0.1993	0.0493	3.3832
11	0.1911	0.0411	3.6550
12	0.1845	0.0345	3.9082
13	0.1791	0.0291	4.1438
14	0.1747	0.0247	4.3624
15	0.1710	0.0210	4.5650
16	0.1680	0.0180	4.7523
17	0.1654	0.0154	4.9251
18	0.1632	0.0132	5.0843
19	0.1613	0.0113	5.2307
20	0.1598	0.0098	5.3651
21	0.1584	0.0084	5.4883
22	0.1573	0.0073	5.6010
23	0.1563	0.0063	5.7040
24	0.1554	0.0054	5.7979
25	0.1547	0.0047	5.8834
26	0.1541	0.0041	5.9612
27	0.1535	0.0035	6.0319
28	0.1531	0.0031	6.0960
29	0.1527	0.0027	6.1541
30	0.1523	0.0023	6.2066
31	0.1520	0.0020	6.2541
32	0.1517	0.0017	6.2970
33	0.1515	0.0015	6.3357
34	0.1513	0.0013	6.3705
35	0.1511	0.0011	6.4019
40	0.1506	0.0006	6.5168
45	0.1503	0.0003	6.5830
50	0.1501	0.0001	6.6205
∞	0.1500	0.0000	6.6667

TABLE C-8 Values of 20% Compound Interest Factors

Number of periods n	Future worth factors			Present worth factors		
	Single-amount F/P	Uniform-series F/A	Gradient-series F/G	Single-amount P/F	Uniform-series P/A	Gradient-series P/G
1	1.2000	1.000	0.00	0.8333	0.833	0.000
2	1.4400	2.200	1.00	0.6944	1.528	0.694
3	1.7280	3.640	3.20	0.5787	2.106	1.852
4	2.0736	5.368	6.84	0.4823	2.589	3.299
5	2.4883	7.442	12.21	0.4019	2.991	4.906
6	2.9860	9.930	19.65	0.3349	3.326	6.581
7	3.5832	12.916	29.58	0.2791	3.605	8.255
8	4.2998	16.499	42.50	0.2326	3.837	9.883
9	5.1598	20.799	58.99	0.1938	4.031	11.434
10	6.1917	25.959	79.79	0.1615	4.192	12.887
11	7.4301	32.150	105.75	0.1346	4.327	14.233
12	8.9161	39.581	137.90	0.1122	4.439	15.467
13	10.6993	48.497	177.48	0.0935	4.533	16.588
14	12.8392	59.196	225.98	0.0779	4.611	17.601
15	15.4070	72.035	285.18	0.0649	4.675	18.509
16	18.4884	87.442	357.21	0.0541	4.730	19.321
17	22.1861	105.931	444.65	0.0451	4.775	20.042
18	26.6233	128.117	550.58	0.0376	4.812	20.680
19	31.9480	154.740	678.70	0.0313	4.844	21.244
20	38.3376	186.688	833.44	0.0261	4.870	21.739
21	46.0051	225.026	1020.13	0.0217	4.891	22.174
22	55.2061	271.031	1245.15	0.0181	4.909	22.555
23	66.2474	326.237	1516.18	0.0151	4.925	22.887
24	79.4968	392.484	1842.42	0.0126	4.937	23.176
25	95.3962	471.981	2234.91	0.0105	4.948	23.428
26	114.4755	567.377	2706.89	0.0087	4.956	23.646
27	137.3706	681.853	3274.26	0.0073	4.964	23.835
28	164.8447	819.223	3956.12	0.0061	4.970	23.999
29	197.8136	984.068	4775.34	0.0051	4.975	24.141
30	237.3763	1181.882	5759.41	0.0042	4.979	24.263
∞	∞	∞	∞	0.0000	5.000	25.000

TABLE C-8 Values of 20% Compound Interest Factors (continued)

Number of periods n	Annuity factors		
	Present-amount A/P	Future amount A/F	Gradient-series A/G
1	1.2000	1.0000	0.0000
2	0.6546	0.4546	0.4546
3	0.4747	0.2747	0.8791
4	0.3863	0.1863	1.2742
5	0.3344	0.1344	1.6405
6	0.3007	0.1007	1.9788
7	0.2774	0.0774	2.2902
8	0.2606	0.0606	2.5756
9	0.2481	0.0481	2.8364
10	0.2385	0.0385	3.0739
11	0.2311	0.0311	3.2893
12	0.2253	0.0253	3.4841
13	0.2206	0.0206	3.6597
14	0.2169	0.0169	3.8175
15	0.2139	0.0139	3.9589
16	0.2114	0.0114	4.0851
17	0.2095	0.0095	4.1976
18	0.2078	0.0078	4.2975
19	0.2065	0.0065	4.3861
20	0.2054	0.0054	4.4644
21	0.2045	0.0045	4.5334
22	0.2037	0.0037	4.5942
23	0.2031	0.0031	4.6475
24	0.2026	0.0026	4.6943
25	0.2021	0.0021	4.7352
26	0.2018	0.0018	4.7709
27	0.2015	0.0015	4.8020
28	0.2012	0.0012	4.8291
29	0.2010	0.0010	4.8527
30	0.2009	0.0009	4.8731
∞	0.2000	0.0000	5.0000

TABLE C-9 Values of 25% Compound Interest Factors

Number of periods n	Future worth factors			Present worth factors		
	Single-amount F/P	Uniform-series F/A	Gradient-series F/G	Single-amount P/F	Uniform-series P/A	Gradient-series P/G
1	1.2500	1.000	0.00	0.8000	0.800	0.000
2	1.5625	2.250	1.00	0.6400	1.440	0.640
3	1.9531	3.813	3.25	0.5120	1.952	1.664
4	2.4414	5.766	7.06	0.4096	2.362	2.893
5	3.0518	8.207	12.83	0.3277	2.689	4.204
6	3.8147	11.259	21.04	0.2621	2.951	5.514
7	4.7684	15.073	32.29	0.2097	3.161	6.773
8	5.9605	19.842	47.37	0.1678	3.329	7.947
9	7.4506	25.802	67.21	0.1342	3.463	9.021
10	9.3132	33.253	93.01	0.1074	3.571	9.987
11	11.6415	42.566	126.26	0.0859	3.656	10.846
12	14.5519	54.208	168.83	0.0687	3.725	11.602
13	18.1899	68.760	223.04	0.0550	3.780	12.262
14	22.7374	86.949	291.80	0.0440	3.824	12.833
15	28.4217	109.687	378.75	0.0352	3.859	13.326
16	35.5271	138.109	488.43	0.0281	3.887	13.748
17	44.4089	173.636	626.54	0.0225	3.910	14.108
18	55.5112	218.045	800.18	0.0180	3.928	14.415
19	69.3889	273.556	1018.22	0.0144	3.942	14.674
20	86.7362	342.945	1291.78	0.0115	3.954	14.893
21	108.4202	429.681	1634.72	0.0092	3.963	15.078
22	135.5253	538.101	2064.40	0.0074	3.970	15.233
23	169.4066	673.626	2602.51	0.0059	3.976	15.362
24	211.7582	843.033	3276.13	0.0047	3.981	15.471
25	264.6978	1054.791	4119.16	0.0038	3.985	15.562
26	330.8722	1319.489	5173.96	0.0030	3.988	15.637
27	413.5903	1650.361	6493.44	0.0024	3.990	15.700
28	516.9879	2063.952	8143.81	0.0019	3.992	15.752
29	646.2349	2580.939	10207.76	0.0015	3.994	15.796
30	807.7936	3227.174	12788.70	0.0012	3.995	15.832
∞	∞	∞	∞	0.0000	4.000	16.000

TABLE C-9   Values of 25% Compound Interest Factors (continued)

Number of periods n	Annuity factors		
	Present-amount A/P	Future-amount A/F	Gradient-series A/G
1	1.2500	1.0000	0.0000
2	0.6945	0.4445	0.4445
3	0.5123	0.2623	0.8525
4	0.4235	0.1735	1.2249
5	0.3719	0.1219	1.5631
6	0.3388	0.0888	1.8683
7	0.3164	0.0664	2.1424
8	0.3004	0.0504	2.3873
9	0.2888	0.0388	2.6048
10	0.2801	0.0301	2.7971
11	0.2735	0.0235	2.9663
12	0.2685	0.0185	3.1145
13	0.2646	0.0146	3.2438
14	0.2615	0.0115	3.3560
15	0.2591	0.0091	3.4530
16	0.2573	0.0073	3.5366
17	0.2558	0.0058	3.6084
18	0.2546	0.0046	3.6698
19	0.2537	0.0037	3.7222
20	0.2529	0.0029	3.7667
21	0.2523	0.0023	3.8045
22	0.2519	0.0019	3.8365
23	0.2515	0.0015	3.8634
24	0.2512	0.0012	3.8861
25	0.2510	0.0010	3.9052
26	0.2508	0.0008	3.9212
27	0.2506	0.0006	3.9346
28	0.2505	0.0005	3.9457
29	0.2504	0.0004	3.9551
30	0.2503	0.0003	3.9628
∞	0.2500	0.0000	4.0000

TABLE C-10   Values of 30% Compound Interest Factors

Number of periods n	Future worth factors			Present worth factors		
	Single-amount F/P	Uniform-series F/A	Gradient-series F/G	Single-amount P/F	Uniform-series P/A	Gradient-series P/G
1	1.3000	1.000	0.00	0.7692	0.769	0.000
2	1.6900	2.300	1.00	0.5917	1.361	0.592
3	2.1970	3.990	3.30	0.4552	1.816	1.502
4	2.8561	6.187	7.29	0.3501	2.166	2.552
5	3.7129	9.043	13.48	0.2693	2.436	3.630
6	4.8268	12.756	22.52	0.2072	2.643	4.666
7	6.2749	17.583	35.28	0.1594	2.802	5.622
8	8.1573	23.858	52.86	0.1226	2.925	6.480
9	10.6045	32.015	76.72	0.0943	3.019	7.234
10	13.7858	42.619	108.73	0.0725	3.092	7.887
11	17.9216	56.405	151.35	0.0558	3.147	8.445
12	23.2981	74.327	207.76	0.0429	3.190	8.917
13	30.2875	97.625	282.08	0.0330	3.223	9.314
14	39.3738	127.913	379.71	0.0254	3.249	9.644
15	51.1859	167.286	507.62	0.0195	3.268	9.917
16	66.5417	218.472	674.91	0.0150	3.283	10.143
17	86.5042	285.014	893.38	0.0116	3.295	10.328
18	112.4554	371.518	1178.39	0.0089	3.304	10.479
19	146.1920	483.973	1549.91	0.0068	3.311	10.602
20	190.0496	630.165	2033.88	0.0053	3.316	10.702
21	247.0645	820.215	2664.05	0.0040	3.320	10.783
22	321.1839	1067.280	3484.27	0.0031	3.323	10.848
23	417.5391	1388.464	4551.55	0.0024	3.325	10.901
24	542.8008	1806.003	5940.01	0.0018	3.327	10.943
25	705.6410	2348.803	7746.01	0.0014	3.329	10.977
26	917.3333	3054.444	10094.81	0.0011	3.330	11.005
27	1192.5333	3971.778	13149.26	0.0008	3.331	11.026
28	1550.2933	5164.311	17121.04	0.0006	3.331	11.044
29	2015.3813	6714.604	22285.35	0.0005	3.332	11.058
30	2619.9956	8729.985	28999.95	0.0004	3.332	11.069
∞	∞	∞	∞	0.0000	3.333	11.111

TABLE C-10 Values of 30% Compound Interest Factors (continued)

Number of periods *n*	Annuity factors		
	Present-amount A/P	Future-amount A/F	Gradient-series A/G
1	1.3000	1.0000	0.0000
2	0.7348	0.4348	0.4348
3	0.5506	0.2506	0.8271
4	0.4616	0.1616	1.1783
5	0.4106	0.1106	1.4903
6	0.3784	0.0784	1.7655
7	0.3569	0.0569	2.0063
8	0.3419	0.0419	2.2156
9	0.3312	0.0312	2.3963
10	0.3235	0.0235	2.5512
11	0.3177	0.0177	2.6833
12	0.3135	0.0135	2.7952
13	0.3103	0.0103	2.8895
14	0.3078	0.0078	2.9685
15	0.3060	0.0060	3.0345
16	0.3046	0.0046	3.0892
17	0.3035	0.0035	3.1345
18	0.3027	0.0027	3.1718
19	0.3021	0.0021	3.2025
20	0.3016	0.0016	3.2276
21	0.3012	0.0012	3.2480
22	0.3009	0.0009	3.2646
23	0.3007	0.0007	3.2781
24	0.3006	0.0006	3.2890
25	0.3004	0.0004	3.2979
26	0.3003	0.0003	3.3050
27	0.3003	0.0003	3.3107
28	0.3002	0.0002	3.3153
29	0.3002	0.0002	3.3189
30	0.3001	0.0001	3.3219
∞	0.3000	0.0000	3.3333

TABLE C-11 Values of 40% Compound Interest Factors

Number of periods n	Future worth factors			Present worth factors		
	Single-amount F/P	Uniform-series F/A	Gradient-series F/G	Single-amount P/F	Uniform-series P/A	Gradient-series P/G
1	1.4000	1.000	0.00	0.7143	0.714	0.000
2	1.9600	2.400	1.00	0.5102	1.224	0.510
3	2.7440	4.360	3.40	0.3644	1.589	1.239
4	3.8416	7.104	7.76	0.2603	1.849	2.020
5	5.3782	10.946	14.86	0.1859	2.035	2.764
6	7.5295	16.324	25.81	0.1328	2.168	3.428
7	10.5414	23.853	42.13	0.0949	2.263	3.997
8	14.7579	34.395	65.99	0.0678	2.331	4.471
9	20.6610	49.153	100.38	0.0484	2.379	4.858
10	28.9255	69.814	149.53	0.0346	2.414	5.170
11	40.4957	98.739	219.35	0.0247	2.438	5.417
12	56.6939	139.235	318.09	0.0176	2.456	5.611
13	79.3715	195.929	457.32	0.0126	2.469	5.762
14	111.1201	275.300	653.25	0.0090	2.478	5.879
15	155.5681	386.420	928.55	0.0064	2.484	5.969
16	217.7953	541.988	1314.97	0.0046	2.489	6.038
17	304.9135	759.784	1856.96	0.0033	2.492	6.090
18	426.8789	1064.697	2616.74	0.0023	2.494	6.130
19	597.6304	1491.576	3681.44	0.0017	2.496	6.160
20	836.6826	2089.206	5173.02	0.0012	2.497	6.183
∞	∞	∞	∞	0.0000	2.500	6.250

TABLE C-11   Values of 40% Compound Interest Factors (continued)

Number of periods n	Annuity factors		
	Present-amount A/P	Future-amount A/F	Gradient-series A/G
1	1.4000	1.0000	0.0000
2	0.8167	0.4167	0.4167
3	0.6294	0.2294	0.7798
4	0.5408	0.1408	1.0924
5	0.4914	0.0914	1.3580
6	0.4613	0.0613	1.5811
7	0.4419	0.0419	1.7664
8	0.4291	0.0291	1.9185
9	0.4204	0.0204	2.0423
10	0.4143	0.0143	2.1419
11	0.4101	0.0101	2.2215
12	0.4072	0.0072	2.2845
13	0.4051	0.0051	2.3341
14	0.4036	0.0036	2.3729
15	0.4026	0.0026	2.4030
16	0.4019	0.0019	2.4262
17	0.4013	0.0013	2.4441
18	0.4009	0.0009	2.4577
19	0.4007	0.0007	2.4682
20	0.4005	0.0005	2.4761
∞	0.4000	0.0000	2.5000

TABLE C-12   Values of 50% Compound Interest Factors

Number of periods n	Future worth factors			Present worth factors		
	Single-amount F/P	Uniform-series F/A	Gradient-series F/G	Single-amount P/F	Uniform-series P/A	Gradient-series P/G
1	1.5000	1.000	0.00	0.6667	0.667	0.000
2	2.2500	2.500	1.00	0.4444	1.111	0.444
3	3.3750	4.750	3.50	0.2963	1.407	1.037
4	5.0625	8.125	8.25	0.1975	1.605	1.630
5	7.5938	13.188	16.38	0.1317	1.737	2.156
6	11.3906	20.781	29.56	0.0878	1.824	2.595
7	17.0859	32.172	50.34	0.0585	1.883	2.947
8	25.6289	49.258	82.52	0.0390	1.922	3.220
9	38.4434	74.887	131.77	0.0260	1.948	3.428
10	57.6650	113.330	206.66	0.0173	1.965	3.584
11	86.4976	170.995	319.99	0.0116	1.977	3.699
12	129.7463	257.493	490.99	0.0077	1.985	3.784
13	194.6195	387.239	748.48	0.0051	1.990	3.846
14	291.9293	581.859	1135.72	0.0034	1.993	3.890
15	437.8939	873.788	1717.58	0.0023	1.995	3.922
16	656.8408	1311.682	2591.36	0.0015	1.997	3.945
17	985.2613	1968.523	3903.05	0.0010	1.998	3.961
18	1477.8919	2953.784	5871.57	0.0007	1.999	3.973
19	2216.8378	4431.676	8825.35	0.0005	1.999	3.981
20	3325.2567	6648.513	13257.03	0.0003	1.999	3.987
∞	∞	∞	∞	0.0000	2.000	4.000

TABLE C-12   Values of 50% Compound Interest Factors (continued)

Number of periods n	Annuity factors		
	Present-amount A/P	Future-amount A/F	Gradient-series A/G
1	1.5000	1.0000	0.0000
2	0.9000	0.4000	0.4000
3	0.7105	0.2105	0.7369
4	0.6231	0.1231	1.0154
5	0.5758	0.0758	1.2417
6	0.5481	0.0481	1.4226
7	0.5311	0.0311	1.5648
8	0.5203	0.0203	1.6752
9	0.5134	0.0134	1.7596
10	0.5088	0.0088	1.8235
11	0.5059	0.0059	1.8714
12	0.5039	0.0039	1.9068
13	0.5026	0.0026	1.9329
14	0.5017	0.0017	1.9519
15	0.5012	0.0012	1.9657
16	0.5008	0.0008	1.9756
17	0.5005	0.0005	1.9827
18	0.5003	0.0003	1.9878
19	0.5002	0.0002	1.9914
20	0.5002	0.0002	1.9940
∞	0.5000	0.0000	2.0000

Bibliography

American Telephone and Telegraph Company, *Engineering Economics*, 2d ed., New York, 1963.

Barish, N. N., *Economic Analysis for Engineering and Managerial Decision-Making*, McGraw-Hill Book Company, New York, 1962.

Bierman, H. and S. Smidt, *The Capital Budgeting Decision*, 4th ed., The Macmillan Company, New York, 1975.

Bracken, J. and C. J. Christenson, *Tables for Use in Analyzing Business Decisions*, Richard D. Irwin, Inc., Homewood, Ill., 1965.

Canada, J. R., *Intermediate Economic Analysis for Management and Engineering*, Prentice-Hall, Inc., Englewood Cliffs, N.J., 1971.

Dean, J., *Capital Budgeting*, Columbia University Press, New York, 1951.

—— *Managerial Economics*, Prentice-Hall, Inc., Englewood Cliffs, N.J., 1951.

De Garmo, E. P. and J. R. Canada, *Engineering Economy*, 5th ed., The Macmillan Company, New York, 1973.

English, J. M., *Cost Effectiveness*, John Wiley & Sons, Inc., New York, 1968.

Fabrycky, W. J. and G. J. Thuesen, *Economic Decision Analysis*, Prentice-Hall, Inc., Englewood Cliffs, N.J., 1974.

Fleischer, G. A., *Capital Allocation Theory*, Appleton-Century-Crofts, Inc., New York, 1969.

Gillis, F. E., *Managerial Economics: Decision Making Under Certainty for Business and Engineering*, Addison-Wesley Publishing Company, Reading, Mass., 1969.

Grant, E. L. and W. G. Ireson, *Principles of Engineering Economy*, 6th ed., The Ronald Press Company, New York, 1976.

Jeynes, P. H., *Profitability and Economic Choice*, The Iowa State University Press, Ames, Iowa, 1968.

Mao, J. C. T., *Quantitative Analysis of Financial Decisions*, W. W. Norton & Company, Inc., New York, 1966.

Morris, W. T., *Engineering Economic Analysis*, Reston Publishing Company, Inc., Reston, Virginia, 1976.

Newman, D. G., *Engineering Economic Analysis*, Engineering Press, San Jose, Cal., 1976.

Oakford, R. V., *Capital Budgeting*, The Ronald Press Company, New York, 1970.

Quirin, G. D., *The Capital Expenditure Decision*, Richard D. Irwin, Inc., Homewood, Ill., 1967.

Reisman, A., *Managerial and Engineering Economics*, Allyn and Bacon, Inc., Boston, 1971.

Riggs, J. L., *Economic Decision Models for Engineers and Managers*, McGraw-Hill Book Company, New York, 1968.

Rosenthal, S. A., *Engineering Economics and Practice*, The Macmillan Company, New York, 1964.

Schweyer, H. E., *Analytical Models for Managerial and Engineering Economics*, Reinhold Publishing Corporation, New York, 1964.

Smith, G. W., *Engineering Economy: Analysis of Capital Expenditures*, 2d ed., The Iowa State University Press, Ames, Iowa, 1973.

Spencer, M. H., *Managerial Economics*, 3d ed., Richard D. Irwin, Inc., Homewood, Ill., 1968.

Stermole, F. J., *Economic Evaluation and Investment Decision Methods*, Investment Evaluations Corporation, Golden, Colorado, 1977.

Stokes, C. J., *Managerial Economics*, Random House, New York, 1969.

Tarquin, A. J. and L. Blank, *Engineering Economy: A Behavioral Approach*, McGraw-Hill Book Company, New York, 1976.

Taylor, G. A., *Managerial and Engineering Economy*, D. van Nostrand Company, Princeton, N.J., 1964.

Terborgh, G., *Business Investment Management*, Machinery and Allied Products Institute, Washington, D.C., 1967.

Thuesen, H. G., W. J. Fabrycky, and G. J. Thuesen, *Engineering Economy*, 4th ed., Prentice-Hall, Inc., Englewood Cliffs, N.J., 1971.

Vandell, R. F. and R. F. Vancil, *Cases in Capital Budgeting*, Richard D. Irwin, Inc., Homewood, Ill., 1962.

Index

Action forks, in decision trees, 411
Addition rule, 379-380
After-tax analyses:
  assumption regarding future replacements in, 267
  determination of tax differences in, 278-282, 293-296
  determination of total taxes in, 261-264, 290-292
  and gains and losses on disposal, 283-287, 345-346
  introductory example of, 261-268
  and investment tax credits, 282-283, 340-341
  in multiple-alternative problems, 290-300, 329-338
  in replacement problems, 278-289, 338-348
  with revenue requirement method, 315-348
  (*See also* Revenue requirement method; Tax determination)
Annual cost method (*see* Uniform annual cost method)
Asset valuation, 168-169
Assets:
  current, 16
  fixed, 16
Average annual cost method (*see* Uniform annual cost method)
Average returns, 194-199, 215-216, 274

Book value:
  definition of, 25
  relevancy of, 35-36
Branches, in decision trees, 411
Break-even analysis:
  description of, 362-363
  evaluation of, 370

Break-even point:
  determination of, 363-369
  interpretation of, 363
Burden rates, 22

Capital costs:
  definition of, 16
  elements of, 16
Capital gains and losses, 283-286, 345-346
Capitalized cost, 167
Cash-flow descriptions:
  and debt repayment expenses, 269-270, 271
  and depreciation expenses, 268-269
  and equity repayment expenses, 269-270
  and interest expenses, 271
  and opportunity costs, 271
  and overhead expenses, 21-23
Cash-flow lines, 26
Chance-event forks, in decision trees, 411
Compound events, 384-387
Compound interest, 58-61
Compound interest factors:
  algebraic expressions for, 439
  derivations of, 425-434
  summary list of, 439
  symbols for, 439
  tables of values for, 440-463
  types of, 63-97
    future-amount annuity factor, 77-79
    gradient-series annuity factor, 94-97
    gradient-series future worth factor, 87-91
    gradient-series present worth factor, 91-94
    present-amount annuity factor, 82-87

Compound interest factors (*continued*):
single-amount future worth factor,
63-65
single-amount present worth factor,
70-72
uniform-series future worth factor,
72-77
uniform-series present worth factor,
79-82
Compounding, frequency of, 61-63
Computers, use of, 239
Constant dollars, estimating in, 392-394
Continuous compounding, 63, 111
Cost of money, 18-20
(*See also* Rate-of-return requirement)
Cost relevancy, 21-23, 125-126
Cumulative cash flows, reversals of sign
in, 242-244
Cumulative probabilities, 390-391
Current assets, 16
Current dollars, estimating in, 392-394

Debt financing, 18
Debt investment, return on, 273
Decision forks, in decision trees, 411
Decision trees:
an application of, 414-422
construction of, 410-416
decision-event chains in, 412-413
evaluation of, 422-423
and time value of money, 420
Declining-balance depreciation, 29-30
Deductible expenses, in tax determination, 23, 259
Dependent events, 380-381, 414-415
Depreciation expense, definition of, 17
Depreciation methods:
double-rate declining-balance, 29-30
straight-line, 24-25
sum-of-the-years-digits, 27-29
Derivations:
of future-amount annuity factor, 427-
430
of gradient-series annuity factor, 430-
434

Derivations (*continued*):
of gradient-series future worth factor,
430-434
of gradient-series present worth factor,
430-434
of present-amount annuity factor,
427-430
of revenue requirement tax factor,
434-438
of revenue requirement tax formula,
434-438
of single-amount future worth factor,
425-427
of single-amount present worth factor,
425-427
of uniform-series future worth factor,
427-430
of uniform-series present worth factor,
427-430
Devaluation expense, 16-17
Discounted cash flow method (*see* Rate
of return method)
Discounting, 420
Double-rate declining-balance depreciation, 29-30
Drucker, Peter F., 422

Economic life:
definition of, 31-32
determination of, 127-128
Economic profit, 123
Effective interest rate, 61-63, 68-70
Effective tax rate, 30, 259-260
Equal time-period requirement:
and assumed replacements, 120-123,
158-166
in discounted cash flow analyses, 188-
190, 212
and forecasted replacements, 118-120,
148-150, 217-220
in future worth analyses, 152
in present worth analyses, 142-143
in rate of return analyses, 188-190, 212
in uniform annual cost analyses, 118-
120

Equity financing, 18
Equity investment, return on (*see* Return
    on equity investment)
Equivalence, 59-61, 66-67
Exhaustive set of events, 380
Expected value, definition of, 381
External rate of return, 151, 234-238
Extra investment, return on (*see* Return
    on extra investment)

Fixed assets, 16
Forks, in decision trees, 411
Frequency of compounding, 61-63
Future-amount annuity factor:
    derivation of, 427-430
    description of, 77-79
    tables of values for, 440-463
Future worth method:
    description of, 150-154, 157-158
    evaluation of, 169-170, 244-245
    interpretation of results from, 151-
        153, 158
    an introductory application of, 150-153
    and multiple-alternative problems, 158
    and replacement problems, 157-158

Gain on disposal, 25, 283-287, 345-346
Gradient, definition of, 88
Gradient series, description of, 88-89
Gradient-series annuity factor:
    derivation of, 430-434
    description of, 94-97
    tables of values for, 440-463
Gradient-series future worth factor:
    derivation of, 430-434
    description of, 87-91
    tables of values for, 440-463
Gradient-series present worth factor:
    derivation of, 430-434
    description of, 91-94
    tables of values for, 440-463
Group accounts (*see* Multiple-asset
    accounts)

Income tax determination (*see* Tax deter-
    mination)
Incremental costs, 22-23
Incremental investment, return on (*see*
    Return on extra investment)
Independent events, 380
Inflation, and cash-flow estimates, 392-
    394
Intangible factors, 5, 123-125, 383, 387,
    391
Interest:
    compound, 58-61
    effective, 61-63, 68-70
    nominal, 61-63
    simple, 57-58
Interest expense, 18
    (*See also* Cost of money; Rate-of-
        return requirement)
Interest factors (*see* Compound interest
    factors)
Interest rate:
    effective, 61-63, 68-70
    nominal, 61-63
    (*See also* Cost of money; Rate-of-
        return requirement)
Internal rate of return, 234-239
Interpolation:
    in interest tables, 65-66
    in rate of return determination, 182,
        184-185
Investment required:
    in currently-owned assets, 32-36
    in new assets, 32
Investment tax credit, 282-283, 340-341
Irreducible factors, 5, 123-125, 383, 387,
    391
Item accounts, 25-26

Long-term gains and losses, 283-284,
    345-346
Loss on disposal, 25, 283-287, 345-346

Magee, John F., 409
Marginal costs, 22-23

Multiple-alternative problems:
  analysis of: with discounted cash flow
    method, 223-234
  with future worth method, 158
  with present worth method, 154-
    156, 158
  with rate of return method, 223-234
  with revenue requirement method,
    329-338
  with uniform annual cost method,
    130
  definition of, 130
  tax determination in, 290-300, 329-338
Multiple-asset accounts, 26
Multiple returns, in rate of return analyses, 240-244
Multiplication rule, 380
Mutually exclusive alternatives, definition of, 1
Mutually exclusive events, 379

No ascertainable return, in rate of return
  analyses, 243-244
Nodes, in decision trees, 411
Nominal interest rate, 61-63
Normal estimates, 388

Operating costs, estimation of, 21-23
Opportunity cost, 18-19
Optimistic estimates, 388
Ordinary gains and losses, 283-286, 345-
  346
Overhead rates, 22

Period-by-period comparisons, in rate
  of return determination, 186-190
Perpetual-service alternatives, analysis of:
  with present worth method, 166-167
  with uniform annual cost method,
    130-134
Pessimistic estimates, 388
Post-audit, 5-6

Present-amount annuity factor:
  derivation of, 427-430
  description of, 82-87
  tables of values for, 440-463
Present worth method:
  and capitalized costs, 167
  description of, 141-150, 154-167
  evaluation of, 169-170, 244-245
  interpretation of results from, 145-
    147, 156-157, 158
  an introductory application of, 141-
    150
  and multiple-alternative problems,
    154-156, 158
  and perpetual-service problems, 166-
    167
  and replacement problems, 154-166
Probability, fundamentals of, 378-381
Public utilities, determination of revenue requirements for, 327-328, 350

Ranking, of investment alternatives, 239,
  394-397
Rate of return, determination of:
  on debt investment, 273
  on equity investment, 271-275, 277
  on extra investment, 185-194
  on total investment, 179-185
  (See also Return on debt investment;
    Return on equity investment; Re-
    turn on extra investment; Return
    on total investment)
Rate of return method:
  advantages of, 244-246
  assumed reinvestment rate in, 234-239
  description of, 207-234
  disadvantages of, 239-244
  interpretation of results from, 209,
    211, 214-217, 222-223
  an introductory application of, 208-220
  and multiple-alternative problems,
    223-234
  and multiple returns, 240-244
  and no ascertainable return, 243-244
  and replacement problems, 220-223

Rate-of-return requirement:
  determination of, 39-45
  reasons for, 37-39
Recurring costs:
  definition of, 15
  examples of, 15-16
Regulated industries, determination of
  revenue requirements for, 327-328,
  350
Reinvestment rates, assumptions regarding, 61, 151, 234-239
Replacement analyses:
  with discounted cash flow method,
    220-223
  with future worth method, 157-158
  with present worth method, 154-166
  with rate of return method, 220-223
  with revenue requirement method,
    338-348
  tax determination in, 278-289, 338-348
  with uniform annual cost method,
    127-130
Replacement cost, relevancy of, 34-35
Replacements:
  assumed, 120-123, 158-166
  forecasted, 118-120, 148-150, 217-220
Retirement analyses (see Replacement
  analyses)
Return on debt investment, 273
Return on equity investment:
  as a decision criterion, 275-277
  determination of: after taxes, 271-275
    before taxes, 277
  as related to return on total investment,
    275-276
Return on extra investment:
  determination of, 185-194
    equating cost expressions in, 190-193
    period-by-period comparisons in,
      186-190
  as an element of an average return,
    194-199, 214-216
  evaluation of calculated value of, 210,
    213, 216, 219
Return on total investment:
  and calculated total annual cost, 113-
    115

Return on total investment (*continued*):
  and calculated total future worth, 153
  and calculated total present worth, 147
  determination of, 179-185
    direct approach to, 180-182
    trial-and-error approach to, 182-185
  as an element of an average return,
    194-199, 214-216
  evaluation of calculated value of, 210,
    211
  as related to return on equity invest-
    ment, 275-276
Revenue requirement method:
  description of, 316-348
  evaluation of, 348-350
  and gains or losses on disposal, 345-346
  interpretation of results from, 324-329
  an introductory application of, 316-324
  and investment tax credits, 340-341
  and multiple-alternative problems,
    329-338
  and non-deductible devaluation ex-
    penses, 343-345
  and regulated industries, 327-328, 350
  and replacement problems, 338-348
  tax factor in, 317-318
  tax formula in, 317-318
Reversal of sign, in cumulative cash
  flows, 242-244
Risk:
  attitude toward, 417
  condition of, 378
Risk analysis, 378-391, 409-423
  with alternative sets of estimates,
    387-391
  with compound events, 384-387, 414-
    422
  decision trees in, 409-423
  evaluation of, 383-384, 387, 391, 422-
    423
  and an expected value problem, 381-
    384
Rollback, in decision trees, 418-420

Sensitivity analysis:
  description of, 370-377

Sensitivity analysis (*continued*):
   evaluation of, 377-378
Short-term gains and losses, 283-284,
   345-346
Sign reversal, in cumulative cash flows,
   242-244
Simple interest, 57-58
Single-amount future worth factor:
   derivation of, 425-427
   description of, 63-65
   tables of values for, 440-463
Single-amount present worth factor:
   derivation of, 425-427
   description of, 70-72
   tables of values for, 440-463
Single-asset accounts, 25-26
Straight-line depreciation, 24-25
Sum-of-the-years-digits depreciation,
   27-29
Surplus revenues, in revenue requirement
   method, 324-326

Tax credit, 282-283, 340-341
Tax-deductible expenses, 23, 259
Tax determination:
   general procedure for, 23, 259
   an introductory example of, 261-264
   in multiple-alternative problems, 290-
      300, 329-338
   in a replacement problem, 278-289,
      338-348
   with revenue requirement tax formula,
      317-319
   (*See also* After-tax analyses)
Tax factor, in revenue requirement
   method, 317-318, 434-438
Tax formula, in revenue requirement
   method, 317-318, 434-438
Tax rate, effective, 30, 259-260

Time lines, 26
Total investment, return on (*see* Return
   on total investment)
Trial-and-error approach, to rate of
   return determination, 182-185, 187-
   188

Uncertainty (*see* Decision trees; Risk
   analysis)
Uniform annual cost method:
   cost relevancy in, 125-126
   description of, 107-134
   evaluation of, 169-170, 244-245
   interpretation of results from, 113-
      116, 125-126
   an introductory application of, 108-
      123
   and multiple-alternative problems, 130
   and perpetual-service alternatives,
      130-134
   and replacement problems, 127-130
Uniform-series future worth factor:
   derivation of, 427-430
   description of, 72-77
   tables of values for, 440-463
Uniform-series present worth factor:
   derivation of, 427-430
   description of, 79-82
   tables of values for, 440-463
Utilities, determination of revenue requirements for, 327-328, 350

Valuation problems, 168-169

Weighted average returns, 194-199, 215-
   216, 274
Working capital, 20

NOTES

NOTES

NOTES

NOTES

NOTES

NOTES

NOTES

NOTES

NOTES

NOTES